INTRODUCTION TO PSYCHOLOGY PART I

INTRODUCTION TO PSYCHOLOGY
PART I

PSY101

EDITED BY JULIE LINDH

Published by SUNY OER Services
Milne Library
State University of New York at Geneseo
Geneseo, NY 14454

Distributed by State University of New York Press

ISBN: 978-1717429032

This book was produced using Pressbooks.com, and PDF rendering was done by PrinceXML.

Contents

About This Book

Your Introduction to Psychology (PSY101) textbook is a compilation of material written by instructors for colleges and universities around the country. The entire compilation is provided through a Creative Commons license. You can access or even copy all the material here, for your own reference, even after the semester ends.

Different Versions:

An electronic version is made available via https://courses.lumenlearning.com/suny-fmcc-intropsych/ and in Blackboard. The electronic version has access to multimedia content including video, PowerPoint, and interactive activities. Also, you may purchase a physical (print) copy at FM's College Store. The print version will have all the same reading material, but not include the multimedia content.

About the Author:

There are many different authors; look to the "Licenses and Attributions" section at the end of each chapter to identify contributors. This compilation was edited by Julie Lindh at Fulton-Montgomery Community College (SUNY).

Module 1: Introduction to Psychology & Psychology Research

Why It Matters: Psychological Foundations

Psychology is the scientific study of mind and behavior. (credit "background": modification of work by Nattachai Noogure; credit "top left": modification of work by U.S. Navy; credit "top middle-left": modification of work by Peter Shanks; credit "top middle-right": modification of work by "devinf"/Flickr; credit "top right": modification of work by Alejandra Quintero Sinisterra; credit "bottom left": modification of work by Gabriel Rocha; credit "bottom middle-left": modification of work by Caleb Roenigk; credit "bottom middle-right": modification of work by Staffan Scherz; credit "bottom right": modification of work by Czech Provincial Reconstruction Team)

Clive Wearing is an accomplished musician who lost his ability to form new memories when he became sick at the age of 46. While he can remember how to play the piano perfectly, he cannot remember what he ate for breakfast just an hour ago (Sacks, 2007). James Wannerton experiences a taste sensation that is associated with the sound of words. His former girlfriend's name tastes like rhubarb (Mundasad, 2013). John Nash is a brilliant mathematician and Nobel Prize winner. However, while he was a professor at MIT, he would tell people that the *New York Times* contained coded messages from extraterrestrial beings that were intended for him. He also began to hear voices and became suspicious of the people around him. Soon thereafter, Nash was diagnosed with schizophrenia and admitted to a state-run mental institution (O'Connor & Robertson, 2002). Nash was the subject of the 2001 movie *A Beautiful Mind*. Why did these people have these experiences? How does the human brain work? And what is the connection between the brain's internal processes and people's external behaviors? This course will introduce you to various ways that the field of psychology has explored these questions.

This module will introduce you to what psychology is and what psychologists do. You'll learn the basic history of the discipline and about the major domains and subdivisions that exist within modern psychology. Lastly, you'll consider what it means to study psychology and what career options are available for those who do.

Module References

American Board of Forensic Psychology. (2014). *Brochure*. Retrieved from http://www.abfp.com/brochure.asp

American Psychological Association. (2014). Retrieved from www.apa.org

American Psychological Association. (2014). *Graduate training and career possibilities in exercise and sport psychology.* Retrieved from http://www.apadivisions.org/division-47/about/resources/training.aspx?item=1

American Psychological Association. (2011). *Psychology as a career.* Retrieved from http://www.apa.org/education/undergrad/psych-career.aspx

Ashliman, D. L. (2001). Cupid and Psyche. In *Folktexts: A library of folktales, folklore, fairy tales, and mythology*. Retrieved from http://www.pitt.edu/~dash/cupid.html

Betancourt, H., & López, S. R. (1993). The study of culture, ethnicity, and race in American psychology. *American Psychologist, 48*, 629–637.

Black, S. R., Spence, S. A., & Omari, S. R. (2004). Contributions of African Americans to the field of psychology. *Journal of Black Studies, 35*, 40–64.

Bulfinch, T. (1855). *The age of fable: Or, stories of gods and heroes.* Boston, MA: Chase, Nichols and Hill.

Buss, D. M. (1989). Sex differences in human mate preferences: Evolutionary hypotheses tested in 37 cultures. *Behavioral and Brain Sciences, 12*, 1–49.

Carlson, N. R. (2013). *Physiology of Behavior* (11th ed.). Boston, MA: Pearson.

Confer, J. C., Easton, J. A., Fleischman, D. S., Goetz, C. D., Lewis, D. M. G., Perilloux, C., & Buss, D. M. (2010). Evolutionary psychology. Controversies, questions, prospects, and limitations. *American Psychologist, 65*, 100–126.

Crawford, M., & Marecek, J. (1989). Psychology reconstructs the female 1968–1988. *Psychology of Women Quarterly, 13*, 147–165.

Danziger, K. (1980). The history of introspection reconsidered. *Journal of the History of the Behavioral Sciences, 16*, 241–262.

Darwin, C. (1871). *Thedescent of man and selection in relation to sex.* London: John Murray.

Darwin, C. (1872). *The expression of the emotions in man and animals.* London: John Murray.

DeAngelis, T. (2010). Fear not. *gradPSYCH Magazine, 8,* 38.

Department of Health and Human Services. (n.d.). Projected future growth of the older population. Retrieved from http://www.aoa.gov/Aging_Statistics/future_growth/future_growth.aspx#age

Endler, J. A. (1986). *Natural Selection in the Wild.* Princeton, NJ: Princeton University Press.

Fogg, N. P., Harrington, P. E., Harrington, T. F., & Shatkin, L. (2012). *College majors handbook with real career paths and payoffs* (3rd ed.). St. Paul, MN: JIST Publishing.

Franko, D. L., et al. (2012). Racial/ethnic differences in adults in randomized clinical trials of binge eating disorder. *Journal of Consulting and Clinical Psychology, 80,* 186–195.

Friedman, H. (2008), Humanistic and positive psychology: The methodological and epistemological divide. *The Humanistic Psychologist, 36,* 113–126.

Gordon, O. E. (1995). *A brief history of psychology.* Retrieved from http://www.psych.utah.edu/gordon/Classes/Psy4905Docs/PsychHistory/index.html#maptop

Greek Myths & Greek Mythology. (2014). *The myth of Psyche and Eros.* Retrieved from http://www.greekmyths-greekmythology.com/psyche-and-eros-myth/

Green, C. D. (2001). Classics in the history of psychology. Retrieved from http://psychclassics.yorku.ca/Krstic/marulic.htm

Greengrass, M. (2004). 100 years of B.F. Skinner. *Monitor on Psychology, 35,* 80.

Halonen, J. S. (2011). *White paper: Are there too many psychology majors?* Prepared for the Staff of the State University System of Florida Board of Governors. Retrieved from http://www.cogdop.org/page_attachments/0000/0200/FLA_White_Paper_for_cogop_posting.pdf

Hock, R. R. (2009). Social psychology. *Forty studies that changed psychology: Explorations into the history of psychological research* (pp. 308–317). Upper Saddle River, NJ: Pearson.

Hoffman, C. (2012). *Careers in clinical, counseling, or school psychology; mental health counseling; clinical social work; marriage & family therapy and related professions.* Retrieved from http://www.indiana.edu/~psyugrad/advising/docs/Careers%20in%20Mental%20Health%20Counseling.pdf

Jang, K. L., Livesly, W. J., & Vernon, P. A. (1996). Heritability of the Big Five personality dimensions and their facets: A twin study. *Journal of Personality, 64,* 577–591.

Johnson, R., & Lubin, G. (2011). College exposed: What majors are most popular, highest paying and most likely to get you a job. *Business Insider.com.* Retrieved from http://www.businessinsider.com/best-college-majors-highest-income-most-employed-georgetwon-study-2011-6?op=1

Knekt, P. P., et al. (2008). Randomized trial on the effectiveness of long- and short-term psycho-dynamic psychotherapy and solution-focused therapy on psychiatric symptoms during a 3-year follow-up. *Psychological Medicine: A Journal of Research In Psychiatry And The Allied Sciences, 38,* 689–703.

Landers, R. N. (2011, June 14). Grad school: Should I get a PhD or Master's in I/O psychology? [Web log post]. Retrieved from http://neoacademic.com/2011/06/14/grad-school-should-i-get-a-ph-d-or-masters-in-io-psychology/#.UuKKLftOnGg

Macdonald, C. (2013). *Health psychology center presents: What is health psychology?* Retrieved from http://healthpsychology.org/what-is-health-psychology/

McCrae, R. R. & Costa, P. T. (2008). Empirical and theoretical status of the five-factor model of personality traits. In G. J. Boyle, G. Matthews, & D. H. Saklofske (Eds.), *The Sage handbook of personality theory and assessment. Vol. 1 Personality theories and models.* London: Sage.

Michalski, D., Kohout, J., Wicherski, M., & Hart, B. (2011). *2009 Doctorate Employment Survey.* APA Center for Workforce Studies. Retrieved from http://www.apa.org/workforce/publications/09-doc-empl/index.aspx

Miller, G. A. (2003). The cognitive revolution: A historical perspective. *Trends in Cognitive Sciences, 7,* 141–144.

Munakata, Y., McClelland, J. L., Johnson, M. H., & Siegler, R. S. (1997). Rethinking infant knowledge: Toward an adaptive process account of successes and failures in object permanence tasks. *Psychological Review, 104,* 689–713.

Mundasad, S. (2013). *Word-taste synaesthesia: Tasting names, places, and Anne Boleyn.* Retrieved from http://www.bbc.co.uk/news/health-21060207

Munsey, C. (2009). More states forgo a postdoc requirement. *Monitor on Psychology, 40,* 10.

National Association of School Psychologists. (n.d.). *Becoming a nationally certified school psychologist (NCSP).* Retrieved from http://www.nasponline.org/CERTIFICATION/becomeNCSP.aspx

Nicolas, S., & Ferrand, L. (1999). Wundt's laboratory at Leipzig in 1891. *History of Psychology, 2,* 194–203.

Norcross, J. C. (n.d.) Clinical versus counseling psychology: What's the diff? Available at http://www.csun.edu/~hcpsy002/Clinical%20Versus%20Counseling%20Psychology.pdf

Norcross, J. C., & Castle, P. H. (2002). Appreciating the PsyD: The facts. *Eye on Psi Chi, 7,* 22–26.

O'Connor, J. J., & Robertson, E. F. (2002). *John Forbes Nash.* Retrieved from http://www-groups.dcs.st-and.ac.uk/~history/Biographies/Nash.html

O'Hara, M. (n.d.). Historic review of humanistic psychology. Retrieved from http://www.ahp-web.org/index.php?option=com_k2&view=item&layout=item&id=14&Itemid=24

Person, E. S. (1980). Sexuality as the mainstay of identity: Psychoanalytic perspectives. *Signs, 5,* 605–630.

Rantanen, J., Metsäpelto, R. L., Feldt, T., Pulkkinen, L., & Kokko, K. (2007). Long-term stability in the Big Five personality traits in adulthood. *Scandinavian Journal of Psychology, 48,* 511–518.

Riggio, R. E. (2013). What is industrial/organizational psychology? *Psychology Today.* Retrieved from http://www.psychologytoday.com/blog/cutting-edge-leadership/201303/what-is-industrialorga-nizational-psychology

Sacks, O. (2007). A neurologists notebook: The abyss, music and amnesia. *The New Yorker.* Retrieved from http://www.newyorker.com/reporting/2007/09/24/070924fa_fact_sacks?currentPage=all

Shedler, J. (2010). The efficacy of psychodynamic psychotherapy. *American Psychologist, 65*(2), 98–109.

Soldz, S., & Vaillant, G. E. (1999). The Big Five personality traits and the life course: A 45-year longitudinal study. *Journal of Research in Personality, 33,* 208–232.

Thorne, B. M., & Henley, T. B. (2005). *Connections in the history and systems of psychology* (3rd ed.). Boston, MA: Houghton Mifflin Company.

Tolman, E. C. (1938). The determiners of behavior at a choice point. *Psychological Review, 45,* 1–41.

U.S. Department of Education, National Center for Education Statistics. (2013). *Digest of Education Statistics, 2012* (NCES 2014-015).

Weisstein, N. (1993). Psychology constructs the female: Or, the fantasy life of the male psychologist (with some attention to the fantasies of his friends, the male biologist and the male anthropologist). *Feminism and Psychology, 3,* 195–210.

Westen, D. (1998). The scientific legacy of Sigmund Freud, toward a psychodynamically informed psychological science. *Psychological Bulletin, 124,* 333–371.

Attributions

The History of Psychology

What you'll learn to do: describe the evolution of psychology and the major pioneers in the field

Figure 1. Plato, Aristotle, and other ancient Greek philosophers examined a wide range of topics relating to what we now consider psychology.

Many cultures throughout history have speculated on the nature of the mind, heart, soul, spirit, and brain. Philosophical interest in behavior and the mind dates back to the ancient civilizations of Egypt, Greece, China, and India, but psychology as a discipline didn't develop until the mid-1800s, when it evolved from the study of philosophy and began in German and American labs. This section will teach you more about the major founding psychologists and their contributions to the development of psychology.

- Define Psychology
- Define structuralism and functionalism and the contributions of Wundt and James in the development of psychology
- Describe Freud's influence on psychology and his major theoretical contributions
- Describe the basic tenets of Gestalt psychology

What is Psychology?

In Greek mythology, Psyche was a mortal woman whose beauty was so great that it rivaled that of the goddess Aphrodite. Aphrodite became so jealous of Psyche that she sent her son, Eros, to make Psyche fall in love with the ugliest man in the world. However, Eros accidentally pricked himself with the tip of his arrow and fell madly in love with Psyche himself. He took Psyche to his palace and showered her with gifts, yet she could never see his face. While visiting Psyche, her sisters roused suspicion in Psyche about her mysterious lover, and eventually, Psyche betrayed Eros' wishes to remain unseen to her. Because of this betrayal, Eros abandoned Psyche. When Psyche appealed to Aphrodite to reunite her with Eros, Aphrodite gave her a series of impossible tasks to complete. Psyche managed to complete all of these trials; ultimately, her perseverance paid off as she was reunited with Eros and was ultimately transformed into a goddess herself (Ashliman, 2001; Greek Myths & Greek Mythology, 2014).

Psyche comes to represent the human soul's triumph over the misfortunes of life in the pursuit of true happiness (Bulfinch, 1855); in fact, the Greek word **psyche** means soul, and it is often represented as a butterfly. The word *psychology* was coined at a time when the concepts of soul and mind were not as clearly distinguished (Green, 2001). The root **–ology** denotes scientific study of, and psychology refers to the scientific study of the mind. Since science studies only observable phenomena and the mind is not directly observable, we expand this definition to the scientific study of mind and behavior.

Figure 2. Antonio Canova's sculpture depicts Eros and Psyche.

The scientific study of any aspect of the world uses the scientific method to acquire knowledge. To apply the scientific method, a researcher with a question about how or why something happens will propose a tentative explanation, called a hypothesis, to explain the phenomenon. A hypothesis is not just any explanation; it should fit into the context of a scientific theory. A scientific theory is a broad explanation or group of explanations for some aspect of the natural world that is consistently supported by evidence over time. A theory is the best understanding that we have of that part of the natural world. Armed with the hypothesis, the researcher then makes observations or, better still, carries out an experiment to test the validity of the hypothesis. That test and its results are then published so that others can check the results or build on them. It is necessary that any explanation in science be testable, which means that the phenomenon must be perceivable and measurable. For example, that a bird sings because it is happy is not a testable hypothesis, since we have no way to measure the happiness of a bird. We must ask a different question, perhaps about the brain state of the bird, since this can be measured. In general, science deals only with matter and energy, that is, those things that can be measured, and it cannot arrive at knowledge about values and morality. This is one reason why our scientific understanding of the mind is so limited, since thoughts, at least as we experience them, are neither matter nor energy. The scientific method is also a form of empiricism. An **empirical method** for acquiring knowledge is one based on observation, including experimentation, rather than a method based only on forms of logical argument or previous authorities.

It was not until the late 1800s that psychology became accepted as its own academic discipline. Before this time, the workings of the mind were considered under the auspices of philosophy. Given that any behavior is, at its roots, biological, some areas of psychology take on aspects of a natural science like biology. No biological organism exists in isolation, and our behavior is influenced by our interactions with others. Therefore, psychology is also a social science.

Psychology is a relatively young science with its experimental roots in the 19th century, compared, for example, to human physiology, which dates much earlier. As mentioned, anyone interested in exploring issues related to the mind generally did so in a philosophical context prior to the 19th century. Two men, working in the 19th century, are generally credited as being the founders of psychology as a science and academic discipline that was distinct from philosophy. Their names were Wilhelm Wundt and William James.

Wundt and Structuralism

Wilhelm Wundt (1832–1920) was a German scientist who was the first person to be referred to as a psychologist. His famous book entitled *Principles of Physiological Psychology* was published in 1873. Wundt viewed psychology as a scientific study of conscious experience, and he believed that the goal of psychology was to identify components of consciousness and how those components combined to result in our conscious experience. Wundt used introspection (he called it "internal perception"), a process by which someone examines their own conscious experience as objectively as possible, making the human mind like any other aspect of nature that a scientist observed. Wundt's version of introspection used only very specific experimental conditions in which an external stimulus was designed to produce a scientifically observable (repeatable) experience of the mind (Danziger, 1980). The first stringent requirement was the use of "trained" or practiced observers, who could immediately observe and report a reaction. The second requirement was the use of repeatable stimuli that always produced the same experience in the subject and allowed the subject to expect and thus be fully attentive to the inner reaction. These experimental requirements were put in place to eliminate "interpretation" in the reporting of internal experiences and to counter the argument that there is no way to know that an individual is observing their mind or consciousness accurately, since it cannot be seen by any other person. This attempt to understand the structure or characteristics of the mind was known as **structuralism.** Wundt established his psychology laboratory at the University at Leipzig in 1879. In this laboratory, Wundt and his students conducted experiments on, for example, reaction times. A subject, sometimes in a room isolated from the scientist, would receive a stimulus such as a light, image, or sound. The subject's reaction to the stimulus would be to push a button, and an apparatus would record the time to reaction. Wundt could measure reaction time to one-thousandth of a second (Nicolas & Ferrand, 1999).

(a)   (b)

Figure 3. (a) Wilhelm Wundt is credited as one of the founders of psychology. He created the first laboratory for psychological research. (b) This photo shows him seated and surrounded by fellow researchers and equipment in his laboratory in Germany.

However, despite his efforts to train individuals in the process of introspection, this process remained highly subjective, and there was very little agreement between individuals. As a result, structuralism fell out of favor with the passing of Wundt's student, Edward Titchener, in 1927 (Gordon, 1995).

James and Functionalism

William James (1842–1910) was the first American psychologist who espoused a different perspective on how psychology should operate. James was introduced to Darwin's theory of evolution by natural selection and accepted it as an explanation of an organism's characteristics. Key to that theory is the idea that natural selection leads to organisms that are adapted to their environment, including their behavior. Adaptation means that a trait of an organism has a function for the survival and reproduction of the individual, because it has been naturally selected. As James saw it, psychology's purpose was to study the function of behavior in the world, and as such, his perspective was known as **functionalism**. Functionalism focused on how mental activities helped an organism fit into its environment. Functionalism has a second, more subtle meaning in that functionalists were more interested in the operation of the whole mind rather than of its individual parts, which were the focus of structuralism. Like Wundt, James believed that introspection could serve as one means by which someone might study mental activities, but James also relied on more objective measures, including the use of various recording devices, and examinations of concrete products of mental activities and of anatomy and physiology (Gordon, 1995).

Figure 4. William James, shown here in a self-portrait, was the first American psychologist.

The Early Schools of Psychology (No Longer Active)		
School of Psychology	**Description**	**Historically Important People**
Structuralism	Focused on understanding the conscious experience through introspection	Wilhelm Wundt
Functionalism	Emphasized how mental activities helped an organism adapt to its environment	William James

Adapted from *Early Schools of Psychology* from the Open Learning Initiative's *Introduction to Psychology.* CC-BY-NC-SA.

Psychoanalytic Theory

Perhaps one of the most influential and well-known figures in psychology's history was Sigmund Freud. Freud (1856–1939) was an Austrian neurologist who was fascinated by patients suffering from "hysteria" and neurosis. Hysteria was an ancient diagnosis for disorders, primarily of women with a wide variety of symptoms, including physical symptoms and emotional disturbances, none of which had an apparent physical cause. Freud theorized that many of his patients' problems arose from the unconscious mind. In Freud's view, the unconscious mind was a repository of feelings and urges of which we have no awareness.

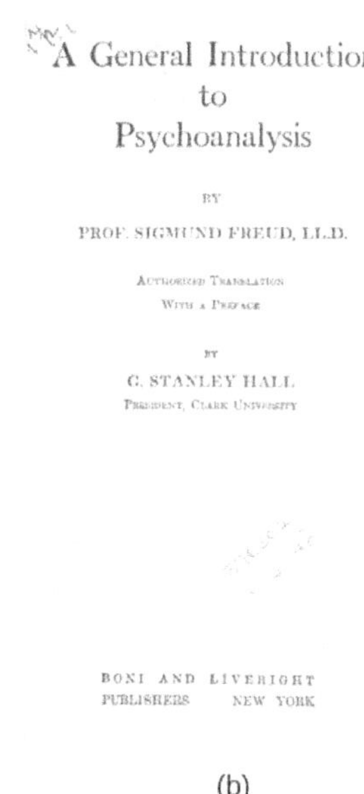

(a)   (b)

Figure 5. (a) Sigmund Freud was a highly influential figure in the history of psychology. (b) One of his many books, A General Introduction to Psychoanalysis, shared his ideas about psychoanalytical therapy; it was published in 1922

Gaining access to the unconscious, then, was crucial to the successful resolution of the patient's problems. According to Freud, the unconscious mind could be accessed through dream analysis, by examinations of the first words that came to people's minds, and through seemingly innocent slips of the tongue. **Psychoanalytic theory** focuses on the role of a person's unconscious, as well as early childhood experiences, and this particular perspective dominated clinical psychology for several decades (Thorne & Henley, 2005).

The Id, Ego, and Superego

Freud's structural model of personality divides the personality into three parts—the id, the ego, and the superego. The id is the unconscious part that is the cauldron of raw drives, such as for sex or aggression. The ego, which has conscious and unconscious elements, is the rational and reasonable part of personality. Its role is to maintain contact with the outside world to keep the individual in touch with society, and to do this it mediates between the conflicting tendencies of the id and the superego. The superego is a person's conscience, which develops early in life and is learned from parents, teachers, and others. Like the ego, the superego has conscious and unconscious elements. When all three parts of the personality are in dynamic equilibrium, the individual is thought to be mentally healthy. However, if the ego is unable to mediate between the id and the superego, an imbalance is believed to occur in the form of psychological distress.

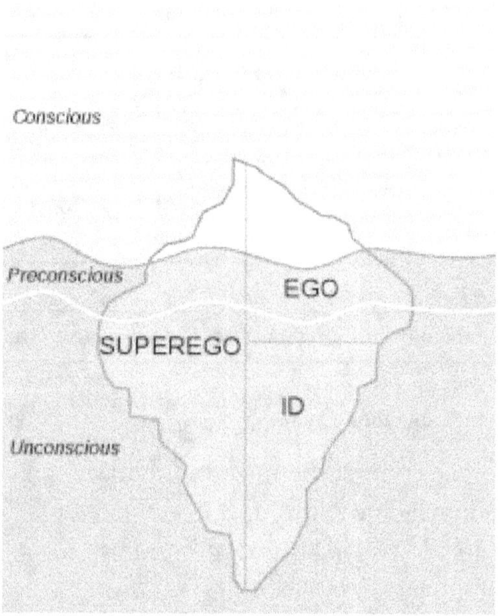

Figure 6. Freud's theory of the unconscious Freud believed that we are only aware of a small amount of our mind's activity, and that most of it remains hidden from us in our unconscious. The information in our unconscious affects our behavior, although we are unaware of it.

Psychosexual Theory of Development

Freud's theories also placed a great deal of emphasis on sexual development. Freud believed that each of us must pass through a series of stages during childhood, and that if we lack proper nurturing during a particular stage, we may become stuck or fixated in that stage. Freud's psychosexual model of development includes five stages: oral, anal, phallic, latency, and genital. According to Freud, children's pleasure-seeking urges are focused on a different area of the body, called an erogenous zone, at each of these five stages. Psychologists today dispute that Freud's psychosexual stages provide a legitimate explanation for how personality develops, but what we can take away from Freud's theory is that personality is shaped, in some part, by experiences we have in childhood.

Freud's ideas were influential, and you will learn more about them when you study lifespan development, personality, and therapy. For instance, many therapists believe strongly in the unconscious and the impact of early childhood experiences on the rest of a person's life. The method of psychoanalysis, which involves the patient talking about their experiences and selves, while not invented by Freud, was certainly popularized by him and is still used today. Many of Freud's other ideas, however, are controversial.

Gestalt Psychology (Wertheimer, Koffka, and Köhler)

Figure 7. When you look at this image, you may see a duck or a rabbit. The sensory information remains the same, but your perception can vary dramatically.

Max Wertheimer (1880–1943), Kurt Koffka (1886–1941), and Wolfgang Köhler (1887–1967) were three German psychologists who immigrated to the United States in the early 20th century to escape Nazi Germany. These men are credited with introducing psychologists in the United States to various Gestalt principles. The word Gestalt roughly translates to "whole;" a major emphasis of Gestalt psychology deals with the fact that although a sensory experience can be broken down into individual parts, how those parts relate to each other as a whole is often what the individual responds to in perception. For example, a song may be made up of individual notes played by different instruments, but the real nature of the song is perceived in the combinations of these notes as they form the melody, rhythm, and harmony. In many ways, this particular perspective would have directly contradicted Wundt's ideas of structuralism (Thorne & Henley, 2005).

Unfortunately, in moving to the United States, these men were forced to abandon much of their work and were unable to continue to conduct research on a large scale. These factors along with the rise of behaviorism (described next) in the United States prevented principles of Gestalt psychology from being as influential in the United States as they had been in their native Germany (Thorne & Henley, 2005). Despite these issues, several Gestalt principles are still very influential today. Considering the human individual as a whole rather than as a sum of individually measured parts became an important foundation in humanistic theory late in the century. The ideas of Gestalt have continued to influence research on sensation and perception.

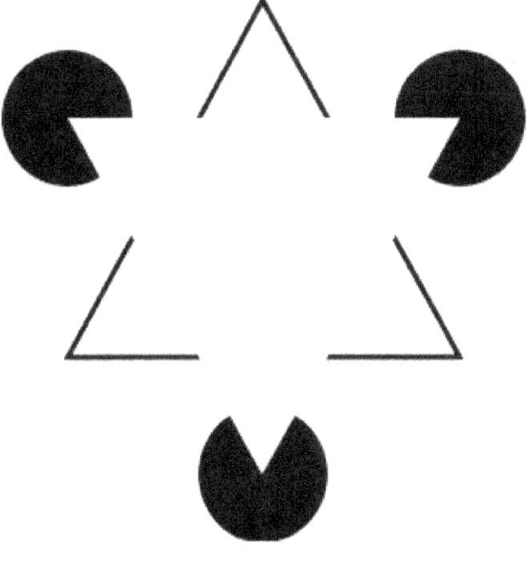

Figure 8. The "invisible" triangle you see here is an example of gestalt perception.

Structuralism, Freud, and the Gestalt psychologists were all concerned in one way or another with describing and understanding inner experience. But other researchers had concerns that inner experience could be a legitimate subject of scientific inquiry and chose instead to exclusively study behavior, the objectively observable outcome of mental processes.

Glossary

empirical method: method for acquiring knowledge based on observation, including experimentation, rather than a method based only on forms of logical argument or previous authorities

functionalism: focused on how mental activities helped an organism adapt to its environment

–ology: suffix that denotes "scientific study of"

psyche: Greek word for soul

psychoanalytic theory: focus on the role of the unconscious in affecting conscious behavior

psychology: scientific study of the mind and behavior

structuralism: understanding the conscious experience through introspection

Attributions

CC licensed content, Original

- Modification and adaptation. **Provided by:** Lumen Learning. **License:** *CC BY-SA: Attribution-ShareAlike*
- Modification, adaptation, and original content. **Provided by:** Lumen Learning. **License:** *CC BY: Attribution*

CC licensed content, Shared previously

- Early Roots of Psychology; The Id, Ego, and Superego and Psychosexual Theory. **Provided by:** Boundless. **Located at:** https://www.boundless.com/psychology/textbooks/boundless-psychology-textbook/introduction-to-psychology-1/introduction-to-the-field-of-psychology-22/early-roots-of-psychology-110-12647/. **License:** *CC BY-SA: Attribution-ShareAlike*

All rights reserved content

- Psychology 101 - Wundt & James: Structuralism & Functionalism - Vook. **Provided by:** VookInc's channel. **Located at:** https://www.youtube.com/watch?v=SW6nm69Z_IE. **License:** *Other.* **License Terms:** Standard YouTube License

The History of Psychology Continued

Learning Objectives

- Define behaviorism and the contributions of Pavlov, Watson, and Skinner to psychology
- Explain the basic tenets of humanism and Maslow's contribution to psychology
- Describe the basics of cognitive psychology and how the cognitive revolution shifted psychology's focus back to the mind
- Summarize the history of psychology, focusing on the major schools of thought

Behavioral Psychology

Early work in the field of behavior was conducted by the Russian physiologist Ivan Pavlov (1849–1936). Pavlov studied a form of learning behavior called a conditioned reflex, in which an animal or human produced a reflex (unconscious) response to a stimulus and, over time, was conditioned to produce the response to a different stimulus that the experimenter associated with the original stimulus. The reflex Pavlov worked with was salivation in response to the presence of food. The salivation reflex could be elicited using a second stimulus, such as a specific sound, that was presented in association with the initial food stimulus several times. Once the response to the second stimulus was "learned," the food stimulus could be omitted. Pavlov's "classical conditioning" is only one form of learning behavior studied by behaviorists.

Figure 1. John B. Watson is known as the father of behaviorism within psychology.

John B. Watson (1878–1958) was an influential American psychologist whose most famous work occurred during the early 20th century at Johns Hopkins University. While Wundt and James were concerned with understanding conscious experience, Watson thought that the study of consciousness was flawed. Because he believed that objective analysis of the mind was impossible, Watson preferred to focus directly on observable behavior and try to bring that behavior under control. Watson was a major proponent of shifting the focus of psychology from the mind to behavior, and this approach of observing and controlling behavior came to be known as **behaviorism**. A major object of study by behaviorists was learned behavior and its interaction with inborn qualities of the organism. Behaviorism commonly used animals in experiments under the assumption that what was learned using animal models could, to some degree, be applied to human behavior. Indeed, Tolman (1938) stated, "I believe that everything important in psychology (except ... such matters as involve society and words) can be investigated in essence through the continued experimental and theoretical analysis of the determiners of rat behavior at a choice-point in a maze."

Behaviorism dominated experimental psychology for several decades, and its influence can still be felt today (Thorne & Henley, 2005). Behaviorism is largely responsible for establishing psychology as a scientific discipline through its objective methods and especially experimentation. In addition, it is used in behavioral and cognitive-behavioral therapy. Behavior modification is commonly used in classroom settings. Behaviorism has also led to research on environmental influences on human behavior.

B. F. Skinner (1904–1990) was an American psychologist. Like Watson, Skinner was a behaviorist, and he concentrated on how behavior was affected by its consequences. Therefore, Skinner spoke of reinforcement and punishment as major factors in driving behavior. As a part of his research, Skinner developed a chamber that allowed the careful study of the principles of modifying behavior through reinforcement and punishment. This device, known as an operant conditioning chamber (or more familiarly, a Skinner box), has remained a crucial resource for researchers studying behavior (Thorne & Henley, 2005).

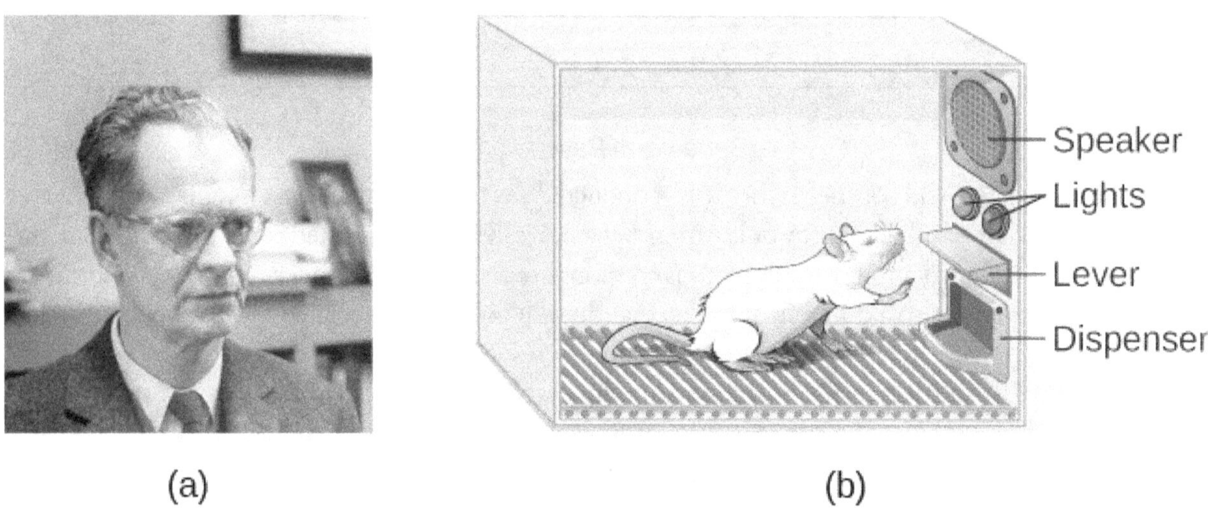

Figure 2. (a) B. F. Skinner is famous for his research on operant conditioning. (b) Modified versions of the operant conditioning chamber, or Skinner box, are still widely used in research settings today. (credit a: modification of work by "Silly rabbit"/Wikimedia Commons)

The Skinner box is a chamber that isolates the subject from the external environment and has a behavior indicator such as a lever or a button. When the animal pushes the button or lever, the box is able to deliver a positive reinforcement of the behavior (such as food) or a punishment (such as a noise) or a token conditioner (such as a light) that is correlated with either the positive reinforcement or punishment.

Skinner's focus on positive and negative reinforcement of learned behaviors had a lasting influence in psychology that has waned somewhat since the growth of research in cognitive psychology. Despite this, conditioned learning is still used in human behavioral modification. Skinner's two widely read and controversial popular science books about the value of operant conditioning for creating happier lives remain as thought-provoking arguments for his approach (Greengrass, 2004).

During the early 20th century, American psychology was dominated by behaviorism and psychoanalysis. However, some psychologists were uncomfortable with what they viewed as limited perspectives being so influential to the field. They objected to the pessimism and determinism (all actions driven by the unconscious) of Freud. They also disliked the reductionism, or simplifying nature, of behaviorism. Behaviorism is also deterministic at its core, because it sees human behavior as entirely determined by a combination of genetics and environment. Some psychologists began to form their own ideas that emphasized personal control, intentionality, and a true predisposition for "good" as important for our self-concept and our behavior. Thus, humanism emerged.

Maslow, Rogers, and Humanism

Humanism is a perspective within psychology that emphasizes the potential for good that is innate to all humans. Two of the most well-known proponents of humanistic psychology are Abraham Maslow and Carl Rogers (O'Hara, n.d.). Abraham Maslow (1908–1970) was an American psychologist who is best known for proposing a hierarchy of human needs in motivating behavior. Although this concept will be discussed in more detail in a later section, a brief overview will be provided here.

Maslow asserted that so long as basic needs necessary for survival were met (e.g., food, water, shelter), higher-level needs (e.g., social needs) would begin to motivate behavior. According to Maslow, the highest-level needs relate to self-actualization, a process by which we achieve our full potential. Obviously, the focus on the positive aspects of human nature that are characteristic of the humanistic perspective is evident (Thorne & Henley, 2005).

Humanistic psychologists rejected, on principle, the research approach based on reductionist experimentation in the tradition of the physical and biological sciences, because it missed the "whole" human being. Beginning with Maslow and Rogers, there was an insistence on a humanistic research program. This program has been largely qualitative (not measurement-based), but there exist a number of quantitative research strains within humanistic psychology, including research on happiness, self-concept, meditation, and the outcomes of humanistic psychotherapy (Friedman, 2008).

Carl Rogers (1902–1987) was also an American psychologist who, like Maslow, emphasized the potential for good that exists within all people. Rogers used a therapeutic technique known as client-centered therapy in helping his clients deal with problematic issues that resulted in their seeking psychotherapy. Unlike a psychoanalytic approach in which the therapist plays an important role in interpreting what conscious behavior reveals about the unconscious mind, client-centered therapy involves the patient taking a lead role in the therapy session. Rogers believed that a therapist needed to display three features to maximize the effectiveness of this particular approach: unconditional positive regard, genuineness, and empathy. Unconditional positive regard refers to the fact that the therapist accepts their client for who they are, no matter what he or she might say. Provided these factors, Rogers believed that people were more than capable of dealing with and working through their own issues (Thorne & Henley, 2005).

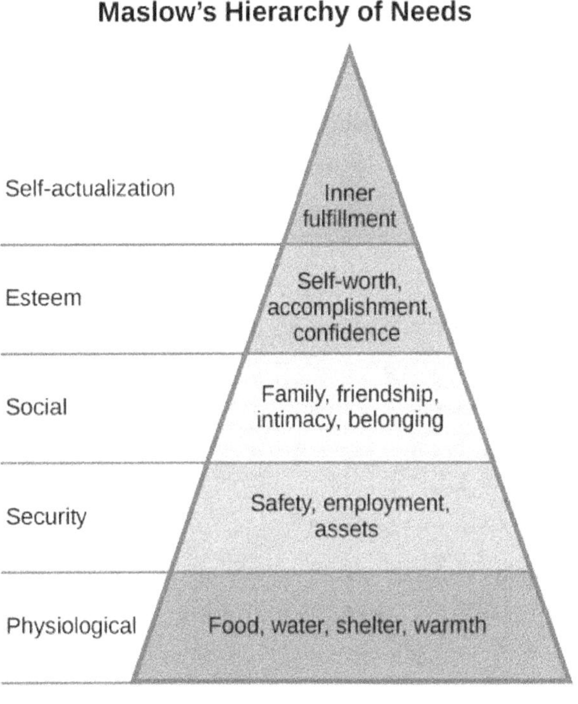

Figure 3.

Humanism has been influential to psychology as a whole. Both Maslow and Rogers are well-known names among students of psychology (you will read more about both men later in this text), and their ideas have influenced many scholars. Furthermore, Rogers' client-centered approach to therapy is still commonly used in psychotherapeutic settings today (O'hara, n.d.).

The Cognitive Revolution

Behaviorism's emphasis on objectivity and focus on external behavior had pulled psychologists' attention away from the mind for a prolonged period of time. The early work of the humanistic psychologists redirected attention to the individual human as a whole, and as a conscious and self-aware being. By the 1950s, new disciplinary perspectives in linguistics, neuroscience, and computer science were emerging, and these areas revived interest in the mind as a focus of scientific inquiry. This particular perspective has come to be known as the cognitive revolution (Miller, 2003). By 1967, Ulric Neisser published the first textbook entitled *Cognitive Psychology*, which served as a core text in cognitive psychology courses around the country (Thorne & Henley, 2005).Although no one person is entirely responsible for starting the cognitive revolution, Noam Chomsky was very influential in the early days of this movement. Chomsky (1928–), an American linguist, was dissatisfied with the influence that behaviorism had had on psychology. He believed that psychology's focus on behavior was short-sighted and that the field had to re-incorporate mental functioning into its purview if it were to offer any meaningful contributions to understanding behavior (Miller, 2003).

European psychology had never really been as influenced by behaviorism as had American psychology; and thus, the cognitive revolution helped reestablish lines of communication between European psychologists and their American counterparts. Furthermore, psychologists began to cooperate with scientists in other fields, like anthropology, linguistics, computer science, and neuroscience, among others. This interdisciplinary approach often was referred to as the cognitive sciences, and the influence and prominence of this particular perspective resonates in modern-day psychology (Miller, 2003).

Noam Chomsky was very influential in beginning the cognitive revolution. In 2010, this mural honoring him was put up in Philadelphia, Pennsylvania. (credit: Robert Moran)

Cognitive Psychology

Cognitive psychology is radically different from previous psychological approaches in that it is characterized by *both* of the following:

1. It accepts the use of the scientific method and generally rejects introspection as a valid method of investigation, unlike phenomenological methods such as Freudian psychoanalysis.

2. It explicitly acknowledges the existence of internal mental states (such as belief, desire, and motivation), unlike behaviorist psychology.

Cognitive theory contends that solutions to problems take the form of algorithms, heuristics, or insights. Major areas of research in cognitive psychology include perception, memory, categorization, knowledge representation, numerical cognition, language, and thinking.

Multicultural Psychology

Culture has important impacts on individuals and social psychology, yet the effects of culture on psychology are under-studied. There is a risk that psychological theories and data derived from white, American settings could be assumed to apply to individuals and social groups from other cultures and this is unlikely to be true (Betancourt & López, 1993). One weakness in the field of cross-cultural psychology is that in looking for differences in psychological attributes across cultures, there remains a need to go beyond simple descriptive statistics (Betancourt & López, 1993). In this sense, it has remained a descriptive science, rather than one seeking to determine cause and effect. For example, a study of characteristics of individuals seeking treatment for a binge eating disorder in Hispanic American, African American, and Caucasian American individuals found significant differences between groups (Franko et al., 2012). The study concluded that results from studying any one of the groups could not be extended to the other groups, and yet potential causes of the differences were not measured.

This history of multicultural psychology in the United States is a long one. The role of African American psychologists in researching the cultural differences between African American individual and social psychology is but one example. In 1920, Cecil Sumner was the first African American to receive a PhD in psychology in the United States. Sumner established a psychology degree program at Howard University, leading to the education of a new generation of African American psychologists (Black, Spence, and Omari, 2004). Much of the work of early African American psychologists (and a general focus of much work in first half of the 20th century in psychology in the United States) was dedicated to testing and intelligence testing in particular (Black et al., 2004). That emphasis has continued, particularly because of the importance of testing in determining opportunities for children, but other areas of exploration in African-American psychology research include learning style, sense of community and belonging, and spiritualism (Black et al., 2004).

The American Psychological Association has several ethnically based organizations for professional psychologists that facilitate interactions among members. Since psychologists belonging to specific ethnic groups or cultures have the most interest in studying the psychology of their communities, these organizations provide an opportunity for the growth of research on the impact of culture on individual and social psychology.

Summary of the History of Psychology

Before the time of Wundt and James, questions about the mind were considered by philosophers. However, both Wundt and James helped create psychology as a distinct scientific discipline. Wundt was a *structuralist*, which meant he believed that our cognitive experience was best understood by breaking that experience into its component parts. He thought this was best accomplished by introspection.

William James was the first American psychologist, and he was a proponent of *functionalism*. This particular perspective focused on how mental activities served as adaptive responses to an organism's environment. Like Wundt, James also relied on introspection; however, his research approach also incorporated more objective measures as well.

Sigmund Freud believed that understanding the unconscious mind was absolutely critical to understand conscious behavior. This was especially true for individuals that he saw who suffered from various hysterias and neuroses. Freud relied on dream analysis, slips of the tongue, and free association as means to access the unconscious. Psychoanalytic theory remained a dominant force in clinical psychology for several decades.

Gestalt psychology was very influential in Europe. Gestalt psychology takes a holistic view of an individual and his experiences. As the Nazis came to power in Germany, Wertheimer, Koffka, and Köhler immigrated to the United States. Although they left their laboratories and their research behind, they did introduce America to Gestalt ideas. Some of the principles of Gestalt psychology are still very influential in the study of sensation and perception.

One of the most influential schools of thought within psychology's history was behaviorism. Behaviorism focused on making psychology an objective science by studying overt behavior and deemphasizing the importance of unobservable mental processes. John Watson is often considered the father of behaviorism, and B. F. Skinner's contributions to our understanding of principles of operant conditioning cannot be underestimated.

As behaviorism and psychoanalytic theory took hold of so many aspects of psychology, some began to become dissatisfied with psychology's picture of human nature. Thus, a humanistic movement within psychology began to take hold. Humanism focuses on the potential of all people for good. Both Maslow and Rogers were influential in shaping humanistic psychology.

During the 1950s, the landscape of psychology began to change. A science of behavior began to shift back to its roots of focus on mental processes. The emergence of neuroscience and computer science aided this transition. Ultimately, the cognitive revolution took hold, and people came to realize that cognition was crucial to a true appreciation and understanding of behavior.

Early Schools of Psychology: Still Active and Advanced Beyond Early Ideas

School of Psychology	Description	Earliest Period	Historically Important People
Psychodynamic Psychology	Focuses on the role of the unconscious and childhood experiences in affecting conscious behavior.	Very late 19th to Early 20th Century	Sigmund Freud, Erik Erikson
Behaviorism	Focuses on observing and controlling behavior through what is observable. Puts an emphasis on learning and conditioning.	Early 20th Century	Ivan Pavlov, John B. Watson, B. F. Skinner
Cognitive Psychology	Focuses not just on behavior, but on on mental processes and internal mental states.	1920s	Ulric Neisser, Noam Chomsky, Jean Piaget, Lev Vygotsky
Humanistic Psychology	Emphasizes the potential for good that is innate to all humans and rejects that psychology should focus on problems and disorders.	1950s	Abraham Maslow, Carl Rogers

Glossary

behaviorism: focus on observing and controlling behavior

humanism: perspective within psychology that emphasizes the potential for good that is innate to all humans

https://assessments.lumenlearning.com/assessments/4802

Attributions

CC licensed content, Original

- Addition of link to learning. **Provided by:** Lumen Learning. **License:** *CC BY: Attribution*

CC licensed content, Shared previously

- History of Psychology. **Authored by:** OpenStax College. **Located at:** http://cnx.org/contents/Sr8Ev5Og@5.48:lAYBvVZM@5/History-of-Psychology. **License:** *CC BY: Attribution.* **License Terms:** Download for free at http://cnx.org/contents/4abf04bf-93a0-45c3-9cbc-2cefd46e68cc@5.48
- Cognitive Psychology. **Provided by:** Boundless. **Located at:** https://www.boundless.com/psychology/textbooks/boundless-psychology-textbook/introduction-to-psychology-1/theoretical-perspectives-in-modern-psychology-23/cognitive-psychology-115-12652/. **License:** *CC BY-SA: Attribution-ShareAlike*
- Early Schools of Psychology: Still Active and Advanced Beyond Early Ideas Table. **Provided by:** Open Learning Initiative. **Located at:** https://oli.cmu.edu/jcourse/workbook/activity/page?context=4c39410080020ca60127b04635de0b80. **Project:** Introduction to Psychology. **License:** *CC BY-NC-SA: Attribution-NonCommercial-ShareAlike*

Domains in Psychology

What you'll learn to do: identify the various approaches, fields, and subfields of psychology along with their major concepts and important figures

This section will provide an overview of the major domains of psychology today, as well as some additional sub-fields and content areas. This is not meant to be an exhaustive listing, but it will provide insight into the major areas of research and practice of modern-day psychologists. You'll come to see that while psychology is defined as the study of the mind and behavior, there are many different types of psychologists who emphasize and apply psychological principles in various ways.

For example, imagine that a woman is diagnosed with depression. What is the cause of the depression? Is it her biology or chemical imbalances in her brain? Evolutionary predispositions? Perhaps it is caused by experiences in her past, or something else that triggered a downward spiral of emotions? Or maybe it is caused by social factors, or cultural expectations? All of these things could, in fact, play a role in her depression. In this section, you'll see how psychologists analyze behavior from a variety of perspectives and better understand the breadth of psychology.

Learning Objectives

- List and define the five major domains, or pillars, of contemporary psychology
- Describe the basic interests and applications of biopsychology and evolutionary psychology
- Describe the basic interests and applications of cognitive psychology
- Describe the basic interests and applications of developmental psychology
- Describe the basic interests and applications of social psychology and personality psychology
- Describe the basic interests and applications of abnormal, clinical, and health psychology
- Define industrial-organizational psychology, sport and exercise psychology, and forensic psychology

Introduction to Contemporary Psychology

Contemporary psychology is a diverse field that is influenced by all of the historical perspectives described in the previous section of reading. Reflective of the discipline's diversity is the diversity seen within the **American Psychological Association** (APA). The APA is a professional organization representing psychologists in the United States. The APA is the largest organization of psychologists in the world, and its mission is to advance and disseminate psychological knowledge for the betterment of people. There are 56 divisions within the APA, representing a wide variety of specialties that range from Societies for the Psychology of Religion and Spirituality to Exercise and Sport Psychology to Behavioral Neuroscience and Comparative Psychology. Reflecting the diversity of the field of psychology itself, members, affiliate members, and associate members span the spectrum from students to doctoral-level psychologists, and come from a variety of places including educational settings, criminal justice, hospitals, the armed forces, and industry (American Psychological Association, 2014).

Link to Learning

Please visit this website to learn about the divisions within the APA. Student resources are also provided by the APA:

- http://www.apa.org/about/division/index.aspx
- http://www.apa.org/about/students.aspx

Psychologists agree that there is no *one* right way to study the way people think or behave. There are, however, various schools of thought that evolved throughout the development of psychology that continue to shape the way we investigate human behavior. For example, some psychologists might attribute a certain behavior to biological factors such as genetics while another psychologist might consider early childhood experiences to be a more likely explanation for the behavior. Many expert psychologists focus their entire careers on just one facet of psychology, such as developmental psychology or cognitive psychology, or even more specifically, newborn intelligence or language processing.

While the field of study is large and vast, this text aims to introduce you to the main topics with psychology. You'll get exposure to the various branches and sub-fields within the discipline and come to understand how they are all interconnected and essential in understanding behavior and mental processes. The five main psychological pillars, or domains, as we will refer to them, are:

1. Domain 1: Biological (includes neuroscience, consciousness, and sensation)

2. Domain 2: Cognitive (includes the study of perception, cognition, memory, and intelligence)

3. Domain 3: Development (includes learning and conditioning, lifespan development, and language)

4. Domain 4: Social and Personality (includes the study of personality, emotion, motivation, gender, and culture)

5. Domain 5: Mental and Physical Health (includes abnormal psychology, therapy, and health psychology)

These five domains cover the main viewpoints, or perspectives, of psychology. These perspectives emphasize certain assumptions about behavior and provide a framework for psychologists in conducting research and analyzing behavior. They include some you have already read about, including Freud's psychodynamic perspective, behaviorism, humanism, and the cognitive approach. Other perspectives include the biological perspective, evolutionary, and socio-cultural perspectives.

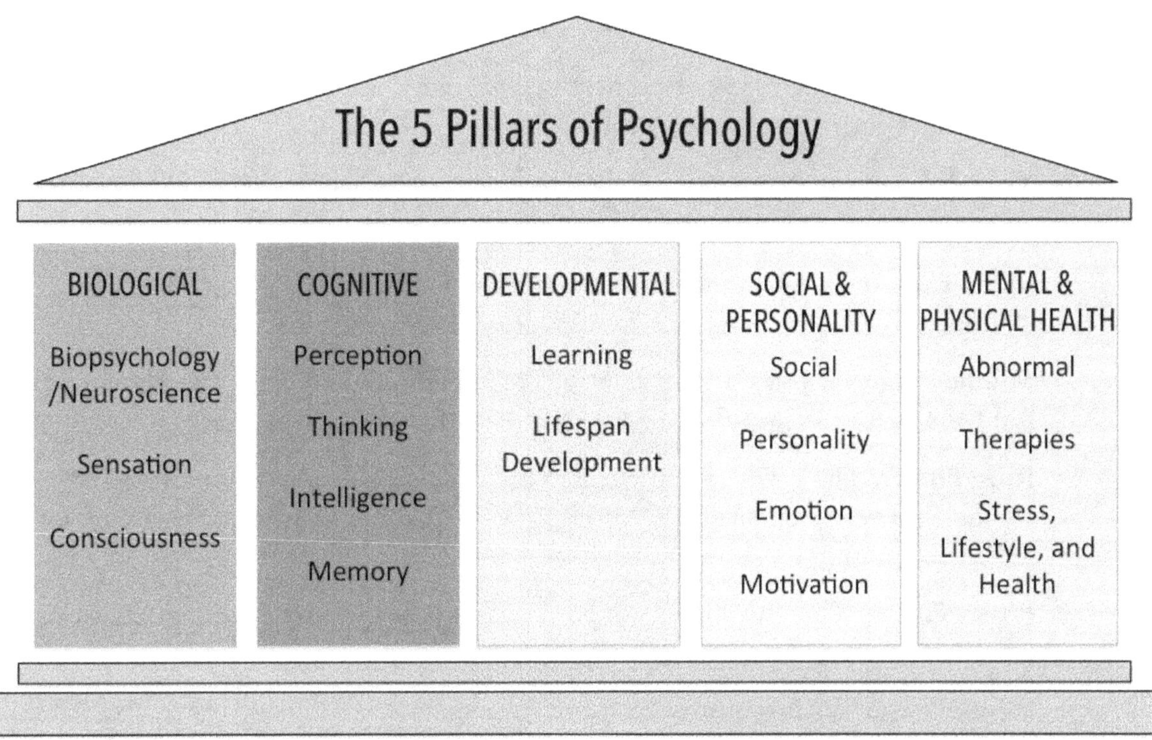

Figure 1. The five pillars, or domains, of psychology. Image adapted from Gurung, R. A., Hackathorn, J., Enns, C., Frantz, S., Cacioppo, J. T., Loop, T., & Freeman, J. E. (2016) article "Strengthening introductory psychology: A new model for teaching the introductory course" from American Psychologist.

Helpful Hints

A neat way to remember the major perspectives in psychology is to think about your hand and associate each finger with a psychological approach:

- **Thumb**: your thumb can move around in PSYCHO ways—it's so versatile! This is the **psychodynamic** perspective.

- **Index Finger**: Tap your finger to the temple of your head as if you were THINKING about something. This is the **cognitive** perspective.

- **Middle Finger:** If you stuck up your middle finger to flip someone off, that would be bad BEHAVIOR in many cultures. This is the **behavioral** perspective.

- **Ring Finger:** This is where you would wear a wedding band. A **humanistic** psychologist would emphasize everyone's potential for marriage, or more likely, for self-actualization.

- **Pinky Finger:** This little finger was born this way—short. Thank your BIOLOGY for that. **Biological** perspective.

- **Palm of hand: Socio-cultural.** In many cultures, giving a high-five is an acceptable greeting.

The Biological Domain

Biopsychology—also known as biological psychology or psychobiology—is the application of the principles of biology to the study of mental processes and behavior. As the name suggests, **biopsychology** explores how our biology influences our behavior. While biological psychology is a broad field, many biological psychologists want to understand how the structure and function of the nervous system is related to behavior. The fields of behavioral neuroscience, cognitive neuroscience, and neuropsychology are all subfields of biological psychology.

The research interests of biological psychologists span a number of domains, including but not limited to, sensory and motor systems, sleep, drug use and abuse, ingestive behavior, reproductive behavior, neurodevelopment, plasticity of the nervous system, and biological correlates of psychological disorders. Given the broad areas of interest falling under the purview of biological psychology, it will probably come as no surprise that individuals from all sorts of backgrounds are involved in this research, including biologists, medical professionals, physiologists, and chemists. This interdisciplinary approach is often referred to as neuroscience, of which biological psychology is a component (Carlson, 2013).

Evolutionary Psychology

While biopsychology typically focuses on the immediate causes of behavior based in the physiology of a human or other animal, evolutionary psychology seeks to study the ultimate biological causes of behavior. To the extent that a behavior is impacted by genetics, a behavior, like any anatomical

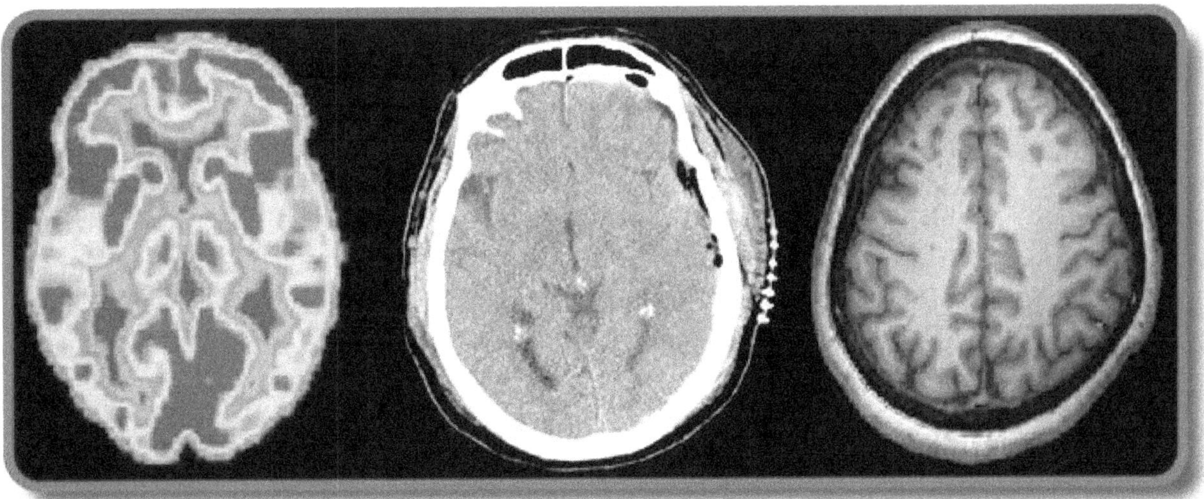

Figure 2. Different brain-imaging techniques provide scientists with insight into different aspects of how the human brain functions. Three types of scans include (left to right) PET scan (positron emission tomography), CT scan (computed tomography), and fMRI (functional magnetic resonance imaging). (credit "left": modification of work by Health and Human Services Department, National Institutes of Health; credit "center": modification of work by "Aceofhearts1968"/Wikimedia Commons; credit "right": modification of work by Kim J, Matthews NL, Park S.)

characteristic of a human or animal, will demonstrate adaption to its surroundings. These surroundings include the physical environment and, since interactions between organisms can be important to survival and reproduction, the social environment. The study of behavior in the context of evolution has its origins with Charles Darwin, the co-discoverer of the theory of evolution by natural selection. Darwin was well aware that behaviors should be adaptive and wrote books titled, *The Descent of Man* (1871) and *The Expression of the Emotions in Man and Animals* (1872), to explore this field.

Evolutionary psychology, and specifically, the evolutionary psychology of humans, has enjoyed a resurgence in recent decades. To be subject to evolution by natural selection, a behavior must have a significant genetic cause. In general, we expect all human cultures to express a behavior if it is caused genetically, since the genetic differences among human groups are small. The approach taken by most evolutionary psychologists is to predict the outcome of a behavior in a particular situation based on evolutionary theory and then to make observations, or conduct experiments, to determine whether the results match the theory. It is important to recognize that these types of studies are not strong evidence that a behavior is adaptive, since they lack information that the behavior is in some part genetic and not entirely cultural (Endler, 1986). Demonstrating that a trait, especially in humans, is naturally selected is extraordinarily difficult; perhaps for this reason, some evolutionary psychologists are content to assume the behaviors they study have genetic determinants (Confer et al., 2010).

One other drawback of evolutionary psychology is that the traits that we possess now evolved under environmental and social conditions far back in human history, and we have a poor understanding of what these conditions were. This makes predictions about what is adaptive for a behavior difficult. Behavioral traits need not be adaptive under current conditions, only under the conditions of the past when they evolved, about which we can only hypothesize.

There are many areas of human behavior for which evolution can make predictions. Examples include memory, mate choice, relationships between kin, friendship and cooperation, parenting, social organization, and status (Confer et al., 2010).

Evolutionary psychologists have had success in finding experimental correspondence between observations and expectations. In one example, in a study of mate preference differences between men and women that spanned 37 cultures, Buss (1989) found that women valued earning potential factors greater than men, and men valued potential reproductive factors (youth and attractiveness) greater than women in their prospective mates. In general, the predictions were in line with the predictions of evolution, although there were deviations in some cultures.

Sensation and Perception

Scientists interested in both physiological aspects of sensory systems as well as in the psychological experience of sensory information work within the area of sensation and perception. As such, sensation and perception research is also quite interdisciplinary. Imagine walking between buildings as you move from one class to another. You are inundated with sights, sounds, touch sensations, and smells. You also experience the temperature of the air around you and maintain your balance as you make your way. These are all factors of interest to someone working in the domain of sensation and perception.

The Cognitive Domain

As mentioned earlier, the cognitive revolution created an impetus for psychologists to focus their attention on better understanding the mind and mental processes that underlie behavior. Thus, **cognitive psychology** is the area of psychology that focuses on studying cognitions, or thoughts, and their relationship to our experiences and our actions. Like biological psychology, cognitive psychology is broad in its scope and often involves collaborations among people from a diverse range of disciplinary backgrounds. This has led some to coin the term cognitive science to describe the interdisciplinary nature of this area of research (Miller, 2003).

Cognitive psychologists have research interests that span a spectrum of topics, ranging from attention to problem solving to language to memory. The approaches used in studying these topics are equally diverse. The bulk of content coverage on cognitive psychology will be covered in the modules in this text on thinking, intelligence, and memory. But given its diversity, various concepts related to cognitive psychology will be covered in other sections such as lifespan development, social psychology, and therapy.

The Developmental Domain

Developmental psychology is the scientific study of development across a lifespan. Developmental psychologists are interested in processes related to physical maturation. However, their focus is not limited to the physical changes associated with aging, as they also focus on changes in cognitive skills, moral reasoning, social behavior, and other psychological attributes. Early developmental psychologists focused primarily on changes that occurred through reaching adulthood, providing enormous insight into the differences in physical, cognitive, and social capacities that exist between very young children and adults. For instance, research by Jean Piaget demonstrated that very young children do not demonstrate object permanence. Object permanence refers to the understanding that physical things continue to exist, even if they are hidden from us. If you were to show an adult a toy, and then hide it behind a curtain, the adult knows that the toy still exists. However, very young infants act as if a hidden object no longer exists. The age at which object permanence is achieved is somewhat controversial (Munakata, McClelland, Johnson, and Siegler, 1997).

While Piaget was focused on cognitive changes during infancy and childhood as we move to adulthood, there is an increasing interest in extending research into the changes that occur much later in life. This may be reflective of changing population demographics of developed nations as a whole. As more and more people live longer lives, the number of people of advanced age will continue to increase. Indeed, it is estimated that there were just over 40 million people aged 65 or older living in the United States in 2010. However, by 2020, this number is expected to increase to about 55 million. By the year 2050, it is estimated that nearly 90 million people in this country will be 65 or older (Department of Health and Human Services, n.d.).

Figure 3. Piaget is best known for his stage theory of cognitive development.

Behavioral Psychology

Another critical field of study under the development domain is that of learning and behaviorism, which you read about already. The primary developments in learning and conditioning came from the work of Ivan Pavlov, John B. Watson, Edward Lee Thorndike, and B. F. Skinner. Contemporary behaviorists apply learning techniques in the form of behavior modification for a variety of mental problems. Learning is seen as behavior change molded by experience; it is accomplished largely through either classical or operant conditioning.

The Social and Personality Psychology Domain

Social psychology is the scientific study of how people's thoughts, feelings, and behaviors are influenced by the actual, imagined, or implied presence of others. This domain of psychology is concerned with the way such feelings, thoughts, beliefs, intentions, and goals are constructed, and how these psychological factors, in turn, influence our interactions with others.

Social psychology typically explains human behavior as a result of the interaction of mental states and immediate social situations. Social psychologists, therefore, examine the factors that lead us to behave in a given way in the presence of others, as well as the conditions under which certain behaviors, actions, and feelings occur. They focus on how people construe or interpret situations and how these interpretations influence their thoughts, feelings, and behaviors (Ross & Nisbett, 1991). Thus, social psychology studies individuals in a social context and how situational variables interact to influence behavior.

Some social psychologists study large-scale sociocultural forces within cultures and societies that affect the thoughts, feelings, and behaviors of individuals. These include forces such as attitudes, child-rearing practices, discrimination and prejudice, ethnic and racial identity, gender roles and norms, family and kinship structures, power dynamics, regional differences, religious beliefs and practices, rituals, and taboos. Several subfields within psychology seek to examine these sociocultural factors that influence human mental states and behavior; among these are social psychology, cultural psychology, cultural-historical psychology, and cross-cultural psychology.

There are many interesting examples of social psychological research, and you will read about many of these in a later in this textbook. Until then, you will be introduced to one of the most controversial psychological studies ever conducted. Stanley Milgram was an American social psychologist who is most famous for research that he conducted on obedience. After the Holocaust, in 1961, a Nazi war criminal, Adolf Eichmann, who was accused of committing mass atrocities, was put on trial. Many people wondered how German soldiers were capable of torturing prisoners in concentration camps, and they were unsatisfied with the excuses given by soldiers that they were simply following orders. At the time, most psychologists agreed that few people would be willing to inflict such extraordinary pain and suffering, simply because they were obeying orders. Milgram decided to conduct research to determine whether or not this was true.

As you will read later in the text, Milgram found that nearly two-thirds of his participants were willing to deliver what they believed to be lethal shocks to another person, simply because they were instructed to do so by an authority figure (in this case, a man dressed in a lab coat). This was in spite of the fact that participants received payment for simply showing up for the research study and could have chosen not to inflict pain or more serious consequences on another person by withdrawing from the study. No one was actually hurt or harmed in any way, Milgram's experiment was a clever ruse that took advantage of research confederates, those

Public Announcement

WE WILL PAY YOU $4.00 FOR ONE HOUR OF YOUR TIME

Persons Needed for a Study of Memory

*We will pay five hundred New Haven men to help us complete a scientific study of memory and learning. The study is being done at Yale University.

*Each person who participates will be paid $4.00 (plus 50c carfare) for approximately 1 hour's time. We need you for only one hour: there are no further obligations. You may choose the time you would like to come (evenings, weekdays, or weekends).

*No special training, education, or experience is needed. We want:

Factory workers	Businessmen	Construction workers
City employees	Clerks	Salespeople
Laborers	Professional people	White-collar workers
Barbers	Telephone workers	Others

All persons must be between the ages of 20 and 50. High school and college students cannot be used.

*If you meet these qualifications, fill out the coupon below and mail it now to Professor Stanley Milgram, Department of Psychology, Yale University, New Haven. You will be notified later of the specific time and place of the study. We reserve the right to decline any application.

*You will be paid $4.00 (plus 50c carfare) as soon as you arrive at the laboratory.

TO:
PROF. STANLEY MILGRAM, DEPARTMENT OF PSYCHOLOGY, YALE UNIVERSITY, NEW HAVEN, CONN. I want to take part in this study of memory and learning. I am between the ages of 20 and 50. I will be paid $4.00 (plus 50c carfare) if I participate.

NAME (Please Print). . . . .

ADDRESS . . . .

TELEPHONE NO. . . . . Best time to call you . . . .

AGE. . . . . OCCUPATION. SEX. . . . . .
CAN YOU COME:

WEEKDAYS . . . . EVENINGS . . . . . . WEEKENDS. . . . .

Figure 4. Stanley Milgram's research demonstrated just how far people will go in obeying orders from an authority figure. This advertisement was used to recruit subjects for his research.

who pretend to be participants in a research study who are actually working for the researcher and have clear, specific directions on how to behave during the research study (Hock, 2009). Milgram's and others' studies that involved deception and potential emotional harm to study participants catalyzed the development of ethical guidelines for conducting psychological research that discourage the use of deception of research subjects, unless it can be argued not to cause harm and, in general, requiring informed consent of participants.

Personality Psychology

Another major field of study within the social and personality domain is, of course, **personality psychology**. Personality refers to the long-standing traits and patterns that propel individuals to consistently think, feel, and behave in specific ways. Our personality is what makes us unique individuals. Each person has an idiosyncratic pattern of enduring, long-term characteristics, and a manner in which they interact with other individuals and the world around them. Our personalities are thought to be long-term, stable, and not easily changed. Personality psychology focuses on

- construction of a coherent picture of the individual and their major psychological processes.

- investigation of individual psychological differences.

- investigation of human nature and psychological similarities between individuals.

Several individuals (e.g., Freud and Maslow) that we have already discussed in our historical overview of psychology, and the American psychologist Gordon Allport, contributed to early theories of personality. These early theorists attempted to explain how an individual's personality develops from his or her given perspective. For example, Freud proposed that personality arose as conflicts between the conscious and unconscious parts of the mind were carried out over the lifespan. Specifically, Freud theorized that an individual went through various psychosexual stages of development. According to Freud, adult personality would result from the resolution of various conflicts that centered on the migration of erogenous (or sexual pleasure-producing) zones from the oral (mouth) to the anus to the phallus to the genitals. Like many of Freud's theories, this particular idea was controversial and did not lend itself to experimental tests (Person, 1980).

More recently, the study of personality has taken on a more quantitative approach. Rather than explaining how personality arises, research is focused on identifying **personality traits**, measuring these traits, and determining how these traits interact in a particular context to determine how a person will behave in any given situation. Personality traits are relatively consistent patterns of thought and behavior, and many have proposed that five trait dimensions are sufficient to capture the variations in personality seen across individuals. These five dimensions are known as the "Big Five" or the Five Factor model, and include dimensions of conscientiousness, agreeableness, neuroticism, openness, and extraversion (shown below). Each of these traits has been demonstrated to be relatively stable over the lifespan (e.g., Rantanen, Metsäpelto, Feldt, Pulkinnen, and Kokko, 2007; Soldz & Vaillant, 1999; McCrae & Costa, 2008) and is influenced by genetics (e.g., Jang, Livesly, and Vernon, 1996). Each of the dimensions of the Five Factor model is shown in this figure. The provided description would describe someone who scored highly on that given dimension. Someone with a lower score on a given dimension could be described in opposite terms.

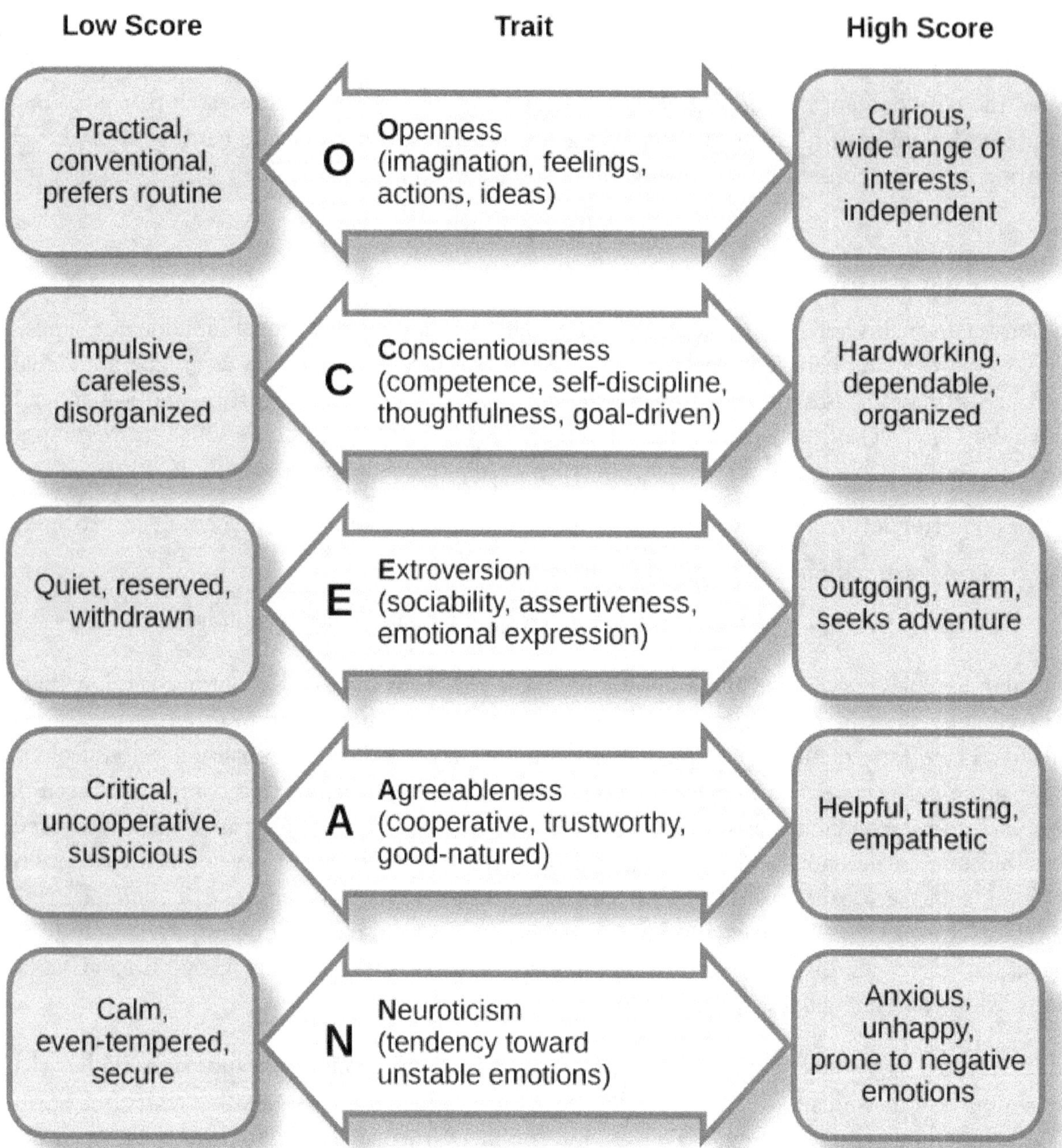

Figure 5. Each of the dimensions of the Five Factor model is shown in this figure. The provided description would describe someone who scored highly on that given dimension. Someone with a lower score on a given dimension could be described in opposite terms.

The Mental and Physical Health Domain

This domain of psychology is what many people think of when they think about psychology—mental disorders and counseling. This includes the study of abnormal psychology, with its focus on abnormal thoughts and behaviors, as well as counseling and treatment methods, and recommendations for coping with stress and living a healthy life.

The names and classifications of mental disorders are listed in the *Diagnostic and Statistical Manual of Mental Disorders* (DSM). The DSM is currently in its 5th edition (DSM-V) and has been designed for use in a wide variety of contexts and across clinical settings (including inpatient, outpatient, partial hospital, clinic, private practice, and primary care). The diagnostic manual includes a total of 237 specific diagnosable disorders, each described in detail, including its symptoms, prevalence, risk factors, and comorbidity. Over time, the number of diagnosable conditions listed in the DSM has grown steadily, prompting criticism from some. Nevertheless, the diagnostic criteria in the DSM are more explicit than those of any other system, which makes the DSM system highly desirable for both clinical diagnosis and research.

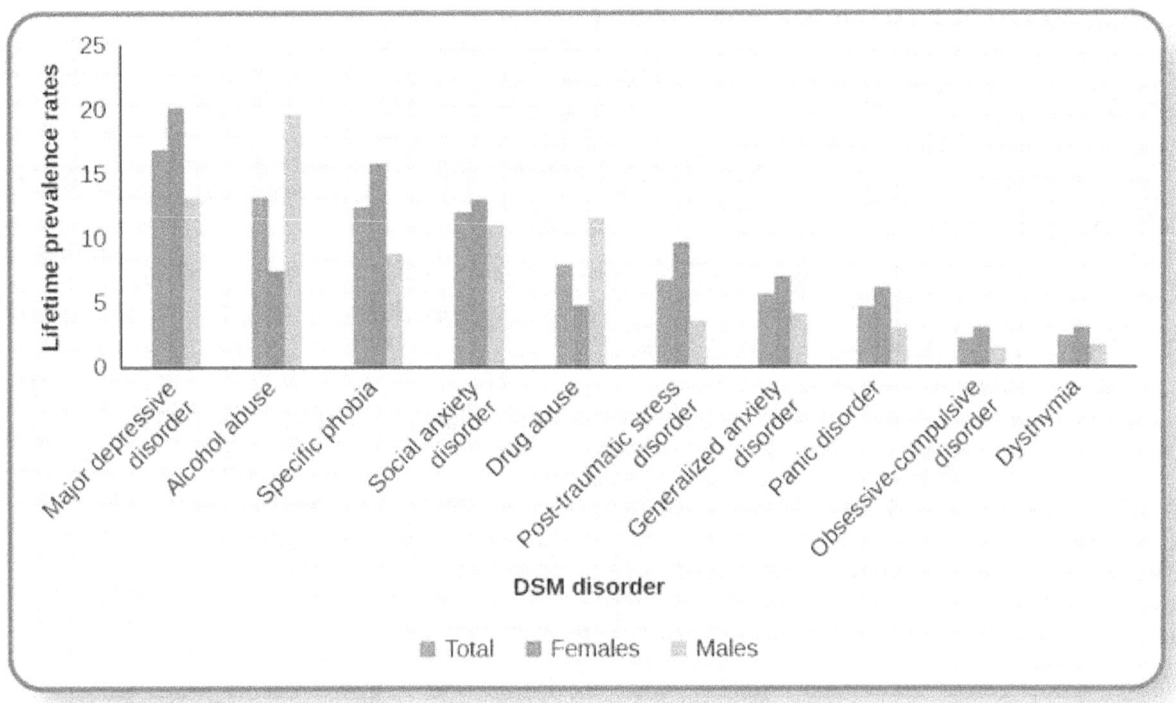

Figure 6. Lifetime prevalence rates for major psychological disorders.

Clinical Psychology

Clinical psychology is the area of psychology that focuses on the diagnosis and treatment of psychological disorders and other problematic patterns of behavior. As such, it is generally considered to be a more applied area within psychology; however, some clinicians are also actively engaged in scientific research. Counseling psychology is a similar discipline that focuses on emotional, social, vocational, and health-related outcomes in individuals who are considered psychologically healthy. As mentioned earlier, both Freud and Rogers provided perspectives that have been influential in shaping how clinicians interact with people seeking psychotherapy. While aspects of the psychoanalytic theory are still found among some of today's therapists who are trained from a psychodynamic perspective, Roger's ideas about client-centered therapy have been especially influential in shaping how many clinicians operate. Furthermore, both behaviorism and the cognitive revolution have shaped clinical practice in the forms of behavioral therapy, cognitive therapy, and cognitive-behavioral therapy. Issues related to the diagnosis and treatment of psychological disorders and problematic patterns of behavior will be discussed in detail later in this textbook.

By far, this is the area of psychology that receives the most attention in popular media, and many people mistakenly assume that all psychology is clinical psychology.

Health Psychology

Health psychology focuses on how health is affected by the interaction of biological, psychological, and sociocultural factors. This particular approach is known as the **biopsychosocial model.** Health psychologists are interested in helping individuals achieve better health through public policy, education, intervention, and research.

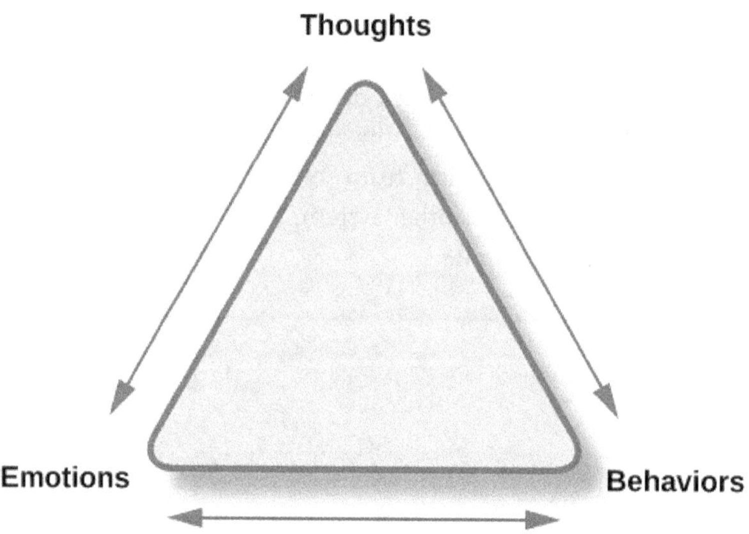

Figure 7. Cognitive-behavioral therapists take cognitive processes and behaviors into account when providing psychotherapy. This is one of several strategies that may be used by practicing clinical psychologists.

Health psychologists might conduct research that explores the relationship between one's genetic makeup, patterns of behavior, relationships, psychological stress, and health. They may research effective ways to motivate people to address patterns of behavior that contribute to poorer health (MacDonald, 2013).

Other Psychological Subfields

Industrial-Organizational Psychology

Industrial-Organizational psychology (I-O psychology) is a subfield of psychology that applies psychological theories, principles, and research findings in industrial and organizational settings. I-O psychologists are often involved in issues related to personnel management, organizational structure, and workplace environment. Businesses often seek the aid of I-O psychologists to make the best hiring decisions as well as to create an environment that results in high levels of employee productivity and efficiency. In addition to its applied nature, I-O psychology also involves conducting scientific research on behavior within I-O settings (Riggio, 2013).

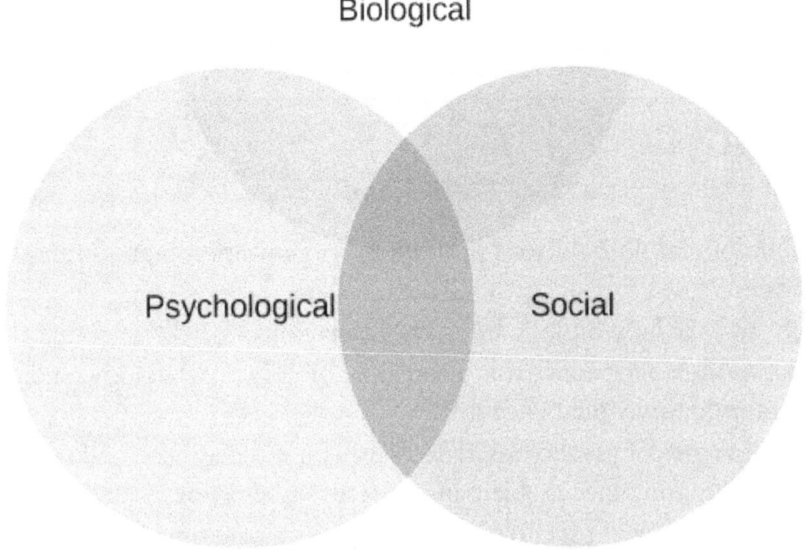

Figure 8. The biopsychosocial model suggests that health/illness is determined by an interaction of these three factors.

Sport and Exercise Psychology

Researchers in **sport and exercise psychology** study the psychological aspects of sport performance, including motivation and performance anxiety, and the effects of sport on mental and emotional well-being. Research is also conducted on similar topics as they relate to physical exercise in general. The discipline also includes topics that are broader than sport and exercise but that are related to interactions between mental and physical performance under demanding conditions, such as fire fighting, military operations, artistic performance, and surgery.

Forensic Psychology

Forensic psychology is a branch of psychology that deals questions of psychology as they arise in the context of the justice system. For example, forensic psychologists (and forensic psychiatrists) will assess a person's competency to stand trial, assess the state of mind of a defendant, act as consultants on child custody cases, consult on sentencing and treatment recommendations, and advise on issues such as eyewitness testimony and children's testimony (American Board of Forensic Psychology, 2014). In these capacities, they will typically act as expert witnesses, called by either side in a court case to provide their research- or experience-based opinions. As expert witnesses, forensic psychologists must have a good understanding of the law and provide information in the context of the legal system rather than just within the realm of psychology. Forensic psychologists are also used in the jury selection process and witness preparation. They may also be involed in providing psychological treatment within the criminal justice system. Criminal profilers are a relatively small proportion of psychologists that act as consultants to law enforcement.

Link to Learning

Check out the APA website for more information on psychological subfields and possible career paths here.

- http://www.apa.org/careers/resources/guides/careers.aspx

Glossary

American Psychological Association: professional organization representing psychologists in the United States

biopsychology: study of how biology influences behavior

biopsychosocial model: perspective that asserts that biology, psychology, and social factors interact to determine an individual's health

clinical psychology: area of psychology that focuses on the diagnosis and treatment of psychological disorders and other problematic patterns of behavior

cognitive psychology: area of psychology that focuses on studying thoughts and their relationship to our experiences and actions

developmental psychology: scientific study of development across a lifespan

forensic psychology: area of psychology that applies the science and practice of psychology to issues within and related to the justice system

personality psychology: study of patterns of thoughts and behaviors that make each individual unique

personality trait: consistent pattern of thought and behavior

sport and exercise psychology: area of psychology that focuses on the interactions between mental and emotional factors and physical performance in sports, exercise, and other activities

https://assessments.lumenlearning.com/assessments/4803

Attributions

Public domain content

- woman at subway. **Authored by:** Eutah Mizushima. **Provided by:** Unsplash. **Located at:** https://www.pexels.com/photo/train-underground-subway-person-7533/. **License:** *Public Domain: No Known Copyright*

Careers in Psychology

Figure 1. An Army psychologist reviewing medical information.

Generally, academic careers in psychology require doctoral degrees. However, there are a number of nonacademic career options for people who have master's degrees in psychology. While people with bachelor's degrees in psychology have more limited psychology-related career options, the skills acquired as a function of an undergraduate education in psychology are useful in a variety of work contexts and are applicable to a wide variety of careers. Basically, studying psychology is never a bad choice!

Learning Objectives

- Explain why an education in psychology is valuable
- Describe educational requirements and career options for the study of psychology

Merits of an Education in Psychology

Often, students take their first psychology course because they are interested in helping others and want to learn more about themselves and why they act the way they do. Sometimes, students take a psychology course because it either satisfies a general education requirement or is required for a program of study such as nursing or pre-med. Many of these students develop such an interest in the area that they go on to declare psychology as their major. As a result, psychology is one of the most popular majors on college campuses across the United States (Johnson & Lubin, 2011). A number of well-known individuals were psychology majors. Just a few famous names on this list are Facebook's creator Mark Zuckerberg, television personality and political satirist Jon Stewart, actress Natalie Portman, and filmmaker Wes Craven (Halonen, 2011). About 6 percent of all bachelor degrees granted in the United States are in the discipline of psychology (U.S. Department of Education, 2013).

Figure 1. Doctoral degrees are generally conferred in formal ceremonies involving special attire and rites. (credit: Public Affairs Office Fort Wainwright)

An education in psychology is valuable for a number of reasons. Psychology students hone critical thinking skills and are trained in the use of the scientific method. Critical thinking is the active application of a set of skills to information for the understanding and evaluation of that information. The evaluation of information—assessing its reliability and usefulness— is an important skill in a world full of competing "facts," many of which are designed to be misleading. For example, critical thinking involves maintaining an attitude of skepticism, recognizing internal biases, making use of logical thinking, asking appropriate questions, and making observations. Psychology students also can develop better communication skills during the course of their undergraduate coursework (American Psychological Association, 2011). Together, these factors increase students' scientific literacy and prepare students to critically evaluate the various sources of information they encounter.

In addition to these broad-based skills, psychology students come to understand the complex factors that shape one's behavior. They appreciate the interaction of our biology, our environment, and our experiences in determining who we are and how we will behave. They learn about basic principles that guide how we think and behave, and they come to recognize the tremendous diversity that exists across individuals and across cultural boundaries (American Psychological Association, 2011).

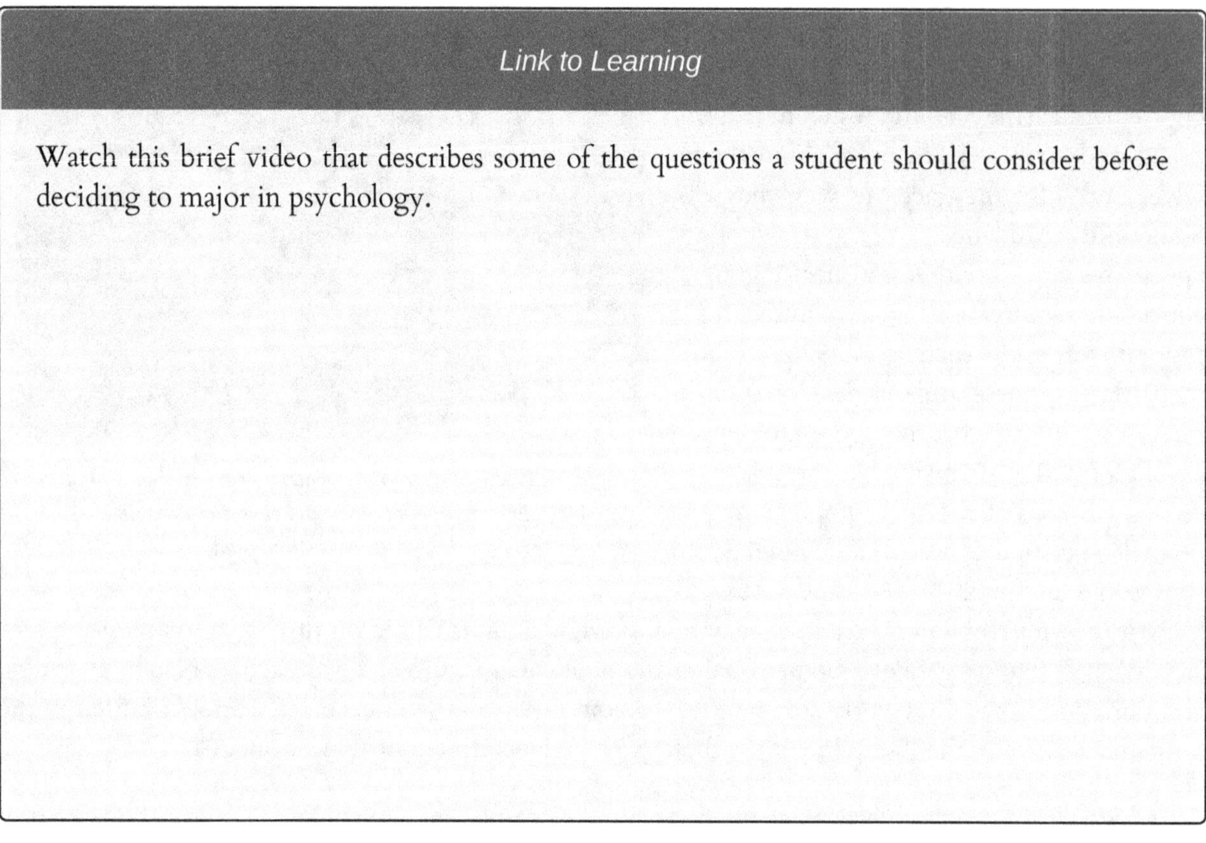

Watch this brief video that describes some of the questions a student should consider before deciding to major in psychology.

Careers in Psychology

Psychologists can work in many different places doing many different things. In general, anyone wishing to continue a career in psychology at a 4-year institution of higher education will have to earn a doctoral degree in psychology for some specialties and at least a master's degree for others. In most areas of psychology, this means earning a PhD in a relevant area of psychology. Literally, PhD refers to a doctor of philosophy degree, but here, philosophy does not refer to the field of philosophy per se. Rather, philosophy in this context refers to many different disciplinary perspectives that would be housed in a traditional college of liberal arts and sciences.

The requirements to earn a PhD vary from country to country and even from school to school, but usually, individuals earning this degree must complete a dissertation. A dissertation is essentially a long research paper or bundled published articles describing research that was conducted as a part of the candidate's doctoral training. In the United States, a dissertation generally has to be defended before a committee of expert reviewers before the degree is conferred. Once someone earns her PhD, she may seek a faculty appointment at a college or university. Being on the faculty of a college or university often involves dividing time between teaching, research, and service to the institution and profession. The amount of time spent on each of these primary responsibilities varies dramatically from school to school, and it is not uncommon for faculty to move from place to place in search of the best personal fit among various academic environments. The previous section detailed some of the major areas that are commonly represented in psychology departments around the country; thus, depending on the training received, an individual could be anything from a biological psychologist to a clinical psychologist in an academic setting.

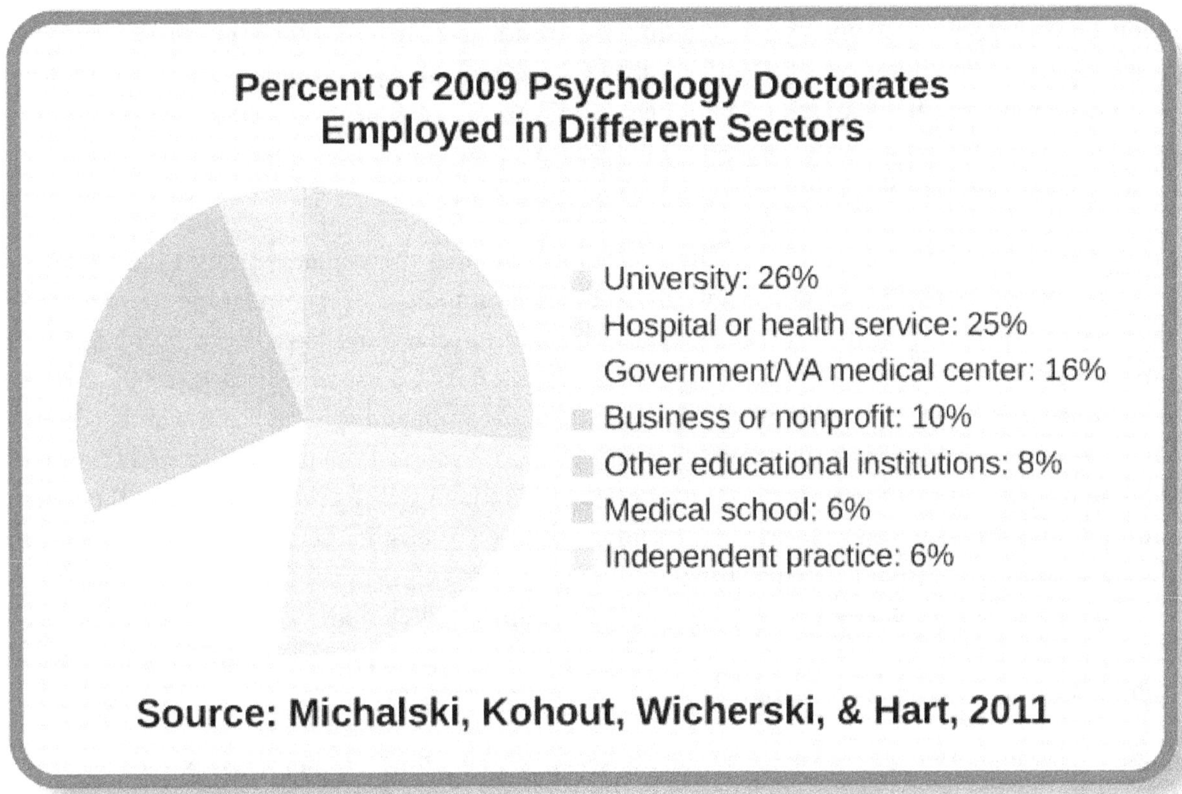

Figure 2. Individuals earning a PhD in psychology have a range of employment options.

Other Careers in Academic Settings

Often times, schools offer more courses in psychology than their full-time faculty can teach. In these cases, it is not uncommon to bring in an adjunct faculty member or instructor. Adjunct faculty members and instructors usually have an advanced degree in psychology, but they often have primary careers outside of academia and serve in this role as a secondary job. Alternatively, they may not hold the doctoral degree required by most 4-year institutions and use these opportunities to gain experience in teaching. Furthermore, many 2-year colleges and schools need faculty to teach their courses in psychology. In general, many of the people who pursue careers at these institutions have master's degrees in psychology, although some PhDs make careers at these institutions as well.

Some people earning PhDs may enjoy research in an academic setting. However, they may not be interested in teaching. These individuals might take on faculty positions that are exclusively devoted to conducting research. This type of position would be more likely an option at large, research-focused universities.

In some areas in psychology, it is common for individuals who have recently earned their PhD to seek out positions in postdoctoral training programs that are available before going on to serve as faculty. In most cases, young scientists will complete one or two postdoctoral programs before applying for a full-time faculty position. Postdoctoral training programs allow young scientists to further develop their research programs and broaden their research skills under the supervision of other professionals in the field.

Career Options Outside of Academics

Individuals who wish to become practicing clinical psychologists have another option for earning a doctoral degree, which is known as a PsyD. A PsyD is a doctor of psychology degree that is increasingly popular among individuals interested in pursuing careers in clinical psychology. PsyD programs generally place less emphasis on research-oriented skills and focus more on application of psychological principles in the clinical context (Norcorss & Castle, 2002).

Regardless of whether earning a PhD or PsyD, in most states, an individual wishing to practice as a licensed clinical or counseling psychologist may complete postdoctoral work under the supervision of a licensed psychologist. Within the last few years, however, several states have begun to remove this requirement, which would allow someone to get an earlier start in his career (Munsey, 2009). After an individual has met the state requirements, his credentials are evaluated to determine whether he can sit for the licensure exam. Only individuals that pass this exam can call themselves licensed clinical or counseling psychologists (Norcross, n.d.). Licensed clinical or counseling psychologists can then work in a number of settings, ranging from private clinical practice to hospital settings. It should be noted that clinical psychologists and psychiatrists do different things and receive different types of education. While both can conduct therapy and counseling, clinical psychologists have a PhD or a PsyD, whereas psychiatrists have a doctor of medicine degree (MD). As such, licensed clinical psychologists can administer and interpret psychological tests, while psychiatrists can prescribe medications.

Individuals earning a PhD can work in a variety of settings, depending on their areas of specialization. For example, someone trained as a biopsychologist might work in a pharmaceutical company to help test the efficacy of a new drug. Someone with a clinical background might become a forensic psychologist and work within the legal system to make recommendations during criminal trials and parole hearings, or serve as an expert in a court case.

While earning a doctoral degree in psychology is a lengthy process, usually taking between 5–6 years of graduate study (DeAngelis, 2010), there are a number of careers that can be attained with a master's degree in psychology. People who wish to provide psychotherapy can become licensed to serve as various types of professional counselors (Hoffman, 2012). Relevant master's degrees are also sufficient for individuals seeking careers as school psychologists (National Association of School Psychologists, n.d.), in some capacities related to sport psychology (American Psychological Association, 2014), or as consultants in various industrial settings (Landers, 2011, June 14). Undergraduate coursework in psychology may be applicable to other careers such as psychiatric social work or psychiatric nursing, where assessments and therapy may be a part of the job.

As mentioned in the opening section of this chapter, an undergraduate education in psychology is associated with a knowledge base and skill set that many employers find quite attractive. It should come as no surprise, then, that individuals earning bachelor's degrees in psychology find themselves in a number of different careers, as shown in the table. Examples of a few such careers can involve serving as case managers, working in sales, working in human resource departments, and teaching in high schools. The rapidly growing realm of healthcare professions is another field in which an education in psychology is helpful and sometimes required. For example, the Medical College Admission Test (MCAT) exam that people must take to be admitted to medical school now includes a section on the psychological foundations of behavior.

Table 1. Top Occupations Employing Graduates with a **BA** in Psychology (Fogg, Harrington, Harrington, & Shatkin, 2012)

Ranking	Occupation
1	Mid- and top-level management (executive, administrator)
2	Sales
3	Social work
4	Other management positions
5	Human resources (personnel, training)
6	Other administrative positions
7	Insurance, real estate, business
8	Marketing and sales
9	Healthcare (nurse, pharmacist, therapist)
10	Finance (accountant, auditor)

Link to Learning

Watch a brief video describing some of the career options available to people earning bachelor's degrees in psychology.

- http://careerplanning.about.com/video/Careers-for-Psychology-Majors.htm

Glossary

dissertation: long research paper about research that was conducted as a part of the candidate's doctoral training

PhD: (doctor of philosophy) doctoral degree conferred in many disciplinary perspectives housed in a traditional college of liberal arts and sciences

postdoctoral training program: allows young scientists to further develop their research programs and broaden their research skills under the supervision of other professionals in the field

PsyD: (doctor of psychology) doctoral degree that places less emphasis on research-oriented skills and focuses more on application of psychological principles in the clinical context

https://assessments.lumenlearning.com/assessments/4804

Attributions

CC licensed content, Shared previously

This is a modified version of OpenStax Psychology. Download the original text for free at https://openstax.org/details/books/psychology

- iDeclare – Why major in Psychology?. **Provided by:** humbiomovies's channel. **Located at:** https://www.youtube.com/watch?v=9hOfn0Xj8cs. **License:** *CC BY: Attribution*

Putting It Together: Psychological Foundations

Learning Objectives

In this module, you learned to

- describe the evolution of psychology and the major pioneers in the field
- identify the various approaches, fields, and subfields of psychology along with their major concepts and important figures
- describe the value of psychology and possible careers paths for those who study psychology

Psychology is a rapidly growing and ever-evolving field of study. In this module, you learned about its roots in early philosophy and the development of psychology as a distinct field of study in the late 1800s. Since that time, various schools of psychology have dominated the scene at different points in time, from structuralism and functionalism, to Freud's psychodynamic theory, behaviorism, humanism, and the cognitive revolution. In modern psychology, researchers and practitioners consider some of these historical approaches but also approach the study of mind and behavior through a variety of lenses, including biological, cognitive, developmental, social, and health perspectives. Watch the following Crash Course Psychology video for a good recap of the topics covered in this module:

Consider a fascinating example of psychological research conducted by is an Assistant Professor of Cognitive Psychology at Oberlin College, Paul Thibodeau. His focus is on language, specifically how people utilize metaphors and analogies, but he did one study on word aversion that he explains in his own words in the following example. As you read it, consider the breadth of coverage that psychologists cover as well as the importance of the scientific method and research to the investigative process. We'll learn more about experiments and psychological research in the next module, but if you could design a psychological study based on the topics that piqued your interested in this text so far, what would it be? Where do your interests lie? Remember, there are nearly endless possibilities for research within the vast field of psychology, and studying the subject will serve to your advantage, no matter your chosen field or career path.

Word Aversion

People Magazine—psycholinguistics' most trusted lexicon—defines "moist" as "the most cringe-worthy word" in American English. When they asked some of the **sexiest men alive** to try and make the word sound sexy, it was pretty clear they could not. **One viewer responded** that the video was "pure sadism" and that the only way to recover would be to "go Oedipal and gouge your eyes out."

There is something interesting going on with this word. Several people have documented the **weirdness** of "moist", **speculated** on why it is aversive, or used the phenomenon for comedic effect.

In a recent **series of studies** published in *PLOS ONE*, several members of my lab and I sought to answer some initial questions about word aversion. Specifically:

1. How prevalent is an aversion to "moist" and who's averse?
2. What does it mean to be averse to a word?
3. And, what makes a word aversive?

Five experiments, conducted over about four years, with almost 2,500 participants from the general population of American English speakers provide some answers.

How prevalent is an aversion to "moist" and who's averse?

On average, about 18 percent of our participants identified as categorically averse to the word. Women, younger people, and those with more education, who tended to score higher on measures of disgust toward bodily function and neuroticism (a personality trait characterized by increased feelings of anxiety, worry, anger and guilt), were particularly likely to find the word unpleasant.

Controlling for these factors, we found no differences in a person's likelihood of finding "moist" aversive based on their political ideology, religiosity, disgust toward sex, or any other personality variables.

What makes a word aversive?

We considered three possible reasons for moist-aversion:

1. Sound. The sound of the word itself may be the cause of peoples' aversion to "moist." Some work in psychology has found that certain sounds are inherently unpleasant—like fingernails scratching a chalkboard. Other work has found evidence of a "facial feedback hypothesis:" "moist" may be aversive because saying the word engages the same facial muscles that contract when we *see* (or smell or hear) something disgusting. This may, in fact, cause people to feel disgusted by saying the word "moist:" patterns of facial muscle constriction not only signal our emotional states to other people, we also learn about ourselves from our unconscious physiological responses to stimuli in the world.

2. Connotation. An alternative possibility is that the word is associated in people's minds with other words or things things that they already find disgusting, like vomit, phlegm, or aspects of sex. Of course, "moist" also has some positive connotations—who doesn't love a moist piece of chocolate cake? So a related possibility might be that the word is aversive because it simultaneously calls to mind positive *and* negative associations. Maybe when someone encounters the word they are hit with images of cake *and* sweaty armpits—not an ideal combination.

3. Social transmission. A final possibility is that the word may have become aversive because of the attention it has received in popular and social media. Word aversion may result from a conscious process of thinking about how certain words are gross. This would suggest that there is a "good" psychological reason for the aversion—that it is grounded in the sound or connotation of the word—but that it is triggered by deliberation and may spread like a virus. Anecdotal evidence for this possibility comes from the growing number of people who seem to find the word unpalatable: as the word gains attention, more and more people seem to find the word aversive. Alternatively, moist-aversion may just be a fad. If so, the "good" psychological reason for the phenomenon might simply be to identify oneself as part of a group—a group of people who find "moist" cringeworthy.

The experiments provided the most support for a combination of the second and third possibilities: that aversion to "moist" may spread socially but it is also grounded in feelings of disgust toward bodily functions.

Here's the evidence for why moist-aversion seems to be tied to disgust toward bodily function. First, recall that people who scored higher on a measure of disgust toward bodily function were more likely to find "moist" aversive. Second, people who identified as categorically averse to "moist" also found words like "phlegm" and "vomit" more aversive than people who didn't have a strong unpleasant reaction to "moist." In contrast, moist-averse participants were not more sensitive to words that had similar phonological properties to "moist" like "foist," "hoist," or "rejoiced" or to words related to sex like "vagina" and "penis" (or a variety of other words related to sex that you can find in the paper).

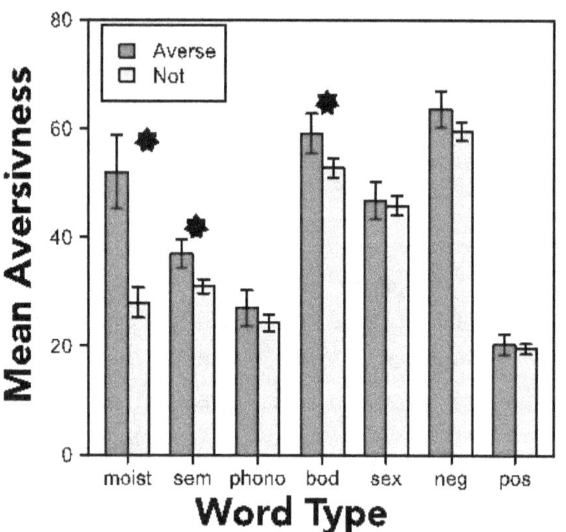

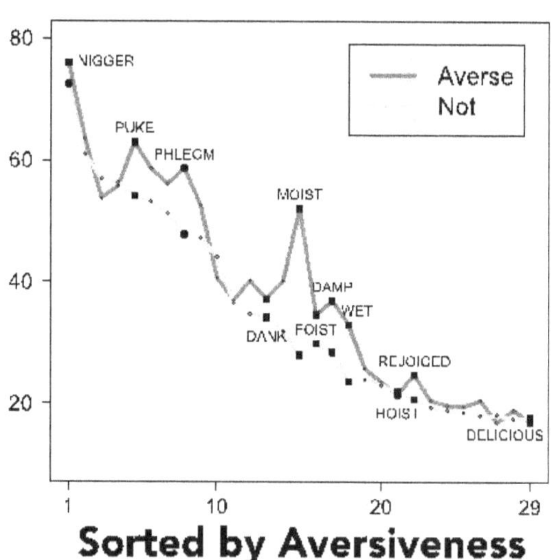

Third, when we used a common statistical technique (latent semantic analysis) to figure out how similar in meaning the words in our set were to "moist," the result was a good predictor of peoples' perceptions of word-averseness. That is, moist-averse participants showed a stronger aversion to words that were related in meaning to "moist," like "wet" and "damp." There was no difference in ratings of aversiveness of words like "hoist" and "love" that are less similar in meaning to "moist."

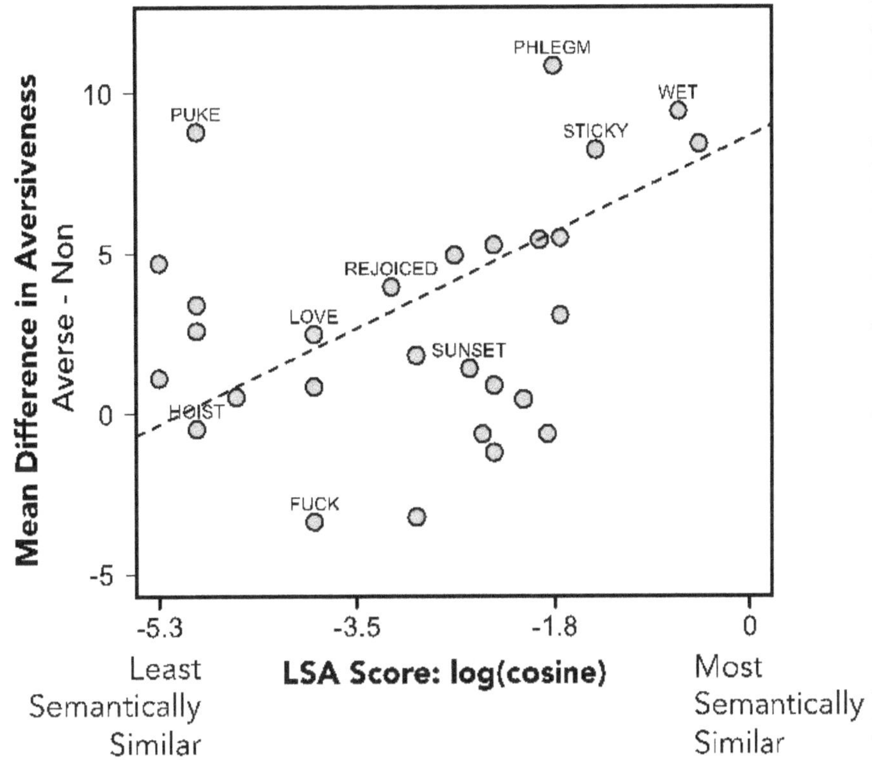

Interestingly, participants' speculation on the cause of moist-aversion was inconsistent with the behavioral data. Often, moist-averse participants pointed to the sound of the word as the source of their aversion. "The 'oy' sound juxtaposed to 'ss' and 'tt.' It's not a word that sounds pleasant. Neither does hoist or foist," wrote one participant. Non-averse participants pointed to the word's association with sex: "It reminds people of sex and vaginas." This kind of data from introspection can be misleading. There is a long history in psychology showing that people regularly don't know why they think and behave the way that they do. In this case, both groups were wrong: people who identified as averse to "moist" may think the sound of the word itself is the cause of their aversion because their reaction is fast and visceral—so it *must* have something to do with the sound of the word. Similarly, although "moist" may have associations to sex, these associations don't seem to be the primary cause of moist-aversion.

The strongest evidence that moist-aversion is transmitted socially and may be triggered by a process of conscious deliberation came from one of our studies that was designed to induce an aversion to the word. One group of people watched the video that was made by *People Magazine*, while another watched a "control" video that showed actors using the word "moist" to describe the taste of cake. After watching the cringe-inducing video, people considered "moist" not only more aversive, but said that it was a word they used relatively infrequently and that the word had a more negative connotation. In other words, watching the video that made "moist" seem aversive shifted the entire profile of the word to be more consistent with the perceptions of people who were already averse to the word.

What do we learn from these studies?

There are a few important lessons to be learned from these studies. Two are fairly obvious: we now have a better sense of what makes the word "moist" aversive and another demonstration that we're not particularly good at reflecting accurately on why we think what we think.

More relevant to broader theories in psychology, the work has implications for theories of language processing and the psychology of disgust. Emotional language is processed differently than "neutral" language: it grabs our attention, engages different parts of the brain, and is more likely to be remembered. This can be good or bad: cake mixes that advertise themselves as "moist" may make some people more likely to buy them because they catch our eye, but they may make us less likely to buy them because of the word's association with disgusting bodily function (an open question).

Disgust is adaptive. If we didn't have an instinct to run away from vomit and diarrhea, disease would spread more easily. But is this instinct biological or do we learn it? Does our culture shape what we find disgusting? This is a complex and nuanced question. Significant work is needed to answer it definitively. But the present studies suggest that, when it comes to the disgust that is elicited by words like "moist," there is an important cultural component—the symbols we use to communicate with one another can become contaminated and elicit disgust by virtue of their association with bodily functions.

Attributions

CC licensed content, Original

- Putting It Together: Psychological Foundations. **Provided by:** Lumen Learning. **License:** *CC BY: Attribution*

CC licensed content, Shared previously

- The Moist Conundrum. **Authored by:** Paul Thibodeau. **Located at:** http://thepsychreport.com/science/moist-conundrum/. **Project:** The Psych Report. **License:** *CC BY-NC-SA: Attribution-NonCommercial-ShareAlike*

All rights reserved content

- Intro to Psychology – Crash Course Psychology #1. **Authored by:** CrashCourse. **Located at:** https://www.youtube.com/watch?v=vo4pMVb0R6M. **License:** *All Rights Reserved.* **License Terms:** Standard YouTube License

Why It Matters: Psychological Research

How does television content impact children's behavior? (credit: modification of work by "antisocialtory"/Flickr)

Have you ever wondered whether the violence you see on television affects your behavior? Are you more likely to behave aggressively in real life after watching people behave violently in dramatic situations on the screen? Or, could seeing fictional violence actually get aggression out of your system, causing you to be more peaceful? How are children influenced by the media they are exposed to? A psychologist interested in the relationship between behavior and exposure to violent images might ask these very questions.

The topic of violence in the media today is contentious. Since ancient times, humans have been concerned about the effects of new technologies on our behaviors and thinking processes. The Greek philosopher Socrates, for example, worried that writing—a new technology at that time—would diminish people's ability to remember because they could rely on written records rather than committing information to memory. In our world of quickly changing technologies, questions about the effects of media continue to emerge. Is it okay to talk on a cell phone while driving? Are headphones good to use in a car? What impact does text messaging have on reaction time while driving? These are types of questions that psychologist David Strayer asks in his lab. Watch this short video to see how he utilizes the scientific method to reach important conclusions regarding technology and driving safety.

How can we go about finding answers that are supported not by mere opinion, but by evidence that we can all agree on? The findings of psychological research can help us navigate issues like this.

Module References

American Academy of Pediatrics, American Academy of Child & Adolescent Psychiatry, American Psychological Association, American Medical Association, American Academy of Family Physicians, American Psychiatric Association. (2000). *Joint statement on the impact of entertainment violence on children.* Retrieved from http://www2.aap.org/advocacy/releases/jstmtevc.htm.

American Cancer Society. (n.d.). History of the cancer prevention studies. Retrieved from http://www.cancer.org/research/researchtopreventcancer/history-cancer-prevention-study

American Psychological Association. (2009). *Publication Manual of the American Psychological Association* (6th ed.). Washington, DC: Author.

American Psychological Association. (n.d.). *Research with animals in psychology.* Retrieved from https://www.apa.org/research/responsible/research-animals.pdf

Arnett, J. (2008). The neglected 95%: Why American psychology needs to become less American. *American Psychologist, 63*(7), 602–614.

Barton, B. A., Eldridge, A. L., Thompson, D., Affenito, S. G., Striegel-Moore, R. H., Franko, D. L., . . . Crockett, S. J. (2005). The relationship of breakfast and cereal consumption to nutrient intake and body mass index: The national heart, lung, and blood institute growth and health study. *Journal of the American Dietetic Association, 105*(9), 1383–1389. Retrieved from http://dx.doi.org/10.1016/j.jada.2005.06.003

Chwalisz, K., Diener, E., & Gallagher, D. (1988). Autonomic arousal feedback and emotional experience: Evidence from the spinal cord injured. *Journal of Personality and Social Psychology, 54,* 820–828.

Clayton, R. R., Cattarello, A. M., & Johnstone, B. M. (1996). The effectiveness of Drug Abuse Resistance Education (Project DARE): 5-year follow-up results. *Preventive Medicine: An International Journal Devoted to Practice and Theory, 25*(3), 307–318. doi:10.1006/pmed.1996.0061

D.A.R.E. (n.d.). D.A.R.E. is substance abuse prevention education and much more! [About page] Retrieved from http://www.dare.org/about-d-a-r-e/

Dominus, S. (2011, May 25). Could conjoined twins share a mind? *New York Times Sunday Magazine.* Retrieved from http://www.nytimes.com/2011/05/29/magazine/could-conjoined-twins-share-a-mind.html?_r=5&hp&

Ennett, S. T., Tobler, N. S., Ringwalt, C. L., & Flewelling, R. L. (1994). How effective is drug abuse resistance education? A meta-analysis of Project DARE outcome evaluations. *American Journal of Public Health, 84*(9), 1394–1401. doi:10.2105/AJPH.84.9.1394

Fanger, S. M., Frankel, L. A., & Hazen, N. (2012). Peer exclusion in preschool children's play: Naturalistic observations in a playground setting. *Merrill-Palmer Quarterly, 58,* 224–254.

Fiedler, K. (2004). Illusory correlation. In R. F. Pohl (Ed.), *Cognitive illusions: A handbook on fallacies and biases in thinking, judgment and memory* (pp. 97–114). New York, NY: Psychology Press.

Frantzen, L. B., Treviño, R. P., Echon, R. M., Garcia-Dominic, O., & DiMarco, N. (2013). Association between frequency of ready-to-eat cereal consumption, nutrient intakes, and body mass index in fourth- to sixth-grade low-income minority children. *Journal of the Academy of Nutrition and Dietetics, 113*(4), 511–519.

Harper, J. (2013, July 5). Ice cream and crime: Where cold cuisine and hot disputes intersect. *The Times-Picayune.* Retrieved from http://www.nola.com/crime/index.ssf/2013/07/ice_cream_and_crime_where_hot.html

Jenkins, W. J., Ruppel, S. E., Kizer, J. B., Yehl, J. L., & Griffin, J. L. (2012). An examination of post 9-11 attitudes towards Arab Americans. *North American Journal of Psychology, 14,* 77–84.

Jones, J. M. (2013, May 13). Same-sex marriage support solidifies above 50% in U.S. *Gallup Politics.* Retrieved from http://www.gallup.com/poll/162398/sex-marriage-support-solidifies-above.aspx

Kobrin, J. L., Patterson, B. F., Shaw, E. J., Mattern, K. D., & Barbuti, S. M. (2008). *Validity of the SAT for predicting first-year college grade point average* (Research Report No. 2008-5). Retrieved from https://research.collegeboard.org/sites/default/files/publications/2012/7/researchreport-2008-5-validity-sat-predicting-first-year-college-grade-point-average.pdf

Lewin, T. (2014, March 5). A new SAT aims to realign with schoolwork. *New York Times.* Retreived from http://www.nytimes.com/2014/03/06/education/major-changes-in-sat-announced-by-college-board.html.

Lowcock, E. C., Cotterchio, M., Anderson, L. N., Boucher, B. A., & El-Sohemy, A. (2013). High coffee intake, but not caffeine, is associated with reduced estrogen receptor negative and post-menopausal breast cancer risk with no effect modification by CYP1A2 genotype. *Nutrition and Cancer, 65*(3), 398–409. doi:10.1080/01635581.2013.768348

Lowry, M., Dean, K., & Manders, K. (2010). The link between sleep quantity and academic performance for the college student. *Sentience: The University of Minnesota Undergraduate Journal of Psychology, 3*(Spring), 16–19. Retrieved from http://www.psych.umn.edu/sentience/files/SENTIENCE_Vol3.pdf

Lynam, D. R., Milich, R., Zimmerman, R., Novak, S. P., Logan, T. K., Martin, C., . . . Clayton, R. (1999). Project DARE: No effects at 10-year follow-up. *Journal of Consulting and Clinical Psychology, 67*(4), 590–593. doi:10.1037/0022-006X.67.4.590

McKie, R. (2010, June 26). Chimps with everything: Jane Goodall's 50 years in the jungle. *The Guardian.* Retrieved from http://www.theguardian.com/science/2010/jun/27/jane-goodall-chimps-africa-interview

Offit, P. (2008). *Autism's false prophets: Bad science, risky medicine, and the search for a cure.* New York: Columbia University Press.

Perkins, H. W., Haines, M. P., & Rice, R. (2005). Misperceiving the college drinking norm and related problems: A nationwide study of exposure to prevention information, perceived norms and student alcohol misuse. *J. Stud. Alcohol, 66*(4), 470–478.

Rimer, S. (2008, September 21). College panel calls for less focus on SATs. *The New York Times.* Retrieved from http://www.nytimes.com/2008/09/22/education/22admissions.html?_r=0

Ringwalt, C., Ennett, S. T., & Holt, K. D. (1991). An outcome evaluation of Project DARE (Drug Abuse Resistance Education). *Health Education Research, 6*(3), 327–337. doi:10.1093/her/6.3.327

Rothstein, J. M. (2004). College performance predictions and the SAT. *Journal of Econometrics, 121,* 297–317.

Rotton, J., & Kelly, I. W. (1985). Much ado about the full moon: A meta-analysis of lunar-lunacy research. *Psychological Bulletin, 97*(2), 286–306. doi:10.1037/0033-2909.97.2.286

Santelices, M. V., & Wilson, M. (2010). Unfair treatment? The case of Freedle, the SAT, and the standardization approach to differential item functioning. *Harvard Education Review, 80,* 106–134.

Sears, D. O. (1986). College sophomores in the laboratory: Influences of a narrow data base on social psychology's view of human nature. *Journal of Personality and Social Psychology, 51,* 515–530.

Tuskegee   University.   (n.d.).   *About   the   USPHS   Syphilis   Study.*   Retrieved   from http://www.tuskegee.edu/about_us/centers_of_excellence/bioethics_center/about_the_usphs_syphilis_study.aspx.

Attributions

- Modification, adaptation, and original content. **Provided by:** Lumen Learning. **License:** *CC BY: Attribution*

The Scientific Method

What you'll learn to do: define and apply the scientific method to psychology

Scientists are engaged in explaining and understanding how the world around them works, and they are able to do so by coming up with theories that generate hypotheses that are testable and falsifiable. Theories that stand up to their tests are retained and refined, while those that do not are discarded or modified. In this way, research enables scientists to separate fact from simple opinion. Having good information generated from research aids in making wise decisions both in public policy and in our personal lives. In this section, you'll see how psychologists use the scientific method to study and understand behavior.

Learning Objectives

- Explain the steps of the scientific method
- Describe why the scientific method is important to psychology
- Summarize the processes of informed consent and debriefing
- Explain how research involving humans or animals is regulated

Scientific research is a critical tool for successfully navigating our complex world. Without it, we would be forced to rely solely on intuition, other people's authority, and blind luck. While many of us feel confident in our abilities to decipher and interact with the world around us, history is filled with examples of how very wrong we can be when we fail to recognize the need for evidence in supporting claims. At various times in history, we would have been certain that the sun revolved around a flat earth, that the earth's continents did not move, and that mental illness was caused by possession (Figure 1). It is through systematic scientific research that we divest ourselves of our preconceived notions and superstitions and gain an objective understanding of ourselves and our world.

The goal of all scientists is to better understand the world around them. Psychologists focus their attention on understanding behavior, as well as the cognitive (mental) and physiological (body) processes that underlie behavior. In contrast to other methods that people use to understand the behavior of others, such as intuition and personal experience, the hallmark of scientific research is that there is evidence to support a claim. Scientific knowledge is empirical: It is grounded in objective, tangible evidence that can be observed time and time again, regardless of who is observing.

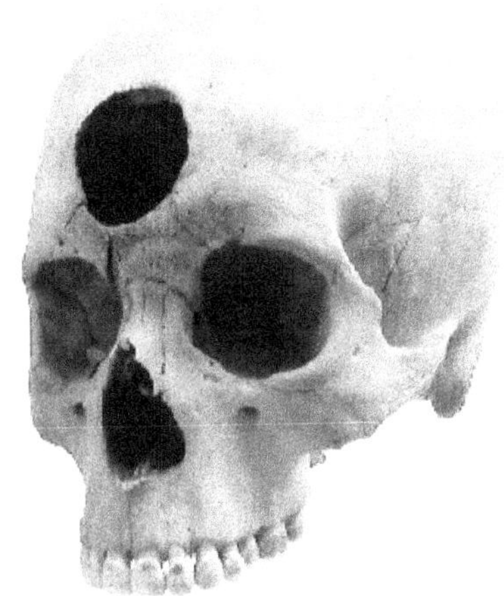

Figure 1. Some of our ancestors, across the world and over the centuries, believed that trephination—the practice of making a hole in the skull, as shown here—allowed evil spirits to leave the body, thus curing mental illness and other disorders. (credit: "taiproject"/Flickr)

While behavior is observable, the mind is not. If someone is crying, we can see behavior. However, the reason for the behavior is more difficult to determine. Is the person crying due to being sad, in pain, or happy? Sometimes we can learn the reason for someone's behavior by simply asking a question, like "Why are you crying?" However, there are situations in which an individual is either uncomfortable or unwilling to answer the question honestly, or is incapable of answering. For example, infants would not be able to explain why they are crying. In such circumstances, the psychologist must be creative in finding ways to better understand behavior. This module explores how scientific knowledge is generated, and how important that knowledge is in forming decisions in our personal lives and in the public domain.

The Process of Scientific Research

Scientific knowledge is advanced through a process known as the scientific method. Basically, ideas (in the form of theories and hypotheses) are tested against the real world (in the form of **empirical** observations), and those empirical observations lead to more ideas that are tested against the real world, and so on.

The basic steps in the scientific method are:

- Observe a natural phenomenon and define a question about it

- Make a hypothesis, or potential solution to the question

- Test the hypothesis

- If the hypothesis is true, find more evidence or find counter-evidence

- If the hypothesis is false, create a new hypothesis or try again

- Draw conclusions and repeat—the scientific method is never-ending, and no result is ever considered perfect

In order to ask an important question that may improve our understanding of the world, a researcher must first observe natural phenomena. By making observations, a researcher can define a useful question. After finding a question to answer, the

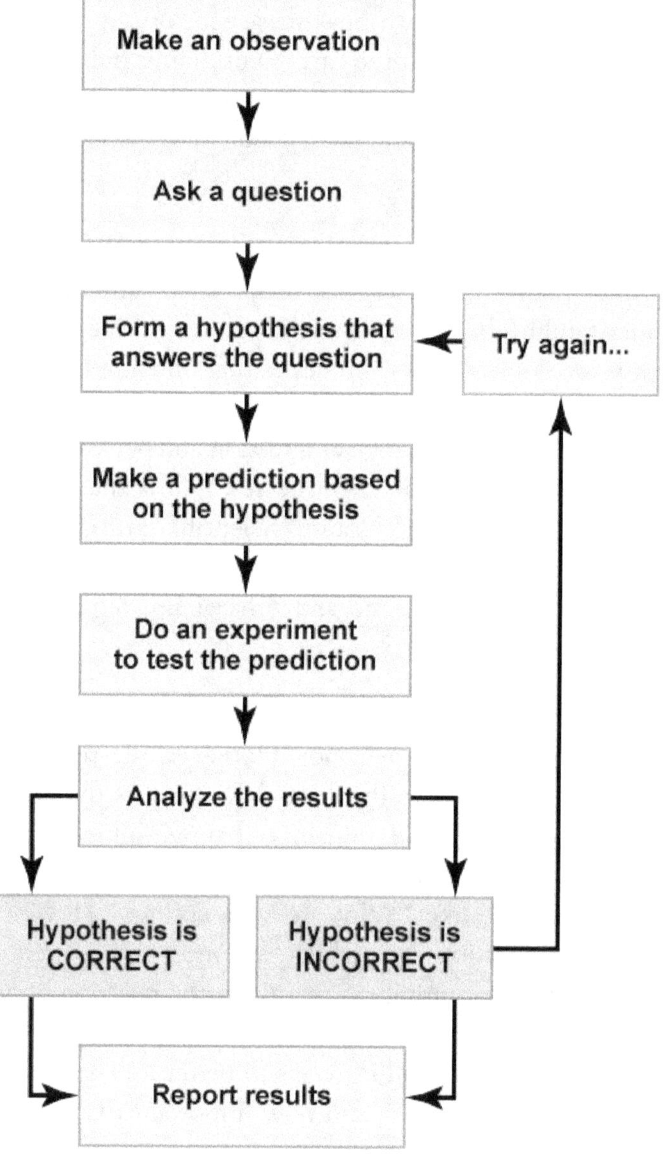

Figure 2. The scientific method is a process for gathering data and processing information. It provides well-defined steps to standardize how scientific knowledge is gathered through a logical, rational problem-solving method.

researcher can then make a prediction (a hypothesis) about what he or she thinks the answer will be. This prediction is usually a statement about the relationship between two or more variables. After making a hypothesis, the researcher will then design an experiment to test his or her hypothesis and evaluate the data gathered. These data will either support or refute the hypothesis. Based on the conclusions drawn from the data, the researcher will then find more evidence to support the hypothesis, look for counter-evidence to further strengthen the hypothesis, revise the hypothesis and create a new experiment, or continue to incorporate the information gathered to answer the research question.

The Basic Principles of the Scientific Method

Two key concepts in the scientific approach are theory and hypothesis. A **theory** is a well-developed set of ideas that propose an explanation for observed phenomena that can be used to make predictions about future observations. A **hypothesis** is a testable prediction that is arrived at logically from a theory. It is often worded as an if-then statement (e.g., if I study all night, I will get a passing grade on the test). The hypothesis is extremely important because it bridges the gap between the realm of ideas and the real world. As specific hypotheses are tested, theories are modified and refined to reflect and incorporate the result of these tests (Figure 2).

Other key components in following the scientific method include verifiability, predictability, falsifiability, and fairness. **Verifiability** means that an experiment must be replicable by another researcher. To achieve verifiability, researchers must make sure to document their methods and clearly explain how their experiment is structured and why it produces certain results.

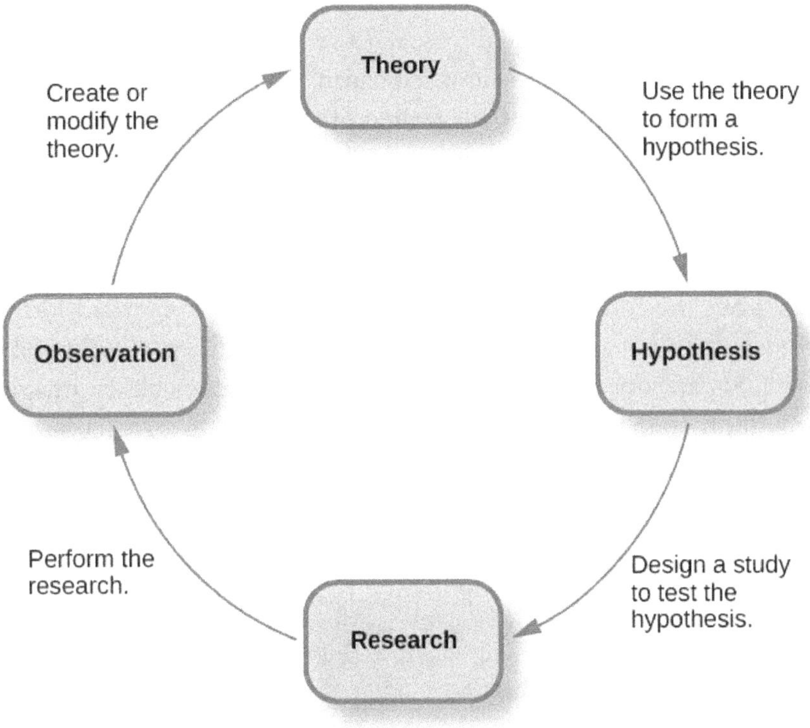

Predictability in a scientific theory implies that the theory should enable us to make predictions about future events. The precision of these predictions is a measure of the strength of the theory.

Figure 3. The scientific method of research includes proposing hypotheses, conducting research, and creating or modifying theories based on results.

Falsifiability refers to whether a hypothesis can disproved. For a hypothesis to be falsifiable, it must be logically possible to make an observation or do a physical experiment that would show that there is no support for the hypothesis. Even when a hypothesis cannot be shown to be false, that does not necessarily mean it is not valid. Future testing may disprove the hypothesis. This does not mean that a hypothesis *has* to be shown to be false, just that it can be tested.

To determine whether a hypothesis is supported or not supported, psychological researchers must conduct hypothesis testing using statistics. Hypothesis testing is a type of statistics that determines the probability of a hypothesis being true or false. If hypothesis testing reveals that results were "statistically significant," this means that there was support for the hypothesis and that the researchers can be reasonably confident that their result was not due to random chance. If the results are not statistically significant, this means that the researchers' hypothesis was not supported.

Fairness implies that all data must be considered when evaluating a hypothesis. A researcher cannot pick and choose what data to keep and what to discard or focus specifically on data that support or do not support a particular hypothesis. All data must be accounted for, even if they invalidate the hypothesis.

Applying the Scientific Method

To see how this process works, let's consider a specific theory and a hypothesis that might be generated from that theory. As you'll learn in a later module, the James-Lange theory of emotion asserts that emotional experience relies on the physiological arousal associated with the emotional state. If you walked out of your home and discovered a very aggressive snake waiting on your doorstep, your heart would begin to race and your stomach churn. According to the James-Lange theory, these physiological changes would result in your feeling of fear. A hypothesis that could be derived from this theory might be that a person who is unaware of the physiological arousal that the sight of the snake elicits will not feel fear.

Remeber that a good scientific hypothesis is falsifiable, or capable of being shown to be incorrect. Recall from the introductory module that Sigmund Freud had lots of interesting ideas to explain various human behaviors (Figure 3). However, a major criticism of Freud's theories is that many of his ideas are not falsifiable; for example, it is impossible to imagine empirical observations that would disprove the existence of the id, the ego, and the superego—the three elements of personality described in Freud's theories. Despite this, Freud's theories are widely taught in introductory psychology texts because of their historical significance for personality psychology and psychotherapy, and these remain the root of all modern forms of therapy.

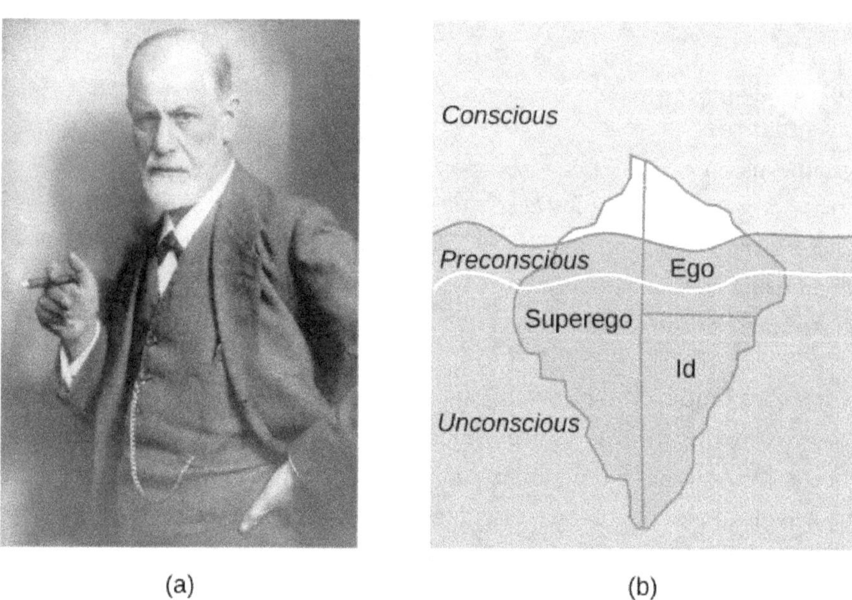

(a)   (b)

Figure 4. Many of the specifics of (a) Freud's theories, such as (b) his division of the mind into id, ego, and superego, have fallen out of favor in recent decades because they are not falsifiable. In broader strokes, his views set the stage for much of psychological thinking today, such as the unconscious nature of the majority of psychological processes.

In contrast, the James-Lange theory does generate falsifiable hypotheses, such as the one described above. Some individuals who suffer significant injuries to their spinal columns are unable to feel the bodily changes that often accompany emotional experiences. Therefore, we could test the hypothesis by determining how emotional experiences differ between individuals who have the ability to detect these changes in their physiological arousal and those who do not. In fact, this research has been conducted and while the emotional experiences of people deprived of an awareness of their physiological arousal may be less intense, they still experience emotion (Chwalisz, Diener, & Gallagher, 1988).

Why the Scientific Method Is Important for Psychology

The use of the scientific method is one of the main features that separates modern psychology from earlier philosophical inquiries about the mind. Compared to chemistry, physics, and other "natural sciences," psychology has long been considered one of the "social sciences" because of the subjective nature of the things it seeks to study. Many of the concepts that psychologists are interested in—such as aspects of the human mind, behavior, and emotions—are subjective and cannot be directly measured. Psychologists often rely instead on behavioral observations and self-reported data, which are considered by some to be illegitimate or lacking in methodological rigor. Applying the scientific method to psychology, therefore, helps to standardize the approach to understanding its very different types of information.

The scientific method allows psychological data to be replicated and confirmed in many instances, under different circumstances, and by a variety of researchers. Through replication of experiments, new generations of psychologists can reduce errors and broaden the applicability of theories. It also allows theories to be tested and validated instead of simply being conjectures that could never be verified or falsified. All of this allows psychologists to gain a stronger understanding of how the human mind works.

Scientific articles published in journals and psychology papers written in the style of the American Psychological Association (i.e., in "APA style") are structured around the scientific method. These papers include an Introduction, which introduces the background information and outlines the hypotheses; a Methods section, which outlines the specifics of how the experiment was conducted to test the hypothesis; a Results section, which includes the statistics that tested the hypothesis and state whether it was supported or not supported, and a Discussion and Conclusion, which state the implications of finding support for, or no support for, the hypothesis. Writing articles and papers that adhere to the scientific method makes it easy for future researchers to repeat the study and attempt to replicate the results.

Today, scientists agree that good research is ethical in nature and is guided by a basic respect for human dignity and safety. However, as you will read in the Tuskegee Syphilis Study, this has not always been the case. Modern researchers must demonstrate that the research they perform is ethically sound. This section presents how ethical considerations affect the design and implementation of research conducted today.

Research Involving Human Participants

Any experiment involving the participation of human subjects is governed by extensive, strict guidelines designed to ensure that the experiment does not result in harm. Any research institution that receives federal support for research involving human participants must have access to an **institutional review board (IRB)**. The IRB is a committee of individuals often made up of members of the institution's administration, scientists, and community members (Figure 1). The purpose of the IRB is to review proposals for research that involves human participants. The IRB reviews these proposals with the principles mentioned above in mind, and generally, approval from the IRB is required in order for the experiment to proceed.

Figure 1. An institution's IRB meets regularly to review experimental proposals that involve human participants. (credit: modification of work by Lowndes Area Knowledge Exchange (LAKE)/Flickr)

An institution's IRB requires several components in any experiment it approves. For one, each participant must sign an informed consent form before they can participate in the experiment. An **informed consent** form provides a written description of what participants can expect during the experiment, including potential risks and implications of the research. It also lets participants know that their involvement is completely voluntary and can be discontinued without penalty at any time. Furthermore, the informed consent guarantees that any data collected in the experiment will remain completely confidential. In cases where research participants are under the age of 18, the parents or legal guardians are required to sign the informed consent form.

While the informed consent form should be as honest as possible in describing exactly what participants will be doing, sometimes deception is necessary to prevent participants' knowledge of the exact research question from affecting the results of the study. **Deception** involves purposely misleading experiment participants in order to maintain the integrity of the experiment, but not to the point where the deception could be considered harmful. For example, if we are interested in how our opinion of someone is affected by their attire, we might use deception in describing the experiment to prevent that knowledge from affecting participants' responses. In cases where deception is involved, participants must receive a full **debriefing** upon conclusion of the study—complete, honest information about the purpose of the experiment, how the data collected will be used, the reasons why deception was necessary, and information about how to obtain additional information about the study.

Dig Deeper: Ethics and the Tuskegee Syphilis Study

Unfortunately, the ethical guidelines that exist for research today were not always applied in the past. In 1932, poor, rural, black, male sharecroppers from Tuskegee, Alabama, were recruited to participate in an experiment conducted by the U.S. Public Health Service, with the aim of studying syphilis in black men (Figure 2). In exchange for free medical care, meals, and burial insurance, 600 men agreed to participate in the study. A little more than half of the men tested positive for syphilis, and they served as the experimental group (given that the researchers could not randomly assign participants to groups, this represents a quasi-experiment). The remaining syphilis-free individuals served as the control group. However, those individuals that tested positive for syphilis were never informed that they had the disease.

While there was no treatment for syphilis when the study began, by 1947 penicillin was recognized as an effective treatment for the disease. Despite this, no penicillin was administered to the participants in this study, and the participants were not allowed to seek treatment at any other facilities if they continued in the study. Over the course of 40 years, many of the participants unknowingly spread syphilis to their wives (and subsequently their children born from their wives) and eventually died because they never received treatment for the disease. This study was discontinued in 1972 when the experiment was discovered by the national press (Tuskegee University, n.d.). The resulting outrage over the experiment led directly to the National Research Act of 1974 and the strict ethical guidelines for research on humans described in this chapter. Why is this study unethical? How were the men who participated and their families harmed as a function of this research?

Visit this website to learn more about the Tuskegee Syphilis Study.

- http://www.tuskegee.edu/about_us/centers_of_excellence/bioethics_center/about_the_usphs_syphilis_study.aspx

---

Research Involving Animal Subjects

Many psychologists conduct research involving animal subjects. Often, these researchers use rodents (Figure 3) or birds as the subjects of their experiments—the APA estimates that 90% of all animal research in psychology uses these species (American Psychological Association, n.d.). Because many

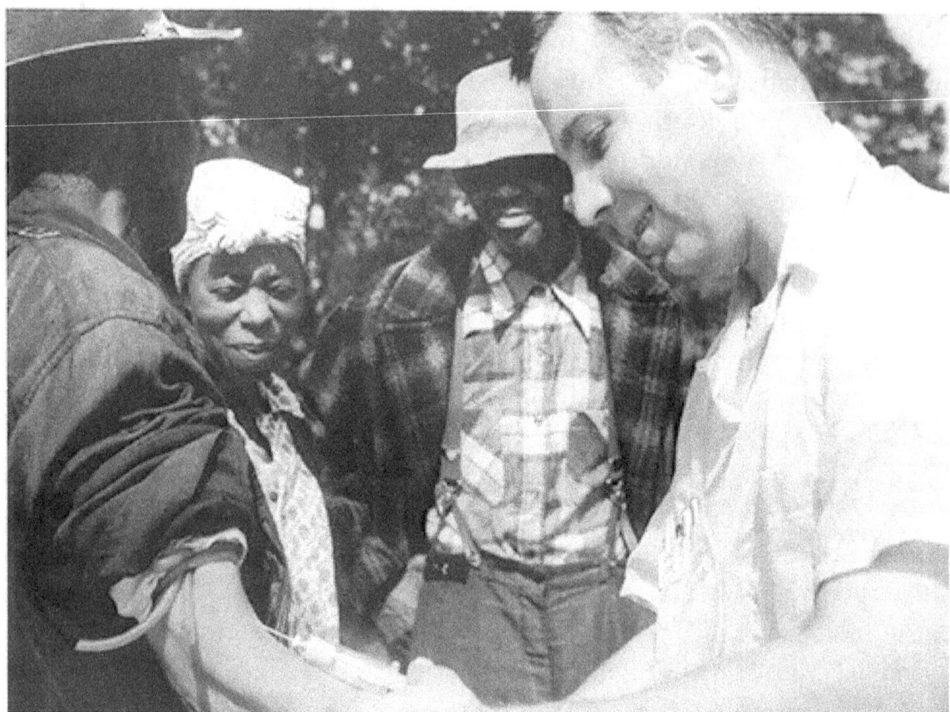

Figure 2. A participant in the Tuskegee Syphilis Study receives an injection.

basic processes in animals are sufficiently similar to those in humans, these animals are acceptable substitutes for research that would be considered unethical in human participants.

This does not mean that animal researchers are immune to ethical concerns. Indeed, the humane and ethical treatment of animal research subjects is a critical aspect of this type of research. Researchers must design their experiments to minimize any pain or distress experienced by animals serving as research subjects.

Whereas IRBs review research proposals that involve human participants, animal experimental proposals are reviewed by an **Institutional Animal Care and Use Committee (IACUC).** An IACUC consists

Figure 3. Rats, like the one shown here, often serve as the subjects of animal research.

of institutional administrators, scientists, veterinarians, and community members. This committee is charged with ensuring that all experimental proposals require the humane treatment of animal research subjects. It also conducts semi-annual inspections of all animal facilities to ensure that the research protocols are being followed. No animal research project can proceed without the committee's approval.

Glossary

debriefing: when an experiment involved deception, participants are told complete and truthful information about the experiment at its conclusion

deception: purposely misleading experiment participants in order to maintain the integrity of the experiment

empirical: grounded in objective, tangible evidence that can be observed time and time again, regardless of who is observing

fairness: implies that all data must be considered when evaluating a hypothesis

falsifiable: able to be disproven by experimental results

hypothesis: (plural: hypotheses) tentative and testable statement about the relationship between two or more variables

informed consent: process of informing a research participant about what to expect during an experiment, any risks involved, and the implications of the research, and then obtaining the person's consent to participate

Institutional Animal Care and Use Committee (IACUC): committee of administrators, scientists, veterinarians, and community members that reviews proposals for research involving human participants

Institutional Review Board (IRB): committee of administrators, scientists, and community members that reviews proposals for research involving human participants

predictability: implies that a theory should enable us to make predictions about future events

theory: well-developed set of ideas that propose an explanation for observed phenomena

verifiability: an experiment must be replicable by another researcher

https://assessments.lumenlearning.com/assessments/4807

Descriptive Research

What you'll learn to do: describe the strengths and weaknesses of descriptive, experimental, and correlational research

If you think about the vast array of fields and topics covered in psychology, you understand that in order to do psychological research, there must be a diverse set of ways to gather data and perform experiments. For example, a biological psychologist might work predominately in a lab setting or alongside a neurologist. A social scientist may set up situational experiments, a health psychologist may administer surveys, and a developmental psychologist may make observations in a classroom. In this section, you'll learn about the various types of research methods that psychologists employ to learn about human behavior.

Psychologists use descriptive, experimental, and correlational methods to conduct research. Descriptive, or qualitative, methods include the case study, naturalistic observation, surveys, archival research, longitudinal research, and cross-sectional research.

Experiments are conducted in order to determine cause-and-effect relationships. In ideal experimental design, the only difference between the experimental and control groups is whether participants are exposed to the experimental manipulation. Each group goes through all phases of the experiment, but each group will experience a different level of the independent variable: the experimental group is exposed to the experimental manipulation, and the control group is not exposed to the experimental manipulation. The researcher then measures the changes that are produced in the dependent variable in each group. Once data is collected from both groups, it is analyzed statistically to determine if there are meaningful differences between the groups.

When scientists passively observe and measure phenomena it is called correlational research. Here, psychologists do not intervene and change behavior, as they do in experiments. In correlational research, they identify patterns of relationships, but usually cannot infer what causes what. Importantly, with correlational research, you can examine only two variables at a time, no more and no less.

More on Research

If you enjoy learning through lectures and want an interesting and comprehensive summary of this section, then click on the link HERE (or on the link below) to watch a lecture given by MIT Professor John Gabrieli. **Start at the 30:45 minute mark** and watch through the end to hear examples of actual psychological studies and how they were analyzed. Listen for references to independent and dependent variables, experimenter bias, and double-blind studies. In the lecture, you'll learn about breaking social norms, "WEIRD" research, why expectations matter, how a warm cup of coffee might make you nicer, why you *should* change your answer on a multiple choice test, and why praise for intelligence won't make you any smarter.

Learning Objectives

- Differentiate between descriptive, experimental, and correlational research
- Explain the strengths and weaknesses of case studies, naturalistic observation, and surveys
- Describe the strength and weaknesses of archival research
- Compare longitudinal and cross-sectional approaches to research

Descriptive Research

There are many research methods available to psychologists in their efforts to understand, describe, and explain behavior and the cognitive and biological processes that underlie it. Some methods rely on observational techniques. Other approaches involve interactions between the researcher and the individuals who are being studied—ranging from a series of simple questions to extensive, in-depth interviews—to well-controlled experiments.

The three main categories of psychological research are descriptive, correlational, and experimental research. Research studies that do not test specific relationships between variables are called **descriptive, or qualitative, studies**. These studies are used to describe general or specific behaviors and attributes that are observed and measured. In the early stages of research it might be difficult to form a hypothesis, especially when there is not any existing literature in the area. In these situations designing an experiment would be premature, as the question of interest is not yet clearly defined as a hypothesis. Often a researcher will begin with a non-experimental approach, such as a descriptive study, to gather more information about the topic before designing an experiment or correlational study to address a specific hypothesis. Descriptive research is distinct from **correlational research**, in which psychologists formally test whether a relationship exists between two or more variables. **Experimental research** goes a step further beyond descriptive and correlational research and randomly assigns people to different conditions, using hypothesis testing to make inferences about how these conditions affect behavior. It aims to determine if one variable directly impacts and causes another. Correlational and experimental research both typically use hypothesis testing, whereas descriptive research does not.

Each of these research methods has unique strengths and weaknesses, and each method may only be appropriate for certain types of research questions. For example, studies that rely primarily on observation produce incredible amounts of information, but the ability to apply this information to the larger population is somewhat limited because of small sample sizes. Survey research, on the other hand, allows researchers to easily collect data from relatively large samples. While this allows for results to be generalized to the larger population more easily, the information that can be collected on any given survey is somewhat limited and subject to problems associated with any type of self-reported data. Some researchers conduct archival research by using existing records. While this can be a fairly inexpensive way to collect data that can provide insight into a number of research questions, researchers using this approach have no control on how or what kind of data was collected.

Correlational research can find a relationship between two variables, but the only way a researcher can claim that the relationship between the variables is cause and effect is to perform an experiment. In experimental research, which will be discussed later in the text, there is a tremendous amount of control over variables of interest. While this is a powerful approach, experiments are often conducted in very artificial settings. This calls into question the validity of experimental findings with regard to how they would apply in real-world settings. In addition, many of the questions that psychologists would like to answer cannot be pursued through experimental research because of ethical concerns.

The three main types of descriptive studies are case studies, naturalistic observation, and surveys.

Case Studies

In 2011, the *New York Times* published a feature story on Krista and Tatiana Hogan, Canadian twin girls. These particular twins are unique because Krista and Tatiana are conjoined twins, connected at the head. There is evidence that the two girls are connected in a part of the brain called the thalamus, which is a major sensory relay center. Most incoming sensory information is sent through the thalamus before reaching higher regions of the cerebral cortex for processing.

> ## Link to Learning
>
> To learn more about Krista and Tatiana, watch this *New York Times* video about their lives.
>
> - http://www.nytimes.com/2011/05/29/magazine/could-conjoined-twins-share-a-mind.html?pagewanted=1&_r=1

The implications of this potential connection mean that it might be possible for one twin to experience the sensations of the other twin. For instance, if Krista is watching a particularly funny television program, Tatiana might smile or laugh even if she is not watching the program. This particular possibility has piqued the interest of many neuroscientists who seek to understand how the brain uses sensory information.

These twins represent an enormous resource in the study of the brain, and since their condition is very rare, it is likely that as long as their family agrees, scientists will follow these girls very closely throughout their lives to gain as much information as possible (Dominus, 2011).

In observational research, scientists are conducting a clinical or **case study** when they focus on one person or just a few individuals. Indeed, some scientists spend their entire careers studying just 10–20 individuals. Why would they do this? Obviously, when they focus their attention on a very small number of people, they can gain a tremendous amount of insight into those cases. The richness of information that is collected in clinical or case studies is unmatched by any other single research method. This allows the researcher to have a very deep understanding of the individuals and the particular phenomenon being studied.

If clinical or case studies provide so much information, why are they not more frequent among researchers? As it turns out, the major benefit of this particular approach is also a weakness. As mentioned earlier, this approach is often used when studying individuals who are interesting to researchers because they have a rare characteristic. Therefore, the individuals who serve as the focus of case studies are not like most other people. If scientists ultimately want to explain all behavior, focusing attention on such a special group of people can make it difficult to generalize any observations to the larger population as a whole. Generalizing refers to the ability to apply the findings of a particular research project to larger segments of society. Again, case studies provide enormous amounts of information, but since the cases are so specific, the potential to apply what's learned to the average person may be very limited.

Naturalistic Observation

If you want to understand how behavior occurs, one of the best ways to gain information is to simply observe the behavior in its natural context. However, people might change their behavior in unexpected ways if they know they are being observed. How do researchers obtain accurate information when people tend to hide their natural behavior? As an example, imagine that your professor asks everyone in your class to raise their hand if they always wash their hands after using the restroom. Chances are that almost everyone in the classroom will raise their hand, but do you think hand washing after every trip to the restroom is really that universal?

This is very similar to the phenomenon mentioned earlier in this chapter: many individuals do not feel comfortable answering a question honestly. But if we are committed to finding out the facts about hand washing, we have other options available to us.

Suppose we send a classmate into the restroom to actually watch whether everyone washes their hands after using the restroom. Will our observer blend into the restroom environment by wearing a white lab coat, sitting with a clipboard, and staring at the sinks? We want our researcher to be inconspicuous—perhaps standing at one of the sinks pretending to put in contact lenses while secretly recording the relevant information. This type of observational study is called **naturalistic observation**: observing behavior in its natural setting. To better understand peer exclusion, Suzanne Fanger collaborated with colleagues at the University of Texas to observe the behavior of preschool children on a playground. How did the observers remain inconspicuous over the duration of the study? They equipped a few of the children with wireless microphones (which the children quickly forgot about) and observed while taking notes from a distance. Also, the children in that particular preschool (a "laboratory preschool") were accustomed to having observers on the playground (Fanger, Frankel, & Hazen, 2012).

It is critical that the observer be as unobtrusive and as inconspicuous as possible: when people know they are being watched, they are less likely to behave naturally. If you have any doubt about this, ask yourself how your driving behavior might differ in two situations: In the first situation, you are driving down a deserted highway during the middle of the day; in the second situation, you are being followed by a police car down the same deserted highway (Figure 1).

It should be pointed out that naturalistic observation is not limited to research involving humans. Indeed, some of the best-known examples of naturalistic observation involve researchers going into the field to observe various

Figure 1. Seeing a police car behind you would probably affect your driving behavior. (credit: Michael Gil)

kinds of animals in their own environments. As with human studies, the researchers maintain their distance and avoid interfering with the animal subjects so as not to influence their natural behaviors. Scientists have used this technique to study social hierarchies and interactions among animals ranging from ground squirrels to gorillas. The information provided by these studies is invaluable in understanding how those animals organize socially and communicate with one another. The anthropologist Jane Goodall, for example, spent nearly five decades observing the behavior of chimpanzees in Africa (Figure 2). As an illustration of the types of concerns that a researcher might encounter in naturalistic observation, some scientists criticized Goodall for giving the chimps names instead of referring to them by numbers—using names was thought to undermine the emotional detachment required for the objectivity of the study (McKie, 2010).

(a)

(b)

Figure 2. (a) Jane Goodall made a career of conducting naturalistic observations of (b) chimpanzee behavior. (credit "Jane Goodall": modification of work by Erik Hersman; "chimpanzee": modification of work by "Afrika Force"/Flickr.com)

The greatest benefit of naturalistic observation is the validity, or accuracy, of information collected unobtrusively in a natural setting. Having individuals behave as they normally would in a given situation means that we have a higher degree of ecological validity, or realism, than we might achieve with other research approaches. Therefore, our ability to **generalize** the findings of the research to real-world situations is enhanced. If done correctly, we need not worry about people or animals modifying their behavior simply because they are being observed. Sometimes, people may assume that reality programs give us a glimpse into authentic human behavior. However, the principle of inconspicuous observation is violated as reality stars are followed by camera crews and are interviewed on camera for personal confessionals. Given that environment, we must doubt how natural and realistic their behaviors are.

The major downside of naturalistic observation is that they are often difficult to set up and control. In our restroom study, what if you stood in the restroom all day prepared to record people's hand washing behavior and no one came in? Or, what if you have been closely observing a troop of gorillas for weeks only to find that they migrated to a new place while you were sleeping in your tent? The benefit of realistic data comes at a cost. As a researcher you have no control of when (or if) you have behavior to observe. In addition, this type of observational research often requires significant investments of time, money, and a good dose of luck.

Sometimes studies involve structured observation. In these cases, people are observed while engaging in set, specific tasks. An excellent example of structured observation comes from Strange Situation by Mary Ainsworth (you will read more about this in the chapter on lifespan development). The Strange Situation is a procedure used to evaluate attachment styles that exist between an infant and caregiver. In this scenario, caregivers bring their infants into a room filled with toys. The Strange Situation involves a number of phases, including a stranger coming into the room, the caregiver leaving the room, and the caregiver's return to the room. The infant's behavior is closely monitored at each phase, but it is the behavior of the infant upon being reunited with the caregiver that is most telling in terms of characterizing the infant's attachment style with the caregiver.

Another potential problem in observational research is **observer bias.** Generally, people who act as observers are closely involved in the research project and may unconsciously skew their observations to fit their research goals or expectations. To protect against this type of bias, researchers should have clear criteria established for the types of behaviors recorded and how those behaviors should be classified. In addition, researchers often compare observations of the same event by multiple observers, in order to test **inter-rater reliability**: a measure of reliability that assesses the consistency of observations by different observers.

Surveys

Often, psychologists develop surveys as a means of gathering data. **Surveys** are lists of questions to be answered by research participants, and can be delivered as paper-and-pencil questionnaires, administered electronically, or conducted verbally (Figure 3). Generally, the survey itself can be completed in a short time, and the ease of administering a survey makes it easy to collect data from a large number of people.

Surveys allow researchers to gather data from larger samples than may be afforded by other research methods. A **sample** is a subset of individuals selected from a **population**, which is the overall group of individuals that the researchers are interested in. Researchers study the sample and seek to generalize their findings to the population.

There is both strength and weakness of the survey in comparison to case studies. By using surveys, we can collect information from a larger sample of people. A larger sample is better able to reflect the actual diversity of the population, thus allowing better generalizability. Therefore, if our sample is suffi-

Figure 3. Surveys can be administered in a number of ways, including electronically administered research, like the survey shown here. (credit: Robert Nyman)

ciently large and diverse, we can assume that the data we collect from the survey can be generalized to the larger population with more certainty than the information collected through a case study. However, given the greater number of people involved, we are not able to collect the same depth of information on each person that would be collected in a case study.

Another potential weakness of surveys is something we touched on earlier in this chapter: People don't always give accurate responses. They may lie, misremember, or answer questions in a way that they think makes them look good. For example, people may report drinking less alcohol than is actually the case.

Any number of research questions can be answered through the use of surveys. One real-world example is the research conducted by Jenkins, Ruppel, Kizer, Yehl, and Griffin (2012) about the backlash against the US Arab-American community following the terrorist attacks of September 11, 2001. Jenkins and colleagues wanted to determine to what extent these negative attitudes toward Arab-Americans still existed nearly a decade after the attacks occurred. In one study, 140 research participants filled out a survey with 10 questions, including questions asking directly about the participant's overt prejudicial attitudes toward people of various ethnicities. The survey also asked indirect questions about how likely the participant would be to interact with a person of a given ethnicity in a variety of settings (such as, "How likely do you think it is that you would introduce yourself to a person of Arab-American descent?"). The results of the research suggested that participants were unwilling to report prejudicial attitudes toward any ethnic group. However, there were significant differences between their pattern of responses to questions about social interaction with Arab-Americans compared to other ethnic groups: they indicated less willingness for social interaction with Arab-Americans compared to the other ethnic groups. This suggested that the participants harbored subtle forms of prejudice against Arab-Americans, despite their assertions that this was not the case (Jenkins et al., 2012).

Archival Research

Some researchers gain access to large amounts of data without interacting with a single research participant. Instead, they use existing records to answer various research questions. This type of research approach is known as archival research. **Archival research** relies on looking at past records or data sets to look for interesting patterns or relationships.

For example, a researcher might access the academic records of all individuals who enrolled in college within the past ten years and calculate how long it took them to complete their degrees, as well as course loads, grades, and extracurricular involvement. Archival research could provide important information about who is most likely to complete their education, and it could help identify important risk factors for struggling students (Figure 1).

In comparing archival research to other research methods, there are several important distinctions. For one, the researcher employing archival research never directly interacts with research participants. Therefore, the investment of time and money to collect data is considerably less with archival research. Additionally, researchers have no control over what information was originally collected. Therefore, research questions have to be tailored so they can be answered within the structure of the existing data sets. There is also no guarantee of consistency between the records from one source to another, which might make comparing and contrasting different data sets problematic.

(a)   (b)

Figure 1. A researcher doing archival research examines records, whether archived as a (a) hardcopy or (b) electronically. (credit "paper files": modification of work by "Newtown graffiti"/Flickr; "computer": modification of work by INPIVIC Family/Flickr)

Longitudinal and Cross-Sectional Research

Sometimes we want to see how people change over time, as in studies of human development and lifespan. When we test the same group of individuals repeatedly over an extended period of time, we are conducting longitudinal research. **Longitudinal** research is a research design in which data-gathering is administered repeatedly over an extended period of time. For example, we may survey a group of individuals about their dietary habits at age 20, retest them a decade later at age 30, and then again at age 40.

Another approach is **cross-sectional** research. In cross-sectional research, a researcher compares multiple segments of the population at the same time. Using the dietary habits example above, the researcher might directly compare different groups of people by age. Instead a group of people for 20 years to see how their dietary habits changed from decade to decade, the researcher would study a group of 20-year-old individuals and compare them to a group of 30-year-old individuals and a group of 40-year-old individuals. While cross-sectional research requires a shorter-term investment, it is also limited by differences that exist between the different generations (or cohorts) that have nothing to do with age per se, but rather reflect the social and cultural experiences of different generations of individuals make them different from one another.

To illustrate this concept, consider the following survey findings. In recent years there has been significant growth in the popular support of same-sex marriage. Many studies on this topic break down survey participants into different age groups. In general, younger people are more supportive of same-sex marriage than are those who are older (Jones, 2013). Does this mean that as we age we become less open to the idea of same-sex marriage, or does this mean that older individuals have different perspectives because of the social climates in which they grew up? Longitudinal research is a powerful approach because the same individuals are involved in the research project over time, which means that the researchers need to be less concerned with differences among cohorts affecting the results of their study.

Often longitudinal studies are employed when researching various diseases in an effort to understand particular risk factors. Such studies often involve tens of thousands of individuals who are followed for several decades. Given the enormous number of people involved in these studies, researchers can feel confident that their findings can be generalized to the larger population. The Cancer Prevention Study-3 (CPS-3) is one of a series of longitudinal studies sponsored by the American Cancer Society aimed at determining predictive risk factors associated with cancer. When participants enter the study, they complete a survey about their lives and family histories, providing information on factors that might cause or prevent the development of cancer. Then every few years the participants receive additional surveys to complete. In the end, hundreds of thousands of participants will be tracked over 20 years to determine which of them develop cancer and which do not.

Clearly, this type of research is important and potentially very informative. For instance, earlier longitudinal studies sponsored by the American Cancer Society provided some of the first scientific demonstrations of the now well-established links between increased rates of cancer and smoking (American Cancer Society, n.d.) (Figure 2).

Figure 2. Longitudinal research like the CPS-3 help us to better understand how smoking is associated with cancer and other diseases. (credit: CDC/Debora Cartagena)

As with any research strategy, longitudinal research is not without limitations. For one, these studies require an incredible time investment by the researcher and research participants. Given that some longitudinal studies take years, if not decades, to complete, the results will not be known for a considerable period of time. In addition to the time demands, these studies also require a substantial financial investment. Many researchers are unable to commit the resources necessary to see a longitudinal project through to the end.

Research participants must also be willing to continue their participation for an extended period of time, and this can be problematic. People move, get married and take new names, get ill, and eventually die. Even without significant life changes, some people may simply choose to discontinue their participation in the project. As a result, the **attrition** rates, or reduction in the number of research participants due to dropouts, in longitudinal studies are quite high and increases over the course of a project. For this reason, researchers using this approach typically recruit many participants fully expecting that a substantial number will drop out before the end. As the study progresses, they continually check whether the sample still represents the larger population, and make adjustments as necessary.

Glossary

archival research: method of research using past records or data sets to answer various research questions, or to search for interesting patterns or relationships

attrition: reduction in number of research participants as some drop out of the study over time

clinical or case study: observational research study focusing on one or a few people

correlational research: tests whether a relationship exists between two or more variables

cross-sectional research: compares multiple segments of a population at a single time

descriptive research: research studies that do not test specific relationships between variables; they are used to describe general or specific behaviors and attributes that are observed and measured

experimental research: tests a hypothesis to determine cause and effect relationships

generalize inferring that the results for a sample apply to the larger population

inter-rater reliability: measure of agreement among observers on how they record and classify a particular event

longitudinal research: studies in which the same group of individuals is surveyed or measured repeatedly over an extended period of time

naturalistic observation: observation of behavior in its natural setting

observer bias: when observations may be skewed to align with observer expectations

population: overall group of individuals that the researchers are interested in

sample: subset of individuals selected from the larger population

survey: list of questions to be answered by research participants—given as paper-and-pencil questionnaires, administered electronically, or conducted verbally—allowing researchers to collect data from a large number of people

Public domain content

- Researchers review documents. **Authored by:** National Cancer Institute. **Provided by:** Wikimedia. **Located at:** https://commons.wikimedia.org/wiki/File:Researchers_review_documents.jpg. **License:** *Public Domain: No Known Copyright*

Correlational Research

Learning Objectives

- Explain what a correlation coefficient tells us about the relationship between variables
- Describe why correlation does not mean causation

Did you know that as sales in ice cream increase, so does the overall rate of crime? Is it possible that indulging in your favorite flavor of ice cream could send you on a crime spree? Or, after committing crime do you think you might decide to treat yourself to a cone? There is no question that a relationship exists between ice cream and crime (e.g., Harper, 2013), but it would be pretty foolish to decide that one thing actually caused the other to occur.

It is much more likely that both ice cream sales and crime rates are related to the temperature outside. When the temperature is warm, there are lots of people out of their houses, interacting with each other, getting annoyed with one another, and sometimes committing crimes. Also, when it is warm outside, we are more likely to seek a cool treat like ice cream. How do we determine if there is indeed a relationship between two things? And when there is a relationship, how can we discern whether it is attributable to coincidence or causation?

Correlational Research

Correlation means that there is a relationship between two or more variables (such as ice cream consumption and crime), but this relationship does not necessarily imply cause and effect. When two variables are correlated, it simply means that as one variable changes, so does the other. We can measure correlation by calculating a statistic known as a correlation coefficient. A **correlation coefficient** is a number from -1 to +1 that indicates the strength and direction of the relationship between variables. The correlation coefficient is usually represented by the letter r.

The number portion of the correlation coefficient indicates the strength of the relationship. The closer the number is to 1 (be it negative or positive), the more strongly related the variables are, and the more predictable changes in one variable will be as the other variable changes. The closer the number is to zero, the weaker the relationship, and the less predictable the relationships between the variables becomes. For instance, a correlation coefficient of 0.9 indicates a far stronger relationship than a correlation coefficient of 0.3. If the variables are not related to one another at all, the correlation coefficient is 0. The example above about ice cream and crime is an example of two variables that we might expect to have no relationship to each other.

The sign—positive or negative—of the correlation coefficient indicates the direction of the relationship (Figure 1). A **positive correlation** means that the variables move in the same direction. Put another way, it means that as one variable increases so does the other, and conversely, when one variable decreases so does the other. **A negative correlation** means that the variables move in opposite directions. If two variables are negatively correlated, a decrease in one variable is associated with an increase in the other and vice versa.

The example of ice cream and crime rates is a positive correlation because both variables increase when temperatures are warmer. Other examples of positive correlations are the relationship between an individual's height and weight or the relationship between a person's age and number of wrinkles. One might expect a negative correlation to exist between someone's tiredness during the day and the number of hours they slept the previous night: the amount of sleep decreases as the feelings of tiredness increase. In a real-world example of negative correlation, student researchers at the University of Minnesota found a weak negative correlation ($r = -0.29$) between the average number of days per week that students got fewer than 5 hours of sleep and their GPA (Lowry, Dean, & Manders, 2010). Keep in mind that a negative correlation is not the same as no correlation. For example, we would probably find no correlation between hours of sleep and shoe size.

As mentioned earlier, correlations have predictive value. Imagine that you are on the admissions committee of a major university. You are faced with a huge number of applications, but you are able to accommodate only a small percentage of the applicant pool. How might you decide who should be admitted? You might try to correlate your current students' college GPA with their scores on standardized tests like the SAT or ACT. By observing which correlations were strongest for your current students, you could use this information to predict relative success of those students who have applied for admission into the university.

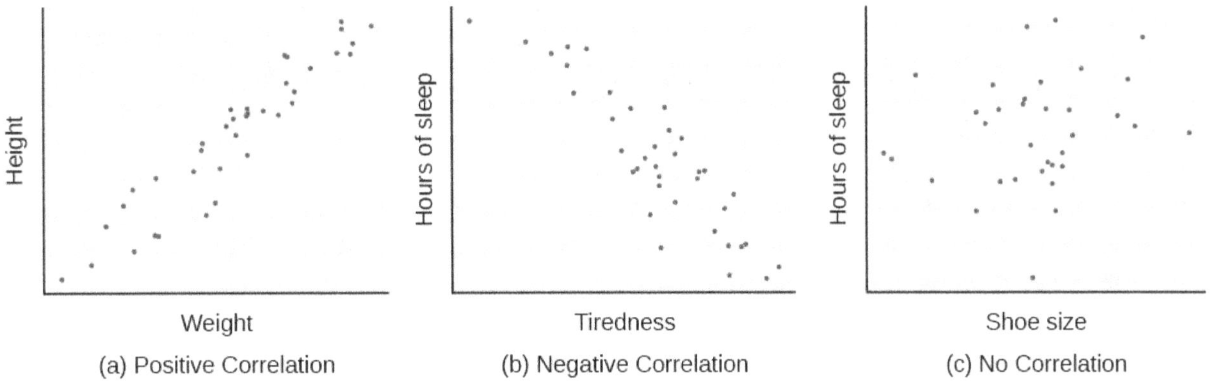

Figure 1. Scatterplots are a graphical view of the strength and direction of correlations. The stronger the correlation, the closer the data points are to a straight line. In these examples, we see that there is (a) a positive correlation between weight and height, (b) a negative correlation between tiredness and hours of sleep, and (c) no correlation between shoe size and hours of sleep.

Link to Learning

Manipulate this interactive scatterplot to practice your understanding of positive and negative correlation.

- http://www.bc.edu/research/intasc/library/correlation.shtml

Correlation Does Not Indicate Causation

Correlational research is useful because it allows us to discover the strength and direction of relationships that exist between two variables. However, correlation is limited because establishing the existence of a relationship tells us little about **cause and effect**. While variables are sometimes correlated because one does cause the other, it could also be that some other factor, a **confounding variable**, is actually causing the systematic movement in our variables of interest. In the ice cream/crime rate example mentioned earlier, temperature is a confounding variable that could account for the relationship between the two variables.

Even when we cannot point to clear confounding variables, we should not assume that a correlation between two variables implies that one variable causes changes in another. This can be frustrating when a cause-and-effect relationship seems clear and intuitive. Think back to our discussion of the research done by the American Cancer Society and how their research projects were some of the first demonstrations of the link between smoking and cancer. It seems reasonable to assume that smoking causes cancer, but if we were limited to **correlational research**, we would be overstepping our bounds by making this assumption.

Unfortunately, people mistakenly make claims of causation as a function of correlations all the time. Such claims are especially common in advertisements and news stories. For example, recent research found that people who eat cereal on a regular basis achieve healthier weights than those who rarely eat cereal (Frantzen, Treviño, Echon, Garcia-Dominic, & DiMarco, 2013; Barton et al., 2005). Guess how the cereal companies report this finding. Does eating cereal really cause an individual to maintain a healthy weight, or are there other possible explanations, such as, someone at a healthy weight is more likely to regularly eat a healthy breakfast than someone who is obese or someone who avoids meals in an attempt to diet (Figure 2)? While correlational research is invaluable in identifying relationships among variables, a major limitation is the inability to establish causality. Psychologists want to make statements about cause and effect, but the only way to do that is to conduct an experiment to answer a research question. The next section describes how scientific experiments incorporate methods that eliminate, or control for, alternative explanations, which allow researchers to explore how changes in one variable cause changes in another variable.

Illusory Correlations

The temptation to make erroneous cause-and-effect statements based on correlational research is not the only way we tend to misinterpret data. We also tend to make the mistake of illusory correlations, especially with unsystematic observations. **Illusory correlations**, or false correlations, occur when people believe that relationships exist between two things when no such relationship exists. One well-known illusory correlation is the supposed effect that the moon's phases have on human behavior. Many people passionately assert that human behavior is affected by the phase of the moon, and specifically, that people act strangely when the moon is full (Figure 3).

Figure 2. Does eating cereal really cause someone to be a healthy weight? (credit: Tim Skillern)

Many people believe that a full moon makes people behave oddly. (credit: Cory Zanker)

There is no denying that the moon exerts a powerful influence on our planet. The ebb and flow of the ocean's tides are tightly tied to the gravitational forces of the moon. Many people believe, therefore, that it is logical that we are affected by the moon as well. After all, our bodies are largely made up of water. A meta-analysis of nearly 40 studies consistently demonstrated, however, that the relationship between the moon and our behavior does not exist (Rotton & Kelly, 1985). While we may pay more attention to odd behavior during the full phase of the moon, the rates of odd behavior remain constant throughout the lunar cycle.

Why are we so apt to believe in illusory correlations like this? Often we read or hear about them and simply accept the information as valid. Or, we have a hunch about how something works and then look for evidence to support that hunch, ignoring evidence that would tell us our hunch is false; this is known as **confirmation bias**. Other times, we find illusory correlations based on the information that comes most easily to mind, even if that information is severely limited. And while we may feel confident that we can use these relationships to better understand and predict the world around us, illusory correlations can have significant drawbacks. For example, research suggests that illusory correlations—in which certain behaviors are inaccurately attributed to certain groups—are involved in the formation of prejudicial attitudes that can ultimately lead to discriminatory behavior (Fiedler, 2004).

Glossary

cause-and-effect relationship: changes in one variable cause the changes in the other variable; can be determined only through an experimental research design

confirmation bias: tendency to ignore evidence that disproves ideas or beliefs

confounding variable: unanticipated outside factor that affects both variables of interest, often giving the false impression that changes in one variable causes changes in the other variable, when, in actuality, the outside factor causes changes in both variables

correlation: relationship between two or more variables; when two variables are correlated, one variable changes as the other does

correlation coefficient: number from -1 to +1, indicating the strength and direction of the relationship between variables, and usually represented by r

illusory correlation: seeing relationships between two things when in reality no such relationship exists

negative correlation: two variables change in different directions, with one becoming larger as the other becomes smaller; a negative correlation is not the same thing as no correlation

positive correlation two variables change in the same direction, both becoming either larger or smaller

This is a modified version of OpenStax Psychology. Download the original text for free at https://openstax.org/details/books/psychology

Attributions

CC licensed content, Shared previously

- Analyzing Findings. **Authored by:** OpenStax College. **Located at:** http://cnx.org/contents/ Sr8Ev5Og@5.49:mfArybye@7/Analyzing-Findings. **License:** *CC BY: Attribution.* **License Terms:** Download for free at http://cnx.org/contents/4abf04bf-93a0-45c3-9cbc-2cefd46e68cc@5.48

All rights reserved content

- Correlation vs. Causality: Freakonomics Movie. **Located at:** https://www.youtube.com/watch?v=lbODqslc4Tg. **License:** *Other.* **License Terms:** Standard YouTube License

Experiments

- Describe the experimental process, including ways to control for bias
- Identify and differentiate between independent and dependent variables

Causality: Conducting Experiments and Using the Data

As you've learned, the only way to establish that there is a cause-and-effect relationship between two variables is to conduct a scientific experiment. **Experiment** has a different meaning in the scientific context than in everyday life. In everyday conversation, we often use it to describe trying something for the first time, such as experimenting with a new hair style or a new food. However, in the scientific context, an experiment has precise requirements for design and implementation.

The Experimental Hypothesis

In order to conduct an experiment, a researcher must have a specific **hypothesis** to be tested. As you've learned, hypotheses can be formulated either through direct observation of the real world or after careful review of previous research. For example, if you think that children should not be allowed to watch violent programming on television because doing so would cause them to behave more violently, then you have basically formulated a hypothesis—namely, that watching violent television programs causes children to behave more violently. How might you have arrived at this particular hypothesis? You may have younger relatives who watch cartoons featuring characters using martial arts to save the world from evildoers, with an impressive array of punching, kicking, and defensive postures. You notice that after watching these programs for a while, your young relatives mimic the fighting behavior of the characters portrayed in the cartoon (Figure 1).

These sorts of personal observations are what often lead us to formulate a specific hypothesis, but we cannot use limited personal observations and anecdotal evidence to rigorously test our hypothesis. Instead, to find out if real-world data supports our hypothesis, we have to conduct an experiment.

Designing an Experiment

The most basic experimental design involves two groups: the experimental group and the control group. The two groups are designed to be the same except for one difference— experimental manipulation. The **experimental group** gets the experimental manipulation—that is, the treatment or variable being tested (in this case, violent TV images)—and the **control group** does not. Since experimental manipulation is the only difference between the experimental and control groups, we can be sure that any differences between the two are due to experimental manipulation rather than chance.

In our example of how violent television programming might affect violent behavior in children, we have the experimental group view violent television programming for a specified time and then measure

Figure 1. Seeing behavior like this right after a child watches violent television programming might lead you to hypothesize that viewing violent television programming leads to an increase in the display of violent behaviors. (credit: Emran Kassim)

their violent behavior. We measure the violent behavior in our control group after they watch nonviolent television programming for the same amount of time. It is important for the control group to be treated similarly to the experimental group, with the exception that the control group does not receive the experimental manipulation. Therefore, we have the control group watch non-violent television programming for the same amount of time as the experimental group.

We also need to precisely define, or operationalize, what is considered violent and nonviolent. An **operational definition** is a description of how we will measure our variables, and it is important in allowing others understand exactly how and what a researcher measures in a particular experiment. In operationalizing violent behavior, we might choose to count only physical acts like kicking or punching as instances of this behavior, or we also may choose to include angry verbal exchanges. Whatever we determine, it is important that we operationalize violent behavior in such a way that anyone who hears about our study for the first time knows exactly what we mean by violence. This aids peoples' ability to interpret our data as well as their capacity to repeat our experiment should they choose to do so.

Once we have operationalized what is considered violent television programming and what is considered violent behavior from our experiment participants, we need to establish how we will run our experiment. In this case, we might have participants watch a 30-minute television program (either violent or nonviolent, depending on their group membership) before sending them out to a playground for an hour where their behavior is observed and the number and type of violent acts is recorded.

Ideally, the people who observe and record the children's behavior are unaware of who was assigned to the experimental or control group, in order to control for experimenter bias. **Experimenter bias** refers to the possibility that a researcher's expectations might skew the results of the study. Remember, conducting an experiment requires a lot of planning, and the people involved in the research project have a vested interest in supporting their hypotheses. If the observers knew which child was in which group, it might influence how much attention they paid to each child's behavior as well as how they interpreted that behavior. By being blind to which child is in which group, we protect against those biases. This situation is a **single-blind study**, meaning that one of the groups (participants) are unaware as to which group they are in (experiment or control group) while the researcher who developed the experiment knows which participants are in each group.

In a **double-blind study**, both the researchers and the participants are blind to group assignments. Why would a researcher want to run a study where no one knows who is in which group? Because by doing so, we can control for both experimenter and participant expectations. If you are familiar with the phrase placebo effect, you already have some idea as to why this is an important consideration. The **placebo effect** occurs when people's expectations or beliefs influence or determine their experience in a given situation. In other words, simply expecting something to happen can actually make it happen.

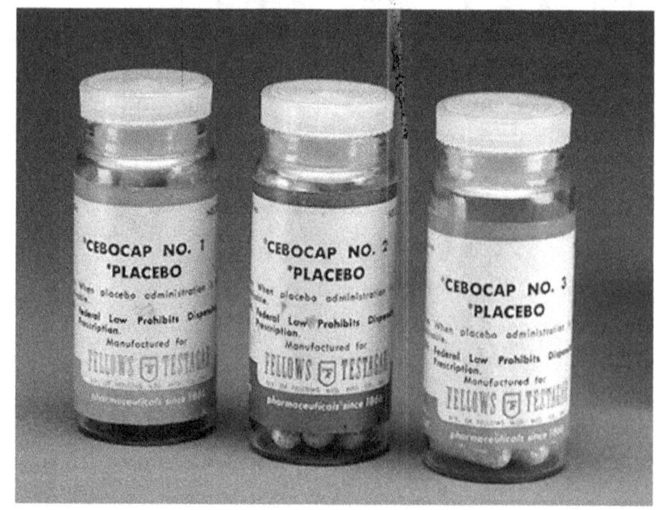

Figure 2. Providing the control group with a placebo treatment protects against bias caused by expectancy. (credit: Elaine and Arthur Shapiro)

The placebo effect is commonly described in terms of testing the effectiveness of a new medication. Imagine that you work in a pharmaceutical company, and you think you have a new drug that is effective in treating depression. To demonstrate that your medication is effective, you run an experiment with two groups: The experimental group receives the medication, and the control group does not. But you don't want participants to know whether they received the drug or not.

Why is that? Imagine that you are a participant in this study, and you have just taken a pill that you think will improve your mood. Because you expect the pill to have an effect, you might feel better simply because you took the pill and not because of any drug actually contained in the pill—this is the placebo effect.

To make sure that any effects on mood are due to the drug and not due to expectations, the control group receives a placebo (in this case a sugar pill). Now everyone gets a pill, and once again neither the researcher nor the experimental participants know who got the drug and who got the sugar pill. Any differences in mood between the experimental and control groups can now be attributed to the drug itself rather than to experimenter bias or participant expectations (Figure 2).

Independent and Dependent Variables

In a research experiment, we strive to study whether changes in one thing cause changes in another. To achieve this, we must pay attention to two important variables, or things that can be changed, in any experimental study: the independent variable and the dependent variable. An **independent variable** is manipulated or controlled by the experimenter. In a well-designed experimental study, the independent variable is the only important difference between the experimental and control groups. In our example of how violent television programs affect children's display of violent behavior, the independent variable is the type of program—violent or nonviolent—viewed by participants in the study (Figure 3). **A dependent variable** is what the researcher measures to see how much effect the independent variable had. In our example, the dependent variable is the number of violent acts displayed by the experimental participants.

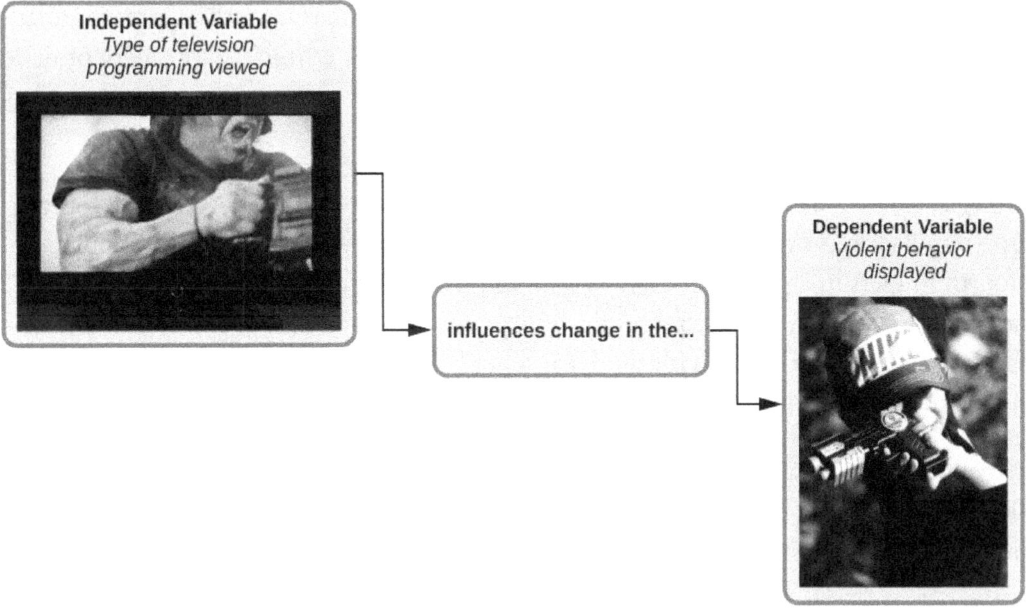

Figure 3. In an experiment, manipulations of the independent variable are expected to result in changes in the dependent variable. (credit "automatic weapon": modification of work by Daniel Oines; credit "toy gun": modification of work by Emran Kassim)

We expect that the dependent variable will change as a function of the independent variable. In other words, the dependent variable *depends* on the independent variable. A good way to think about the relationship between the independent and dependent variables is with this question: What effect does the independent variable have on the dependent variable? Returning to our example, what effect does watching a half hour of violent television programming or nonviolent television programming have on the number of incidents of physical aggression displayed on the playground?

Selecting and Assigning Experimental Participants

Now that our study is designed, we need to obtain a sample of individuals to include in our experiment. Our study involves human participants so we need to determine who to include. **Participants** are the subjects of psychological research, and as the name implies, individuals who are involved in psychological research actively participate in the process. Often, psychological research projects rely on college students to serve as participants. In fact, the vast majority of research in psychology subfields has historically involved students as research participants (Sears, 1986; Arnett, 2008). But are college students truly representative of the general population? College students tend to be younger, more educated, more liberal, and less diverse than the general population. Although using students as test subjects is an accepted practice, relying on such a limited pool of research participants can be problematic because it is difficult to generalize findings to the larger population.

Our hypothetical experiment involves children, and we must first generate a sample of child participants. Samples are used because populations are usually too large to reasonably involve every member in our particular experiment (Figure 4). If possible, we should use a **random sample** (there are other types of samples, but for the purposes of this section, we will focus on random samples). A random sample is a subset of a larger population in which every member of the population has an equal chance of being selected. Random samples are preferred because if the sample is large enough we can be reasonably sure that the participating individuals are representative of the larger population. This means that the percentages of characteristics in the sample—sex, ethnicity, socioeconomic level, and any other characteristics that might affect the results—are close to those percentages in the larger population.

In our example, let's say we decide our population of interest is fourth graders. But all fourth graders is a very large population, so we need to be more specific; instead we might say our population of interest is all fourth graders in a particular city. We should include students from various income brackets, family situations, races, ethnicities, religions, and geographic areas of town. With this more manageable population, we can work with the local schools in selecting a random sample of around 200 fourth graders who we want to participate in our experiment.

In summary, because we cannot test all of the fourth graders in a city, we want to find a group of about 200 that reflects the composition of that city. With a representative group, we can generalize our findings to the larger population without fear of our sample being biased in some way.

Now that we have a sample, the next step of the experimental process is to split the participants into experimental and control groups through random assignment. With **random assignment**, all participants have an equal chance of being assigned to either group. There is statistical software that will randomly assign each of the fourth graders in the sample to either the experimental or the control group.

Random assignment is critical for sound **experimental design**. With sufficiently large samples, random assignment makes it unlikely that there are systematic differences between the groups. So, for instance, it would be very unlikely that we would get one group composed entirely of males, a given ethnic identity, or a given religious ideology. This is important because if the groups were systematically different before the experiment began, we would not know the origin of any differences we find

(a)   (b)

Figure 4. Researchers may work with (a) a large population or (b) a sample group that is a subset of the larger population. (credit "crowd": modification of work by James Cridland; credit "students": modification of work by Laurie Sullivan)

between the groups: Were the differences preexisting, or were they caused by manipulation of the independent variable? Random assignment allows us to assume that any differences observed between experimental and control groups result from the manipulation of the independent variable.

Issues to Consider

While experiments allow scientists to make cause-and-effect claims, they are not without problems. True experiments require the experimenter to manipulate an independent variable, and that can complicate many questions that psychologists might want to address. For instance, imagine that you want to know what effect sex (the independent variable) has on spatial memory (the dependent variable). Although you can certainly look for differences between males and females on a task that taps into spatial memory, you cannot directly control a person's sex. We categorize this type of research approach as quasi-experimental and recognize that we cannot make cause-and-effect claims in these circumstances.

Experimenters are also limited by ethical constraints. For instance, you would not be able to conduct an experiment designed to determine if experiencing abuse as a child leads to lower levels of self-esteem among adults. To conduct such an experiment, you would need to randomly assign some experimental participants to a group that receives abuse, and that experiment would be unethical.

Link to Learning

Learn more about descriptive, correlational, and experimental approaches to psychological research through the following PsychSim Tutorial:

- What's Wrong With This Study
- http://bcs.worthpublishers.com/webpub/Ektron/Myers_Psychology%2010e/ PsychSim5_Tutorials/WhatsWrong/WhatsWrong.htm

Glossary

cause-and-effect relationship: changes in one variable cause the changes in the other variable; can be determined only through an experimental research design

confirmation bias: tendency to ignore evidence that disproves ideas or beliefs

control group: serves as a basis for comparison and controls for chance factors that might influence the results of the study—by holding such factors constant across groups so that the experimental manipulation is the only difference between groups

correlation: relationship between two or more variables; when two variables are correlated, one variable changes as the other does

dependent variable: variable that the researcher measures to see how much effect the independent variable had

double-blind study: experiment in which both the researchers and the participants are blind to group assignments

experimental group: group designed to answer the research question; experimental manipulation is the only difference between the experimental and control groups, so any differences between the two are due to experimental manipulation rather than chance

experimenter bias: researcher expectations skew the results of the study

independent variable: variable that is influenced or controlled by the experimenter; in a sound experimental study, the independent variable is the only important difference between the experimental and control group

operational definition: description of what actions and operations will be used to measure the dependent variables and manipulate the independent variables

participants: subjects of psychological research

placebo effect: people's expectations or beliefs influencing or determining their experience in a given situation

random assignment: method of experimental group assignment in which all participants have an equal chance of being assigned to either group

random sample: subset of a larger population in which every member of the population has an equal chance of being selected

replicate: repeating an experiment using different samples to determine the research's reliability

single-blind study: experiment in which the researcher knows which participants are in the experimental group and which are in the control group

statistical analysis: determines how likely any difference between experimental groups is due to chance

https://assessments.lumenlearning.com/assessments/4808

Attributions

CC licensed content, Original

- Modification, adaptation, addition of link to learning. **Provided by:** Lumen Learning. **License:** *CC BY: Attribution*

CC licensed content, Shared previously

This is a modified version of OpenStax Psychology. Download the original text for free at https://openstax.org/details/books/psychology

- Analyzing Findings. **Authored by:** OpenStax College. **Located at:** http://cnx.org/contents/ Sr8Ev5Og@5.48:mfArybye@7/Analyzing-Findings. **License:** *CC BY: Attribution.* **License Terms:** Download for free at http://cnx.org/contents/4abf04bf-93a0-45c3-9cbc-2cefd46e68cc@5.48

Module 2: Personality

Why It Matters: Personality

What makes two individuals have different personalities? (credit: modification of work by Nicolas Alejandro)

Consider two brothers. One of these siblings will grow up to become a world leader. The other will struggle with alcohol and drugs, eventually spending time in jail. What about each of their personalities propelled them to take the path they did?

Three months before William Jefferson Blythe III was born, his father died in a car accident. He was raised by his mother, Virginia Dell, and grandparents, in Hope, Arkansas. When he turned 4, his mother married Roger Clinton, Jr., an alcoholic who was physically abusive to William's mother. Six years later, Virginia gave birth to another son, Roger. William, who later took the last name Clinton from his stepfather, became the 42nd president of the United States. While Bill Clinton was making his political ascendance, his half-brother, Roger Clinton, was arrested numerous times for drug charges, including possession, conspiracy to distribute cocaine, and driving under the influence, serving time in jail. Two brothers, raised by the same people, took radically different paths in their lives. Why did they make the choices they did? What internal forces shaped their decisions? Personality psychology can help us answer these questions and more.

Module References

Adler, A. (1930). Individual psychology. In C. Murchison (Ed.), *Psychologies of 1930* (pp. 395–405). Worcester, MA: Clark University Press.

Adler, A. (1937). A school girl's exaggeration of her own importance. *International Journal of Individual Psychology, 3*(1), 3–12.

Adler, A. (1956). *The individual psychology of Alfred Adler: A systematic presentation in selections from his writings.* (C. H. Ansbacher & R. Ansbacher, Eds.). New York: Harper.

Adler, A. (1961). The practice and theory of individual psychology. In T. Shipley (Ed.), *Classics in psychology* (pp. 687–714). New York: Philosophical Library

Adler, A. (1964). *Superiority and social interest.* New York: Norton.

Akomolafe, M. J. (2013). Personality characteristics as predictors of academic performance of secondary school students. *Mediterranean Journal of Social Sciences, 4*(2), 657–664.

Allport, G. W. & Odbert, H. S. (1936). Trait-names: A psycho-lexical study. Albany, NY: Psychological Review Company.

Aronow, E., Weiss, K. A., & Rezinkoff, M. (2001). *A practical guide to the Thematic Apperception Test.* Philadelphia: Brunner Routledge.

Bandura, A. (1977). Self-efficacy: Toward a unifying theory of behavioral change. *Psychological Review, 84,* 191–215.

Bandura, A. (1986). *Social foundations of thought and action: A social cognitive theory.* Englewood Cliffs, NJ: Prentice Hall.

Bandura, A. (1995). *Self-efficacy in changing societies.* Cambridge, UK: Cambridge University Press.

Benassi, V. A., Sweeney, P. D., & Dufour, C. L. (1988). Is there a relation between locus of control orientation and depression? *Journal of Abnormal Psychology, 97*(3), 357.

Ben-Porath, Y., & Tellegen, A. (2008). *Minnesota Multiphasic Personality Inventory-2-RF.* Minneapolis, MN: University of Minnesota Press.

Benet-Martínez, V. & Karakitapoglu-Aygun, Z. (2003). The interplay of cultural values and personality in predicting life-satisfaction: Comparing Asian- and European-Americans. *Journal of Cross-Cultural Psychology, 34,* 38–61.

Benet-Martínez, V., & Oishi, S. (2008). Culture and personality. In O. P. John, R.W. Robins, L. A. Pervin (Eds.), *Handbook of personality: Theory and research.* New York: Guildford Press.

Beutler, L. E., Nussbaum, P. D., & Meredith, K. E. (1988). Changing personality patterns of police officers. *Professional Psychology: Research and Practice, 19*(5), 503–507.

Bouchard, T., Jr. (1994). Genes, environment, and personality. *Science, 264,* 1700–1701.

Bouchard, T., Jr., Lykken, D. T., McGue, M., Segal, N. L., & Tellegen, A. (1990). Sources of human psychological differences: The Minnesota Study of Twins Reared Apart. *Science, 250,* 223–228.

Burger, J. (2008). *Personality* (7th ed.). Belmont, CA: Thompson Higher Education.

Carter, J. E., and Heath, B. H. (1990). *Somatotyping: Development and applications.* Cambridge, UK: Cambridge University Press.

Carter, S., Champagne, F., Coates, S., Nercessian, E., Pfaff, D., Schecter, D., & Stern, N. B. (2008). *Development of temperament symposium.* Philoctetes Center, New York.

Cattell, R. B. (1946*). The description and measurement of personality.* New York: Harcourt, Brace, & World.

Cattell, R. B. (1957). *Personality and motivation structure and measurement.* New York: World Book.

Chamorro-Premuzic, T., & Furnham, A. (2008). Personality, intelligence, and approaches to learning as predictors of academic performance. *Personality and Individual Differences, 44,* 1596–1603.

Cheung, F. M., van de Vijver, F. J. R., & Leong, F. T. L. (2011). Toward a new approach to the study of personality in culture. *American Psychologist, 66*(7), 593–603.

Clark, A. L., & Watson, D. (2008). Temperament: An organizing paradigm for trait psychology. In O. P. John, R. W. Robins, & L. A. Previn (Eds.), *Handbook of personality: Theory and research* (3rd ed., pp. 265–286). New York: Guilford Press.

Conrad, N. & Party, M.W. (2012). Conscientiousness and academic performance: A Mediational Analysis. International *Journal for the Scholarship of Teaching and Learning, 6* (1), 1–14.

Cortés, J., & Gatti, F. (1972). Delinquency and crime: A biopsychological approach. New York: Seminar Press.

Costantino, G. (1982). TEMAS: A new technique for personality research assessment of Hispanic children. Hispanic Research Center, Fordham University *Research Bulletin, 5, 3–7.*

Cramer, P. (2004). *Storytelling, narrative, and the Thematic Apperception Test.* New York: Guilford Press.

Damon, S. (1955). Physique and success in military flying. *American Journal of Physical Anthropology, 13*(2), 217–252.

Donnellan, M. B., & Lucas, R. E. (2008). Age differences in the big five across the life span: Evidence from two national samples. *Psychology and Aging, 23*(3), 558–566.

Duzant, R. (2005). *Differences of emotional tone and story length of African American respondents when administered the Contemporized Themes Concerning Blacks test versus the Thematic Apperception Test.* Unpublished doctoral dissertation, The Chicago School of Professional Psychology, Chicago, IL.

Exner, J. E. (2002). *The Rorschach: Basic foundations and principles of interpretation* (Vol. 1). Hoboken, NJ: Wiley.

Eysenck, H. J. (1990). An improvement on personality inventory. *Current Contents: Social and Behavioral Sciences, 22*(18), 20.

Eysenck, H. J. (1992). Four ways five factors are *not* basic. *Personality and Individual Differences, 13,* 667–673.

Eysenck, H. J. (2009). *The biological basis of personality* (3rd ed.). New Brunswick, NJ: Transaction Publishers.

Eysenck, H. J. (1970). *The structure of human personality*. London, UK: Methuen.

Eysenck, S. B. G., & Eysenck, H. J. (1963). The validity of questionnaire and rating assessments of extroversion and neuroticism, and their factorial stability. *British Journal of Psychology, 54,* 51–62.

Eysenck, H. J., & Eysenck, M. W. (1985*). Personality and individual differences: A natural science approach*. New York: Plenum Press.

Eysenck, S. B. G., Eysenck, H. J., & Barrett, P. (1985). A revised version of the psychoticism scale. *Personality and Individual Differences, 6*(1), 21–29.

Fazeli, S. H. (2012). The exploring nature of the assessment instrument of five factors of personality traits in the current studies of personality. *Asian Social Science, 8*(2), 264–275.

Fancher, R. W. (1979). *Pioneers of psychology*. New York: Norton.

Freud, S. (1920). Resistance and suppression. *A general introduction to psychoanalysis* (pp. 248–261). New York: Horace Liveright.

Freud, S. (1923/1949). The ego and the id. London: Hogarth.

Freud, S. (1931/1968). Female sexuality. In J. Strachey (Ed. &Trans.), *The standard edition of the complete psychological works of Sigmund Freud* (Vol. 21). London: Hogarth Press.

Funder, D. C. (2001). Personality. *Annual Review of Psychology, 52,* 197–221.

Hofstede, G. (2001). *Culture's consequences: Comparing values, behaviors, institutions, and organizations across nations* (2nd ed.). Thousand Oaks, CA: Sage.

Holaday, D., Smith, D. A., & Sherry, Alissa. (2010). Sentence completion tests: A review of the literature and results of a survey of members of the society for personality assessment. *Journal of Personality Assessment, 74*(3), 371–383.

Hothersall, D. (1995). *History of psychology*. New York: McGraw-Hill.

Hoy, M. (1997). *Contemporizing of the Themes Concerning Blacks test (C-TCB)*. Alameda, CA: California School of Professional Psychology.

Hoy-Watkins, M., & Jenkins-Moore, V. (2008). The Contemporized-Themes Concerning Blacks Test (C-TCB). In S. R. Jenkins (Ed.), *A Handbook of Clinical Scoring Systems for Thematic Apperceptive Techniques* (pp. 659–698). New York: Lawrence Erlbaum Associates.

Genovese, J. E. C. (2008). Physique correlates with reproductive success in an archival sample of delinquent youth. *Evolutionary Psychology, 6*(3), 369-385.

Jang, K. L., Livesley, W. J., & Vernon, P. A. (1996). Heritability of the big five personality dimensions and their facts: A twin study. *Journal of Personality, 64*(3), 577–591.

Jang, K. L., Livesley, W. J., Ando, J., Yamagata, S., Suzuki, A., Angleitner, A., et al. (2006). Behavioral genetics of the higher-order factors of the Big Five. *Personality and Individual Differences, 41,* 261–272.

Judge, T. A., Livingston, B. A., & Hurst, C. (2012). Do nice guys-and gals- really finish last? The joint effects of sex and agreeableness on income. *Journal of Personality and Social Psychology, 102*(2), 390–407.

Jung, C. G. (1923). *Psychological types.* New York: Harcourt Brace.

Jung, C. G. (1928). *Contributions to analytical psychology.* New York: Harcourt Brace Jovanovich.

Jung, C. G. (1964). *Man and his symbols.* New York: Doubleday and Company.

Jung, C., & Kerenyi, C. (1963). Science of mythology. In R. F. C. Hull (Ed. & Trans.), *Essays on the myth of the divine child and the mysteries of Eleusis.* New York: Harper & Row.

Launer, J. (2005). Anna O. and the 'talking cure.' *QJM: An International Journal of Medicine, 98*(6), 465–466.

Lecci, L. B. & Magnavita, J. J. (2013). *Personality theories: A scientific approach.* San Diego, CA: Bridgepoint Education.

Lefcourt, H. M. (1982). *Locus of control: Current trends in theory and research* (2nd ed.). Hillsdale, NJ: Erlbaum.

Lecci, L. B. & Magnavita, J. J. (2013). *Personality theories: A scientific approach.* San Diego, CA: Bridgepoint Education.

Likert, R. (1932). A technique for the measurement of attitudes. *Archives of Psychology, 140,* 1–55.

Lilienfeld, S. O., Wood, J. M., & Garb, H. N. (2000). The scientific status of projective techniques. *Psychological Science in the Public Interest, 1*(2), 27–66.

Maltby, J., Day, L., & Macaskill, A. (2007). *Personality, individual differences and intelligence* (3rd ed.). UK: Pearson.

Maslow, A. H. (1970). *Motivation and personality.* New York: Harper & Row.

Maslow, A. H. (1950). Self-actualizing people: A study of psychological health. In W. Wolff (Ed.), *Personality Symposia: Symposium 1 on Values* (pp. 11–34). New York: Grune & Stratton.

McCrae, R. R., & Costa, P. T. (1997). Personality trait structure as a human universal. *American Psychologist, 52*(5), 509–516.

McCrae, R. R., et al. (2005). Universal features of personality traits from the observer's perspective: Data from 50 cultures. *Journal of Personality and Social Psychology, 88,* 547–561.

Mischel, W. (1993). *Introduction to personality* (5th ed.). Fort Worth, TX: Harcourt Brace Jovanovich.

Mischel, W., Ayduk, O., Berman, M. G., Casey, B. J., Gotlib, I. H., Jonides, J., et al. (2010). 'Willpower' over the life span: Decomposing self-regulation. *Social Cognitive and Affective Neuroscience, 6*(2), 252–256.

Mischel, W., Ebbesen, E. B., & Raskoff Zeiss, A. (1972). Cognitive and attentional mechanisms of delay in gratification. *Journal of Personality and Social Psychology, 21*(2), 204–218.

Mischel, W., & Shoda, Y. (1995). A cognitive-affective system theory of personality: Reconceptualizing situations, dispositions, dynamics, and invariance in personality structure. *Psychological Review, 102*(2), 246–268.

Mischel, W., Shoda, Y., & Rodriguez, M. L. (1989, May 26). Delay of gratification in children. *Science, 244,* 933-938.

Motley, M. T. (2002). Theory of slips. In E. Erwin (Ed.), *The Freud encyclopedia: Theory, therapy, and culture* (pp. 530–534). New York: Routledge.

Noftle, E. E., & Robins, R. W. (2007). Personality predictors of academic outcomes: Big Five correlates of GPA and SAT scores. *Personality Processes and Individual Differences, 93,* 116–130.

Noga, A. (2007). *Passions and tempers: A history of the humors.* New York: Harper Collins.

Oyserman, D., Coon, H., & Kemmelmier, M. (2002). Rethinking individualism and collectivism: Evaluation of theoretical assumptions and meta-analyses. *Psychological Bulletin, 128,* 3–72.

Parnell, R.W. (1958). *Behavior and physique: An introduction to practical somatometry.* London, UK: Edward Arnold Publishers LTD.

Peterson, J., Liivamagi, J., & Koskel, S. (2006). Associations between temperament types and body build in 17–22 year-old Estonian female students. *Papers on Anthropology, 25,* 142–149.

Piotrowski, Z. A. (1987). *Perceptanalysis: The Rorschach method fundamentally reworked, expanded and systematized.* London, UK: Routledge.

Rafter, N. (2007). Somatotyping, antimodernism, and the production of criminological knowledge. *Criminology, 45,* 805–833.

Rentfrow, P. J., Gosling, S. D., Jokela, M., Stillwell, D. J., Kosinski, M., & Potter, J. (2013, October 14). Divided we stand: Three psychological regions of the United States and their political, economic, social, and health correlates. *Journal of Personality and Social Psychology, 105*(6), 996–1012.

Roesler, C. (2012). Are archetypes transmitted more by culture than biology? Questions arising from conceptualizations of the archetype. *Journal of Analytical Psychology, 57*(2), 223–246.

Rogers, C. (1980). *A way of being.* Boston, MA: Houghton Mifflin.

Rosenbaum, R. (1995, January 15). The great Ivy League posture photo scandal. *The New York Times,* pp. A26.

Rothbart, M. K. (2011). *Becoming who we are: Temperament and personality in development.* New York: Guilford Press.

Rothbart, M. K., Ahadi, S. A., & Evans, D. E. (2000). Temperament and personality: Origins and outcomes. *Journal of Personality and Social Psychology, 78*(1), 122–135.

Rothbart, M. K., & Derryberry, D. (1981). Development of individual differences in temperament. In M. E. Lamb & A. L. Brown (Eds.), *Advances in developmental psychology* (Vol. 1, pp. 37–86). Hillsdale, NJ: Erlbaum.

Rothbart, M. K., Sheese, B. E., Rueda, M. R., & Posner, M. I. (2011). Developing mechanisms of self-regulation in early life. *Emotion Review, 3*(2), 207–213.

Rotter, J. (1966). Generalized expectancies for internal versus external control of reinforcements. *Psychological Monographs, 80,* 609.

Rotter, J. B., & Rafferty, J. E. (1950). *Manual the Rotter Incomplete Sentences Blank College Form.* New York: The Psychological Corporation.

Sanford, R. N., Adkins, M. M., Miller, R. B., & Cobb, E. A. (1943). Physique, personality, and scholarship: A cooperative study of school children. *Monographs of the Society for Research in Child Development, 8*(1), 705.

Schmitt, D. P., Allik, J., McCrae, R. R., & Benet-Martinez, V. (2007). The geographic distribution of Big Five personality traits: Patterns and profiles of human self-description across 56 nations. *Journal of Cross-Cultural Psychology, 38,* 173–212.

Scott, J. (2005). *Electra after Freud: Myth and culture.* Ithaca: Cornell University Press.

Segal, N. L. (2012). *Born together-reared apart: The landmark Minnesota Twin Study.* Cambridge, MA: Harvard University Press.

Sheldon, W. H. (1940). *The varieties of human physique: An introduction to constitutional psychology.* New York: Harper and Row.

Sheldon, W. H. (1942). *The varieties of temperament: A psychology of constitutional differences.* New York: Harper and Row.

Sheldon, W.H. (1949). Varieties of delinquent youth: An introduction to constitutional psychology. New York: Harper and Brothers.

Skinner, B. F. (1953). *Science and human behavior.* New York: The Free Press.

Sotirova-Kohli, M., Opwis, K., Roesler, C., Smith, S. M., Rosen, D. H., Vaid, J., & Djnov, V. (2013). Symbol/meaning paired-associate recall: An "archetypal memory" advantage? *Behavioral Sciences, 3,* 541–561. Retrieved from http://www2.cnr.edu/home/araia/Myth_%20Body.pdf

Stelmack, R. M., & Stalikas, A. (1991). Galen and the humour theory of temperament. *Personal Individual Difference, 12*(3), 255–263.

Terracciano A., McCrae R. R., Brant L. J., Costa P. T., Jr. (2005). Hierarchical linear modeling analyses of the NEO-PI-R scales in the Baltimore Longitudinal Study of Aging. *Psychology and Aging, 20,* 493–506.

Thomas, A., & Chess, S. (1977). *Temperament and development.* New York: Brunner/Mazel.

Tok, S. (2011). The big five personality traits and risky sport participation. *Social Behavior and Personality: An International Journal, 39*(8), 1105–1111.

Triandis, H. C. (1995). *Individualism and collectivism.* Boulder, CO: Westview.

Triandis, H. C., & Suh, E. M. (2002). Cultural influences on personality. *Annual Review of Psychology, 53,* 133–160.

Wagerman, S. A., & Funder, D. C. (2007). Acquaintance reports of personality and academic achievement: A case for conscientiousness. *Journal of Research in Personality, 41,* 221–229.

Watson, D., & Clark, L. A. (1984). Negative affectivity: The disposition to experience aversive emotional states. *Psychological Bulletin, 96,* 465–490.

Weiner, I. B. (2003). *Principles of Rorschach interpretation.* Mahwah, N.J.: Lawrence Erlbaum.

Whyte, C. (1980). An integrated counseling and learning center. In K. V. Lauridsen (Ed.), *Examining the scope of learning centers* (pp. 33–43). San Francisco, CA: Jossey-Bass.

Whyte, C. (1978). Effective counseling methods for high-risk college freshmen. *Measurement and Evaluation in Guidance, 6*(4), 198–200.

Whyte, C. B. (1977). High-risk college freshman and locus of control. *The Humanist Educator, 16*(1), 2–5.

Williams, R. L. (1972). Themes Concerning Blacks: Manual. St. Louis, MO: Williams.

Wundt, W. (1874/1886). *Elements du psychologie, physiologique* (2ieme tome). [Elements of physiological psychology, Vol. 2]. (E. Rouvier, Trans.). Paris: Ancienne Librairie Germer Bailliere et Cie.

Yang, K. S. (2006). Indigenous personality research: The Chinese case. In U. Kim, K.-S. Yang, & K.-K. Hwang (Eds.), *Indigenous and cultural psychology: Understanding people in context* (pp. 285–314). New York: Springer.

Young-Eisendrath, P. (1995). *Myth and body: Pandora's legacy in a post-modern world.* Retrieved from http://www2.cnr.edu/home/araia/Myth_%20Body.pdf

Attributions

CC licensed content, Shared previously

- Introduction to Personality. **Authored by:** OpenStax College. **Located at:** http://cnx.org/contents/ Sr8Ev5Og@5.52:X7lIv6fX@5/Introduction. **License:** *CC BY: Attribution.* **License Terms:** Download for free at http://cnx.org/content/col11629/latest/.

Personality and the Psychodynamic Perspective

What you'll learn to do: define personality and the contributions of Freud and neo-Freudians to personality theory

Sigmund Freud presented the first comprehensive theory of personality. He was also the first to recognize that much of our mental life takes place outside of our conscious awareness. He proposed three components to our personality: the id, ego, and superego. The job of the ego is to balance the sexual and aggressive drives of the id with the moral ideal of the superego. Freud also said that personality develops through a series of psychosexual stages. In each stage, pleasure focuses on a specific erogenous zone. Failure to resolve a stage can lead one to become fixated in that stage, leading to unhealthy personality traits. Successful resolution of the stages leads to a healthy adult.

The neo-Freudians were psychologists whose work followed from Freud's. They generally agreed with Freud that childhood experiences matter, but they decreased the emphasis on sex and focused more on the social environment and effects of culture on personality. Some of the notable neo-Freudians are Alfred Adler, Carl Jung, Erik Erikson, and Karen Horney. The neo-Freudian approaches have been criticized, because they tend to be philosophical rather than based on sound scientific research. You'll learn about Freud and the neo-Freudian perspectives on personality in this section. Watch this CrashCourse video for an excellent overview of these concepts:

- Define personality and describe early theories about personality development
- Describe the assumptions of the psychodynamic perspective on personality development, including the id, ego, and superego
- Define and describe the defense mechanisms
- Define and describe the psychosexual stages of personality development

What is Personality?

Personality refers to the long-standing traits and patterns that propel individuals to consistently think, feel, and behave in specific ways. Our personality is what makes us unique individuals. Each person has an idiosyncratic pattern of enduring, long-term characteristics and a manner in which he or she interacts with other individuals and the world around them. Our personalities are thought to be long term, stable, and not easily changed. The word *personality* comes from the Latin word *persona*. In the ancient world, a persona was a mask worn by an actor. While we tend to think of a mask as being worn to conceal one's identity, the theatrical mask was originally used to either represent or project a specific personality trait of a character (Figure 1).

Historical Perspectives

The concept of personality has been studied for at least 2,000 years, beginning with Hippocrates in 370 BCE (Fazeli, 2012). Hippocrates theorized that personality traits and human behaviors are based on four separate

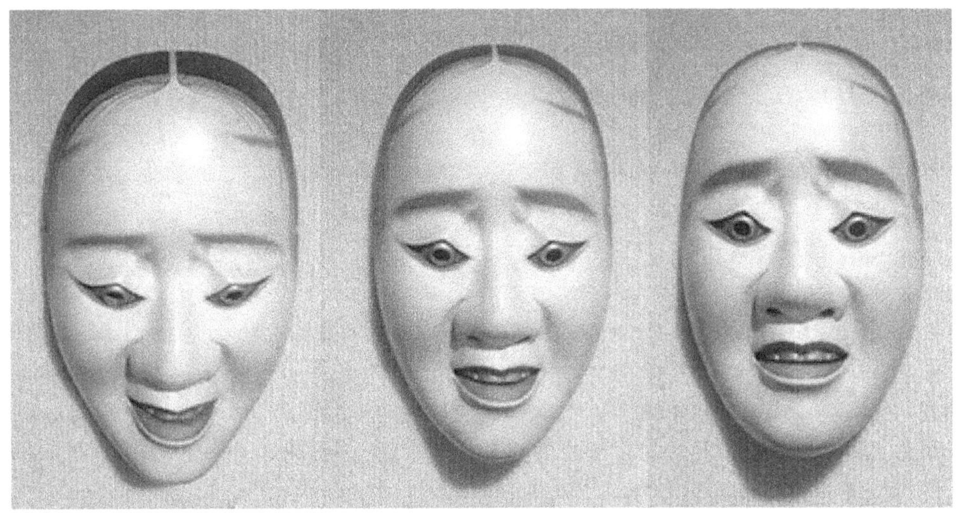

Figure 1. Happy, sad, impatient, shy, fearful, curious, helpful. What characteristics describe your personality?

temperaments associated with four fluids ("humors") of the body: choleric temperament (yellow bile from the liver), melancholic temperament (black bile from the kidneys), sanguine temperament (red blood from the heart), and phlegmatic temperament (white phlegm from the lungs) (Clark & Watson, 2008; Eysenck & Eysenck, 1985; Lecci & Magnavita, 2013; Noga, 2007). Centuries later, the influential Greek physician and philosopher Galen built on Hippocrates's theory, suggesting that both diseases and personality differences could be explained by imbalances in the humors and that each person exhibits one of the four temperaments. For example, the choleric person is passionate, ambitious, and bold; the melancholic person is reserved, anxious, and unhappy; the sanguine person is joyful, eager, and optimistic; and the phlegmatic person is calm, reliable, and thoughtful (Clark & Watson, 2008; Stelmack & Stalikas, 1991). Galen's theory was prevalent for over 1,000 years and continued to be popular through the Middle Ages.

In 1780, Franz Gall, a German physician, proposed that the distances between bumps on the skull reveal a person's personality traits, character, and mental abilities (Figure 2). According to Gall, measuring these distances revealed the sizes of the brain areas underneath, providing information that could be used to determine whether a person was friendly, prideful, murderous, kind, good with languages, and so on. Initially, phrenology was very popular; however, it was soon discredited for lack of empirical support and has long been relegated to the status of pseudoscience (Fancher, 1979).

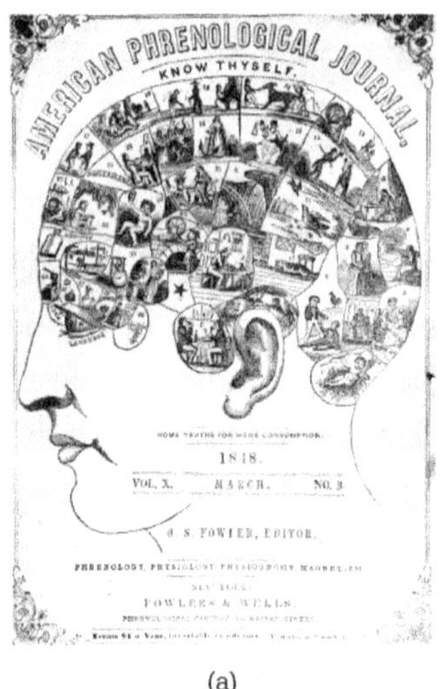

(a)

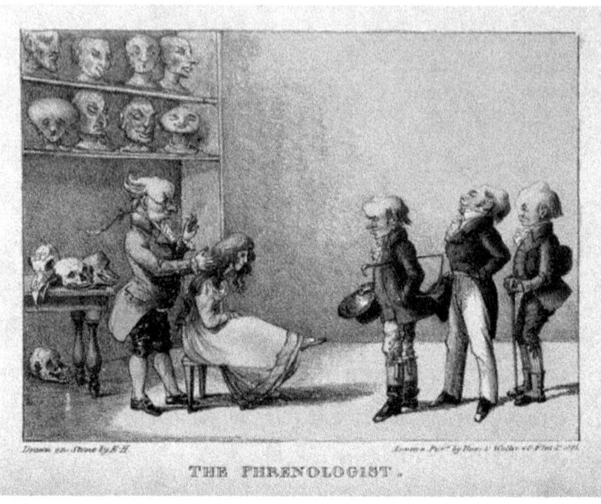

(b)

In the centuries after Galen, other researchers contributed to the development of his four primary temperament types, most prominently Immanuel Kant (in the 18th century) and psychologist Wilhelm Wundt (in the 19th century) (Eysenck, 2009; Stelmack

Figure 2. The pseudoscience of measuring the areas of a person's skull is known as phrenology. (a) Gall developed a chart that depicted which areas of the skull corresponded to particular personality traits or characteristics (Hothersall, 1995). (b) An 1825 lithograph depicts Gall examining the skull of a young woman. (credit b: modification of work by Wellcome Library, London)

& Stalikas, 1991; Wundt, 1874/1886) (Figure 3). Kant agreed with Galen that everyone could be sorted into one of the four temperaments and that there was no overlap between the four categories (Eysenck, 2009). He developed a list of traits that could be used to describe the personality of a person from each of the four temperaments. However, Wundt suggested that a better description of personality could be achieved using two major axes: emotional/nonemotional and changeable/unchangeable. The first axis separated strong from weak emotions (the melancholic and choleric temperaments from the phlegmatic and sanguine). The second axis divided the changeable temperaments (choleric and sanguine) from the unchangeable ones (melancholic and phlegmatic) (Eysenck, 2009).

Sigmund Freud's psychodynamic perspective of personality was the first comprehensive theory of personality, explaining a wide variety of both normal and abnormal behaviors. According to Freud, unconscious drives influenced by sex and aggression, along with childhood sexuality, are the forces that influence our personality. Freud attracted many followers who modified his ideas to create new theories about personality. These theorists, referred to as neo-Freudians, generally agreed with Freud that childhood experiences matter, but they reduced the emphasis on sex and focused more on the social environment and effects of culture on personality. The perspective of personality proposed by Freud and his followers was the dominant theory of personality for the first half of the 20th century.

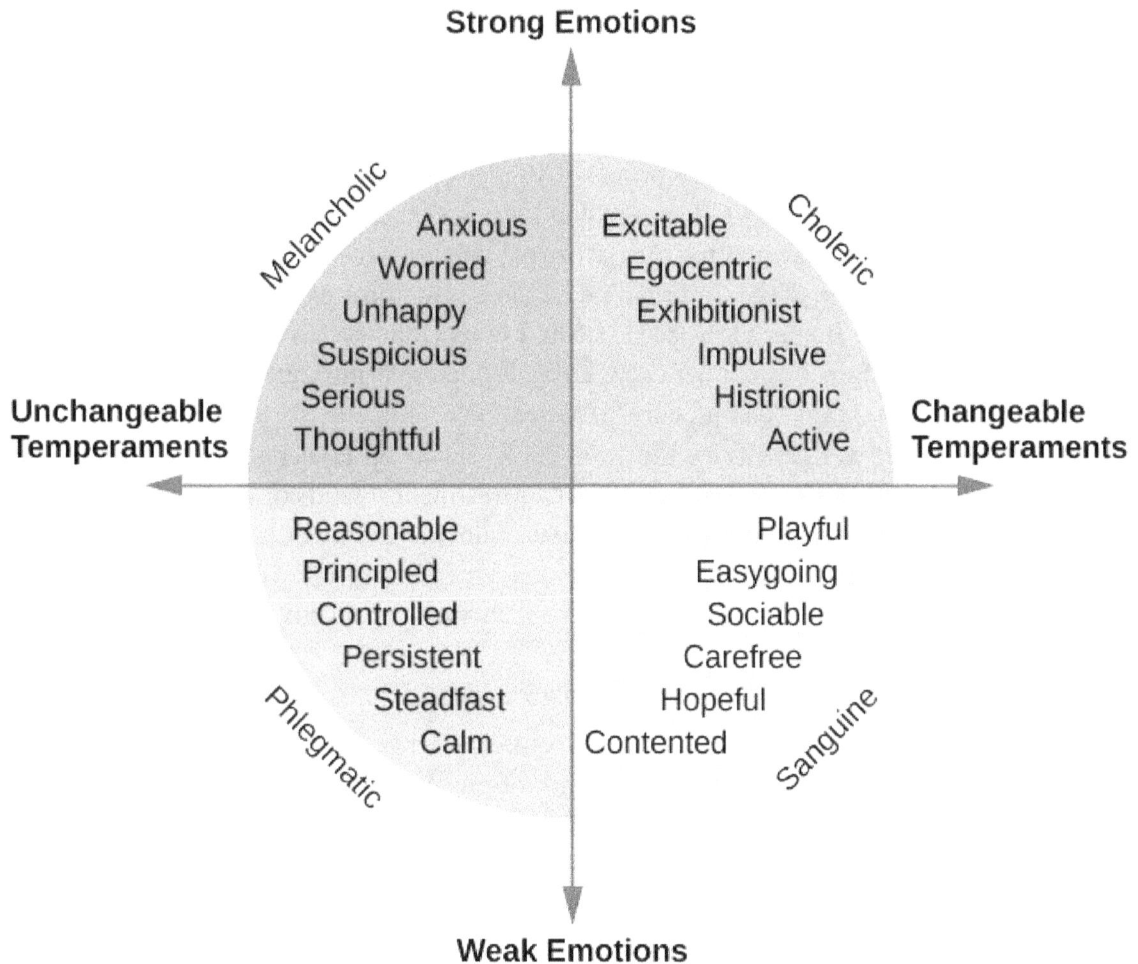

Figure 3. Developed from Galen's theory of the four temperaments, Kant proposed trait words to describe each temperament. Wundt later suggested the arrangement of the traits on two major axes.

Other major theories then emerged, including the learning, humanistic, biological, evolutionary, trait, and cultural perspectives. In this module, we will explore these various perspectives on personality in depth.

> ### Link to Learning
>
> View this video for a brief overview of some of the psychological perspectives on personality.
>
> - https://www.youtube.com/watch?v=X3CaKQWWe_U

Freud and the Psychodynamic Perspective

Sigmund Freud (1856–1939) is probably the most controversial and misunderstood psychological theorist. When reading Freud's theories, it is important to remember that he was a medical doctor, not a psychologist. There was no such thing as a degree in psychology at the time that he received his education, which can help us understand some of the controversy over his theories today. However, Freud was the first to systematically study and theorize the workings of the unconscious mind in the manner that we associate with modern psychology.

In the early years of his career, Freud worked with Josef Breuer, a Viennese physician. During this time, Freud became intrigued by the story of one of Breuer's patients, Bertha Pappenheim, who was referred to by the pseudonym Anna O. (Launer, 2005). Anna O. had been caring for her dying father when she began to experience symptoms such as partial paralysis, headaches, blurred vision, amnesia, and hallucinations (Launer, 2005). In Freud's day, these symptoms were commonly referred to as hysteria. Anna O. turned to Breuer for help. He spent 2 years (1880–1882) treating Anna O. and discovered that allowing her to talk about her experiences seemed to bring some relief of her symptoms. Anna O. called his treatment the "talking cure" (Launer, 2005). Despite the fact the Freud never met Anna O., her story served as the basis for the 1895 book, *Studies on Hysteria*, which he co-authored with Breuer. Based on Breuer's description of Anna O.'s treatment, Freud concluded that hysteria was the result of sexual abuse in childhood and that these traumatic experiences had been hidden from consciousness. Breuer disagreed with Freud, which soon ended their work together. However, Freud continued to work to refine talk therapy and build his theory on personality.

Levels of Consciousness

To explain the concept of conscious versus unconscious experience, Freud compared the mind to an iceberg (Figure 4). He said that only about one-tenth of our mind is **conscious**, and the rest of our mind is unconscious. Our **unconscious** refers to that mental activity of which we are unaware and are unable to access (Freud, 1923). According to Freud, unacceptable urges and desires are kept in our unconscious through a process called repression. For example, we sometimes say things that we don't intend to say by unintentionally substituting another word for the one we meant. You've probably heard of a Freudian slip, the term used to describe this. Freud suggested that slips of the tongue are actually sexual or aggressive urges, accidentally slipping out of our unconscious. Speech errors such as this are quite common. Seeing them as a reflection of unconscious desires, linguists today have found that slips of the tongue tend to occur when we are tired, nervous, or not at our optimal level of cognitive functioning (Motley, 2002).

According to Freud, our personality develops from a conflict between two forces: our biological aggressive and pleasure-seeking drives versus our internal (socialized) control over these drives. Our personality is the result of our efforts to balance these two competing forces. Freud suggested that we can understand this by imagining three interacting systems within our minds. He called them the id, ego, and superego (Figure 5).

The unconscious **id** contains our most primitive drives or urges, and is present from birth. It directs impulses for hunger, thirst, and sex. Freud believed that the id operates on what he called the "pleasure principle," in which the id seeks immediate gratification. Through social interactions with parents and others in a child's environment, the ego and superego develop to help control the id. The **superego** develops as a child interacts with others, learning the social rules for right and wrong. The superego acts as our conscience; it is our moral compass that tells us how we should behave. It strives for perfection and judges our behavior, leading to feelings of pride or—when we fall short of the ideal—feelings of guilt. In contrast to the instinctual id and the rule-based superego, the **ego** is the rational part of

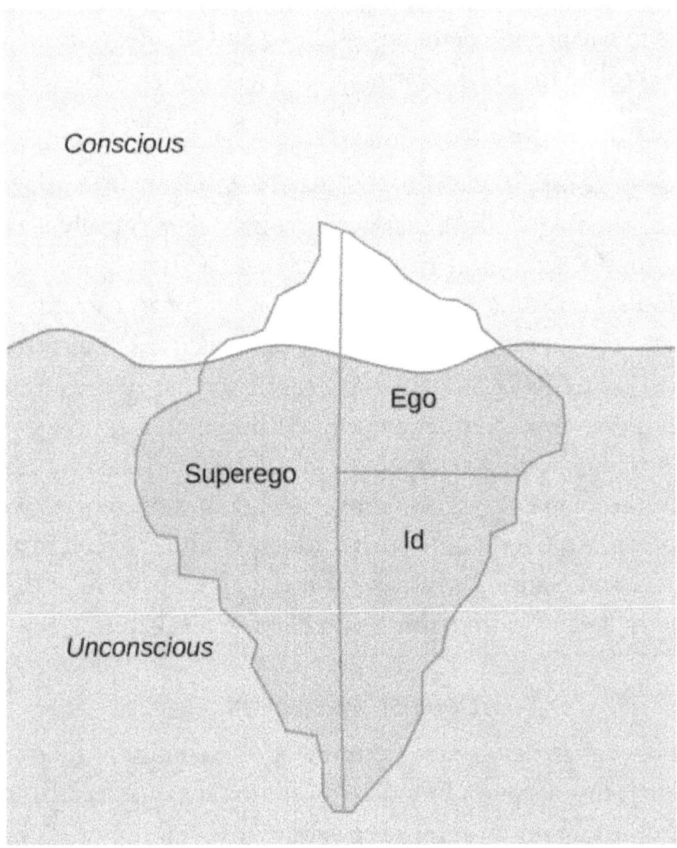

Figure 4. Freud believed that we are only aware of a small amount of our mind's activities and that most of it remains hidden from us in our unconscious. The information in our unconscious affects our behavior, although we are unaware of it.

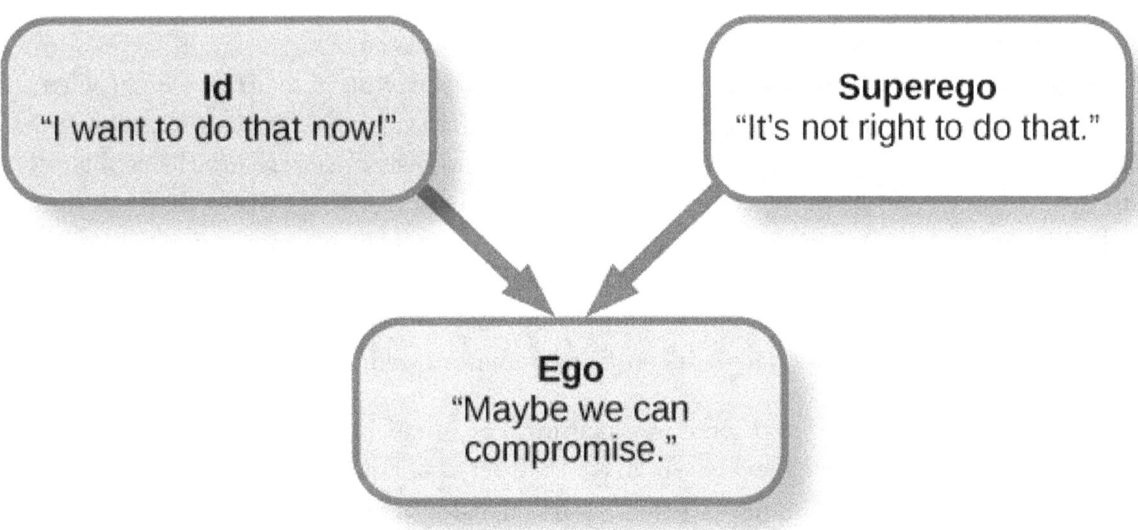

Figure 5. The job of the ego, or self, is to balance the aggressive/pleasure-seeking drives of the id with the moral control of the superego.

our personality. It's what Freud considered to be the self, and it is the part of our personality that is seen by others. Its job is to balance the demands of the id and superego in the context of reality; thus, it operates on what Freud called the "reality principle." The ego helps the id satisfy its desires in a realistic way.

The id and superego are in constant conflict, because the id wants instant gratification regardless of the consequences, but the superego tells us that we must behave in socially acceptable ways. Thus, the ego's job is to find the middle ground. It helps satisfy the id's desires in a rational way that will not lead us to feelings of guilt. According to Freud, a person who has a strong ego, which can balance the demands of the id and the superego, has a healthy personality. Freud maintained that imbalances in the system can lead to **neurosis** (a tendency to experience negative emotions), anxiety disorders, or unhealthy behaviors. For example, a person who is dominated by their id might be narcissistic and impulsive. A person with a dominant superego might be controlled by feelings of guilt and deny themselves even socially acceptable pleasures; conversely, if the superego is weak or absent, a person might become a psychopath. An overly dominant superego might be seen in an over-controlled individual whose rational grasp on reality is so strong that they are unaware of their emotional needs, or, in a neurotic who is overly defensive (overusing ego defense mechanisms).

Defense Mechanisms

Freud believed that feelings of anxiety result from the ego's inability to mediate the conflict between the id and superego. When this happens, Freud believed that the ego seeks to restore balance through various protective measures known as **defense mechanisms** (Figure 6). When certain events, feelings, or yearnings cause an individual anxiety, the individual wishes to reduce that anxiety. To do that, the individual's unconscious mind uses ego defense mechanisms, unconscious protective behaviors that aim to reduce anxiety. The ego, usually conscious, resorts to unconscious strivings to protect the ego from being overwhelmed by anxiety. When we use defense mechanisms, we are unaware that we are using them. Further, they operate in various ways that distort reality. According to Freud, we all use ego defense mechanisms.

While everyone uses defense mechanisms, Freud believed that overuse of them may be problematic. For example, let's say Joe Smith is a high school football player. Deep down, Joe feels sexually attracted to males. His conscious belief is that being gay is immoral and that if he were gay, his family would disown him and he would be ostracized by his peers. Therefore, there is a conflict between his conscious beliefs (being gay is wrong and will result in being ostracized) and his unconscious urges (attraction to males). The idea that he might be gay causes Joe to have feelings of anxiety. How can he decrease his anxiety? Joe may find himself acting very "macho," making gay jokes, and picking on a school peer who is gay. This way, Joe's unconscious impulses are further submerged.

There are several different types of defense mechanisms. For instance, in repression, anxiety-causing memories from consciousness are blocked. As an analogy, let's say your car is making a strange noise, but because you do not have the money to get it fixed, you just turn up the radio so that you no longer hear the strange noise. Eventually you forget about it. Similarly, in the human psyche, if a memory is too overwhelming to deal with, it might be **repressed** and thus removed from conscious awareness (Freud, 1920). This repressed memory might cause symptoms in other areas.

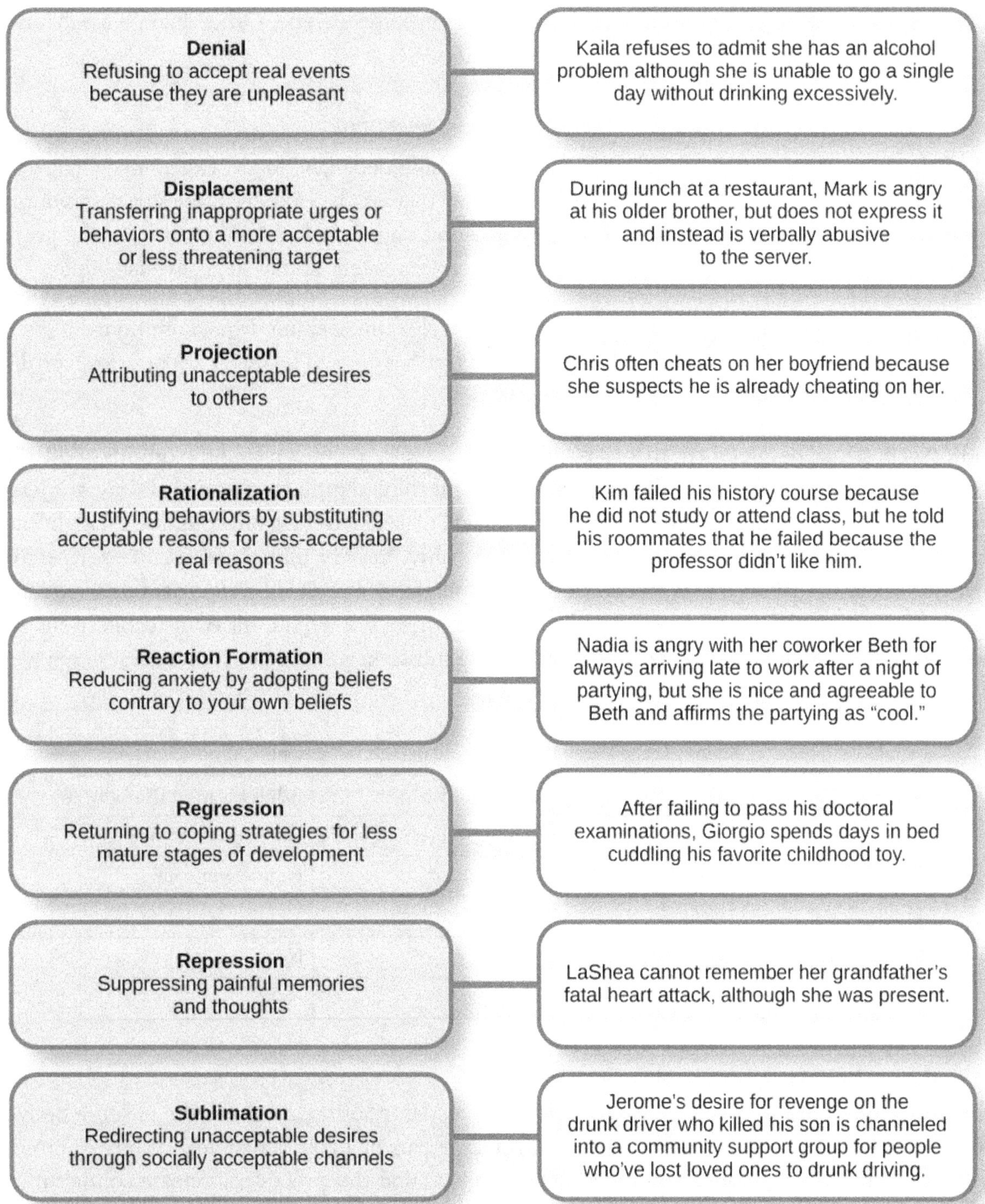

Figure 6. Defense mechanisms are unconscious protective behaviors that work to reduce anxiety.

Another defense mechanism is **reaction formation**, in which someone expresses feelings, thoughts, and behaviors opposite to their inclinations. In the above example, Joe made fun of a homosexual peer while himself being attracted to males. In **regression**, an individual acts much younger than their age. For example, a four-year-old child who resents the arrival of a newborn sibling may act like a baby and revert to drinking out of a bottle. In **projection**, a person refuses to acknowledge her own unconscious feelings and instead sees those feelings in someone else. Other defense mechanisms include **rationalization, displacement,** and **sublimation.**

Stages of Psychosexual Development

Freud believed that personality develops during early childhood: Childhood experiences shape our personalities as well as our behavior as adults. He asserted that we develop via a series of stages during childhood. Each of us must pass through these childhood stages, and if we do not have the proper nurturing and parenting during a stage, we will be stuck, or fixated, in that stage, even as adults.

In each **psychosexual stage of development**, the child's pleasure-seeking urges, coming from the id, are focused on a different area of the body, called an erogenous zone. The stages are oral, anal, phallic, latency, and genital (Table 1).

Freud's psychosexual development theory is quite controversial. To understand the origins of the theory, it is helpful to be familiar with the political, social, and cultural influences of Freud's day in Vienna at the turn of the 20th century. During this era, a climate of sexual repression, combined with limited understanding and education surrounding human sexuality, heavily influenced Freud's perspective. Given that sex was a taboo topic, Freud assumed that negative emotional states (neuroses) stemmed from suppression of unconscious sexual and aggressive urges. For Freud, his own recollections and interpretations of patients' experiences and dreams were sufficient proof that psychosexual stages were universal events in early childhood.

Table 1. Freud's Stages of Psychosexual Development

Stage	Age (years)	Erogenous Zone	Major Conflict	Adult Fixation Example
Oral	0–1	Mouth	Weaning off breast or bottle	Smoking, overeating
Anal	1–3	Anus	Toilet training	Neatness, messiness
Phallic	3–6	Genitals	Oedipus/Electra complex	Vanity, overambition
Latency	6–12	None	None	None
Genital	12+	Genitals	None	None

Oral Stage

In the **oral stage** (birth to 1 year), pleasure is focused on the mouth. Eating and the pleasure derived from sucking (nipples, pacifiers, and thumbs) play a large part in a baby's first year of life. At around 1 year of age, babies are weaned from the bottle or breast, and this process can create conflict if not handled properly by caregivers. According to Freud, an adult who smokes, drinks, overeats, or bites her nails is fixated in the oral stage of her psychosexual development; she may have been weaned too early or too late, resulting in these fixation tendencies, all of which seek to ease anxiety.

Anal Stage

After passing through the oral stage, children enter what Freud termed the **anal stage** (1–3 years). In this stage, children experience pleasure in their bowel and bladder movements, so it makes sense that the conflict in this stage is over toilet training. Freud suggested that success at the anal stage depended on how parents handled toilet training. Parents who offer praise and rewards encourage positive results and can help children feel competent. Parents who are harsh in toilet training can cause a child to become fixated at the anal stage, leading to the development of an anal-retentive personality. The anal-retentive personality is stingy and stubborn, has a compulsive need for order and neatness, and might be considered a perfectionist. If parents are too lenient in toilet training, the child might also become fixated and display an anal-expulsive personality. The anal-expulsive personality is messy, careless, disorganized, and prone to emotional outbursts.

Phallic Stage

Freud's third stage of psychosexual development is the **phallic stage** (3–6 years), corresponding to the age when children become aware of their bodies and recognize the differences between boys and girls. The erogenous zone in this stage is the genitals. Conflict arises when the child feels a desire for the opposite-sex parent, and jealousy and hatred toward the same-sex parent. For boys, this is called the Oedipus complex, involving a boy's desire for his mother and his urge to replace his father who is seen as a rival for the mother's attention. At the same time, the boy is afraid his father will punish him for his feelings, so he experiences *castration anxiety*. The Oedipus complex is successfully resolved when the boy begins to identify with his father as an indirect way to have the mother. Failure to resolve the Oedipus complex may result in fixation and development of a personality that might be described as vain and overly ambitious.

Girls experience a comparable conflict in the phallic stage—the Electra complex. The Electra complex, while often attributed to Freud, was actually proposed by Freud's protégé, Carl Jung (Jung & Kerenyi, 1963). A girl desires the attention of her father and wishes to take her mother's place. Jung also said that girls are angry with the mother for not providing them with a penis—hence the term *penis envy*. While Freud initially embraced the Electra complex as a parallel to the Oedipus complex, he later rejected it, yet it remains as a cornerstone of Freudian theory, thanks in part to academics in the field (Freud, 1931/1968; Scott, 2005).

Latency Period

Following the phallic stage of psychosexual development is a period known as the **latency period** (6 years to puberty). This period is not considered a stage, because sexual feelings are dormant as children focus on other pursuits, such as school, friendships, hobbies, and sports. Children generally engage in activities with peers of the same sex, which serves to consolidate a child's gender-role identity.

Genital Stage

The final stage is the **genital stage** (from puberty on). In this stage, there is a sexual reawakening as the incestuous urges resurface. The young person redirects these urges to other, more socially acceptable partners (who often resemble the other-sex parent). People in this stage have mature sexual interests, which for Freud meant a strong desire for the opposite sex. Individuals who successfully completed the previous stages, reaching the genital stage with no fixations, are said to be well-balanced, healthy adults.

While most of Freud's ideas have not found support in modern research, we cannot discount the contributions that Freud has made to the field of psychology. It was Freud who pointed out that a large part of our mental life is influenced by the experiences of early childhood and takes place outside of our conscious awareness; his theories paved the way for others.

Freud's Theories Today

Empirical research assessing psychodynamic concepts has produced mixed results, with some concepts receiving good empirical support, and others not faring as well. For example, the notion that we express strong sexual feelings from a very early age, as the psychosexual stage model suggests, has not held up to empirical scrutiny. On the other hand, the idea that there are dependent, control-oriented, and competitive personality types—an idea also derived from the psychosexual stage model—does seem useful.

Many ideas from the psychodynamic perspective have been studied empirically. Luborsky and Barrett (2006) reviewed much of this research; other useful reviews are provided by Bornstein (2005), Gerber (2007), and Huprich (2009). For now, let's look at three psychodynamic hypotheses that have received strong empirical support.

- *Unconscious processes influence our behavior as the psychodynamic perspective predicts.* We perceive and process much more information than we realize, and much of our behavior is shaped by feelings and motives of which we are, at best, only partially aware (Bornstein, 2009, 2010). Evidence for the importance of unconscious influences is so compelling that it has become a central element of contemporary cognitive and social psychology (Robinson & Gordon, 2011).

- *We all use ego defenses and they help determine our psychological adjustment and physical health.* People really do differ in the degree that they rely on different ego defenses—so much so that researchers now study each person's "defense style" (the unique constellation of defenses that we use). It turns out that certain defenses are more adaptive than others: Rationalization and sublimation are healthier (psychologically speaking) than repression and reaction formation (Cramer, 2006). Denial is, quite literally, bad for your health, because people who use denial tend to ignore symptoms of illness until it's too late (Bond, 2004).

- *Mental representations of self and others do indeed serve as blueprints for later relationships.*Dozens have studies have shown that mental images of our parents, and other significant figures, really do shape our expectations for later friendships and romantic relationships. The idea that you choose a romantic partner who resembles mom or dad is a myth, but it's true that you expect to be treated by others as you were treated by your parents early in life (Silverstein, 2007; Wachtel, 1997).

Glossary

anal stage: psychosexual stage in which children experience pleasure in their bowel and bladder movements

conscious: mental activity (thoughts, feelings, and memories) that we can access at any time

defense mechanism: unconscious protective behaviors designed to reduce ego anxiety

displacement: ego defense mechanism in which a person transfers inappropriate urges or behaviors toward a more acceptable or less threatening target

ego: aspect of personality that represents the self, or the part of one's personality that is visible to others

genital stage: psychosexual stage in which the focus is on mature sexual interests

id: aspect of personality that consists of our most primitive drives or urges, including impulses for hunger, thirst, and sex

latency period: psychosexual stage in which sexual feelings are dormant

neurosis: tendency to experience negative emotions

oral stage: psychosexual stage in which an infant's pleasure is focused on the mouth

phallic stage: psychosexual stage in which the focus is on the genitals

personality: long-standing traits and patterns that propel individuals to consistently think, feel, and behave in specific ways

projection: ego defense mechanism in which a person confronted with anxiety disguises their unacceptable urges or behaviors by attributing them to other people

psychosexual stages of development: stages of child development in which a child's pleasure-seeking urges are focused on specific areas of the body called erogenous zones

rationalization: ego defense mechanism in which a person confronted with anxiety makes excuses to justify behavior

reaction formation: ego defense mechanism in which a person confronted with anxiety swaps unacceptable urges or behaviors for their opposites

regression: ego defense mechanism in which a person confronted with anxiety returns to a more immature behavioral state

repression: ego defense mechanism in which anxiety-related thoughts and memories are kept in the unconscious

sublimation: ego defense mechanism in which unacceptable urges are channeled into more appropriate activities

superego: aspect of the personality that serves as one's moral compass, or conscience

unconscious: mental activity of which we are unaware and unable to access

Sr8Ev5Og@5.52:YJjSZ1SS@5/What-Is-Personality#Figure_11_01_FourTemper. **License:** *CC BY: Attribution.* **License Terms:** Download for free at http://cnx.org/content/col11629/latest/.

- Freud's Theories Today. **Authored by:** Robert Bornstein . **Provided by:** Adelphi University. **Located at:** http://nobaproject.com/modules/the-psychodynamic-perspective. **Project:** The Noba Project. **License:** *CC BY-NC-SA: Attribution-NonCommercial-ShareAlike*

All rights reserved content

- Rorschach & Freudians: Crash Course Psychology #21. **Provided by:** CrashCourse. **Located at:** https://www.youtube.com/watch?v=mUELAiHbCxc&feature=youtu.be&list=PL8dPuuaLjXtOPRKzVLY0jJY-uHOH9KVU6. **License:** *Other.* **License Terms:** Standard YouTube License

Neo-Freudians: Adler, Erikson, Jung, and Horney

Freud attracted many followers who modified his ideas to create new theories about personality. These theorists, referred to as neo-Freudians, generally agreed with Freud that childhood experiences matter, but deemphasized sex, focusing more on the social environment and effects of culture on personality. Four notable neo-Freudians include Alfred Adler, Erik Erikson, Carl Jung (pronounced "Yoong"), and Karen Horney (pronounced "HORN-eye").

Alfred Adler

Alfred Adler, a colleague of Freud's and the first president of the Vienna Psychoanalytical Society (Freud's inner circle of colleagues), was the first major theorist to break away from Freud (Figure 1). He subsequently founded a school of psychology called **individual psychology**, which focuses on our drive to compensate for feelings of inferiority. Adler (1937, 1956) proposed the concept of the **inferiority complex**. An inferiority complex refers to a person's feelings that they lack worth and don't measure up to the standards of others or of society. Adler's ideas about inferiority represent a major difference between his thinking and Freud's. Freud believed that we are motivated by sexual and aggressive urges, but Adler (1930, 1961) believed that feelings of inferiority in childhood are what drive people to attempt to gain superiority and that this striving is the force behind all of our thoughts, emotions, and behaviors.

Figure 1. Alfred Adler proposed the concept of the inferiority complex.

Adler also believed in the importance of social connections, seeing childhood development emerging through social development rather than the sexual stages Freud outlined. Adler noted the inter-relatedness of humanity and the need to work together for the betterment of all. He said, "The happiness of mankind lies in working together, in living as if each individual had set himself the task of contributing to the common welfare" (Adler, 1964, p. 255) with the main goal of psychology being "to recognize the equal rights and equality of others" (Adler, 1961, p. 691).

With these ideas, Adler identified three fundamental social tasks that all of us must experience: occupational tasks (careers), societal tasks (friendship), and love tasks (finding an intimate partner for a long-term relationship). Rather than focus on sexual or aggressive motives for behavior as Freud did, Adler focused on social motives. He also emphasized conscious rather than unconscious motivation, since he believed that the three fundamental social tasks are explicitly known and pursued. That is not to say that Adler did not also believe in unconscious processes—he did—but he felt that conscious processes were more important.

One of Adler's major contributions to personality psychology was the idea that our birth order shapes our personality. He proposed that older siblings, who start out as the focus of their parents' attention but must share that attention once a new child joins the family, compensate by becoming overachievers. The youngest children, according to Adler, may be spoiled, leaving the middle child with the opportunity to minimize the negative dynamics of the youngest and oldest children. Despite popular attention, research has not conclusively confirmed Adler's hypotheses about birth order.

Link to Learning

One of Adler's major contributions to personality psychology was the idea that our birth order shapes our personality. Follow this link to view a summary of birth order theory.

- http://www.bestpsychologydegrees.com/birth-order/

Erik Erikson

As an art school dropout with an uncertain future, young Erik Erikson met Freud's daughter, Anna Freud, while he was tutoring the children of an American couple undergoing psychoanalysis in Vienna. It was Anna Freud who encouraged Erikson to study psychoanalysis. Erikson received his diploma from the Vienna Psychoanalytic Institute in 1933, and as Nazism spread across Europe, he fled the country and immigrated to the United States that same year. As you learned when you studied lifespan development, Erikson later proposed a psychosocial theory of development, suggesting that an individual's personality develops throughout the lifespan—a departure from Freud's view that personality is fixed in early life. In his theory, Erikson emphasized the social relationships that are important at each stage of personality development, in contrast to Freud's emphasis on sex. Erikson identified eight stages, each of which represents a conflict or developmental task (Table 1). The development of a healthy personality and a sense of competence depend on the successful completion of each task.

Table 1. Erikson's Psychosocial Stages of Development

Stage	Age (years)	Developmental Task	Description
1	0–1	Trust vs. mistrust	Trust (or mistrust) that basic needs, such as nourishment and affection, will be met
2	1–3	Autonomy vs. shame/doubt	Sense of independence in many tasks develops
3	3–6	Initiative vs. guilt	Take initiative on some activities, may develop guilt when success not met or boundaries overstepped
4	7–11	Industry vs. inferiority	Develop self-confidence in abilities when competent or sense of inferiority when not
5	12–18	Identity vs. confusion	Experiment with and develop identity and roles
6	19–29	Intimacy vs. isolation	Establish intimacy and relationships with others
7	30–64	Generativity vs. stagnation	Contribute to society and be part of a family
8	65–	Integrity vs. despair	Assess and make sense of life and meaning of contributions

Carl Jung

Carl Jung (Figure 2) was a Swiss psychiatrist and protégé of Freud, who later split off from Freud and developed his own theory, which he called analytical psychology. The focus of analytical psychology is on working to balance opposing forces of conscious and unconscious thought, and experience within one's personality. According to Jung, this work is a continuous learning process—mainly occurring in the second half of life—of becoming aware of unconscious elements and integrating them into consciousness.

Jung's split from Freud was based on two major disagreements. First, Jung, like Adler and Erikson, did not accept that sexual drive was the primary motivator in a person's mental life. Second, although Jung agreed with Freud's concept of a personal unconscious, he thought it to be incomplete. In addition to the personal unconscious, Jung focused on the collective unconscious.

The **collective unconscious** is a universal version of the personal unconscious, holding mental patterns, or memory traces, which are common to all of us (Jung, 1928). These ancestral memories, which Jung called **archetypes**, are represented by universal themes in various cultures, as expressed through literature, art, and dreams (Jung). Jung said that these themes reflect common experiences of people the world over, such as facing death, becoming independent, and striving for mastery. Jung (1964) believed that through biology, each person is handed down the same themes and that the same types of symbols—such as the hero, the maiden, the sage, and the trickster—are present in the folklore and fairy tales of every culture. In Jung's view, the task of integrating these unconscious archetypal aspects of the self is part of the self-realization process in the second half of life. With this orientation toward self-realization, Jung parted ways with Freud's belief that personality is determined solely by past events and anticipated the humanistic movement with its emphasis on self-actualization and orientation toward the future.

Figure 2. Carl Jung was interested in exploring the collective unconscious.

Jung also proposed two attitudes or approaches toward life: extroversion and introversion (Jung, 1923) (Table 2). These ideas are considered Jung's most important contributions to the field of personality psychology, as almost all models of personality now include these concepts. If you are an extrovert, then you are a person who is energized by being outgoing and socially oriented: You derive your energy from being around others. If you are an introvert, then you are a person who may be quiet and reserved, or you may be social, but your energy is derived from your inner psychic activity. Jung believed a balance between extroversion and introversion best served the goal of self-realization.

Table 2. Introverts and Extroverts

Introvert	Extrovert
Energized by being alone	Energized by being with others
Avoids attention	Seeks attention
Speaks slowly and softly	Speaks quickly and loudly
Thinks before speaking	Thinks out loud
Stays on one topic	Jumps from topic to topic
Prefers written communication	Prefers verbal communication
Pays attention easily	Distractible
Cautious	Acts first, thinks later

Another concept proposed by Jung was the **persona**, which he referred to as a mask that we adopt. According to Jung, we consciously create this persona; however, it is derived from both our conscious experiences and our collective unconscious. What is the purpose of the persona? Jung believed that it is a compromise between who we really are (our true self) and what society expects us to be. We hide those parts of ourselves that are not aligned with society's expectations.

Connect the Concepts: Are Archetypes Genetically Based?

Jung proposed that human responses to archetypes are similar to instinctual responses in animals. One criticism of Jung is that there is no evidence that archetypes are biologically based or similar to animal instincts (Roesler, 2012). Jung formulated his ideas about 100 years ago, and great advances have been made in the field of genetics since that time. We've found that human babies are born with certain capacities, including the ability to acquire language. However, we've also found that symbolic information (such as archetypes) is not encoded on the genome and that babies cannot decode symbolism, refuting the idea of a biological basis to archetypes. Rather than being seen as purely biological, more recent research suggests that archetypes emerge directly from our experiences and are reflections of linguistic or cultural characteristics (Young-Eisendrath, 1995). Today, most Jungian scholars believe that the collective unconscious and archetypes are based on both innate and environmental influences, with the differences being in the role and degree of each (Sotirova-Kohli et al., 2013).

Karen Horney

Karen Horney was one of the first women trained as a Freudian psychoanalyst. During the Great Depression, Horney moved from Germany to the United States, and subsequently moved away from Freud's teachings. Like Jung, Horney believed that each individual has the potential for self-realization and that the goal of psychoanalysis should be moving toward a healthy self rather than exploring early childhood patterns of dysfunction. Horney also disagreed with the Freudian idea that girls have penis envy and are jealous of male biological features. According to Horney, any jealousy is most likely culturally based, due to the greater privileges that males often have, meaning that the differences between men's and women's personalities are culturally based, not biologically based. She further suggested that men have womb envy, because they cannot give birth.Horney's theories focused on the role of unconscious anxiety. She suggested that normal growth can be blocked by basic anxiety stemming from needs not being met, such as childhood experiences of loneliness and/or isolation. How do children learn to handle this anxiety? Horney suggested three styles of coping (Table 3). The first coping style, *moving toward people*, relies on affiliation and dependence. These children become dependent on their parents and other caregivers in an effort to receive attention and affection, which provides relief from anxiety (Burger, 2008). When these children grow up, they tend to use this same coping strategy to deal with relationships, expressing an intense need for love and acceptance (Burger, 2008). The second coping style, *moving against people*, relies on aggression and assertiveness. Children with this coping style find that fighting is the best way to deal with an unhappy home situation, and they deal with their feelings of insecurity by bullying other children (Burger, 2008). As adults, people with this coping style tend to lash out with hurtful comments and exploit others (Burger, 2008). The third coping style, *moving away from people*, centers on detachment and isolation. These children handle their anxiety by withdrawing from the world. They need privacy and tend to be self-sufficient. When these children are adults, they continue to avoid such things as love and friendship, and they also tend to gravitate toward careers that require little interaction with others (Burger, 2008).

Table 3. Horney's Coping Styles

Coping Style	Description	Example
Moving toward people	Affiliation and dependence	Child seeking positive attention and affection from parent; adult needing love
Moving against people	Aggression and manipulation	Child fighting or bullying other children; adult who is abrasive and verbally hurtful, or who exploits others
Moving away from people	Detachment and isolation	Child withdrawn from the world and isolated; adult loner

Horney believed these three styles are ways in which people typically cope with day-to-day problems; however, the three coping styles can become neurotic strategies if they are used rigidly and compulsively, leading a person to become alienated from others.

Glossary

analytical psychology: Jung's theory focusing on the balance of opposing forces within one's personality and the significance of the collective unconscious

archetype: pattern that exists in our collective unconscious across cultures and societies

collective unconscious: common psychological tendencies that have been passed down from one generation to the next

individual psychology: school of psychology proposed by Adler that focuses on our drive to compensate for feelings of inferiority

inferiority complex: refers to a person's feelings that they lack worth and don't measure up to others' or to society's standard

https://assessments.lumenlearning.com/assessments/4856
Attributions

Explaining Personality: Learning and Humanistic Approaches

What you'll learn to do: describe and differentiate between personality theories

Beyond Freud and the Neo-Freudians, there are many other approaches that work to explain personality. In this section, you'll learn about the behavioral, humanistic, biological, trait, and cultural perspectives. Watch this video for an overview about the main philosophical approaches to studying personality:

Learning Objectives

- Describe the learning perspective on personality, including the concepts of reciprocal determinism, self-efficacy, locus of control, and the person-situation debate
- Explain the contributions of humanists Abraham Maslow and Carl Rogers to personality development

Learning Approaches

In contrast to the psychodynamic approaches of Freud and the neo-Freudians, which relate personality to inner (and hidden) processes, the learning approaches focus only on observable behavior. This illustrates one significant advantage of the learning approaches to personality over psychodynamics: Because learning approaches involve observable, measurable phenomena, they can be scientifically tested.

The Behavioral Perspective

Behaviorists do not believe in biological determinism: They do not see personality traits as inborn. Instead, they view personality as significantly shaped by the reinforcements and consequences outside of the organism. In other words, people behave in a consistent manner based on prior learning. B. F. Skinner, a strict behaviorist, believed that environment was solely responsible for all behavior, including the enduring, consistent behavior patterns studied by personality theorists.

As you may recall from your study on the psychology of learning, Skinner proposed that we demonstrate consistent behavior patterns because we have developed certain response tendencies (Skinner, 1953). In other words, we *learn* to behave in particular ways. We increase the behaviors that lead to positive consequences, and we decrease the behaviors that lead to negative consequences. Skinner disagreed with Freud's idea that personality is fixed in childhood. He argued that personality develops over our entire life, not only in the first few years. Our responses can change as we come across new situations; therefore, we can expect more variability over time in personality than Freud would anticipate. For example, consider a young woman, Greta, a risk taker. She drives fast and participates in dangerous sports such as hang gliding and kiteboarding. But after she gets married and has children, the system of reinforcements and punishments in her environment changes. Speeding and extreme sports are no longer reinforced, so she no longer engages in those behaviors. In fact, Greta now describes herself as a cautious person.

The Social-Cognitive Perspective

Albert Bandura agreed with Skinner that personality develops through learning. He disagreed, however, with Skinner's strict behaviorist approach to personality development, because he felt that thinking and reasoning are important components of learning. He presented a social-cognitive theory of personality that emphasizes both learning and cognition as sources of individual differences in personality. In social-cognitive theory, the concepts of reciprocal determinism, observational learning, and self-efficacy all play a part in personality development.

Reciprocal Determinism

In contrast to Skinner's idea that the environment alone determines behavior, Bandura (1990) proposed the concept of reciprocal determinism, in which cognitive processes, behavior, and context all interact, each factor influencing and being influenced by the others simultaneously (Figure 1). *Cognitive processes* refer to all characteristics previously learned, including beliefs, expectations, and personality characteristics. *Behavior* refers to anything that we do that may be rewarded or punished. Finally, the *context* in which the behavior occurs refers to the environment or situation, which includes rewarding/punishing stimuli.

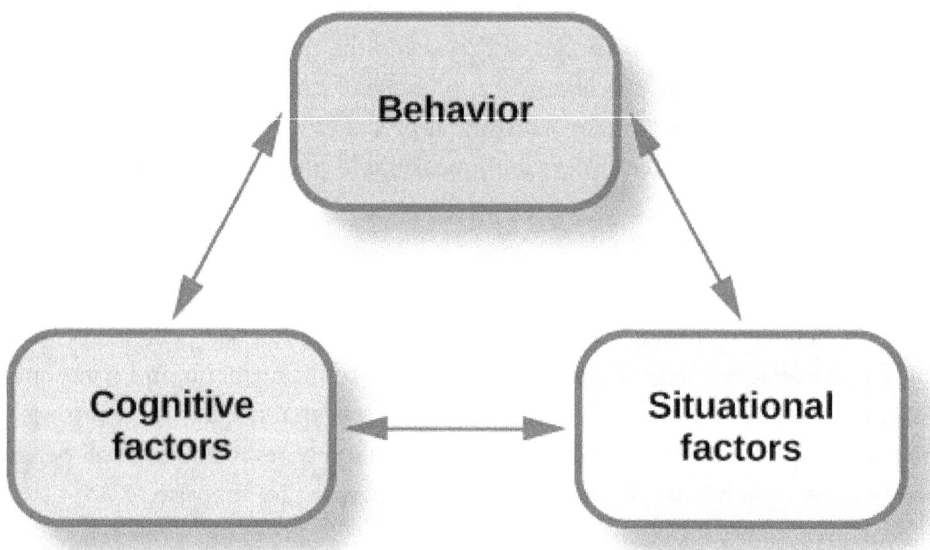

Figure 1. Bandura proposed the idea of reciprocal determinism: Our behavior, cognitive processes, and situational context all influence each other.

Consider, for example, that you're at a festival and one of the attractions is bungee jumping from a bridge. Do you do it? In this example, the behavior is bungee jumping. Cognitive factors that might influence this behavior include your beliefs and values, and your past experiences with similar behaviors. Finally, context refers to the reward structure for the behavior. According to reciprocal determinism, all of these factors are in play.

Observational Learning

Bandura's key contribution to learning theory was the idea that much learning is vicarious. We learn by observing someone else's behavior and its consequences, which Bandura called observational learning. He felt that this type of learning also plays a part in the development of our personality. Just as we learn individual behaviors, we learn new behavior patterns when we see them performed by other people or models. Drawing on the behaviorists' ideas about reinforcement, Bandura suggested that whether we choose to imitate a model's behavior depends on whether we see the model reinforced or punished. Through observational learning, we come to learn what behaviors are acceptable and rewarded in our culture, and we also learn to inhibit deviant or socially unacceptable behaviors by seeing what behaviors are punished.

We can see the principles of reciprocal determinism at work in observational learning. For example, personal factors determine which behaviors in the environment a person chooses to imitate, and those environmental events in turn are processed cognitively according to other personal factors.

Self-Efficacy

Bandura (1977, 1995) has studied a number of cognitive and personal factors that affect learning and personality development, and most recently has focused on the concept of self-efficacy. **Self-efficacy** is our level of confidence in our own abilities, developed through our social experiences. Self-efficacy affects how we approach challenges and reach goals. In observational learning, self-efficacy is a cognitive factor that affects which behaviors we choose to imitate as well as our success in performing those behaviors.

People who have high self-efficacy believe that their goals are within reach, have a positive view of challenges seeing them as tasks to be mastered, develop a deep interest in and strong commitment to the activities in which they are involved, and quickly recover from setbacks. Conversely, people with low self-efficacy avoid challenging tasks because they doubt their ability to be successful, tend to focus on failure and negative outcomes, and lose confidence in their abilities if they experience setbacks. Feelings of self-efficacy can be specific to certain situations. For instance, a student might feel confident in her ability in English class but much less so in math class.

Julian Rotter and Locus of Control

Julian Rotter (1966) proposed the concept of locus of control, another cognitive factor that affects learning and personality development. Distinct from self-efficacy, which involves our belief in our own abilities, **locus of control** refers to our beliefs about the power we have over our lives. In Rotter's view, people possess either an internal or an external locus of control (Figure 2). Those of us with an **internal locus of control** ("internals") tend to believe that most of our outcomes are the direct result of our efforts. Those of us with an **external locus of control** ("externals") tend to believe that our outcomes are outside of our control. Externals see their lives as being controlled by other people, luck, or chance. For example, say you didn't spend much time studying for your psychology test and went out to dinner with friends instead. When you receive your test score, you see that you earned a D. If you possess an internal locus of control, you would most likely admit that you failed because you didn't spend enough time studying and decide to study more for the next test. On the other hand, if you possess an external locus of control, you might conclude that the test was too hard and not bother studying for the next test, because you figure you will fail it anyway. Researchers have found that people with an internal locus of control perform better academically, achieve more in their careers, are more independent, are healthier, are better able to cope, and are less depressed than people who have an external locus of control (Benassi, Sweeney, & Durfour, 1988; Lefcourt, 1982; Maltby, Day, & Macaskill, 2007; Whyte, 1977, 1978, 1980).

Figure 2. Locus of control occurs on a continuum from internal to external.

Walter Mischel and the Person-Situation Debate

Walter Mischel was a student of Julian Rotter and taught for years at Stanford, where he was a colleague of Albert Bandura. Mischel surveyed several decades of empirical psychological literature regarding trait prediction of behavior, and his conclusion shook the foundations of personality psychology. Mischel found that the data did not support the central principle of the field—that a person's personality traits are consistent across situations. His report triggered a decades-long period of self-examination, known as the person-situation debate, among personality psychologists.

Mischel suggested that perhaps we were looking for consistency in the wrong places. He found that although behavior was inconsistent across different situations, it was much more consistent within situations—so that a person's behavior in one situation would likely be repeated in a similar one. And as you will see next regarding his famous "marshmallow test," Mischel also found that behavior is consistent in equivalent situations across time.

One of Mischel's most notable contributions to personality psychology was his ideas on self-regulation. According to Lecci & Magnavita (2013), "Self-regulation is the process of identifying a goal or set of goals and, in pursuing these goals, using both internal (e.g., thoughts and affect) and external (e.g., responses of anything or anyone in the environment) feedback to maximize goal attainment" (p. 6.3). Self-regulation is also known as will power. When we talk about will power, we tend to think of it as the ability to delay gratification. For example, Bettina's teenage daughter made strawberry cupcakes, and they looked delicious. However, Bettina forfeited the pleasure of eating one, because she is training for a 5K race and wants to be fit and do well in the race. Would you be able to resist getting a small reward now in order to get a larger reward later? This is the question Mischel investigated in his now-classic marshmallow test.

Mischel designed a study to assess self-regulation in young children. In the marshmallow study, Mischel and his colleagues placed a preschool child in a room with one marshmallow on the table. The child was told that he could either eat the marshmallow now, or wait until the researcher returned to the room and then he could have two marshmallows (Mischel, Ebbesen & Raskoff, 1972). This was repeated with hundreds of preschoolers. What Mischel and his team found was that young children differ in their degree of self-control. Mischel and his colleagues continued to follow this group of preschoolers through high school, and what do you think they discovered? The children who had more self-control in preschool (the ones who waited for the bigger reward) were more successful in high school. They had higher SAT scores, had positive peer relationships, and were less likely to have substance abuse issues; as adults, they also had more stable marriages (Mischel, Shoda, & Rodriguez,

1989; Mischel et al., 2010). On the other hand, those children who had poor self-control in preschool (the ones who grabbed the one marshmallow) were not as successful in high school, and they were found to have academic and behavioral problems.

> ### Link to Learning
>
> To learn more about the marshmallow test, watch Joachim de Posada's TEDTalk video.
>
> - https://www.youtube.com/watch?v=M0yhHKWUa0g

Today, the debate is mostly resolved, and most psychologists consider both the situation and personal factors in understanding behavior. For Mischel (1993), people are situation processors. The children in the marshmallow test each processed, or interpreted, the rewards structure of that situation in their own way. Mischel's approach to personality stresses the importance of both the situation and the way the person perceives the situation. Instead of behavior being determined by the situation, people use cognitive processes to interpret the situation and then behave in accordance with that interpretation.

Humanistic Approaches

As the "third force" in psychology, **humanism** is touted as a reaction both to the pessimistic determinism of psychoanalysis, with its emphasis on psychological disturbance, and to the behaviorists' view of humans passively reacting to the environment, which has been criticized as making people out to be personality-less robots. It does not suggest that psychoanalytic, behaviorist, and other points of view are incorrect but argues that these perspectives do not recognize the depth and meaning of human experience, and fail to recognize the innate capacity for self-directed change and transforming personal experiences. This perspective focuses on how healthy people develop. One pioneering humanist, Abraham Maslow, studied people who he considered to be healthy, creative, and productive, including Albert Einstein, Eleanor Roosevelt, Thomas Jefferson, Abraham Lincoln, and others. Maslow (1950, 1970) found that such people share similar characteristics, such as being open, creative, loving, spontaneous, compassionate, concerned for others, and accepting of themselves. When you studied motivation, you learned about one of the best-known humanistic theories, Maslow's hierarchy of needs theory, in which Maslow proposes that human beings have certain needs in common and that these needs must be met in a certain order. The highest need is the need for self-actualization, which is the achievement of our fullest potential.

Another humanistic theorist was Carl Rogers. One of Rogers's main ideas about personality regards **self-concept**, our thoughts and feelings about ourselves. How would you respond to the question, "Who am I?" Your answer can show how you see yourself. If your response is primarily positive, then you tend to feel good about who you are, and you see the world as a safe and positive place. If your response is mainly negative, then you may feel unhappy with who you are. Rogers further divided the self into two categories: the ideal self and the real self. The **ideal self** is the person that you would like to be; the **real self** is the person you actually are. Rogers focused on the idea that we need to achieve consistency between these two selves. We experience **congruence** when our thoughts about our real self and ideal self are very similar—in other words, when our self-concept is accurate.

High congruence leads to a greater sense of self-worth and a healthy, productive life. Parents can help their children achieve this by giving them unconditional positive regard, or unconditional love. According to Rogers (1980), "As persons are accepted and prized, they tend to develop a more caring attitude towards themselves" (p. 116). People raised in an environment of unconditional positive regard, in which no preconceived conditions of worth are present, have the opportunity to fully actualize. When people are raised in an environment of *conditional positive regard,* in which worth and love are only given under certain conditions, they must match or achieve those conditions in order to receive the love or positive regard they yearn for. Their ideal self is thereby determined by others based on these conditions, and they are forced to develop outside of their own true actualizing tendency; this contributes to **incongruence** and a greater gap between the real self and the ideal self. Both Rogers's and Maslow's theories focus on individual choices and do not believe that biology is deterministic.

Unconditional Positive Regard

In the development of the self-concept, Rogers elevated the importance of *unconditional positive regard,* or unconditional love. Personality Development and the Self-Concept

Rogers based his theories of personality development on humanistic psychology and theories of subjective experience. He believed that everyone exists in a constantly changing world of experiences that they are at the center of. A person reacts to changes in their phenomenal field, which includes external objects and people as well as internal thoughts and emotions.

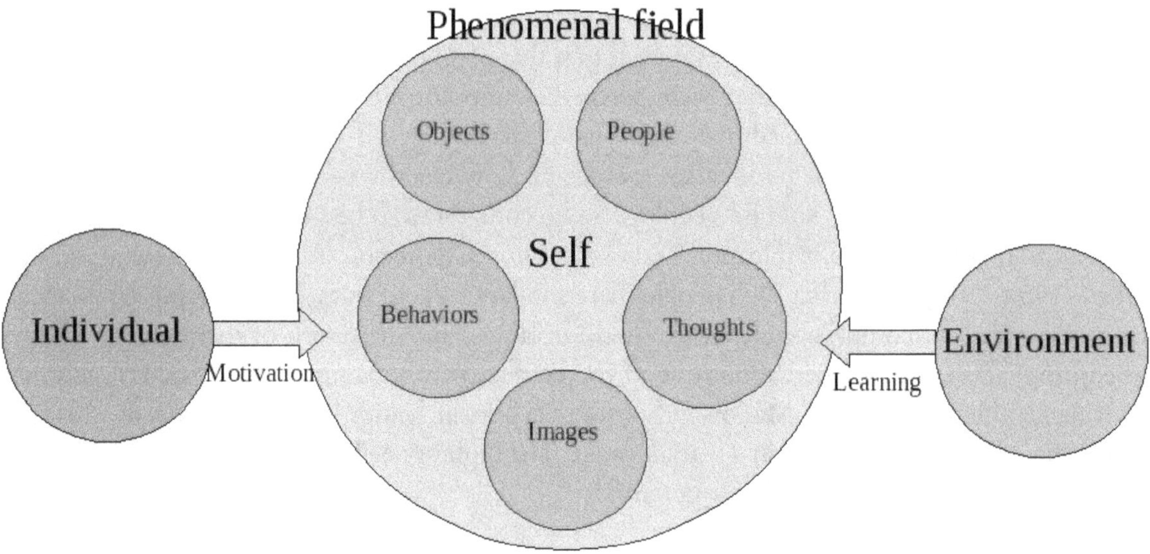

Figure 3 The phenomenal field refers to a person's subjective reality, which includes external objects and people as well as internal thoughts and emotions. The person's motivations and environments both act on their phenomenal field.

Rogers believed that all behavior is motivated by self-actualizing tendencies, which drive a person to achieve at their highest level. As a result of their interactions with the environment and others, an individual forms a structure of the self or *self-concept*—an organized, fluid, conceptual pattern of concepts and values related to the self. If a person has a positive self-concept, they tend to feel good about who they are and often see the world as a safe and positive place. If they have a negative self-concept, they may feel unhappy with who they are.

"The Good Life"

Rogers described life in terms of principles rather than stages of development. These principles exist in fluid processes rather than static states. He claimed that a fully functioning person would continually aim to fulfill his or her potential in each of these processes, achieving what he called *"the good life."* These people would allow personality and self-concept to emanate from experience. He found that fully functioning individuals had several traits or tendencies in common:

1. A growing openness to experience–they move away from defensiveness.

2. An increasingly existential lifestyle–living each moment fully, rather than distorting the moment to fit personality or self-concept.

3. Increasing organismic trust–they trust their own judgment and their ability to choose behavior that is appropriate for each moment.

4. Freedom of choice–they are not restricted by incongruence and are able to make a wide range of choices more fluently. They believe that they play a role in determining their own behavior and so feel responsible for their own behavior.

5. Higher levels of creativity–they will be more creative in the way they adapt to their own circumstances without feeling a need to conform.

6. Reliability and constructiveness–they can be trusted to act constructively. Even aggressive needs will be matched and balanced by intrinsic goodness in congruent individuals.

7. A rich full life–they will experience joy and pain, love and heartbreak, fear and courage more intensely.

Criticisms of Rogers' Theories

Like Maslow's theories, Rogers' were criticized for their lack of empirical evidence used in research. The holistic approach of humanism allows for a great deal of variation but does not identify enough constant variables to be researched with true accuracy. Psychologists also worry that such an extreme focus on the subjective experience of the individual does little to explain or appreciate the impact of society on personality development.

<table>
<tr><td>

Glossary

congruence: state of being in which our thoughts about our real and ideal selves are very similar

ideal self: person we would like to be

incongruence: state of being in which there is a great discrepancy between our real and ideal selves

locus of control: beliefs about the power we have over our lives; an external locus of control is the belief that our outcomes are outside of our control; an internal locus of control is the belief that we control our own outcomes

real self: person who we actually are

reciprocal determinism: belief that one's environment can determine behavior, but at the same time, people can influence the environment with both their thoughts and behaviors

social-cognitive theory: Bandura's theory of personality that emphasizes both cognition and learning as sources of individual differences in personality

self-concept: our thoughts and feelings about ourselves

self-efficacy: someone's level of confidence in their own abilities

</td></tr>
</table>

Attributions

CC licensed content, Original

- Modification, adaptation, and original content. **Provided by:** Lumen Learning. **License:** *CC BY: Attribution*

CC licensed content, Shared previously

- Explaining Personality. **Authored by:** OpenStax College. **Located at:** http://cnx.org/contents/ Sr8Ev5Og@5.52:bT_lgq6S@5/Learning-Approaches. **License:** *CC BY: Attribution.* **License Terms:** Download for free at http://cnx.org/contents/4abf04bf-93a0-45c3-9cbc-2cefd46e68cc@5.48

All rights reserved content

- What's Personality All About. **Authored by:** Ken Tangem. **Located at:** https://www.youtube.com/ watch?v=rvE0uHX3guk. **License:** *Other.* **License Terms:** Standard YouTube License

Explaining Personality: Biological Approaches and Trait Theories

Learning Objectives

- Explain biological approaches to understanding personality, including the findings of the Minnesota Study of Twins Reared Apart, heritability, and temperament

- Discuss the early trait theories of Cattell and Eysenck

- Describe the Big Five factors and categorize someone who is high and low on each of the five traits

- Discuss personality differences of people from collectivist and individualist cultures and compare the cultural-comparative approach, the indigenous approach, and the combined approach to studying personality

Biological Approaches

How much of our personality is in-born and biological, and how much is influenced by the environment and culture we are raised in? Psychologists who favor the biological approach believe that inherited predispositions as well as physiological processes can be used to explain differences in our personalities (Burger, 2008).

In the field of behavioral genetics, the Minnesota Study of Twins Reared Apart—a well-known study of the genetic basis for personality—conducted research with twins from 1979 to 1999. In studying 350 pairs of twins, including pairs of identical and fraternal twins reared together and apart, researchers found that identical twins, whether raised together or apart, have very similar personalities (Bouchard, 1994; Bouchard, Lykken, McGue, Segal, & Tellegen, 1990; Segal, 2012). These findings suggest the heritability of some personality traits. **Heritability** refers to the proportion of difference among people that is attributed to genetics. Some of the traits that the study reported as having more than a 0.50 heritability ratio include leadership, obedience to authority, a sense of well-being, alienation, resistance to stress, and fearfulness. The implication is that some aspects of our personalities are largely controlled by genetics; however, it's important to point out that traits are not determined by a single gene, but by a combination of many genes, as well as by epigenetic factors that control whether the genes are expressed.

Temperament

Most contemporary psychologists believe temperament has a biological basis due to its appearance very early in our lives (Rothbart, 2011). As you learned when you studied lifespan development, Thomas and Chess (1977) found that babies could be categorized into one of three temperaments: easy, difficult, or slow to warm up. However, environmental factors (family interactions, for example) and maturation can affect the ways in which children's personalities are expressed (Carter et al., 2008).

Research suggests that there are two dimensions of our temperament that are important parts of our adult personality—*reactivity* and *self-regulation* (Rothbart, Ahadi, & Evans, 2000). Reactivity refers to how we respond to new or challenging environmental stimuli; self-regulation refers to our ability to control that response (Rothbart & Derryberry, 1981; Rothbart, Sheese, Rueda, & Posner, 2011). For example, one person may immediately respond to new stimuli with a high level of anxiety, while another barely notices it.

Connect the Concepts: Body Type and Temperament

Is there an association between your body type and your temperament? The constitutional perspective, which examines the relationship between the structure of the human body and behavior, seeks to answer this question (Genovese, 2008). The first comprehensive system of constitutional psychology was proposed by American psychologist William H. Sheldon (1940, 1942). He believed that your body type can be linked to your personality. Sheldon's life's work was spent observing human bodies and temperaments. Based on his observations and interviews of hundreds of people, he proposed three body/personality types, which he called somatotypes. The three somatotypes are ectomorphs, endomorphs, and mesomorphs (Figure 1). Ectomorphs are thin with a small bone structure and very little fat on their bodies. According to Sheldon, the ectomorph personality is anxious, self-conscious, artistic, thoughtful, quiet, and private. They enjoy intellectual stimulation and feel uncomfortable in social situations. Actors Adrien Brody and Nicole Kidman would be characterized as ectomorphs. Endomorphs are the opposite of ectomorphs. Endomorphs have narrow shoulders and wide hips, and carry extra fat on their round bodies. Sheldon described endomorphs as being relaxed, comfortable, good-humored, even-tempered, sociable, and tolerant. Endomorphs enjoy affection and detest disapproval. Queen Latifah and Jack Black would be considered endomorphs. The third somatotype is the mesomorph. This body type falls between the ectomorph and the endomorph. Mesomorphs have large bone structure, well-defined muscles, broad shoulders, narrow waists, and attractive, strong bodies. According to Sheldon, mesomorphs are adventurous, assertive, competitive, and fearless. They are curious and enjoy trying new things, but can also be obnoxious and aggressive. Channing Tatum and Scarlett Johannson would likely be mesomorphs.

Sheldon (1949) also conducted further research into somatotypes and criminality. He measured the physical proportions of hundreds of juvenile delinquent boys in comparison to male college students, and found that problem youth were primarily mesomorphs. Why might this be? Perhaps it's because they are quick to anger and don't have the restraint demonstrated by ectomorphs. Maybe it's because a person with a mesomorphic body type reflects high levels of testosterone, which may lead to more aggressive behavior. Can you think of other explanations for Sheldon's findings?

Sheldon's method of somatotyping is not without criticism, as it has been considered largely subjective (Carter & Heath, 1990; Cortés & Gatti, 1972; Parnell, 1958). More systematic and controlled research methods did not support his findings (Eysenck, 1970). Consequently, it's not uncommon to see his theory labeled as pseudoscience, much like Gall's theory of phrenology (Rafter, 2007; Rosenbaum, 1995). However, studies involving correlations between somatotype, temperament, and children's school performance (Sanford et al., 1943; Parnell); somatotype and performance of pilots during wartime (Damon, 1955); and somatotype and temperament (Peterson, Liivamagi, & Koskel, 2006) did support his theory.

Trait Theories

Trait theorists believe personality can be understood via the approach that all people have certain **traits,** or characteristic ways of behaving. Do you tend to be sociable or shy? Passive or aggressive? Optimistic or pessimistic? Moody or even-tempered? Early trait theorists tried to describe all human

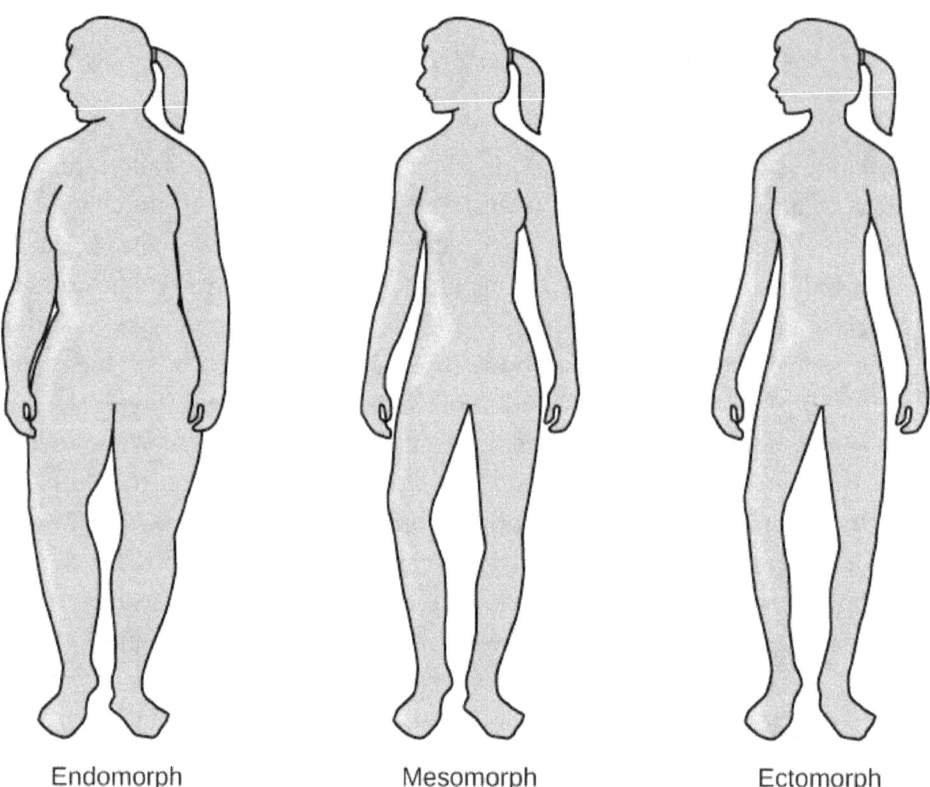

Figure 1. Sheldon proposed three somatotypes: endomorphs, mesomorphs, and ectomorphs. Do you think Sheldon's ideas about somatotypes are generally accurate about most people?

personality traits. For example, one trait theorist, Gordon Allport (Allport & Odbert, 1936), found 4,500 words in the English language that could describe people. He organized these personality traits into three categories: cardinal traits, central traits, and secondary traits. A cardinal trait is one that dominates your entire personality, and hence your life—such as Ebenezer Scrooge's greed and Mother Theresa's altruism. Cardinal traits are not very common: Few people have personalities dominated by a single trait. Instead, our personalities typically are composed of multiple traits. Central traits are those that make up our personalities (such as loyal, kind, agreeable, friendly, sneaky, wild, and grouchy). Secondary traits are those that are not quite as obvious or as consistent as central traits. They are present under specific circumstances and include preferences and attitudes. For example, one person gets angry when people try to tickle him; another can only sleep on the left side of the bed; and yet another always orders her salad dressing on the side. And you—although not normally an anxious person—feel nervous before making a speech in front of your English class.

In an effort to make the list of traits more manageable, Raymond Cattell (1946, 1957) narrowed down the list to about 171 traits. However, saying that a trait is either present or absent does not accurately reflect a person's uniqueness, because all of our personalities are actually made up of the same traits; we differ only in the degree to which each trait is expressed. Cattell (1957) identified 16 factors or dimensions of personality: warmth, reasoning, emotional stability, dominance, liveliness, rule-consciousness, social boldness, sensitivity, vigilance, abstractedness, privateness, apprehension, openness to change, self-reliance, perfectionism, and tension (Table 1). He developed a personality assessment based on these 16 factors, called the 16PF. Instead of a trait being present or absent, each dimension is scored over a continuum, from high to low. For example, your level of warmth describes how warm, caring, and nice to others you are. If you score low on this index, you tend to be more distant and cold. A high score on this index signifies you are supportive and comforting.

Table 1. Personality Factors Measured by the 16PF Questionnaire

Factor	Low Score	High Score
Warmth	Reserved, detached	Outgoing, supportive
Intellect	Concrete thinker	Analytical
Emotional stability	Moody, irritable	Stable, calm
Aggressiveness	Docile, submissive	Controlling, dominant
Liveliness	Somber, prudent	Adventurous, spontaneous
Dutifulness	Unreliable	Conscientious
Social assertiveness	Shy, restrained	Uninhibited, bold
Sensitivity	Tough-minded	Sensitive, caring
Paranoia	Trusting	Suspicious
Abstractness	Conventional	Imaginative
Introversion	Open, straightforward	Private, shrewd
Anxiety	Confident	Apprehensive
Openmindedness	Closeminded, traditional	Curious, experimental
Independence	Outgoing, social	Self-sufficient
Perfectionism	Disorganized, casual	Organized, precise
Tension	Relaxed	Stressed

Link to Learning

Follow this link to an assessment based on Cattell's 16PF questionnaire to see which personality traits dominate your personality.

- http://personality-testing.info/tests/16PF.php

Figure 2. Hans and Sybil Eysenck believed that our personality traits are influenced by our genetic inheritance. (credit: "Sirswindon"/Wikimedia Commons)

Psychologists Hans and Sybil Eysenck were personality theorists (Figure 2) who focused on **temperament**, the inborn, genetically based personality differences that you studied earlier in the module. They believed personality is largely governed by biology. The Eysencks (Eysenck, 1990, 1992; Eysenck & Eysenck, 1963) viewed people as having two specific personality dimensions: extroversion/introversion and neuroticism/stability.

According to their theory, people high on the trait of extroversion are sociable and outgoing, and readily connect with others, whereas people high on the trait of introversion have a higher need to be alone, engage in solitary behaviors, and limit their interactions with others. In the neuroticism/stability dimension, people high on neuroticism tend to be anxious; they tend to have an overactive sympathetic nervous system and, even with low stress, their bodies and emotional state tend to go into a flight-or-fight reaction. In contrast, people high on stability tend to need more stimulation to activate their flight-or-fight reaction and are considered more emotionally stable. Based on these two dimensions, the Eysencks' theory divides people into four quadrants. These quadrants are sometimes compared with the four temperaments described by the Greeks: melancholic, choleric, phlegmatic, and sanguine (Figure 3).

Later, the Eysencks added a third dimension: psychoticism versus superego control (Eysenck, Eysenck & Barrett, 1985). In this dimension, people who are high on psychoticism tend to be independent thinkers, cold, nonconformists, impulsive, antisocial, and hostile, whereas people who are high on superego control tend to have high impulse control—they are more altruistic, empathetic, cooperative, and conventional (Eysenck, Eysenck & Barrett, 1985).

The Big 5

While Cattell's 16 factors may be too broad, the Eysenck's two-factor system has been criticized for being too narrow. Another personality theory, called the **Five Factor Model**, effectively hits a middle ground, with its five factors referred to as the Big Five personality traits. It is the most popular theory in personality psychology today and the most accurate approximation of the basic trait dimensions (Funder, 2001). The five traits are openness to experience, conscientiousness, extroversion, agreeableness, and neuroticism (Figure 4). A helpful way to remember the traits is by using the mnemonic OCEAN.

In the Five Factor Model, each person has each trait, but they occur along a spectrum. Openness to experience is characterized by imagination, feelings, actions, and ideas. People who score high on this trait tend to be curious and have a wide range of interests. Conscientiousness is characterized by competence, self-discipline, thoughtfulness, and achievement-striving (goal-directed behavior). People who score high on this trait are hardworking and dependable. Numerous studies have found a positive correlation between conscientiousness and academic success (Akomolafe, 2013; Chamorro-Premuzic & Furnham, 2008; Conrad & Patry, 2012; Noftle & Robins, 2007; Wagerman & Funder, 2007). Extroversion is characterized by sociability, assertiveness, excitement-seeking, and emotional

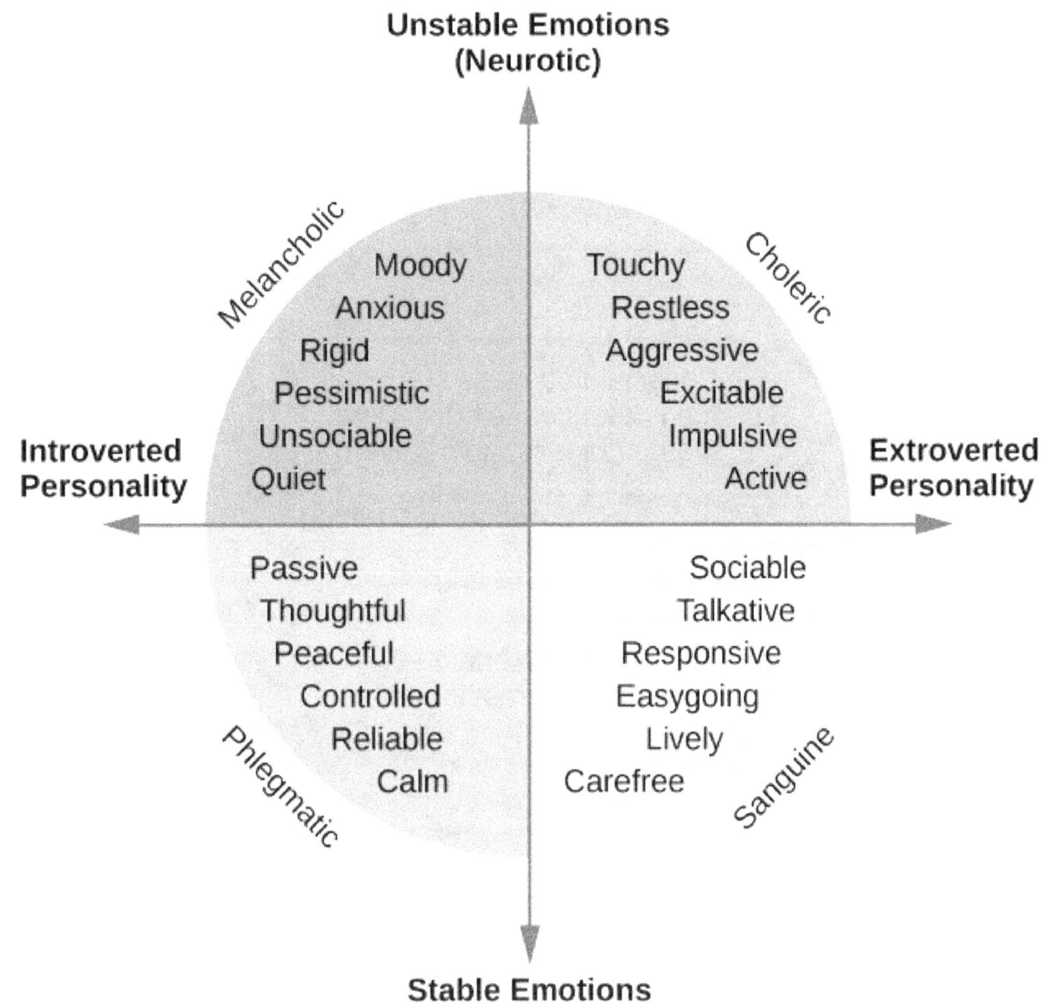

Figure 3. The Eysencks described two factors to account for variations in our personalities: extroversion/introversion and emotional stability/instability.

expression. People who score high on this trait are usually described as outgoing and warm. Not surprisingly, people who score high on both extroversion and openness are more likely to participate in adventure and risky sports due to their curious and excitement-seeking nature (Tok, 2011). The fourth trait is agreeableness, which is the tendency to be pleasant, cooperative, trustworthy, and good-natured. People who score low on agreeableness tend to be described as rude and uncooperative, yet one recent study reported that men who scored low on this trait actually earned more money than men who were considered more agreeable (Judge, Livingston, & Hurst, 2012). The last of the Big Five traits is neuroticism, which is the tendency to experience negative emotions. People high on neuroticism tend to experience emotional instability and are characterized as angry, impulsive, and hostile. Watson and Clark (1984) found that people reporting high levels of neuroticism also tend to report feeling anxious and unhappy. In contrast, people who score low in neuroticism tend to be calm and even-tempered.

The Big Five personality factors each represent a range between two extremes. In reality, most of us tend to lie somewhere midway along the continuum of each factor, rather than at polar ends. It's important to note that the Big Five traits are relatively stable over our lifespan, with some tendency

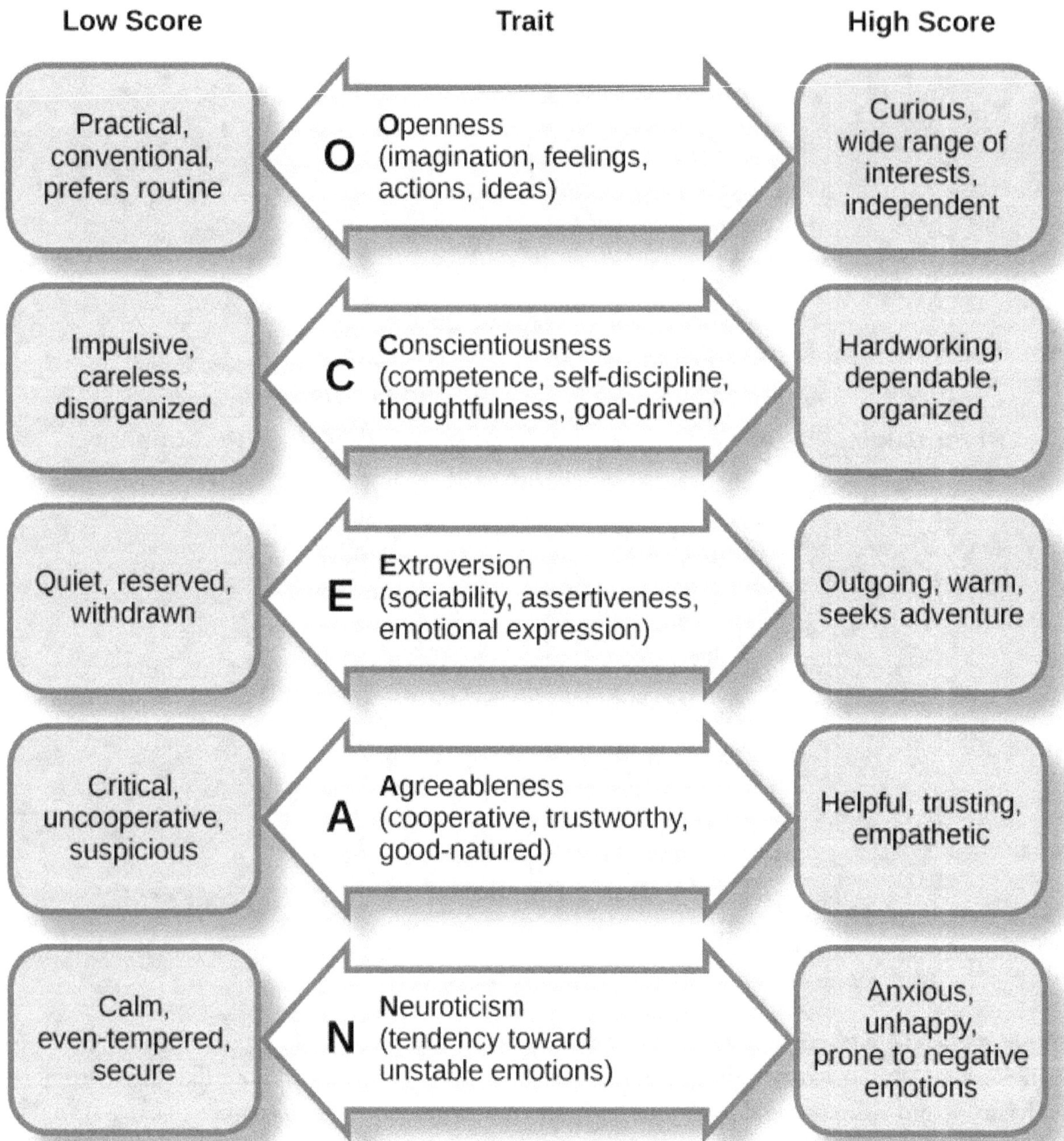

Figure 4. In the Five Factor Model, each person has five traits, each scored on a continuum from high to low. In the center column, notice that the first letter of each trait spells the mnemonic OCEAN.

for the traits to increase or decrease slightly. Researchers have found that conscientiousness increases through young adulthood into middle age, as we become better able to manage our personal relationships and careers (Donnellan & Lucas, 2008). Agreeableness also increases with age, peaking between 50 to 70 years (Terracciano, McCrae, Brant, & Costa, 2005). Neuroticism and extroversion tend to decline slightly with age (Donnellan & Lucas; Terracciano et al.). Additionally, The Big Five traits have been shown to exist across ethnicities, cultures, and ages, and may have substantial biological and genetic components (Jang, Livesley, & Vernon, 1996; Jang et al., 2006; McCrae & Costa, 1997; Schmitt et al., 2007).

Cultural Understandings of Personality

As you have learned in this module, personality is shaped by both genetic and environmental factors. The culture in which you live is one of the most important environmental factors that shapes your personality (Triandis & Suh, 2002). The term **culture** refers to all of the beliefs, customs, art, and traditions of a particular society. Culture is transmitted to people through language as well as through the modeling of culturally acceptable and nonacceptable behaviors that are either rewarded or punished (Triandis & Suh, 2002). With these ideas in mind, personality psychologists have become interested in the role of culture in understanding personality. They ask whether personality traits are the same across cultures or if there are variations. It appears that there are both universal and culture-specific aspects that account for variation in people's personalities.

Why might it be important to consider cultural influences on personality? Western ideas about personality may not be applicable to other cultures (Benet-Martinez & Oishi, 2008). In fact, there is evidence that the strength of personality traits varies across cultures. Let's take a look at some of the Big Five factors (conscientiousness, neuroticism, openness, and extroversion) across cultures. As you will learn when you study social psychology, Asian cultures are more collectivist, and people in these cultures tend to be less extroverted. People in Central and South American cultures tend to score higher on openness to experience, whereas Europeans score higher on neuroticism (Benet-Martinez & Karakitapoglu-Aygun, 2003).

According to this study, there also seem to be regional personality differences within the United States (Figure 5). Researchers analyzed responses from over 1.5 million individuals in the United States and found that there are three distinct regional personality clusters: Cluster 1, which is in the Upper Midwest and Deep South, is dominated by people who fall into the "friendly and conventional" personality; Cluster 2, which includes the West, is dominated by people who are more relaxed, emotionally stable, calm, and creative; and Cluster 3, which includes the Northeast, has more people who are stressed, irritable, and depressed. People who live in Clusters 2 and 3 are also generally more open (Rentfrow et al., 2013).

One explanation for the regional differences is **selective migration** (Rentfrow et al., 2013). Selective migration is the concept that people choose to move to places that are compatible with their personalities and needs. For example, a person high on the agreeable scale would likely want to live near family and friends, and would choose to settle or remain in such an area. In contrast, someone high on openness would prefer to settle in a place that is recognized as diverse and innovative (such as California).

Personality Clusters in the Continental United States

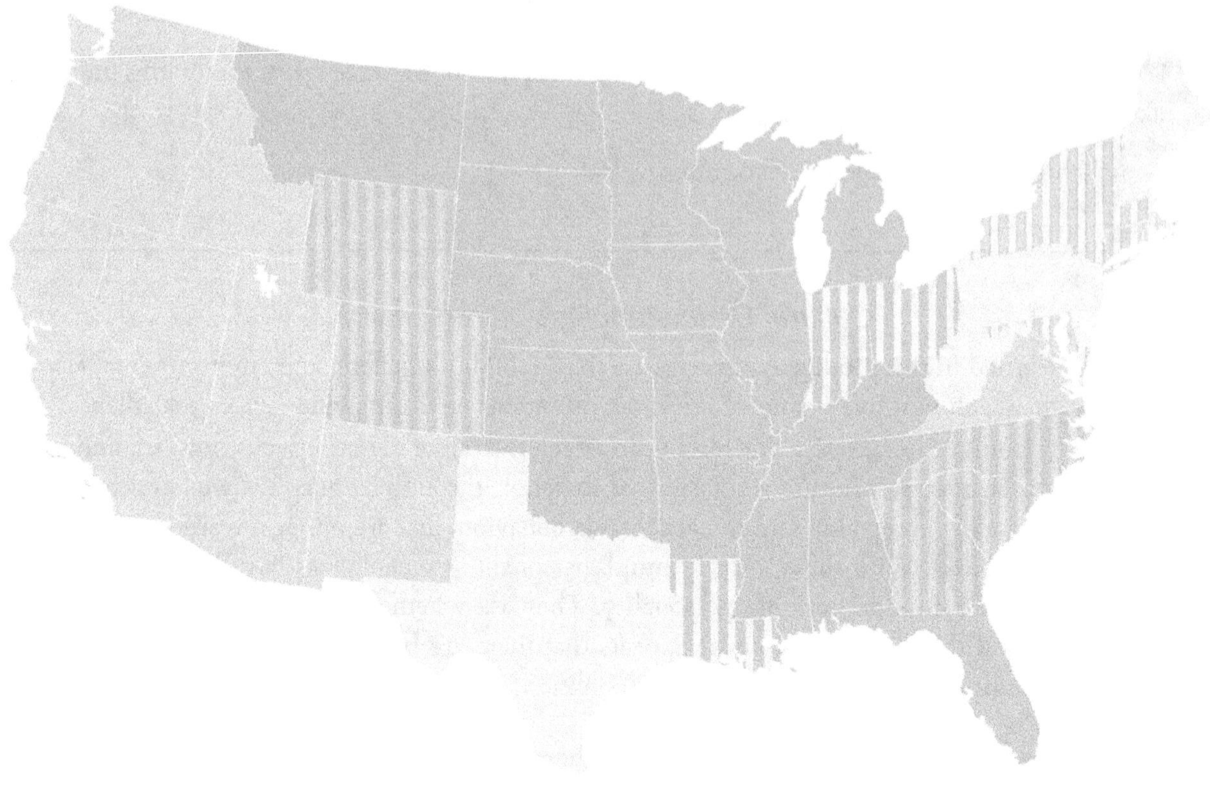

Figure 5. Researchers found three distinct regional personality clusters in the United States. People tend to be friendly and conventional in the Upper Midwest and Deep South; relaxed, emotionally stable, and creative in the West; and stressed, irritable, and depressed in the Northeast (Rentfrow et al., 2013).

Personality in Individualist and Collectivist Cultures

Individualist cultures and collectivist cultures place emphasis on different basic values. People who live in individualist cultures tend to believe that independence, competition, and personal achievement are important. Individuals in Western nations such as the United States, England, and Australia score high on individualism (Oyserman, Coon, & Kemmelmier, 2002). People who live in collectivist cultures value social harmony, respectfulness, and group needs over individual needs. Individuals who live in countries in Asia, Africa, and South America score high on collectivism (Hofstede, 2001; Triandis, 1995). These values influence personality. For example, Yang (2006) found that people in individualist cultures displayed more personally oriented personality traits, whereas people in collectivist cultures displayed more socially oriented personality traits.

Approaches to Studying Personality in a Cultural Context

There are three approaches that can be used to study personality in a cultural context, the *cultural-comparative approach*; the *indigenous approach*; and the *combined approach*, which incorporates elements of both views. Since ideas about personality have a Western basis, the cultural-comparative approach seeks to test Western ideas about personality in other cultures to determine whether they can be generalized and if they have cultural validity (Cheung van de Vijver, & Leong, 2011). For example, recall from the previous section on the trait perspective that researchers used the cultural-comparative approach to test the universality of McCrae and Costa's Five Factor Model. They found applicability in numerous cultures around the world, with the Big Five traits being stable in many cultures (McCrae & Costa, 1997; McCrae et al., 2005). The indigenous approach came about in reaction to the dominance of Western approaches to the study of personality in non-Western settings (Cheung et al., 2011). Because Western-based personality assessments cannot fully capture the personality constructs of other cultures, the indigenous model has led to the development of personality assessment instruments that are based on constructs relevant to the culture being studied (Cheung et al., 2011). The third approach to cross-cultural studies of personality is the combined approach, which serves as a bridge between Western and indigenous psychology as a way of understanding both universal and cultural variations in personality (Cheung et al., 2011).

Glossary

culture: all of the beliefs, customs, art, and traditions of a particular society

Five Factor Model: theory that personality is composed of five factors or traits, including openness, conscientiousness, extroversion, agreeableness, and neuroticism

heritability: proportion of difference among people that is attributed to genetics

selective migration: concept that people choose to move to places that are compatible with their personalities and needs

temperament: how a person reacts to the world, including their activity level, starting when they are very young

traits: characteristic ways of behaving

---

https://assessments.lumenlearning.com/assessments/4857

Personality Assessment

What you'll learn to do: explain the use and purpose of common personality tests

Personality tests are techniques designed to measure one's personality. They are used to diagnose psychological problems as well as to screen candidates for college and employment. There are two types of personality tests: self-report inventories and projective tests. The MMPI is one of the most common self-report inventories. It asks a series of true/false questions that are designed to provide a clinical profile of an individual. Projective tests use ambiguous images or other ambiguous stimuli to assess an individual's unconscious fears, desires, and challenges. The Rorschach Inkblot Test, the TAT, the RISB, and the C-TCB are all forms of projective tests.

Learning Objectives

- Describe different types of personality tests, including the Minnesota Multiphasic Personality Inventory and common projective tests

Roberto, Mikhail, and Nat are college friends and all want to be police officers. Roberto is quiet and shy, lacks self-confidence, and usually follows others. He is a kind person, but lacks motivation. Mikhail is loud and boisterous, a leader. He works hard, but is impulsive and drinks too much on the weekends. Nat is thoughtful and well liked. He is trustworthy, but sometimes he has difficulty making quick decisions. Of these three men, who would make the best police officer? What qualities and personality factors make someone a good police officer? What makes someone a bad or dangerous police officer?

A police officer's job is very high in stress, and law enforcement agencies want to make sure they hire the right people. Personality testing is often used for this purpose—to screen applicants for employment and job training. Personality tests are also used in criminal cases and custody battles, and to assess psychological disorders. This section explores the best known among the many different types of personality tests.

Self-Report Inventories

Self-report inventories are a kind of objective test used to assess personality. They typically use multiple-choice items or numbered scales, which represent a range from 1 (strongly disagree) to 5 (strongly agree). They often are called Likert scales after their developer, Rensis Likert (1932) (Figure 1).

	Strongly Disagree	Somewhat Disagree	No Opinion	Somewhat Agree	Strongly Agree
I am easygoing.	O	O	O	O	O
I have high standards.	O	O	O	O	O
I enjoy time alone.	O	O	O	O	O
I work well with others.	O	O	O	O	O
I dislike confrontation.	O	O	O	O	O
I prefer crowds over intimacy.	O	O	O	O	O

Figure 1. If you've ever taken a survey, you are probably familiar with Likert-type scale questions. Most personality inventories employ these types of response scales.

One of the most widely used personality inventories is the Minnesota Multiphasic Personality Inventory (MMPI), first published in 1943, with 504 true/false questions, and updated to the MMPI-2 in 1989, with 567 questions. The original MMPI was based on a small, limited sample, composed mostly of Minnesota farmers and psychiatric patients; the revised inventory was based on a more representative, national sample to allow for better standardization. The MMPI-2 takes 1–2 hours to complete. Responses are scored to produce a clinical profile composed of 10 scales: hypochondriasis, depression, hysteria, psychopathic deviance (social deviance), masculinity versus femininity, paranoia, psychasthenia (obsessive/compulsive qualities), schizophrenia, hypomania, and social introversion. There is also a scale to ascertain risk factors for alcohol abuse. In 2008, the test was again revised, using more advanced methods, to the MMPI-2-RF. This version takes about one-half the time to complete and has only 338 questions (Figure 2). Despite the new test's advantages, the MMPI-2 is more established and is still more widely used. Typically, the tests are administered by computer. Although the MMPI was originally developed to assist in the clinical diagnosis of psychological disorders, it is now also used for occupational screening, such as in law enforcement, and in college, career, and marital counseling (Ben-Porath & Tellegen, 2008).

	True	False
1. I like gardening magazines.	O	O
2. I am unhappy with my sex life.	O	O
3. I feel like no one understands me.	O	O
4. I think I would enjoy the work of a teacher.	O	O
5. I am not easily awakened by noise.	O	O

Figure 2. These true/false questions resemble the kinds of questions you would find on the MMPI.

In addition to clinical scales, the tests also have validity and reliability scales. (Recall the concepts of reliability and validity from your study of psychological research.) One of the validity scales, the Lie Scale (or "L" Scale), consists of 15 items and is used to ascertain whether the respondent is "faking good" (underreporting psychological problems to appear healthier). For example, if someone responds "yes" to a number of unrealistically positive items such as "I have never told a lie," they may be trying to "fake good" or appear better than they actually are.

Reliability scales test an instrument's consistency over time, assuring that if you take the MMPI-2-RF today and then again 5 years later, your two scores will be similar. Beutler, Nussbaum, and Meredith (1988) gave the MMPI to newly recruited police officers and then to the same police officers 2 years later. After 2 years on the job, police officers' responses indicated an increased vulnerability to alcoholism, somatic symptoms (vague, unexplained physical complaints), and anxiety. When the test was given an additional 2 years later (4 years after starting on the job), the results suggested high risk for alcohol-related difficulties.

Projective Tests

Another method for assessment of personality is **projective testing**. This kind of test relies on one of the defense mechanisms proposed by Freud—projection—as a way to assess unconscious processes. During this type of testing, a series of ambiguous cards is shown to the person being tested, who then is encouraged to project his feelings, impulses, and desires onto the cards—by telling a story, interpreting an image, or completing a sentence. Many projective tests have undergone standardization procedures (for example, Exner, 2002) and can be used to access whether someone has unusual thoughts or a high level of anxiety, or is likely to become volatile. Some examples of projective tests are the Rorschach Inkblot Test, the Thematic Apperception Test (TAT), the Contemporized-Themes Concerning Blacks test, the TEMAS (Tell-Me-A-Story), and the Rotter Incomplete Sentence Blank (RISB).

The **Rorschach Inkblot Test** was developed in 1921 by a Swiss psychologist named Hermann Rorschach (pronounced "ROAR-shock"). It is a series of symmetrical inkblot cards that are presented to a client by a psychologist. Upon presentation of each card, the psychologist asks the client, "What might this be?" What the test-taker sees reveals unconscious feelings and struggles (Piotrowski, 1987; Weiner, 2003). The Rorschach has been standardized using the Exner system and is effective in measuring depression, psychosis, and anxiety.

A second projective test is the **Thematic Apperception Test (TAT)**, created in the 1930s by Henry Murray, an American psychologist, and a psychoanalyst named Christiana Morgan. A person taking the TAT is shown 8–12 ambiguous pictures and is asked to tell a story about each picture. The stories give insight into their social world, revealing hopes, fears, interests, and goals. The storytelling format helps to lower a person's resistance divulging unconscious personal details (Cramer, 2004). The TAT has been used in clinical settings to evaluate psychological disorders; more recently, it has been used in counseling settings to help clients gain a better understanding of themselves and achieve personal growth. Standardization of test administration is virtually nonexistent among clinicians, and the test tends to be modest to low on validity and reliability (Aronow, Weiss, & Rezinkoff, 2001; Lilienfeld, Wood, & Garb, 2000). Despite these shortcomings, the TAT has been one of the most widely used projective tests.

A third projective test is the **Rotter Incomplete Sentence Blank (RISB)** developed by Julian Rotter in 1950 (recall his theory of locus of control, covered earlier in this chapter). There are three forms of this test for use with different age groups: the school form, the college form, and the adult form. The tests include 40 incomplete sentences that people are asked to complete as quickly as possible (Figure 3). The average time for completing the test is approximately 20 minutes, as responses are only 1–2 words in length. This test is similar to a word association test, and like other types of projective tests, it is presumed that responses will reveal desires, fears, and struggles. The RISB is used in screening college students for adjustment problems and in career counseling (Holaday, Smith, & Sherry, 2010; Rotter & Rafferty 1950).

For many decades, these traditional projective tests have been used in cross-cultural personality assessments. However, it was found that test bias limited their usefulness (Hoy-Watkins & Jenkins-Moore, 2008). It is difficult to assess the personalities and lifestyles of members of widely divergent ethnic/cultural groups using personality instruments based on data from a single culture or race (Hoy-Watkins & Jenkins-Moore, 2008). For example, when the TAT was used with African-American test takers, the result was often shorter story length and low levels of cultural identification (Duzant, 2005). Therefore, it was vital to develop other personality assessments that explored factors such as race, language, and level of acculturation (Hoy-Watkins & Jenkins-Moore, 2008). To address this need, Robert Williams developed the first culturally specific projective test designed to reflect the everyday life experiences of African Americans (Hoy-Watkins & Jenkins-Moore, 2008). The updated version

1. I feel...	
2. I regret...	
3. At home...	
4. My mother...	
5. My greatest worry...	

Figure 3. These incomplete sentences resemble the types of questions on the RISB. How would you complete these sentences?

of the instrument is the **Contemporized–Themes Concerning Blacks Test (C-TCB)** (Williams, 1972). The C-TCB contains 20 color images that show scenes of African-American lifestyles. When the C-TCB was compared with the TAT for African Americans, it was found that use of the C-TCB led to increased story length, higher degrees of positive feelings, and stronger identification with the C-TCB (Hoy, 1997; Hoy-Watkins & Jenkins-Moore, 2008).

The **TEMAS Multicultural Thematic Apperception Test** is another tool designed to be culturally relevant to minority groups, especially Hispanic youths. TEMAS—standing for "Tell Me a Story" but also a play on the Spanish word *temas* (themes)—uses images and storytelling cues that relate to minority culture (Constantino, 1982).

Glossary

Contemporized-Themes Concerning Blacks Test (C-TCB): projective test designed to be culturally relevant to African Americans, using images that relate to African-American culture

Minnesota Multiphasic Personality Inventory (MMPI): personality test composed of a series of true/false questions in order to establish a clinical profile of an individual

Projective test: personality assessment in which a person responds to ambiguous stimuli, revealing hidden feelings, impulses, and desires

Rorschach Inkblot Test: projective test that employs a series of symmetrical inkblot cards that are presented to a client by a psychologist in an effort to reveal the person's unconscious desires, fears, and struggles

Rotter Incomplete Sentence Blank (RISB): projective test that is similar to a word association test in which a person completes sentences in order to reveal their unconscious desires, fears, and struggles

TEMAS Multicultural Thematic Apperception Test: projective test designed to be culturally relevant to minority groups, especially Hispanic youths, using images and storytelling that relate to minority culture

Thematic Apperception Test (TAT): projective test in which people are presented with ambiguous images, and they then make up stories to go with the images in an effort to uncover their unconscious desires, fears, and struggles

https://assessments.lumenlearning.com/assessments/4858
Attributions

Putting It Together: Personality

In this module, you learned to

- define personality and the contributions of Freud and neo-Freudians to personality theory

- describe and differentiate between personality theories

- explain the use and purpose of common personality tests

Personality psychology is about how individuals differ from each other in their characteristic ways of thinking, feeling, and behaving. In this module, you examined some of the foundational theories that explain personality and learned about personality testing today. Some of the most interesting questions about personality attributes involve issues of stability and change. Are shy children destined to become shy adults? Are the typical personality attributes of adults different from the typical attributes of adolescents? Do people become more self-controlled and better able to manage their negative emotions as they become adults? What mechanisms explain personality stability and what mechanisms account for personality change?

Remember that the Big Five personality traits include:

- extraversion (attributes such as assertive, confident, independent, outgoing, and sociable),

- agreeableness (attributes such as cooperative, kind, modest, and trusting),

- conscientiousness (attributes such as hard working, dutiful, self-controlled, and goal-oriented),

- neuroticism (attributes such as anxious, tense, moody, and easily angered),

- openness (attributes such as artistic, curious, inventive, and open-minded).

The Big Five is one of the most common ways of organizing the vast range of personality attributes that seem to distinguish one person from the next. In a meta-analysis of several studies of the Big Five test, Roberts, Walton, and Viechtbauer found that in general, average levels of extraversion (especially the attributes linked to self-confidence and independence), agreeableness, and conscientiousness appear to increase with age whereas neuroticism appears to decrease with age (Roberts et al., 2006). Openness also declines with age, especially after mid-life (Roberts et al., 2006). These changes are often viewed as positive trends given that higher levels of agreeableness and conscientiousness and lower levels of neuroticism are associated with seemingly desirable outcomes such as increased relationship stability and quality, greater success at work, better health, a reduced risk of criminality and mental health problems, and even decreased mortality. This pattern of positive average changes in personality attributes is known as the maturity principle of adult personality development (Caspi,

Roberts, & Shiner, 2005). The basic idea is that attributes associated with positive adaptation and attributes associated with the successful fulfillment of adult roles tend to increase during adulthood in terms of their average levels.

Beyond providing insights into the general outline of adult personality development, Roberts et al. (2006) found that young adulthood (the period between the ages of 18 and the late 20s) was the most active time in the lifespan for observing average changes, although average differences in personality attributes were observed across the lifespan. Such a result might be surprising in light of the intuition that adolescence is a time of personality change and maturation. However, young adulthood is typically a time in the lifespan that includes a number of life changes in terms of finishing school, starting a career, committing to romantic partnerships, and parenthood (Donnellan, Conger, & Burzette, 2007; Rindfuss, 1991). Finding that young adulthood is an active time for personality development provides circumstantial evidence that adult roles might generate pressures for certain patterns of personality development. Indeed, this is one potential explanation for the maturity principle of personality development.

It should be emphasized again that average trends are summaries that do not necessarily apply to all individuals. Some people do not conform to the maturity principle. The possibility of exceptions to general trends is the reason it is necessary to study individual patterns of personality development. The methods for this kind of research are becoming increasingly popular (e.g., Vaidya, Gray, Haig, Mroczek, & Watson, 2008) and existing studies suggest that personality changes differ across people (Roberts & Mroczek, 2008). These new research methods work best when researchers collect more than two waves of longitudinal data covering longer spans of time. This kind of research design is still somewhat uncommon in psychological studies but it will likely characterize the future of research on personality stability.

So, while personality is still considered relatively stable over the lifespan, take hope, as it is not set in stone. Many personality attributes are linked to life experiences in a mutually reinforcing cycle: Personality attributes seem to shape environmental contexts, and those contexts often then accentuate and reinforce those very personality attributes. Even so, personality change or transformation is possible because individuals respond to their environments.

Attributions

- Man adjusting tie. **Authored by:** Alex France. **Provided by:** Flickr. **Located at:** https://www.flickr.com/photos/alexfrance/3221301604/. **License:** *CC BY-SA: Attribution-ShareAlike*

Module 3: Lifespan Development

Why It Matters: Introduction to Lifespan Development

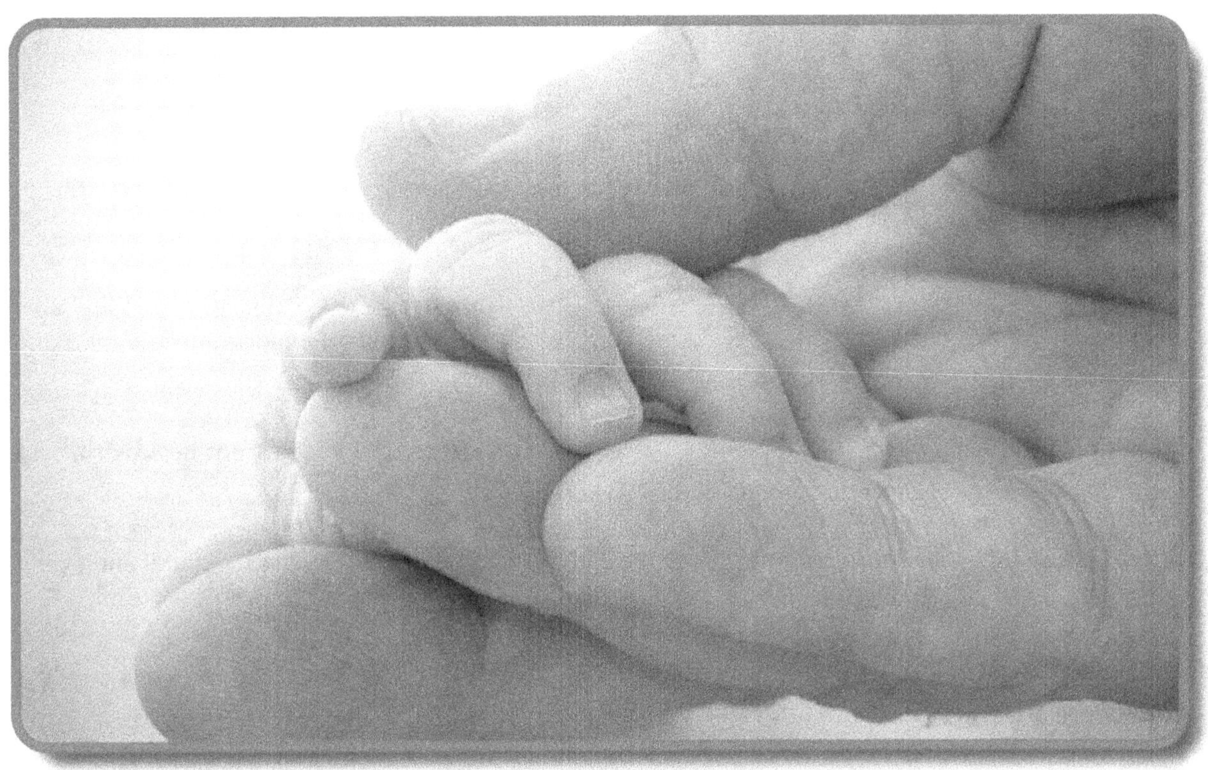

Figure 1. How have you changed since childhood? How are you the same? What will your life be like 25 years from now? Fifty years from now? Lifespan development studies how you change as well as how you remain the same over the course of your life. (credit: modification of work by Giles Cook)

Welcome to the story of your life. In this module we will explore the fascinating tale of how you have grown and developed into the person you are today. We will also look at some ideas about who you will grow into tomorrow. Yours is a story of lifespan development (Figure 1), from the start of life to the end.

The process of human growth and development is more obvious in infancy and childhood, yet your development is happening this moment and will continue, minute by minute, for the rest of your life. Who you are today and who you will be in the future depends on a blend of genetics, environment, culture, relationships, and more, as you continue through each phase of life. You have experienced firsthand much of what is discussed in this module. Now consider what psychological science has to say about your physical, cognitive, and psychosocial development, from the womb to the tomb.

Module References

Ainsworth, M. D. S., & Bell, S. M. (1970). Attachment, exploration, and separation: Illustrated by the behavior of one-year-olds in a strange situation. *Child Development, 41,* 49–67.

Ainsworth, M. D. S., Blehar, M. C., Waters, E., & Wall, S. (1978). *Patterns of attachment: A psychological study of the strange situation.* Hillsdale, NJ: Erlbaum.

American Academy of Pediatrics. (2007). The importance of play in promoting healthy child development and maintaining strong parent-child bonds. *Pediatrics, 199*(1), 182–191.

Amsterdam, B. (1972). Mirror image reactions before age two. *Developmental Psychobiology, 5,* 297–305.

Archer, J. (1992). *Ethology and human development.* New York, NY: Harvester Wheatsheaf.

Arnett, J. (2000). Emerging adulthood: A theory of development from the late teens through the twenties. *American Psychologist, 55*(5), 469–480.

Ashley, S. J., Magnuson, S. I., Omnell, L. M., & Clarren, S. K. (1999). Fetal alcohol syndrome: Changes in craniofacial form with age, cognition, and timing of ethanol exposure in the macaque. *Teratology, 59*(3), 163–172.

Bahr, S. J., & Hoffman, J. P. (2010). Parenting style, religiosity, peers, and adolescent heavy drinking. *Journal of Studies on Alcohol and Drugs, 71,* 539–543.

Baillargeon, R. (2004). Infants' reasoning about hidden objects: Evidence for event-general and event-specific expectations. *Developmental Science, 7*(4), 391–424.

Baillargeon, R. (1987). Young infants' reasoning about the physical and spatial properties of a hidden object. *Cognitive Development, 2*(3), 179–200.

Baillargeon, R., Li, J., Gertner, Y., & Wu, D. (2011). How do infants reason about physical events. *The Wiley-Blackwell handbook of childhood cognitive development, 2,* 11–48.

Barber, B. K. (1994). Cultural, family, and person contexts of parent-adolescent conflict. *Journal of Marriage and the Family, 56,* 375–386.

Basseches, M. (1984). Dialectical thinking as metasystematic form of cognitive organization. In M. L. Commons, F. A. Richards, & C. Armon (Eds.), *Beyond formal operations: Late adolescent and adult cognitive development* (pp. 216–238). New York, NY: Praeger.

Baumrind, D. (1971). Current patterns of parental authority. *Developmental Psychology, 4*(1, Pt. 2), 1–103. doi:10.1037/h0030372

Baumrind, D. (1991). The influence of parenting style on adolescent competence and substance use. *Journal of Early Adolescence, 11*(1), 56–95.

Bayley, N., & Oden, M. H. (1955). The maintenance of intellectual ability in gifted adults. *Journal of Gerontology, 10,* 91–107.

Bjorklund, D. F. (1987). A note on neonatal imitation. *Developmental Review, 7,* 86–92.

Blossom, M., & Morgan, J.L. (2006). Does the face say what the mouth says? A study of infants' sensitivity to visual prosody. In *30th annual Boston University conference on language development, Somerville, MA.*

Bogartz, R. S., Shinskey, J. L., & Schilling, T. (2000). *Infancy, 1*(4), 403–428.

Bowlby, J. (1969). *Attachment and loss: Attachment* (Vol. 1). New York, NY: Basic Books.

Bowlby, J. (1988). *A secure base: Parent-child attachment and health human development.* New York, NY: Basic Books.

Brumley, R., Enquidanos, S., Jamison, P., Seitz, R., Morgenstern, N., Saito, S., . . . Gonzalez, J. (2007). Increased satisfaction with care and lower costs: Results of a randomized trial of in-home palliative care. *Journal of the American Geriatric Society, 55*(7), 993–1000.

Brumley, R. D., Enquidanos, S., & Cherin, D. A. (2003). Effectiveness of a home-based palliative care program for end-of-life. *Journal of Palliative Medicine, 6*(5), 715–724.

Callaghan, T. C., Rochat, P., Lillard, A., Claux, M.L., Odden, H., Itakura, S., . . . Singh, S. (2005). Synchrony in the onset of mental-state reasoning. *Psychological Science, 16*, 378–384.

Carel, J-C., Lahlou, N., Roger, M., & Chaussain, J. L. (2004). Precocious puberty and statural growth. *Human Reproduction Update, 10*(2), 135–147.

Carstensen, L. L. (1992). Social and emotional patterns in adulthood: Support for socioemotional selectivity. *Psychology and Aging, 7*(3), 331–338.

Case, R. (1985). *Intellectual development: Birth to Adulthood.* New York, NY: Academic.

Casey, B. J., Tottenham, N., Liston, C., & Durston, S. (2005). Imaging the developing brain: What have we learned about cognitive development? *TRENDS in Cognitive Sciences, 19*(3), 104–110.

Centers for Disease Control and Prevention. (2013). *Smoking during pregnancy.* Retrieved from http://www.cdc.gov/tobacco/basic_information/health_effects/pregnancy/

Chick, K., Heilman-Houser, R., & Hunter, M. (2002). The impact of child care on gender role development and gender stereotypes. *Early Childhood Education Journal, 29*(3), 149–154.

Chomsky, N. (1957). *Syntactic structures.* The Hague, Netherlands: Mouton.

Clements, R. (2004). An investigation of the status of outdoor play. *Contemporary Issues in Early Childhood, 5*(1), 68–80.

Commons, M. L., & Bresette, L. M. (2006). Illuminating major creative scientific innovators with postformal stages. In C. Hoare (Ed.), *Handbook of adult development and learning* (pp. 255–280). New York, NY: Oxford University Press.

Connor, S. R., Pyenson, B., Fitch, K., Spence, C., & Iwasaki, K. (2007). Comparing hospice and non-hospice patient survival among patients who die within a three-year window. *Journal of Pain and Symptom Management, 33*(3), 238–246.

Courage, M. L., & Howe, M. L. (2002). From infant to child: The dynamics of cognitive change in the second year of life. *Psychological Bulletin, 128*, 250–277.

Curtiss, S. (1981). Dissociations between language and cognition: Cases and implications. *Journal of Autism and Developmental Disorders, 11*(1), 15–30.

Darling, N. (1999). *Parenting style and its correlates.* Retrieved from ERIC database (EDO-PS-99-3) http://ecap.crc.illinois.edu/eecearchive/digests/1999/darlin99.pdf

de Hevia, M. D., & Spelke, E. S. (2010). Number-space mapping in human infants. *Psychological Science, 21*(5), 653–660.

Dennett, D. (1987). *The intentional stance.* Cambridge, MA: MIT Press.

Diamond, A. (2009). The interplay of biology and the environment broadly defined. *Developmental Psychology, 45*(1), 1–8.

Donenberg, G. R., Wilson, H. W., Emerson, E., Bryant, F. B. (2002). Holding the line with a watchful eye: The impact of perceived parental permissiveness and parental monitoring on risky sexual behavior among adolescents in psychiatric care. *AIDS Education Prevention, 14*(2), 138–157.

Dornbusch, S. M., Ritter, P. L., Leiderman, P. H., Roberts, D. F., & Fraleigh, M. J. (1987). The relation of parenting style to adolescent school performance. *Child Development, 58*(5), 1244–1257.

Duncan, G. J., & Magnuson, K. A. (2005). Can family socioeconomic resources account for racial and ethnic test score gaps? *The Future of Children, 15*(1), 35–54.

Erikson, E. H. (1963). *Childhood and Society* (2nd ed.). New York, NY: Norton.

Erikson, E. H. (1968). *Identity: Youth and crisis.* New York, NY: Norton.

Ferrer, M., & Fugate, A. (2003). *Helping your school-age child develop a healthy self-concept.* Retrieved from http://edis.ifas.ufl.edu/fy570#FOOTNOTE_2

Figdor, E., & Kaeser, L. (1998). Concerns mount over punitive approaches to substance abuse among pregnant women. *The Guttmacher Report on Public Policy 1*(5), 3–5.

Fischer, K. W., Yan, Z., & Stewart, J. (2003). Adult cognitive development: Dynamics in the developmental web. In J. Valsiner & K Connolly (Eds.), *Handbook of developmental psychology* (pp. 491–516). Thousand Oaks, CA: Sage Publications.

Flannery, D. J., Rowe, D. C., & Gulley, B. L. (1993). Impact of pubertal status, timing, and age on adolescent sexual experience and delinquency. *Journal of Adolescent Research, 8*, 21–40.

Freud, S. (1909). Analysis of a phobia in a five-year-old boy. In *Collected Papers: Volume 111, Case Histories (1949)* (pp. 149–289). Hogarth Press: London.

Fromkin, V., Krashen, S., Curtiss, S., Rigler, D., & Rigler, M. (1974). The development of language in Genie: A case of language acquisition beyond the critical period. *Brain and Language, 1*, 81–107.

Galambos, N. L., & Almeida, D. M. (1992). Does parent-adolescent conflict increase in early adolescence? *Journal of Marriage and the Family, 54*, 737–747.

Ganger, J., & Brent, M.R. (2004). Reexamining the vocabulary spurt. *Developmental Psychology, 40*(4), 621–632.

Ge, X., Conger, R. D., & Elder, G. H. (2001). Pubertal transition, stressful life events, and the emergence of gender differences in adolescent depressive symptoms. *Developmental Psychology, 37*, 404–417.

Gervai, J. (2009). Environmental and genetic influences on early attachment. *Child and Adolescent Psychiatry and Mental Health, 3*, 25.

Gesell, A. (1933). Maturation and the patterning of behavior. In C. Murchison (Ed.), *A handbook of child psychology* (2nd ed., pp. 209–235). Worcester, MA: Clark University Press.

Gesell, A. (1939). *Biographies of child development*. New York, NY: Paul B. Hoeber.

Gesell, A. (1940). *The first five years of life*. New York, NY: Harper.

Gesell, A., & Ilg, F. L. (1946). *The child from five to ten*. New York, NY: Harper.

Gilligan, C. (1982). *In a different voice: Psychological theory and women's development*. Cambridge, MA: Harvard University Press.

Gleitman, L.R., & Newport, E. L. (1995). The invention of language by children: Environmental and biological influences on the acquisition of language. In D.N. Osherson , L.R. Gleitman, & M. Liberman (Eds.), *An invitation to cognitive science: Language* (pp. 1–24). Cambridge, MA: The MIT Press.

Gleitman, L. R., & Newport, E. L. (1995). The invention of language by children: Environmental and biological influences on the acquisition of language. In L. R. Gleitman & M. Liberman (Eds.), *An invitation to cognitive science, Vol. 1: Language.* (2nd ed.) (pp. 1–24). Cambridge, MA: MIT Press.

Godkin, M., Krant, M., & Doster, N. (1984). The impact of hospice care on families. *International Journal of Psychiatry in Medicine, 13*, 153–165.

Graber, J. A., Lewinsohn, P. M., Seeley, J. R., & Brooks-Gunn, J. (1997). Is psychopathology associated with the timing of pubertal development? *Journal of the Academy of Child and Adolescent Psychiatry, 36*, 1768–1776.

Hair, E. C., Moore, K. A., Garrett, S. B., Kinukawa, A., Lippman, L., & Michelson, E. (2005). The parent-adolescent relationship scale. In L. Lippman (Ed.), *Conceptualizing and Measuring Indicators of Positive Development: What Do Children Need to Fluorish?* (pp. 183–202). New York, NY: Kluwer Academic/Plenum Press.

Hall, S. S. (2004, May). The good egg. *Discover,* 30–39.

Hall, G. S. (1904). *Adolescence.* New York, NY: Appleton.

Harlow, H. (1958). The nature of love. *American Psychologist, 13,* 673–685.

Harris, J. R. (2009). *The nurture assumption: Why children turn out the way they do* (2nd ed.). New York, NY: Free Press.

Hart, B., & Risley, T. R. (2003). The early catastrophe: The 30 million word gap. *American Educator, 27*(1), 4–9.

Hatch, E. (1983). *Psycholinguistics: A second language perspective.* Rowley, MA: Newbury House.

Hertzog, C., Kramer, A. F., Wilson, R. S., & Lindenberger, U. (2009). Enrichment effects on adult cognitive development. *Psychological Science in the Public Interest, 9*(1), 1–65.

Hood, R. W., Jr., Spilka, B., Hunsberger, B., & Corsuch, R. (1996). *The psychology of religion: An empirical approach* (2nd ed.). New York, NY: Guilford.

Huebler, F. (2005, December 14). International education statistics [Web log post]. Retrieved from http://huebler.blogspot.com/2005/12/age-and-level-of-education-in-nigeria.html

Hutchinson, N. (2011). A geographically informed vision of skills development. *Geographical Education, 24,* 15.

Huttenlocher, P. R., & Dabholkar, A. S. (1997). Regional differences in synaptogenesis in human cerebral cortex. *Journal of Comparative Neurology, 387*(2), 167–178.

Iverson, J.M., & Goldin-Meadow, S. (2005). Gesture paves the way for language development. *Psychological Science, 16*(5), 367–71.

Iyengar, S. S., Wells, R. E., & Schwartz, B. (2006). Doing better but feeling worse: Looking for the best job undermines satisfaction. *Psychological Science, 17,* 143–150.

Jos, P. H., Marshall, M. F., & Perlmutter, M. (1995). The Charleston policy on cocaine use during pregnancy: A cautionary tale. *The Journal of Law, Medicine & Ethics, 23*(2), 120–128.

Kaltiala-Heino, R. A., Rimpela, M., Rissanen, A., & Rantanen, P. (2001). Early puberty and early sexual activity are associated with bulimic-type eating pathology in middle adolescence. *Journal of Adolescent Health, 28,* 346–352.

Kaplan, H., & Dove, H. (1987). Infant development among the Aché of Eastern Paraguay. *Developmental Psychology, 23*, 190–198.

Karasik, L. B., Adolph, K. E., Tamis-LeMonda, C. S., & Bornstein, M. H. (2010). WEIRD Walking: Cross-cultural research on motor development. *Behavioral & Brain Sciences, 33*(2-3), 95–96.

Karnik, S., & Kanekar, A. (2012). Childhood obesity: A global public health crisis. *International Journal of Preventive Medicine, 3*(1), 1–7.

Kohlberg, L. (1969). Stage and sequence: The cognitive-developmental approach to socialization. In D. A. Goslin (Ed.), *Handbook of socialization theory and research* (p. 379). Chicago, IL: Rand McNally.

Kolb, B., & Whishaw, I. Q. (2009). *Fundamentals of human neuropsychology*. New York, NY: Worth.

Kübler-Ross, E. (1969). *On death and dying*. New York, NY: Macmillan.

Labouvie-Vief, G., & Diehl, M. (1999). Self and personality development. In J. C. Cavanaugh & S. K. Whitbourne (Eds.), *Gerontology: An interdisciplinary perspective* (pp. 238–268). New York, NY: Oxford University Press.

Larson, E. B., Wang, L., Bowen, J. D., McCormick, W. C., Teri, L., Crane, P., & Kukull, W. (2006). Exercise is associated with reduced risk for incident dementia among persons 65 years of age or older. *Annals of Internal Medicine, 144*, 73–81.

Lee, V. E., & Burkam, D. T. (2002). *Inequality at the starting gate: Social background differences in achievement as children begin school*. Washington, DC: Economic Policy Institute.

Lobo, I. (2008) Environmental influences on gene expression. *Nature Education 1*(1), 39.

Loop, E. (2013). *Major milestones in cognitive development in early childhood*. Retrieved from http://everydaylife.globalpost.com/major-milestones-cognitive-development-early-childhood-4625.html

Maccoby, E. (1980). *Social development: Psychological growth and the parent-child relationship*. New York, NY: Harcourt Brace Jovanovich.

MacFarlane, A. (1978, February). What a baby knows. *Human Nature*, 74–81.

Maier, S. E., & West, J. R. (2001). Drinking patterns and alcohol-related birth defects. *Alcohol Research & Health, 25*(3), 168–174.

Main, M., & Solomon, J. (1990). Procedures for identifying infants as disorganized/disoriented during the Ainsworth Strange Situation. In M. T. Greenberg, D. Cicchetti, & E. M. Cummings (Eds.), *Attachment in the Preschool Years* (pp. 121–160). Chicago, IL: University of Chicago Press.

Markus, H. R., Ryff, C. D., Curan, K., & Palmersheim, K. A. (2004). In their own words: Well-being at midlife among high school-educated and college-educated adults. In O. G. Brim, C. D. Ryff, & R. C. Kessler (Eds.), *How healthy are we? A national study of well-being at midlife* (pp. 273–319). Chicago, IL: University of Chicago Press.

McIntosh, D. N., Silver, R. C., & Wortman, C. B. (1993). Religion's role in adjustment to a negative life event: Coping with the loss of a child. *Journal of Personality and Social Psychology, 65*, 812–821.

McMillan, S. C., Small, B. J., Weitzner, M., Schonwetter, R., Tittle, M., Moody, L., & Haley, W. E. (2006). Impact of coping skills intervention with family caregivers of hospice patients with cancer. *Cancer, 106*(1), 214-222.

Miklikowska, M., Duriez, B., & Soenens, B. (2011). Family roots of empathy-related characteristics: The role of perceived maternal and paternal need support in adolescence. *Developmental Psychology, 47*(5), 1342–1352.

Mills, M., & Melhuish, E. (1974). Recognition of mother's voice in early infancy. *Nature, 252*, 123–124.

Mohr, R. D., & Zoghi, C. (2006). Is job enrichment really enriching? (U.S. Bureau of Labor Statistics Working Paper 389). Washington, DC: U.S. Bureau of Labor Statistics. Retrieved from http://www.bls.gov/ore/pdf/ec060010.pdf

Moore, K. A., Guzman, L., Hair, E. C., Lippman, L., & Garrett, S. B. (2004). Parent-teen relationships and interactions: Far more positive than not. *Child Trends Research Brief, 2004-25*. Washington, DC: Child Trends.

National Institutes of Health. (2013). *What is prenatal care and why is it important?* Retrieved from http://www.nichd.nih.gov/health/topics/pregnancy/conditioninfo/Pages/prenatal-care.aspx

Nolen-Hoeksema, S., & Larson, J. (1999). *Coping with loss.* Mahweh, NJ: Erlbaum.

Overman, W. H., Bachevalier, J., Turner, M., & Peuster, A. (1992). Object recognition versus object discrimination: Comparison between human infants and infant monkeys. *Behavioral Neuroscience, 106*, 15–29.

Paloutzian, R. F. (1996). *Invitation to the psychology of religion.* Boston, MA: Allyn & Bacon.

Parent, J., Forehand, R., Merchant, M. J., Edwards, M. C., Conners-Burrow, N. A., Long, N., & Jones, D. J. (2011). The relation of harsh and permissive discipline with child disruptive behaviors: Does child gender make a difference in an at-risk sample? *Journal of Family Violence, 26*, 527–533.

Piaget, J. (1954). *The construction of reality in the child.* New York: Basic Books.

Pickens, J. (1994). Full-term and preterm infants' perception of face-voice synchrony. *Infant Behavior and Development, 17*, 447–455.

Piaget, J. (1930). *The child's conception of the world.* New York, NY: Harcourt, Brace & World.

Piaget, J. (1932). *The moral judgment of the child*. New York, NY: Harcourt, Brace & World.

Podewils, L. J., Guallar, E., Kuller, L. H., Fried, L. P., Lopez, O. L., Carlson, M., & Lyketsos, C. G. (2005). Physical activity, APOE genotype, and dementia risk: Findings from the Cardiovascular Health Cognition Study. *American Journal of Epidemiology, 161*, 639–651.

Pollack, W., & Shuster, T. (2000). *Real boys' voices*. New York, NY: Random House.

Rhodes, R. L., Mitchell, S. L., Miller, S. C., Connor, S. R., & Teno, J. M. (2008). Bereaved family members' evaluation of hospice care: What factors influence overall satisfaction with services? *Journal of Pain and Symptom Management, 35*, 365–371.

Risley, T. R., & Hart, B. (2006). Promoting early language development. In N. F. Watt, C. Ayoub, R. H. Bradley, J. E. Puma, & W. A. LeBoeuf (Eds.), *The crisis in youth mental health: Early intervention programs and policies* (Vol. 4, pp. 83–88). Westport, CT: Praeger.

Rothbaum, R., Weisz, J., Pott, M., Miyake, K., & Morelli, G. (2000). Attachment and culture: Security in the United States and Japan. *American Psychologist, 55*, 1093–1104.

Russell, S. T., Crockett, L. J., & Chao, R. (Eds.). (2010). Asian American parenting and parent-adolescent relationships. In R. Levesque (Series Ed.), *Advancing responsible adolescent development*. New York, NY: Springer.

Ryff, C. D., & Singer, B. (2009). Understanding healthy aging: Key components and their integration. In V. L. Bengtson, D. Gans., N. M. Putney, & M. Silverstein. (Eds.), *Handbook of theories of aging* (2nd ed., pp. 117–144). New York, NY: Springer.

Samarel, N. (1991). *Caring for life after death*. Washington, DC: Hemisphere.

Sanson, A., & Rothbart, M. K. (1995). Child temperament and parenting. In M. Bornstein (Ed.), *Applied and practical parenting* (Vol. 4, pp. 299–321). Mahwah, NJ: Lawrence Erlbaum.

Schechter, C., & Byeb, B. (2007). Preliminary evidence for the impact of mixed-income preschools on low-income children's language growth. *Early Childhood Research Quarterly, 22*, 137–146.

Shamay-Tsoory, S. G., Tomer, R., & Aharon-Peretz, J. (2005). The neuroanatomical basis of understanding sarcasm and its relationship to social cognition. *Neuropsychology, 19*(3), 288–300.

Shanahan, L., McHale, S. M., Osgood, D. W., & Crouter, A. C. (2007). Conflict frequency with mothers and fathers from middle childhood to late adolescence: Within and between family comparisons. *Developmental Psychology, 43*, 539–550.

Siegler, R. S. (2005). *Children's thinking* (4th ed). Mahwah, NJ: Erlbaum.

Siegler, R. S. (2006). Microgenetic analyses of learning. In D. Kuhn & R. S. Siegler (Eds.), *Handbook of child psychology: Cognition, perception, and language* (6th ed., Vol. 2). New York: Wiley.

Sinnott, J. D. (1998). *The development of logic in adulthood: Postformal thought and its applications*. New York, NY: Springer.

Small, M. F. (1999). *Our babies, ourselves: How biology and culture shape the way we parent*. New York, NY: Anchor Books.

Spelke, E.S., & Cortelyou, A. (1981). Perceptual aspects of social knowing: Looking and listening in infancy. In M.E. Lamb & L.R. Sherrod (Eds.), *Infant social cognition: Empirical and theoretical considerations* (pp. 61–83). Hillsdale, NJ: Erlbaum.

Steinberg, L., & Morris, A. S. (2001). Adolescent development. *Annual Review of Psychology, 52,* 83–110.

Sterns, H. L., & Huyck, M. H. (2001). The role of work in midlife. In M. Lachman (Ed.), *The handbook of midlife development* (pp. 447–486). New York, NY:Wiley.

Steven L. Youngentob, et. al. (2007). Experience-induced fetal plasticity: The effect of gestational ethanol exposure on the behavioral and neurophysiologic olfactory response to ethanol odor in early postnatal and adult rats. *Behavioral Neuroscience, 121*(6), 1293–1305.

Stork, F. C., & Widdowson, D. A. (1974). *Learning about linguistics*. London, UK: Hutchinson Ltd.

Streissguth, A. P., Bookstein, F. L., Barr, H. M., Sampson, P. D., O'Malley, K., & Young, J. K. (2004). Risk factors for adverse life outcomes in fetal alcohol syndrome and fetal alcohol effects. *Developmental and Behavioral Pediatrics, 25*(4), 228–238.

Striegel-Moore, R. H., & Cachelin, F. M. (1999). Body image concerns and disordered eating in adolescent girls: Risk and protective factors. In N. G. Johnson, M. C. Roberts, & J. Worell (Eds.), *Beyond appearance: A new look at adolescent girls*. Washington, DC: American Psychological Association

Tanner, J. M. (1978). *Fetus into man: Physical growth from conception to maturity*. Cambridge, MA: Harvard University Press.

Temel, J. S., Greer, J. A., Muzikansky, A., Gallagher, E. R., Admane, S., Jackson, V. A. . . . Lynch, T. J. (2010). Early palliative care for patients with metastic non-small-cell lung cancer. *New England Journal of Medicine, 363*, 733–742.

Thomas, A. (1984). Temperament research: Where we are, where we are going. *Merrill-Palmer Quarterly, 30*(2), 103–109.

Tran, T. D., & Kelly, S. J. (2003). Critical periods for ethanol-induced cell loss in the hippocampal formation. *Neurotoxicology and Teratology, 25*(5), 519–528.

Umberson, D., Pudrovska, T., & Reczek, C. (2010). Parenthood, childlessness, and well-being: A life course perspective. *Journal of Marriage and the Family, 72*(3), 612–629.

United Nations Educational, Scientific and Cultural Organization. (2013, June). *UIS Fact Sheet: Schooling for millions of children jeopardized by reductions in aid*. Montreal, Canada: UNESCO Institute for Statistics.

Vaillant, G. E. (2002). *Aging well*. New York, NY: Little Brown & Co.

Van der Graaff, J., Branje, S., De Wied, M., Hawk, S., Van Lier, P., & Meeus, W. (2013). Perspective taking and empathetic concern in adolescence: Gender differences in developmental changes. *Developmental Psychology, 50*(3), 881.

van Ijzendoorn, M. H., & Sagi-Schwartz, A. (2008). Cross-cultural patterns of attachment: Universal and contextual dimensions. In J. Cassidy & P. R. Shaver (Eds.), *Handbook of attachment*. New York, NY: Guilford.

Vouloumanos, A., & Werker, J. F. (2004). Tuned to the signal: The privileged status of speech for young infants. *Developmental Science, 7*, 270–276.

WHO Multicentre Growth Reference Study Group. (2006). *WHO Child growth standards: Methods and development: Length/height-for-age, weight-for-age, weight-for-length, weight-for-height and body mass index-for-age*. Geneva, Switzerland: World Health Organization.

Winerman, L. (2011). Closing the achievement gap. *Monitor of Psychology, 42*(8), 36.

Wortman, J. H., & Park, C. L. (2008). Religion and spirituality in adjustment following bereavement: An integrative review. *Death Studies*

Attributions

CC licensed content, Shared previously

What Is Lifespan Development?

What you'll learn to do: compare and contrast theories lifespan development theories

Lifespan development explores how we change and grow from conception to death. This field of psychology is studied by developmental psychologists. They view development as a lifelong process that can be studied scientifically across three developmental domains: physical, cognitive development, and psychosocial.

There are many theories regarding how babies and children grow and develop into happy, healthy adults. Sigmund Freud suggested that we pass through a series of psychosexual stages in which our energy is focused on certain erogenous zones on the body. Eric Erikson modified Freud's ideas and suggested a theory of psychosocial development. Erikson said that our social interactions and successful completion of social tasks shape our sense of self. Jean Piaget proposed a theory of cognitive development that explains how children think and reason as they move through various stages. Finally, Lawrence Kohlberg turned his attention to moral development. He said that we pass through three levels of moral thinking that build on our cognitive development. You'll learn about each of these theories in this section.

Learning Objectives

- Describe the three major issues in development: continuity and discontinuity, one common course of development or many unique courses of development, and nature versus nurture

My heart leaps up when I behold
A rainbow in the sky:
So was it when my life began;
So is it now I am a man;
So be it when I shall grow old,
Or let me die!
The Child is father of the Man;
And I could wish my days to be
Bound each to each by natural piety. (Wordsworth, 1802)

In this poem, William Wordsworth writes, "the child is father of the man." What does this seemingly incongruous statement mean, and what does it have to do with lifespan development? Wordsworth might be suggesting that the person he is as an adult depends largely on the experiences he had in childhood. Consider the following questions: To what extent is the adult you are today influenced by the child you once were? To what extent is a child fundamentally different from the adult he grows up to be?

These are the types of questions developmental psychologists try to answer, by studying how humans change and grow from conception through childhood, adolescence, adulthood, and death. They view development as a lifelong process that can be studied scientifically across three developmental domains—physical, cognitive, and psychosocial development. Physical development involves growth and changes in the body and brain, the senses, motor skills, and health and wellness. Cognitive development involves learning, attention, memory, language, thinking, reasoning, and creativity. Psychosocial development involves emotions, personality, and social relationships. We refer to these domains throughout the module.

Connect the Concepts: Research Methods in Developmental Psychology

You've learned about a variety of research methods used by psychologists. Developmental psychologists use many of these approaches in order to better understand how individuals change mentally and physically over time. These methods include naturalistic observations, case studies, surveys, and experiments, among others.

Naturalistic observations involve observing behavior in its natural context. A developmental psychologist might observe how children behave on a playground, at a daycare center, or in the child's own home. While this research approach provides a glimpse into how children behave in their natural settings, researchers have very little control over the types and/or frequencies of displayed behavior.

In a case study, developmental psychologists collect a great deal of information from one individual in order to better understand physical and psychological changes over the lifespan. This particular approach is an excellent way to better understand individuals, who are exceptional in some way, but it is especially prone to researcher bias in interpretation, and it is difficult to generalize conclusions to the larger population.

In one classic example of this research method being applied to a study of lifespan development Sigmund Freud analyzed the development of a child known as "Little Hans" (Freud, 1909/1949). Freud's findings helped inform his theories of psychosexual development in children, which you will learn about later in this module. Little Genie, the subject of a case study discussed in the module on thinking and intelligence, provides another example of how psychologists examine developmental milestones through detailed research on a single individual. In Genie's case, her neglectful and abusive upbringing led to her being unable to speak until, at age 13, she was removed from that harmful environment. As she learned to use language, psychologists were able to compare how her language acquisition abilities differed when occurring in her late-stage development compared to the typical acquisition of those skills during the ages of infancy through early childhood (Fromkin, Krashen, Curtiss, Rigler, & Rigler, 1974; Curtiss, 1981).

The survey method asks individuals to self-report important information about their thoughts, experiences, and beliefs. This particular method can provide large amounts of information in relatively short amounts of time; however, validity of data collected in this way relies on honest self-reporting, and the data is relatively shallow when compared to the depth of information collected in a case study.

Experiments involve significant control over extraneous variables and manipulation of the independent variable. As such, experimental research allows developmental psychologists to make causal statements about certain variables that are important for the developmental process. Because experimental research must occur in a controlled environment, researchers must be cautious about whether behaviors observed in the laboratory translate to an individual's natural environment.

Later in this module, you will learn about several experiments in which toddlers and young children observe scenes or actions so that researchers can determine at what age specific cognitive abilities develop. For example, children may observe a quantity of liquid poured from a short, fat glass into a tall, skinny glass. As the experimenters question the children about what occurred, the subjects' answers help psychologists understand at what age a child begins to comprehend that the volume of liquid remained the same although the shapes of the containers differs.

Across these three domains—physical, cognitive, and psychosocial—the **normative approach** to development is also discussed. This approach asks, "What is normal development?" In the early decades of the 20th century, normative psychologists studied large numbers of children at various ages to determine norms (i.e., average ages) of when most children reach specific developmental milestones in each of the three domains (Gesell, 1933, 1939, 1940; Gesell & Ilg, 1946; Hall, 1904). Although children develop at slightly different rates, we can use these age-related averages as general guidelines to compare children with same-age peers to determine the approximate ages they should reach specific normative events called **developmental milestones** (e.g., crawling, walking, writing, dressing, naming colors, speaking in sentences, and starting puberty).

Not all normative events are universal, meaning they are not experienced by all individuals across all cultures. Biological milestones, such as puberty, tend to be universal, but social milestones, such as the age when children begin formal schooling, are not necessarily universal; instead, they affect most individuals in a particular **culture** (Gesell & Ilg, 1946). For example, in developed countries children begin school around 5 or 6 years old, but in developing countries, like Nigeria, children often enter school at an advanced age, if at all (Huebler, 2005; United Nations Educational, Scientific, and Cultural Organization [UNESCO], 2013).

To better understand the normative approach, imagine two new mothers, Louisa and Kimberly, who are close friends and have children around the same age. Louisa's daughter is 14 months old, and Kimberly's son is 12 months old. According to the normative approach, the average age a child starts to walk is 12 months. However, at 14 months Louisa's daughter still isn't walking. She tells Kimberly she is worried that something might be wrong with her baby. Kimberly is surprised because her son started walking when he was only 10 months old. Should Louisa be worried? Should she be concerned if her daughter is not walking by 15 months or 18 months?

Link to Learning

The Centers for Disease Control and Prevention (CDC) describes the developmental milestones for children from 2 months through 5 years old. After reviewing the information, take this quiz to see how well you recall what you've learned. If you are a parent with concerns about your child's development, contact your pediatrician.

- http://www.cdc.gov/ncbddd/actearly/milestones/

Issues in Developmental Psychology

There are many different theoretical approaches regarding human development. As we evaluate them in this module, recall that developmental psychology focuses on how people change, and keep in mind that all the approaches that we present in this module address questions of change: Is the change smooth or uneven (continuous versus discontinuous)? Is this pattern of change the same for everyone, or are there many different patterns of change (one course of development versus many courses)? How do genetics and environment interact to influence development (nature versus nurture)?

Is Development Continuous or Discontinuous?

Continuous development views development as a cumulative process, gradually improving on existing skills (Figure 1). With this type of development, there is gradual change. Consider, for example, a child's physical growth: adding inches to her height year by year. In contrast, theorists who view development as **discontinuous** believe that development takes place in unique stages: It occurs at specific times or ages. With this type of development, the change is more sudden, such as an infant's ability to conceive object permanence.

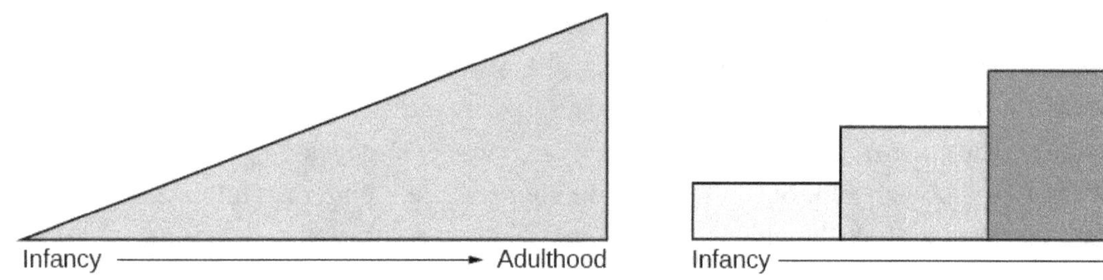

Figure 1. The concept of continuous development can be visualized as a smooth slope of progression, whereas discontinuous development sees growth in more discrete stages.

Is There One Course of Development or Many?

Is development essentially the same, or universal, for all children (i.e., there is one course of development) or does development follow a different course for each child, depending on the child's specific genetics and environment (i.e., there are many courses of development)? Do people across the world share more similarities or more differences in their development? How much do culture and genetics influence a child's behavior?

Stage theories hold that the sequence of development is universal. For example, in cross-cultural studies of language development, children from around the world reach language milestones in a similar sequence (Gleitman & Newport, 1995). Infants in all cultures coo before they babble. They begin babbling at about the same age and utter their first word around 12 months old. Yet we live in diverse contexts that have a unique effect on each of us. For example, researchers once believed that motor development follows one course for all children regardless of culture. However, child care practices vary by culture, and different practices have been found to accelerate or inhibit achievement of developmental milestones such as sitting, crawling, and walking (Karasik, Adolph, Tamis-LeMonda, & Bornstein, 2010).

For instance, let's look at the Aché society in Paraguay. They spend a significant amount of time foraging in forests. While foraging, Aché mothers carry their young children, rarely putting them down in order to protect them from getting hurt in the forest. Consequently, their children walk much later: They walk around 23–25 months old, in comparison to infants in Western cultures who begin to walk around 12 months old. However, as Aché children become older, they are allowed more freedom to move about, and by about age 9, their motor skills surpass those of U.S. children of the same age: Aché children are able to climb trees up to 25 feet tall and use machetes to chop their way through the forest (Kaplan & Dove, 1987). As you can see, our development is influenced by multiple contexts, so the timing of basic motor functions may vary across cultures. However, the functions themselves are present in all societies (Figure 2).

(a)　　　　　　　　　　　　　　　　　(b)

Figure 2. All children across the world love to play. Whether in (a) Florida or (b) South Africa, children enjoy exploring sand, sunshine, and the sea. (credit a: modification of work by "Visit St. Pete/Clearwater"/Flickr; credit b: modification of work by "stringer_bel"/Flickr)

How Do Nature and Nurture Influence Development?

Are we who we are because of nature (biology and genetics), or are we who we are because of nurture (our environment and culture)? This longstanding question is known in psychology as the nature versus nurture debate. It seeks to understand how our personalities and traits are the product of our genetic makeup and biological factors, and how they are shaped by our environment, including our parents, peers, and culture. For instance, why do biological children sometimes act like their parents—is it because of genetics or because of early childhood environment and what the child has learned from the parents? What about children who are adopted—are they more like their biological families or more like their adoptive families? And how can siblings from the same family be so different?

We are all born with specific genetic traits inherited from our parents, such as eye color, height, and certain personality traits. Beyond our basic genotype, however, there is a deep interaction between our genes and our environment: Our unique experiences in our environment influence whether and how particular traits are expressed, and at the same time, our genes influence how we interact with our environment (Diamond, 2009; Lobo, 2008). This module will show that there is a reciprocal interaction between nature and nurture as they both shape who we become, but the debate continues as to the relative contributions of each.

Dig Deeper: The Achievement Gap: How Does Socioeconomic Status Affect Development?

The achievement gap refers to the persistent difference in grades, test scores, and graduation rates that exist among students of different ethnicities, races, and—in certain subjects—sexes (Winerman, 2011). Research suggests that these achievement gaps are strongly influenced by differences in socioeconomic factors that exist among the families of these children. While the researchers acknowledge that programs aimed at reducing such socioeconomic discrepancies would likely aid in equalizing the aptitude and performance of children from different backgrounds, they recognize that such large-scale interventions would be difficult to achieve. Therefore, it is recommended that programs aimed at fostering aptitude and achievement among disadvantaged children may be the best option for dealing with issues related to academic achievement gaps (Duncan & Magnuson, 2005).

Low-income children perform significantly more poorly than their middle- and high-income peers on a number of educational variables: They have significantly lower standardized test scores, graduation rates, and college entrance rates, and they have much higher school dropout rates. There have been attempts to correct the achievement gap through state and federal legislation, but what if the problems start before the children even enter school?

Psychologists Betty Hart and Todd Risley (2006) spent their careers looking at early language ability and progression of children in various income levels. In one longitudinal study, they found that although all the parents in the study engaged and interacted with their children, middle- and high-income parents interacted with their children differently than low-income parents. After analyzing 1,300 hours of parent-child interactions, the researchers found that middle- and high-income parents talk to their children significantly more, starting when the children are infants. By 3 years old, high-income children knew almost double the number of words known by their low-income counterparts, and they had heard an estimated total of 30 million more words than the low-income counterparts (Hart & Risley, 2003). And the gaps only become more pronounced. Before entering kindergarten, high-income children score 60% higher on achievement tests than their low-income peers (Lee & Burkam, 2002).

There are solutions to this problem. At the University of Chicago, experts are working with low-income families, visiting them at their homes, and encouraging them to speak more to their children on a daily and hourly basis. Other experts are designing preschools in which students from diverse economic backgrounds are placed in the same classroom. In this research, low-income children made significant gains in their language development, likely as a result of attending the specialized preschool (Schechter & Byeb, 2007). What other methods or interventions could be used to decrease the achievement gap? What types of activities could be implemented to help the children of your community or a neighboring community?

Glossary

cognitive development: domain of lifespan development that examines learning, attention, memory, language, thinking, reasoning, and creativity

continuous development: view that development is a cumulative process: gradually improving on existing skills

developmental milestone: approximate ages at which children reach specific normative events

discontinuous development: view that development takes place in unique stages, which happen at specific times or ages

nature: genes and biology

normative approach: study of development using norms, or average ages, when most children reach specific developmental milestones

nurture: environment and culture

physical development: domain of lifespan development that examines growth and changes in the body and brain, the senses, motor skills, and health and wellness

psychosocial development: domain of lifespan development that examines emotions, personality, and social relationships

Attributions

CC licensed content, Original

- Modification, adaptation, and original content. **Provided by:** Lumen Learning. **License:** *CC BY: Attribution*

CC licensed content, Shared previously

- What is Lifespan Development?. **Authored by:** OpenStax College. **Located at:** http://cnx.org/contents/Sr8Ev5Og@5.52:-4PGiivG@5/What-Is-Lifespan-Development. **License:** *CC BY: Attribution*. **License Terms:** Download for free at http://cnx.org/content/col11629/latest/.

Psychosexual and Psychosocial Theories of Development

Psychosexual Theory of Development

Sigmund Freud (1856–1939) believed that personality develops during early childhood. For Freud, childhood experiences shape our personalities and behavior as adults. Freud viewed development as discontinuous; he believed that each of us must pass through a serious of stages during childhood, and that if we lack proper nurturance and parenting during a stage, we may become stuck, or fixated, in that stage. Freud's stages are called the stages of **psychosexual development**. According to Freud, children's pleasure-seeking urges are focused on a different area of the body, called an erogenous zone, at each of the five stages of development: oral, anal, phallic, latency, and genital.

While most of Freud's ideas have not found support in modern research, we cannot discount the contributions that Freud has made to the field of psychology. Psychologists today dispute Freud's psychosexual stages as a legitimate explanation for how one's personality develops, but what we can take away from Freud's theory is that personality is shaped, in some part, by experiences we have in childhood. These stages are discussed in detail in the module on personality.

Psychosocial Theory of Development

Erik Erikson (1902–1994) (Figure 1), another stage theorist, took Freud's theory and modified it as psychosocial theory. Erikson's **psychosocial development theory** emphasizes the social nature of our development rather than its sexual nature. While Freud believed that personality is shaped only in childhood, Erikson proposed that personality development takes place all through the lifespan. Erikson suggested that how we interact with others is what affects our sense of self, or what he called the ego identity.

Erikson proposed that we are motivated by a need to achieve competence in certain areas of our lives. According to psychosocial theory, we experience eight stages of development over our lifespan, from infancy through late adulthood. At each stage there is a conflict, or task, that we need to resolve. Successful completion of each developmental task results in a sense of competence and a healthy personality. Failure to master these tasks leads to feelings of inadequacy.

According to Erikson (1963), trust is the basis of our development during infancy (birth to 12 months). Therefore, the primary task of this stage is trust versus mistrust. Infants are dependent upon their caregivers, so caregivers who are responsive and sensitive to their infant's needs help their baby to develop a sense of trust; their baby will see the world as a safe, predictable place. Unresponsive caregivers who do not meet their baby's needs can engender feelings of anxiety, fear, and mistrust; their baby may see the world as unpredictable.

Figure 1. Erik Erikson proposed the psychosocial theory of development. In each stage of Erikson's theory, there is a psychosocial task that we must master in order to feel a sense of competence.

As toddlers (ages 1–3 years) begin to explore their world, they learn that they can control their actions and act on the environment to get results. They begin to show clear preferences for certain elements of the environment, such as food, toys, and clothing. A toddler's main task is to resolve the issue of autonomy versus shame and doubt, by working to establish independence. This is the "me do it" stage. For example, we might observe a budding sense of autonomy in a 2-year-old child who wants to choose her clothes and dress herself. Although her outfits might not be appropriate for the situation, her input in such basic decisions has an effect on her sense of independence. If denied the opportunity to act on her environment, she may begin to doubt her abilities, which could lead to low self-esteem and feelings of shame.

Once children reach the preschool stage (ages 3–6 years), they are capable of initiating activities and asserting control over their world through social interactions and play. According to Erikson, preschool children must resolve the task of initiative versus guilt. By learning to plan and achieve goals while interacting with others, preschool children can master this task. Those who do will develop self-confidence and feel a sense of purpose. Those who are unsuccessful at this stage—with their initiative misfiring or stifled—may develop feelings of guilt. How might over-controlling parents stifle a child's initiative?

During the elementary school stage (ages 6–12), children face the task of industry versus inferiority. Children begin to compare themselves to their peers to see how they measure up. They either develop a sense of pride and accomplishment in their schoolwork, sports, social activities, and family life, or they feel inferior and inadequate when they don't measure up. What are some things parents and teachers can do to help children develop a sense of competence and a belief in themselves and their abilities?

In adolescence (ages 12–18), children face the task of identity versus role confusion. According to Erikson, an adolescent's main task is developing a sense of self. Adolescents struggle with questions such as "Who am I?" and "What do I want to do with my life?" Along the way, most adolescents try on many different selves to see which ones fit. Adolescents who are successful at this stage have a strong sense of identity and are able to remain true to their beliefs and values in the face of problems and other people's perspectives. What happens to apathetic adolescents, who do not make a conscious search for identity, or those who are pressured to conform to their parents' ideas for the future? These teens will have a weak sense of self and experience role confusion. They are unsure of their identity and confused about the future.

People in early adulthood (i.e., 20s through early 40s) are concerned with intimacy versus isolation. After we have developed a sense of self in adolescence, we are ready to share our life with others. Erikson said that we must have a strong sense of self before developing intimate relationships with others. Adults who do not develop a positive self-concept in adolescence may experience feelings of loneliness and emotional isolation.

When people reach their 40s, they enter the time known as middle adulthood, which extends to the mid-60s. The social task of middle adulthood is generativity versus stagnation. Generativity involves finding your life's work and contributing to the development of others, through activities such as volunteering, mentoring, and raising children. Those who do not master this task may experience stagnation, having little connection with others and little interest in productivity and self-improvement.

From the mid-60s to the end of life, we are in the period of development known as late adulthood. Erikson's task at this stage is called integrity versus despair. He said that people in late adulthood reflect on their lives and feel either a sense of satisfaction or a sense of failure. People who feel proud of their accomplishments feel a sense of integrity, and they can look back on their lives with few regrets. However, people who are not successful at this stage may feel as if their life has been wasted. They focus on what "would have," "should have," and "could have" been. They face the end of their lives with feelings of bitterness, depression, and despair. Table 1 summarizes the stages of Erikson's theory.

Table 1. Erikson's Psychosocial Stages of Development

Stage	Age (years)	Developmental Task	Description
1	0–1	Trust vs. mistrust	Trust (or mistrust) that basic needs, such as nourishment and affection, will be met
2	1–3	Autonomy vs. shame/doubt	Develop a sense of independence in many tasks
3	3–6	Initiative vs. guilt	Take initiative on some activities—may develop guilt when unsuccessful or boundaries overstepped
4	7–11	Industry vs. inferiority	Develop self-confidence in abilities when competent or sense of inferiority when not
5	12–18	Identity vs. confusion	Experiment with and develop identity and roles
6	19–29	Intimacy vs. isolation	Establish intimacy and relationships with others
7	30–64	Generativity vs. stagnation	Contribute to society and be part of a family
8	65–	Integrity vs. despair	Assess and make sense of life and meaning of contributions

Glossary

psychosexual development: process proposed by Freud in which pleasure-seeking urges focus on different erogenous zones of the body as humans move through five stages of life

psychosocial development: process proposed by Erikson in which social tasks are mastered as humans move through eight stages of life from infancy to adulthood

Attributions

CC licensed content, Specific attribution

- Lifespan Theories. **Authored by:** OpenStax College. **Located at:** http://cnx.org/contents/ Sr8Ev5Og@5.52:Edod3PQm@5/Lifespan-Theories. **License:** *CC BY: Attribution.* **License Terms:** Download for free at http://cnx.org/content/col11629/latest/.

Cognitive Development

Learning Objectives

- Give examples of behavior and key vocabulary in each of Piaget's stages of cognitive development

Cognitive Theory of Development

Jean Piaget (1896–1980) is another stage theorist who studied childhood development (Figure 1). Instead of approaching development from a psychoanalytical or psychosocial perspective, Piaget focused on children's cognitive growth. He believed that thinking is a central aspect of development and that children are naturally inquisitive. However, he said that children do not think and reason like adults (Piaget, 1930, 1932). His theory of cognitive development holds that our cognitive abilities develop through specific stages, which exemplifies the discontinuity approach to development. As we progress to a new stage, there is a distinct shift in how we think and reason.

Piaget said that children develop schemata to help them under-stand the world. **Schemata** are concepts (mental models) that are used to help us categorize and interpret information. By the time children have reached adulthood, they have created schemata for almost everything. When children learn new information, they adjust their schemata through two processes: assimilation and accommodation. First, they assimilate new information or expe-riences in terms of their current schemata: **assimilation** is when they take in information that is comparable to what they already know. **Accommodation** describes when they change their schemata based on new information. This process continues as children interact with their environment.

Figure 1. Jean Piaget spent over 50 years studying children and how their minds develop.

For example, 2-year-old Blake learned the schema for dogs because his family has a Labrador retriever. When Blake sees other dogs in his picture books, he says, "Look mommy, dog!" Thus, he has assimilated them into his schema for dogs. One day, Blake sees a sheep for the first time and says, "Look mommy, dog!" Having a basic schema that a dog is an animal with four legs and fur, Blake thinks all furry, four-legged creatures are dogs. When Blake's mom tells him that the animal he sees is a sheep, not a dog, Blake must accom-modate his schema for dogs to include more information based on his new experiences. Blake's schema for dog was too broad, since not all furry, four-legged creatures are dogs. He now modifies his schema for dogs and forms a new one for sheep.

Like Freud and Erikson, Piaget thought development unfolds in a series of stages approximately associated with age ranges. He proposed a theory of cognitive development that unfolds in four stages: sensorimotor, preoperational, concrete operational, and formal operational.

Table 1. Piaget's Stages of Cognitive Development

Age (years)	Stage	Description	Developmental issues
0–2	Sensorimotor	World experienced through senses and actions	Object permanence Stranger anxiety
2–6	Preoperational	Use words and images to represent things, but lack logical reasoning	Pretend play Egocentrism Language development
7–11	Concrete operational	Understand concrete events and analogies logically; perform arithmetical operations	Conservation Mathematical transformations
12–	Formal operational	Formal operations Utilize abstract reasoning	Abstract logic Moral reasoning

The first stage is the **sensorimotor** stage, which lasts from birth to about 2 years old. During this stage, children learn about the world through their senses and motor behavior. Young children put objects in their mouths to see if the items are edible, and once they can grasp objects, they may shake or bang them to see if they make sounds. Between 5 and 8 months old, the child develops **object permanence**, which is the understanding that even if something is out of sight, it still exists (Bogartz, Shinskey, & Schilling, 2000). According to Piaget, young infants do not remember an object after it has been removed from sight. Piaget studied infants' reactions when a toy was first shown to an infant and then hidden under a blanket. Infants who had already developed object permanence would reach for the hidden toy, indicating that they knew it still existed, whereas infants who had not developed object permanence would appear confused.

Link to Learning

Please take a few minutes to view this brief video demonstrating different children's ability to understand object permanence:

In Piaget's view, around the same time children develop object permanence, they also begin to exhibit stranger anxiety, which is a fear of unfamiliar people. Babies may demonstrate this by crying and turning away from a stranger, by clinging to a caregiver, or by attempting to reach their arms toward familiar faces such as parents. Stranger anxiety results when a child is unable to assimilate the stranger into an existing schema; therefore, she can't predict what her experience with that stranger will be like, which results in a fear response.

Piaget's second stage is the **preoperational stage**, which is from approximately 2 to 7 years old. In this stage, children can use symbols to represent words, images, and ideas, which is why children in this stage engage in pretend play. A child's arms might become airplane wings as he zooms around the room, or a child with a stick might become a brave knight with a sword. Children also begin to use language in the preoperational stage, but they cannot understand adult logic or mentally manipulate information (the term *operational* refers to logical manipulation of information, so children at this stage are considered to be *pre*-operational). Children's logic is based on their own personal knowledge of the world so far, rather than on conventional knowledge. For example, dad gave a slice of pizza to 10-year-old Keiko and another slice to her 3-year-old brother, Kenny. Kenny's pizza slice was cut into five pieces, so Kenny told his sister that he got more pizza than she did. Children in this stage cannot perform mental operations because they have not developed an understanding of **conservation**, which is the idea that even if you change the appearance of something, it is still equal in size as long as nothing has been removed or added.

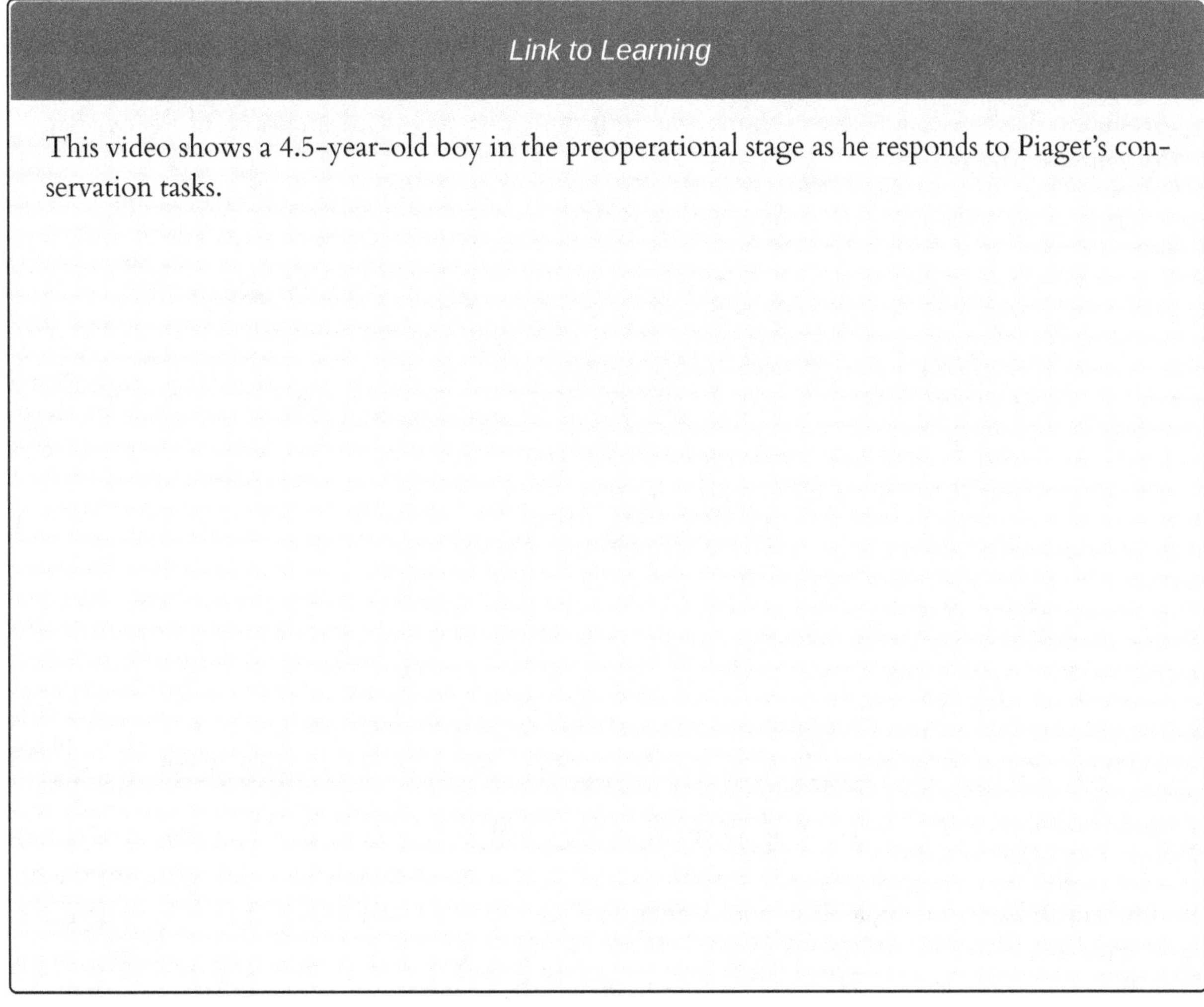

This video shows a 4.5-year-old boy in the preoperational stage as he responds to Piaget's conservation tasks.

During this stage, we also expect children to display **egocentrism**, which means that the child is not able to take the perspective of others. A child at this stage thinks that everyone sees, thinks, and feels just as they do. Let's look at Kenny and Keiko again. Keiko's birthday is coming up, so their mom takes Kenny to the toy store to choose a present for his sister. He selects an Iron Man action figure for her, thinking that if he likes the toy, his sister will too. An egocentric child is not able to infer the perspective of other people and instead attributes his own perspective. At some point during this stage and typically between 3 and 5 years old, children come to understand that people have thoughts, feelings, and beliefs that are different from their own. This is known as **theory-of-mind** (TOM).

Piaget developed the Three-Mountain Task to determine the level of egocentrism displayed by children. Children view a 3-dimensional mountain scene from one viewpoint, and are asked what another person at a different viewpoint would see in the same scene. Watch the Three-Mountain Task in action in this short vide from the University of Minnesota and the Science Museum of Minnesota.

Piaget's third stage is the **concrete operational stage**, which occurs from about 7 to 11 years old. In this stage, children can think logically about real (concrete) events; they have a firm grasp on the use of numbers and start to employ memory strategies. They can perform mathematical operations and understand transformations, such as addition is the opposite of subtraction, and multiplication is the opposite of division. In this stage, children also master the concept of conservation: Even if something changes shape, its mass, volume, and number stay the same. For example, if you pour water from a tall, thin glass to a short, fat glass, you still have the same amount of water. Remember Keiko and Kenny and the pizza? How did Keiko know that Kenny was wrong when he said that he had more pizza?

Children in the concrete operational stage also understand the principle of **reversibility**, which means that objects can be changed and then returned back to their original form or condition. Take, for example, water that you poured into the short, fat glass: You can pour water from the fat glass back to the thin glass and still have the same amount (minus a couple of drops).

The fourth, and last, stage in Piaget's theory is the **formal operational stage**, which is from about age 11 to adulthood. Whereas children in the concrete operational stage are able to think logically only about concrete events, children in the formal operational stage can also deal with abstract ideas and hypothetical situations. Children in this stage can use abstract thinking to problem solve, look at alternative solutions, and test these solutions. In adolescence, a renewed egocentrism occurs. For example, a 15-year-old with a very small pimple on her face might think it is huge and incredibly visible, under the mistaken impression that others must share her perceptions.

Beyond Formal Operational Thought

As with other major contributors of theories of development, several of Piaget's ideas have come under criticism based on the results of further research. For example, several contemporary studies support a model of development that is more continuous than Piaget's discrete stages (Courage & Howe, 2002; Siegler, 2005, 2006). Many others suggest that children reach cognitive milestones earlier than Piaget describes (Baillargeon, 2004; de Hevia & Spelke, 2010).

According to Piaget, the highest level of cognitive development is formal operational thought, which develops between 11 and 20 years old. However, many developmental psychologists disagree with Piaget, suggesting a fifth stage of cognitive development, known as the postformal stage (Basseches, 1984; Commons & Bresette, 2006; Sinnott, 1998). In postformal thinking, decisions are made based on situations and circumstances, and logic is integrated with emotion as adults develop principles that depend on contexts. One way that we can see the difference between an adult in postformal thought and an adolescent in formal operations is in terms of how they handle emotionally charged issues.

It seems that once we reach adulthood our problem solving abilities change: As we attempt to solve problems, we tend to think more deeply about many areas of our lives, such as relationships, work, and politics (Labouvie-Vief & Diehl, 1999). Because of this, postformal thinkers are able to draw on past experiences to help them solve new problems. Problem-solving strategies using postformal thought vary, depending on the situation. What does this mean? Adults can recognize, for example, that what seems to be an ideal solution to a problem at work involving a disagreement with a colleague may not be the best solution to a disagreement with a significant other.

Glossary

assimilation: adjustment of a schema by adding information similar to what is already known

accommodation: adjustment of a schema by changing a scheme to accommodate new information different from what was already known

concrete operational stage: third stage in Piaget's theory of cognitive development; from about 7 to 11 years old, children can think logically about real (concrete) events

conservation: idea that even if you change the appearance of something, it is still equal in size, volume, or number as long as nothing is added or removed

egocentrism: preoperational child's difficulty in taking the perspective of others

formal operational stage: final stage in Piaget's theory of cognitive development; from age 11 and up, children are able to deal with abstract ideas and hypothetical situations

object permanence: idea that even if something is out of sight, it still exists

preoperational stage: second stage in Piaget's theory of cognitive development; from ages 2 to 7, children learn to use symbols and language but do not understand mental operations and often think illogically

schema: (plural = schemata) concept (mental model) that is used to help us categorize and interpret information

sensorimotor stage: first stage in Piaget's theory of cognitive development; from birth through age 2, a child learns about the world through senses and motor behavior

theory-of-mind: the understanding that people have thoughts, feelings, and beliefs that are different from our own

Attributions

CC licensed content, Original

- Modification and adaptation, addition of video link. **Provided by:** Lumen Learning. **License:** *CC BY: Attribution*

CC licensed content, Specific attribution

- Lifespan Theories. **Authored by:** OpenStax. **Located at:** http://cnx.org/contents/Sr8Ev5Og@5.52:Edod3PQm@5/Lifespan-Theories. **License:** *CC BY: Attribution*. **License Terms:** Download for free at http://cnx.org/content/col11629/latest/.

All rights reserved content

- Piaget – Stage 1 – Sensorimotor stage : Object Permanence. **Authored by:** Geert Stienissen. **Located at:** https://www.youtube.com/watch?v=NCdLNuP7OA8. **License:** *Other*. **License Terms:** Standard YouTube License

- A typical child on Piaget's conservation tasks. **Authored by:** munakatay. **Located at:** https://www.youtube.com/watch?v=gnArvcWaH6I. **License:** *Other*. **License Terms:** Standard YouTube License

- Piaget's Mountains Task. **Authored by:** UofMNCYFC. **Located at:** https://www.youtube.com/watch?v=v4oYOjVDgo0. **License:** *Other*. **License Terms:** Standard YouTube License

Moral Development

Learning ObjectiveS

- Describe Kohlberg's theory of moral development and the stages of reasoning
- Explain the procedure, results, and implications of Hamlin and Wynn's research on moral reasoning in infants

Theory of Moral Development

A major task beginning in childhood and continuing into adolescence is discerning right from wrong. Psychologist Lawrence Kohlberg (1927–1987) extended upon the foundation that Piaget built regarding cognitive development. Kohlberg believed that moral development, like cognitive development, follows a series of stages. To develop this theory, Kohlberg posed moral dilemmas to people of all ages, and then he analyzed their answers to find evidence of their particular stage of moral development. Before reading about the stages, take a minute to consider how you would answer one of Kohlberg's best-known moral dilemmas, commonly known as the Heinz dilemma:

> In Europe, a woman was near death from a special kind of cancer. There was one drug that the doctors thought might save her. It was a form of radium that a druggist in the same town had recently discovered. The drug was expensive to make, but the druggist was charging ten times what the drug cost him to make. He paid $200 for the radium and charged $2,000 for a small dose of the drug. The sick woman's husband, Heinz, went to everyone he knew to borrow the money, but he could only get together about $1,000, which is half of what it cost. He told the druggist that his wife was dying and asked him to sell it cheaper or let him pay later. But the druggist said: "No, I discovered the drug and I'm going to make money from it." So Heinz got desperate and broke into the man's store to steal the drug for his wife. Should the husband have done that? (Kohlberg, 1969, p. 379)

How would you answer this dilemma? Kohlberg was not interested in whether you answer yes or no to the dilemma: Instead, he was interested in the reasoning behind your answer.

After presenting people with this and various other moral dilemmas, Kohlberg reviewed people's responses and placed them in different **stages of moral reasoning** (Figure 1). According to Kohlberg, an individual progresses from the capacity for pre-conventional morality (before age 9) to the capacity for conventional morality (early adolescence), and toward attaining post-conventional morality (once formal operational thought is attained), which only a few fully achieve. Kohlberg placed in the highest stage responses that reflected the reasoning that Heinz should steal the drug because his wife's life is more important than the pharmacist making money. The value of a human life overrides the pharmacist's greed.

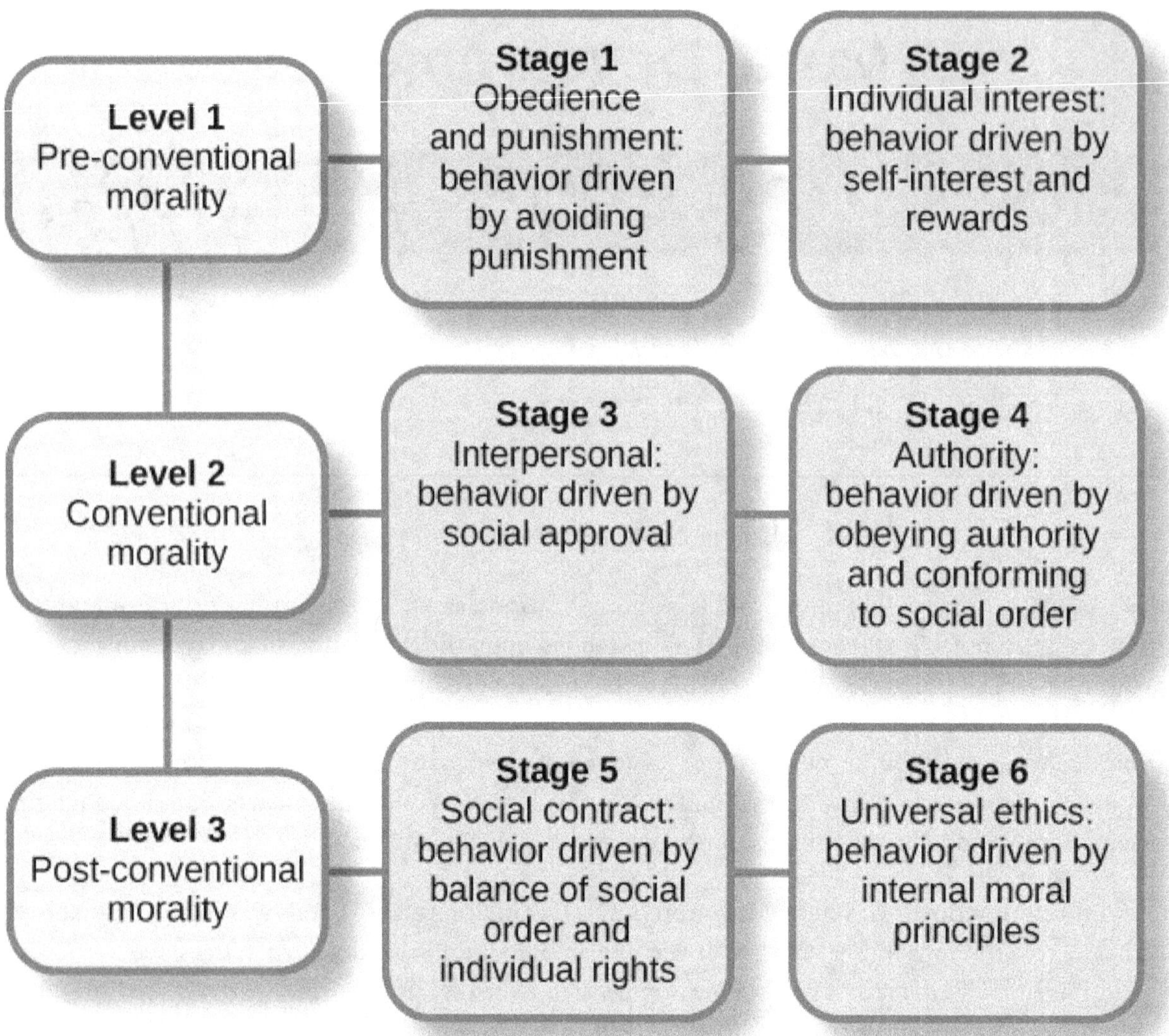

Figure 1. Kohlberg identified three levels of moral reasoning: pre-conventional, conventional, and post-conventional: Each level is associated with increasingly complex stages of moral development.

It is important to realize that even those people who have the most sophisticated, post-conventional reasons for some choices may make other choices for the simplest of pre-conventional reasons. Many psychologists agree with Kohlberg's theory of moral development but point out that moral reasoning is very different from moral behavior. Sometimes what we say we would do in a situation is not what we actually do in that situation. In other words, we might "talk the talk," but not "walk the walk."

How does this theory apply to males and females? Kohlberg (1969) felt that more males than females move past stage four in their moral development. He went on to note that women seem to be deficient in their moral reasoning abilities. These ideas were not well received by Carol Gilligan, a research assistant of Kohlberg, who consequently developed her own ideas of moral development. In her groundbreaking book, *In a Different Voice: Psychological Theory and Women's Development*, Gilligan (1982) criticized her former mentor's theory because it was based only on upper class white men and boys. She argued that women are not deficient in their moral reasoning—she proposed that males and females reason differently. Girls and women focus more on staying connected and the importance of interpersonal relationships. Therefore, in the Heinz dilemma, many girls and women respond that Heinz should not steal the medicine. Their reasoning is that if he steals the medicine, is arrested, and is put in jail, then he and his wife will be separated, and she could die while he is still in prison.

The Foundation of Moral Reasoning in Infants

The work of Lawrence Kohlberg was an important start to modern research on moral development and reasoning. However, Kohlberg relied on a specific method: he presented moral dilemmas (like the Heinz problem) and asked children and adults to explain what they would do and—more importantly—why they would act in that particular way. Kohlberg found that children tended to make choices based on avoiding punishment and gaining

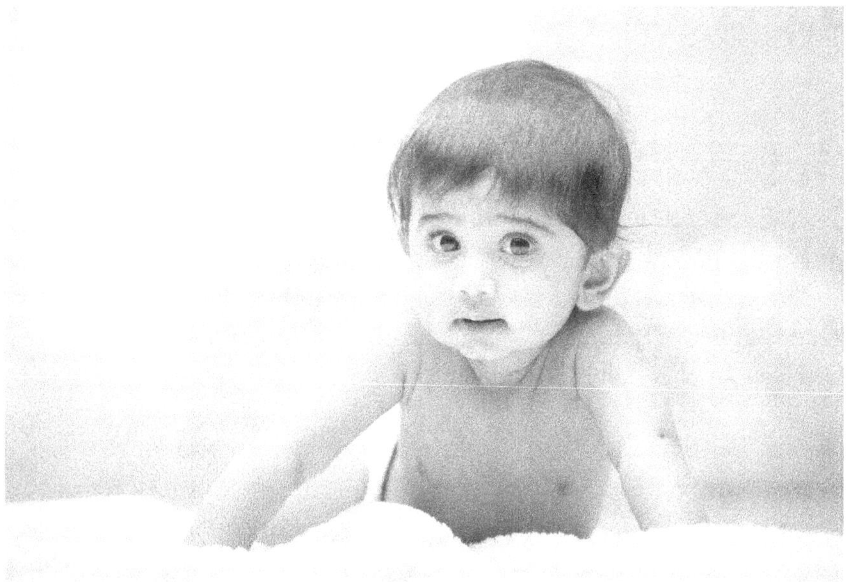

Figure 2. Maybe babies know more than we think they do!

praise. But children are at a disadvantage compared to adults when they must rely on language to convey their inner thoughts and emotional reactions, so what they say may not adequately capture the complexity of their thinking.

Starting in the 1980s, developmental psychologists created new methods for studying the thought processes of children, even of infants long before they acquire language. One particularly effective method is to present children with puppet shows, which grab their attention, and then record non-verbal behaviors, such as looking and choosing, to identify children's preferences or interests.

A research group at Yale University has been using the puppet show technique to study moral thinking of children for much of the past decade. What they have discovered has given us a glimpse of surprisingly complex thought processes that may serve as the foundation of moral reasoning.

EXPERIMENT 1: Do children prefer givers or takers?

In 2011, J. Kiley Hamlin and Karen Wynn put on puppet shows for very young children: 5-month-old infants. The infants watch a puppet bouncing a ball. We'll call this puppet the "bouncer puppet." Two other puppets stand at the back of the stage, one to left and the other to the right. After a few bounces, the ball gets away from the bouncer puppet and rolls to the side of the stage toward one of the other puppets. This puppet grabs the ball. The bouncer puppet turns toward the ball and opens its arms, as if asking for the ball back.

This is where the puppet show gets interesting (for a young infant, anyway!). Sometimes, the puppet with the ball rolls it back to the bouncer puppet. This is the "giver puppet" condition. Other times, the infant sees a different ending. As the bouncer puppet opens its arms to ask for the ball, the puppet with the ball turns and runs away with it. This is the "taker puppet" condition. Although the giver and taker puppets are two copies of the same animal doll, they are easily distinguished because they are wearing different colored shirts, and color is a quality that infants easily distinguish and remember. It looks like this:

https://s3-us-west-2.amazonaws.com/oerfiles/Psychology/Bouncerhelper.mp4

Each infant sees both conditions: the giver condition and the taker condition. Just after the end of the second puppet show (i.e., the second condition), a new researcher, who doesn't know which puppet was the giver and which was the taker, sits in front of the infant with the giver puppet in one hand and the taker puppet in the other. The 5-month-old infants are allowed to reach for a puppet. The one the child reaches out to touch is considered the preferred puppet.

Remember that Lawrence Kohlberg thought that children at this age—and, in fact, through 9 years of age—are primarily motivated to avoid punishment and seek rewards. Neither Kohlberg nor Carol Gilligan nor Jean Piaget was likely to predict that infants would develop preferences based on the type of behavior shown by other individuals.

Work It Out

The puppet show is over and the experimenter is holding the two dolls—the giver puppet and the taker puppet—in front of the infant. The reaching behavior of the infant is being videotaped for later analysis.

What do you think? Make a prediction about the results of this study—which should reflect your own "theory" of children's ability to judge and care about the types of behavior others display. Do you think infants will choose the taker or the giver puppet? Do you expect the results to be significant? Explain your answer in the text box below:

[practice-area rows="4"][/practice-area]

INSTRUCTIONS: Adjust the pink bar on the left to show the percentage of infants who reached for the giver puppet. The yellow bar on the right will automatically adjust to make the total (sum of both bars) equal 100%.

Here are the results from Experiment 1:

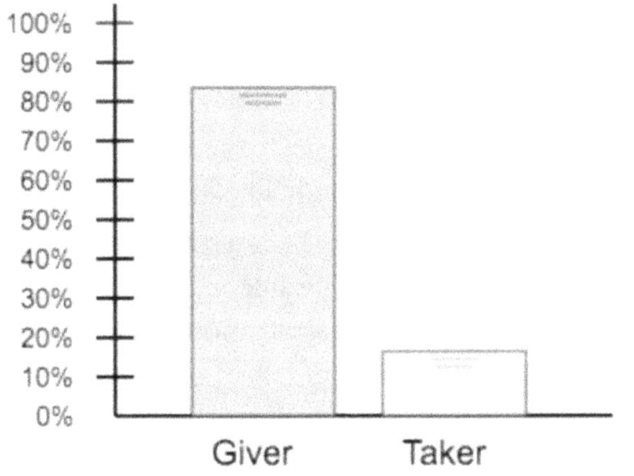

Figure 3. Results from experiment 1.

Experiment 1 suggests that these 5-month-old infants are not just passive observers in the world. They notice what others do and, if we are interpreting the results of experiments like this one correctly, they distinguish helpful behaviors ("prosocial behaviors") from behaviors that hurt others ("antisocial behaviors"). But they do more that that. They are attracted to those who are acting in a prosocial way, and they reject those who act in an antisocial way.

These researchers also tested infants who were only 3-months old. These infants were so immature that they did not yet have good control of their arms, so the experimenter could not use "reaching for one of the puppets" as the dependent variable, as they did with the 5-month-olds. Three-month-old infants can control where they look quite well, and previous research has indicated that very young infants will look longer at objects they want. The researchers showed these very young infants the same puppet shows that were described above and then, during the choice phase, they recorded which puppet (giver or taker) the 3-month-olds looked at longer. The results were very similar to those found with the 5-month-olds. A strong majority of younger infants (92%) looked longer at the giver puppet than the taker puppet.

But this isn't the end of the story…

EXPERIMENT 2: Do infants judge others based on their behavior?

In the research world, the early attempts to study something, when the researchers work to develop a solid and reliable research procedure, is often the most challenging time. Once the researcher works through initial problems and issues and begins to get consistent results, he or she can gain a deeper understanding by adding new variables or testing different groups of subjects (e.g., older children or children with some interesting psychological characteristics).

The study you just read about is an example of a simple, basic study. The researchers found that infants preferred puppets that help another puppet (the puppet in the giver condition) over puppets that are not nice to another puppet (the puppet in the taker condition). A common sense interpretation of this simple result is that infants like nice behavior and they dislike hurtful behavior. And perhaps that is as complicated as an 8-month-old infant's thoughts can be. But maybe not.

Dr. Hamlin and her colleagues wondered if infants might consider more factors when judging an event. Adults generally prefer situations where good things happen to someone rather than something harmful. However, when adults see someone do something bad, they may find satisfaction in seeing that person punished by having something bad happen to him or her. In a nutshell: good things should happen to good people and bad things should happen to bad people. This is what is called "just world" thinking, where people get what they deserve.

In the study we will call Experiment 2, Hamlin's team tested 8-month-old infants and repeated the procedures from Experiment 1 with a major addition. In Experiment 1 (described above), the puppet bouncing the ball was a neutral character, neither good nor bad. In Experiment 2, the infants saw 2 different shows. First, they saw the bouncer puppet either helping or hindering another puppet. Then, they watched the same ball-bouncing puppet show. Here is what happened:

- Puppet Show #1: A puppet is trying to open a box, but cannot quite succeed. Two puppets stand in the background. For some infants, as the first puppet struggles to open the box, one of the puppets in the back comes forward and helps to open the box. This is the helper puppet. For other children, as the first puppet struggles, a puppet comes from the back and jumps on the box, slamming it shut. This is the hinderer puppet. Each infant sees only a helper or a hinderer—not both. Here is a video showing the helper puppet situation:

https://s3-us-west-2.amazonaws.com/oerfiles/Psychology/Boxlidhelper.mp4

- Puppet Show #2: Just after the infants have watched the first show, the second puppet show begins. This is the show that you read about in Experiment 1. The only thing that is new is that the bouncer puppet, the one that loses the ball, is either the helper puppet from Puppet Show #1 or the hinderer puppet from Puppet Show #1. Each infant sees this puppet lose the ball to a giver, who returns the ball, and to a taker, who runs off with the ball.

This video shows both of the shows. In show #1, the duck is trying to open a box and the elephant in the yellow shirt helps the duck, while the elephant in the red shirt hinders the duck. In show #2, the same elephant in the yellow shirt is now bouncing a ball. After dropping the ball, the moose in the green shirt gives it back to him, while the moose in the red shirt takes it away.

So far we have concluded that even young babies prefer the "nice" puppet and show a preference for a puppet who helps another puppet. But this only happened when the bouncer puppet was the Helper from the first puppet show. What if, instead of the nice elephant in the yellow shirt bouncing the ball, the elephant in the red shirt (the one who jumped on the duck's box, remember?) was the one bouncing the ball? Imagine the same scenario: the mean elephant in red shirt is bouncing the ball, he drops it, and the moose in the green shirt gives it to him or the moose in the red shirt takes it away.

So now things are getting interesting, right? Do 8-month old infants understand the concepts of revenge or justice? We must always be careful when labeling behaviors of children (or animals) with characteristics we use for human adults. In the description above, we have talked of "nice puppets" and "mean puppets" and used other loaded terms. It is tempting to interpret the choices of the 8-month-olds as a kind of revenge motive: the bad guy gets its just desserts (the hinderer puppet has its ball stolen) and the good guy gets its just reward (the helper puppet is itself helped by the giver). Maybe that is what is going on, but we encourage you to consider these very sophisticated types of thinking as merely one hypothesis. Remember the facts—what did the puppets do and what choices did the infants make?—without committing yourself to the adult-level interpretation.

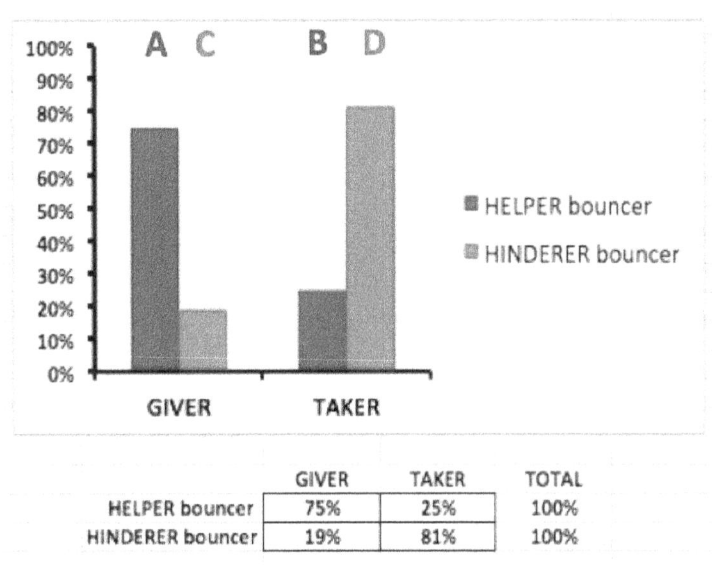

	GIVER	TAKER	TOTAL
HELPER bouncer	75%	25%	100%
HINDERER bouncer	19%	81%	100%

Figure 4. This bar graph shows the results of Experiment 2 for 8-month-old infants. The blue bars show the preferences for the infants who saw the Helper from the first show as the bouncer in the second. Bar A is taller than Bar B, showing the greater choice of the Giver than the Taker puppet. The red bars show the reverse effect. The babies strongly preferred the Taker (Bar C) to the Giver (Bar D) when the puppet bouncing the ball had been the Hinderer, who jumped on the box in the first show.

The researchers believe that this type of thinking, which is remarkably sophisticated, takes some cognitive development. They tested 5-month-olds using the same procedures, and the results with these younger infants was different. The 5-month-olds showed an overwhelming preference for the giver puppets, regardless of who was bouncing the ball. Maybe it is too complex for them to understand that the bouncer puppet in the second show was the same puppet from the first show, Or perhaps their memory processes are too fragile to hold onto information for that length of time. Possibly the "revenge" motive is too advanced a way of thinking. Or maybe something else is going on. What is clear is that 5-month-olds and 8-month-olds respond differently to the situations tested in the second experiment.

EXPERIMENT 3: Do infants judge others based on their preferences?

Across the first two experiments, infants appear to prefer puppets (and, by extension, maybe people, as well) that are helpful over those that are not helpful. Experiment 2 complicated our story a bit, but it still appears that prosocial behavior is attractive to infants and antisocial behavior is unattractive. But another experiment, again using the bouncing ball show, suggests that infants as young as 8-months of age may have some other motives that are less altruistic than the first two experiments indicate.

In a study by Hamlin, Mahanjan, Liberman, and Wynn from 2013, 9-month-old infants watched the bouncing ball show, but with a new twist.

At the beginning of the experiment—**Phase 1**—the infants were given a choice between graham crackers and green beans. The experimenters determined which food the infant preferred.

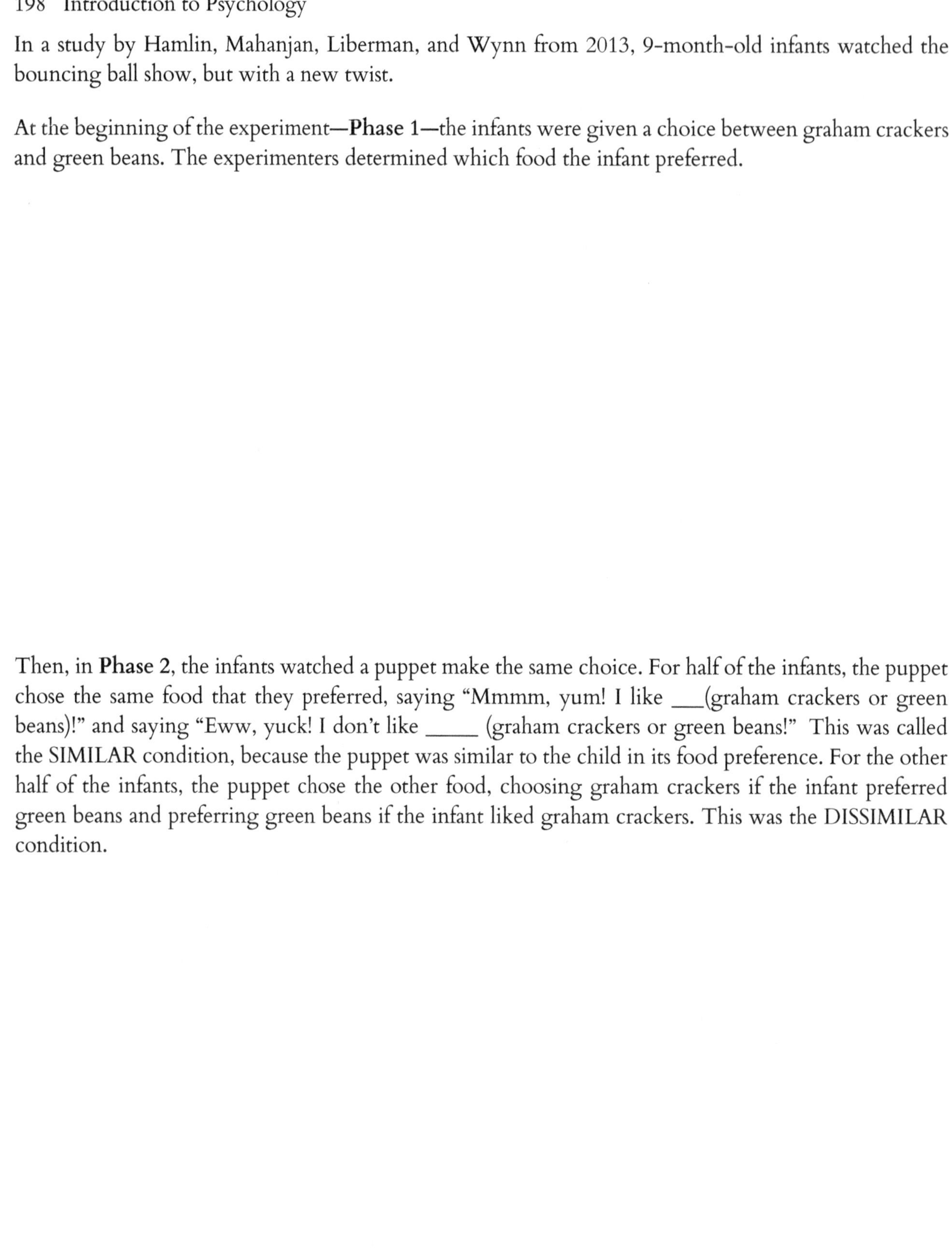

Then, in **Phase 2**, the infants watched a puppet make the same choice. For half of the infants, the puppet chose the same food that they preferred, saying "Mmmm, yum! I like ___(graham crackers or green beans)!" and saying "Eww, yuck! I don't like _____ (graham crackers or green beans!" This was called the SIMILAR condition, because the puppet was similar to the child in its food preference. For the other half of the infants, the puppet chose the other food, choosing graham crackers if the infant preferred green beans and preferring green beans if the infant liked graham crackers. This was the DISSIMILAR condition.

Why did experimenters do this? They wanted to know if young children form in-groups and out-groups by perceiving some people as being like them and other people as being unlike them. The experimenters noted in their research introduction that we (adults) are influenced by our perception that others are similar to us or not like us. We tend to project positive qualities—being trustworthy, intelligent, kind—on people we perceive as similar to ourselves, and people we see as unlike us are seen as having negative qualities—being relatively untrustworthy, unintelligent, and unkind.[1]

Of course, there is a big difference between claiming that adults use similarity to make judgments about others and saying that infants less than a year of age do the same thing. However, the researchers note that some recent research has suggested that infants less than a year old are more likely to develop peer friendships with other infants who "share their own food, clothing or toy preferences" compared to those who don't.

So, back to the experiment. In **Phase 3**, the infants either saw a similar puppet (one that chose the food the baby preferred) or a dissimilar puppet (one that chose the food the baby did not prefer) bouncing the ball. As in the other experiments, the ball got away from the bouncer and rolled to the back of the stage. In one instance, the giver puppet returned the ball and, in the other instance, the other puppet ran away with the ball. Finally, in **Phase 4**, the 9-month-old baby was shown the giver and taker puppet and the experimenters recorded which of the two puppets the baby preferred (reached out to touch). This video shows the dog in the light blue shirt giving the ball back to the red bunny that preferred graham crackers.

---

1. The experimenters support these claims by citing the following studies: (1) DeBruine, L.M. Facial resemblance enhances trust: Proceedings of the Royal Society of London B, 2002, 269: 1307-1312. (2) Brewer, M.B. In-group bias in the minimal intergroup situation: A cognitive-motivational analysis. Psychological Bulletin, 1979, 86: 307-324. (3) Doise, W., Cspely, G., Dann, and others. An experimental investigation into the formation of intergroup representation. European Journal of Social Psychology, 1972, 2: 202-204.

Here is a summary of the four phases in Experiment 3:

- Phase 1: The infant chooses graham crackers or green beans.
- Phase 2: The bouncer puppets chooses graham crackers or green beans.
    - Similar condition: The bouncer chooses the same food that the infant chose.
    - Dissimilar condition: The bouncer chooses the food that the infant did not choose.
- Phase 3: This is the same bouncing ball experiment that you have been reading about.
    - Remember that each child sees both the Giver and Taker shows.
- Phase 4: This is the same choice—Giver or Taker—that was the final phase in the other two experiments

Work It Out

Now make predictions for the results. Here is a matrix picture of the design of the experiment:

		OTHER PUPPET in SHOW	
		GIVER puppet	**TAKER puppet**
BOUNCER	**SIMILAR to child**	A	B
food choice	**DISSIMILAR from child**	C	D

INSTRUCTIONS: Adjust bars A and C to make your predictions. Bar A represents the "nice" puppet who gave the ball to the bouncer puppet that liked the same food as the child, while bar B represents the "mean" puppet who took the ball away from the bouncer puppet who liked the same food as the child. Bar C represents the "nice" puppet who gave the ball back to the puppet who did not like the same food as the child, and bar D represents the puppet who took the ball away from the puppet who did not like the same food.

As before, move the bars on the left to indicate the percentage of infants preferring the giver puppet in the similar condition (purple bars) and in the dissimilar condition (green bars). The bars on the right will adjust to make the total in each of the similarity conditions equal 100%.

After you have recorded your predictions, click the "Show Answer" link to see the results from the experiment.

Here are the results from Experiment 3:

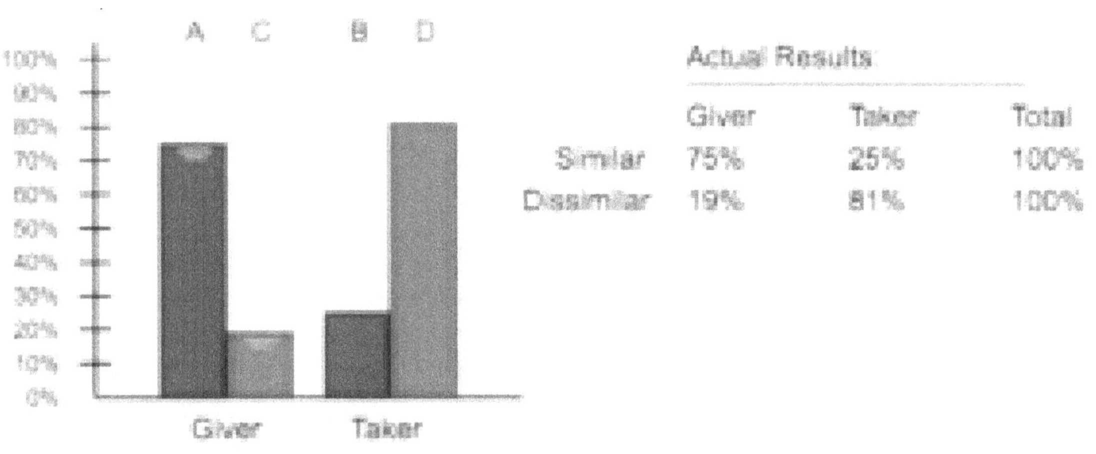

Figure 5. Results from experiment 3.

These results are similar to those for the 8-month-olds in the previous experiment. But remember that, in this experiment, the variable that distinguishes the two bouncer puppets was a food choice, not the prosocial or antisocial behavior in Experiment 2. If we take the results from Experiments 2 and 3 together, the results here suggest that the similar puppet is being treated as if it is nice or good. Puppets that treat this similar puppet in a nice way are preferred. Conversely, the dissimilar puppets are treated as if they have done something negative and puppets that treat these dissimilar puppets badly are preferred.

The experimenters also tested an older group of babies that were 14-months-old. The results for these older babies were consistent with the 9-month-old and, if anything, the effects were stronger. Their results showed that all infants preferred when the giver puppet was nice to the puppet that was similar to them and all infants preferred when puppets were mean to the puppet that was dissimilar to them.

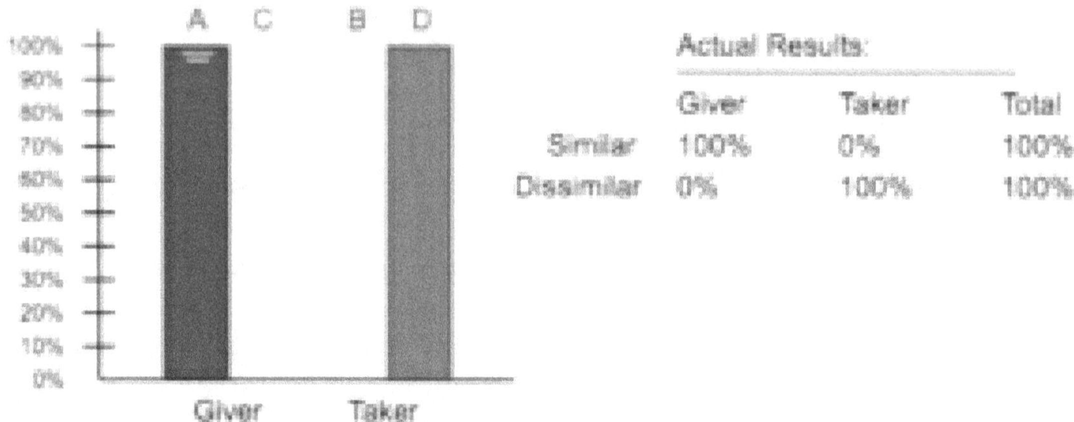

Figure 6. These bar graphs show the results of the experiment when 14-month olds were tested. 100% of the children chose the puppet that gave the ball back to the puppet that was similar to them, and 100% of children chose the puppet that took the ball away from the puppet that had a different preference than they did.

CONCLUSIONS

This exercise started with a reminder that Lawrence Kohlberg found that children went through a long developmental process in their moral reasoning. Based on children's reasoning aloud about moral dilemmas, Kohlberg concluded that children younger than about 8 or 9 years of age make moral decisions based on avoiding punishment and receiving praise. Neither his research nor that of most others in the 1970s and 1980s suggested that young children would use multiple sources of information and judgments about the meaning of behaviors in their thinking what sorts of behaviors are better or worse.

If Dr. Hamlin and her colleagues are right, then infants are much more sophisticated and complex in their thinking about the world than these earlier researchers thought. In Dr. Hamlin's view, infants like good things to happen to good puppets and people, and bad things to happen to bad puppets and people. Experiment 3 suggests that they make judgments about more than helping and harming behavior. They prefer others who are like them (green beans vs. graham crackers) and they don't mind if others who are not like them have unpleasant experiences.

The research we have been reviewing is just part of an impressive set of research on infant thinking. The ideas that the researchers have developed are intriguing and they are consistent with the modern view of the infant as an active, creative thinker. At the same time, remember that science doesn't rest on an early set of explanations based on a small set of complicated experiments. Science pushed beyond what we currently know and believe. This starts with curiosity on your part. Are the experimenters correct in interpreting reaching behavior as showing a preference or is something else going on? Do infants really prefer prosocial behaviors to antisocial behaviors, or is there some other explanation for their preferences? How else could we test moral judgments of infants without using puppet shows? The next generation of creative scientists will push beyond what we know now, with new research methods and new ideas about the mind.

We'll give Dr. Hamlin the last word. Here is part of her conclusion section from an article that summarizes some of the research we have been studying: "In sum, recent developmental research supports the claim that at least some aspects of human morality are innate…Indeed, these early tendencies are far from shallow, mechanical predispositions to behave well or knee-jerk reactions to particular states of the world. Infant moral inclinations are sophisticated, flexible, and surprisingly consistent with adults' moral inclinations, incorporating aspects of moral goodness, evaluation, and retaliation. " [Hamlin, 2013, p. 191]

Key Takeaways

stage of moral reasoning: process proposed by Kohlberg; humans move through three stages of moral development

https://assessments.lumenlearning.com/assessments/4845

Attributions

CC licensed content, Original

- Psychology in Real Life: Moral Reasoning. **Authored by:** Patrick Carroll for Lumen Learning. **Provided by:** Lumen Learning. **License:** *CC BY: Attribution*
- Similar/Dissimilar Puppet Preference Example. **Provided by:** UBCHamlinLab . **Located at:** https://www.youtube.com/watch?v=aT4ljlQw-Io. **License:** *All Rights Reserved*

CC licensed content, Shared previously

- Picture of baby. **Authored by:** adtkedia . **Located at:** https://pixabay.com/p-1709003/?no_redirect. **License:** *CC0: No Rights Reserved*

All rights reserved content

- Videos shared with permission from Kiley Hamlin. **Provided by:** The University of British Columbia: Vancouver Campus. **Located at:** http://cic.psych.ubc.ca/media-videos/. **License:** *All Rights Reserved*
- Babies want bad behavior punished video. **Authored by:** Kiley Hamlin. **Provided by:** Live Science. **Located at:** http://www.livescience.com/17205-babies-bad-behavior-punished.html. **License:** *All Rights Reserved*
- Graham Cracker Choice. **Provided by:** UBCHamlinLab. **Located at:** https://www.youtube.com/watch?v=VY005Pia4uA. **License:** *All Rights Reserved*
- Nice Blue Dog. **Provided by:** UBCHamlinLab . **Located at:** https://www.youtube.com/watch?v=Ijiru5ggPVQ. **License:** *All Rights Reserved*

Prenatal Development

What you'll learn to do: explain the physical, cognitive, and emotional development that occurs from infancy through childhood

Think about the miraculous development that occurs during childhood in order for a tiny zygote to grow into a walking, talking, thinking child. Newborn infants only weigh about 7.5 pounds but their physical, cognitive, and psychosocial skills grow and change as they move through developmental stages. In this section, you'll learn about many of these changes. Some of these key concepts are discussed (as well as others you learned about previously) in the following CrashCourse Psychology video:

Learning Objectives

- Describe the stages of prenatal development and the significance of prenatal care
- Define and differentiate between various infant reflexes

As discussed at the beginning of this module, developmental psychologists often divide our development into three areas: physical development, cognitive development, and psychosocial development. Mirroring Erikson's stages, lifespan development is divided into different stages that are based on age. We will discuss prenatal, infant, child, adolescent, and adult development.

Prenatal Development

How did you come to be who you are? From beginning as a one-cell structure to your birth, your **prenatal development** occurred in an orderly and delicate sequence.

There are three stages of prenatal development: germinal, embryonic, and fetal. Let's take a look at what happens to the developing baby in each of these stages.

Germinal Stage (Weeks 1–2)

In the discussion of biopsychology earlier in the book, you learned about genetics and DNA. A mother and father's DNA is passed on to the child at the moment of conception. Conception occurs when sperm fertilizes an egg and forms a **zygote** (Figure 1). A zygote begins as a one-cell structure that is created when a sperm and egg merge. The genetic makeup and sex of the baby are set at this point. During the first week after conception, the zygote divides and multiplies, going from a one-cell structure to two cells, then four cells, then eight cells, and so on. This process of cell division is called mitosis. **Mitosis** is a fragile process, and fewer than one-half of all zygotes survive beyond the first two weeks (Hall, 2004). After 5 days of mitosis there are 100 cells, and after 9 months there are billions of cells. As the cells divide, they become more specialized, forming different organs and body parts. In the germinal stage, the mass of cells has yet to attach itself to the lining of the mother's uterus. Once it does, the next stage begins.

Embryonic Stage (Weeks 3–8)

After the zygote divides for about 7–10 days and has 150 cells, it travels down the fallopian tubes and implants itself in the lining of the uterus. Upon implantation, this multi-cellular organism is called an **embryo.** Now blood vessels grow, forming the placenta. The **placenta** is a structure connected to the uterus that provides nourishment and oxygen from the mother to the developing embryo via the umbilical cord. Basic structures of the embryo start to develop into areas that will become the head, chest, and abdomen. During the embryonic stage, the heart begins

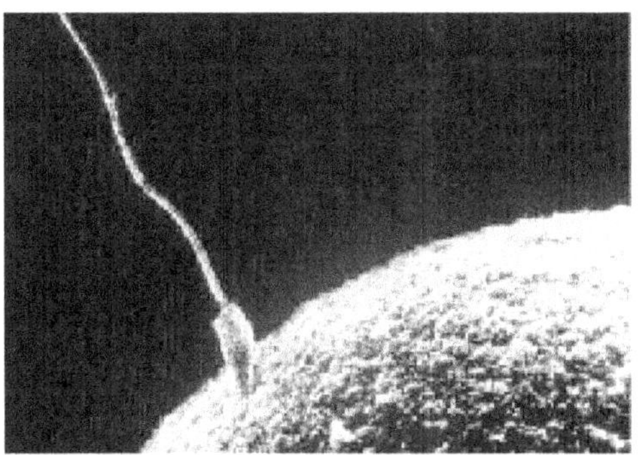

Figure 1. Sperm and ovum fuse at the point of conception.

to beat and organs form and begin to function. The neural tube forms along the back of the embryo, developing into the spinal cord and brain.

Fetal Stage (Weeks 9–40)

When the organism is about nine weeks old, the embryo is called a fetus. At this stage, the fetus is about the size of a kidney bean and begins to take on the recognizable form of a human being as the "tail" begins to disappear.

From 9–12 weeks, the sex organs begin to differentiate. At about 16 weeks, the fetus is approximately 4.5 inches long. Fingers and toes are fully developed, and fingerprints are visible. By the time the fetus reaches the sixth month of development (24 weeks), it weighs up to 1.4 pounds. Hearing has developed, so the fetus can respond to sounds. The internal organs, such as the lungs, heart, stomach, and intestines, have formed enough that a fetus born prematurely at this point has a chance to survive outside of the mother's womb. Throughout the fetal stage the brain continues to grow and develop, nearly doubling in size from weeks 16 to 28. Around 36 weeks, the fetus is almost ready for birth. It weighs about 6 pounds and is about 18.5 inches long, and by week 37 all of the fetus's organ systems are developed enough that it could survive outside the mother's uterus without many of the risks associated with premature birth. The fetus continues to gain weight and grow in length until approximately 40 weeks. By then, the fetus has very little room to move around and birth becomes imminent. The progression through the stages is shown in Figure 2.

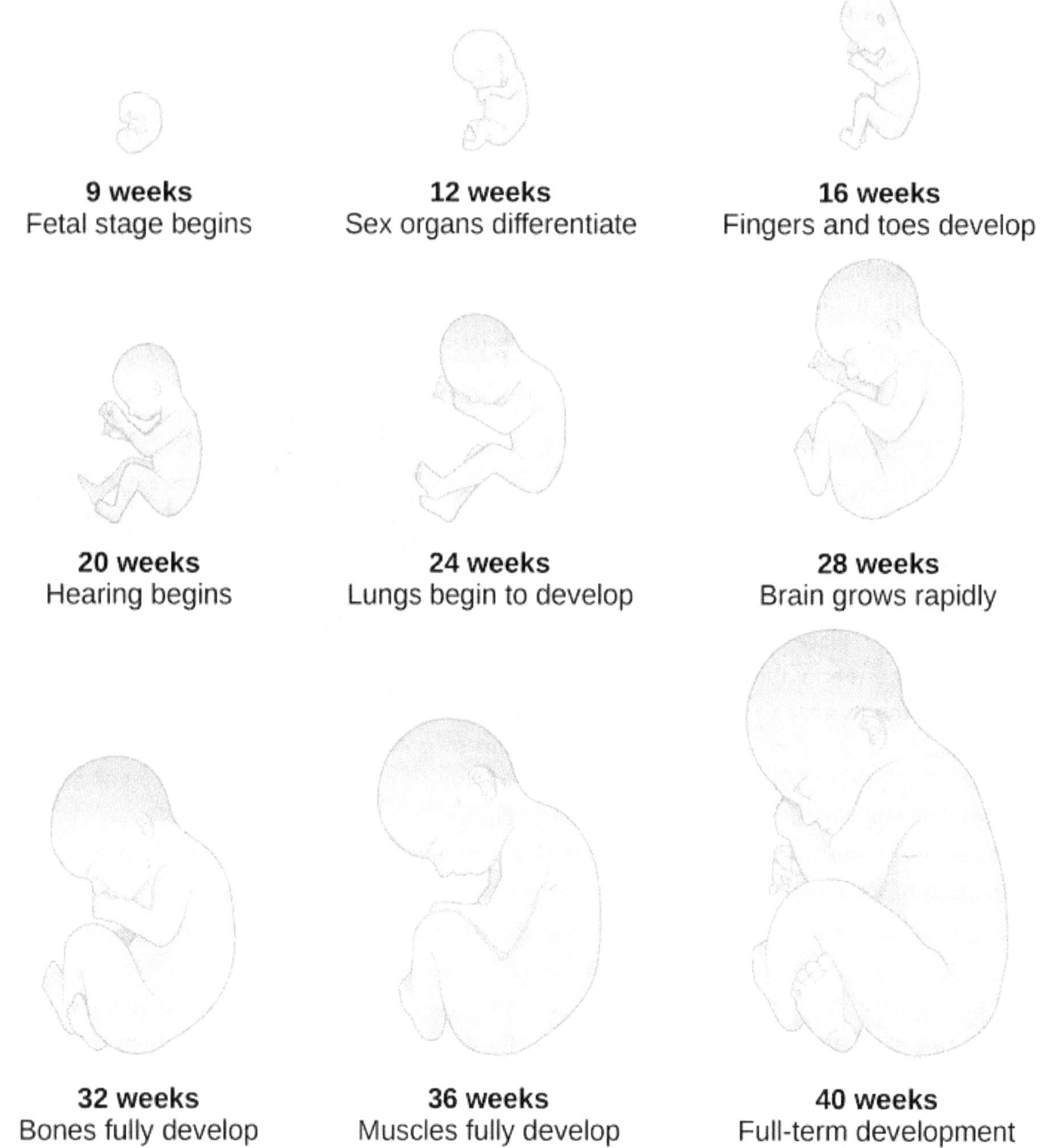

Figure 2. During the fetal stage, the baby's brain develops and the body adds size and weight, until the fetus reaches full-term development.

Prenatal Influences

During each prenatal stage, genetic and environmental factors can affect development. The developing fetus is completely dependent on the mother for life. It is important that the mother takes good care of herself and receives **prenatal care**, which is medical care during pregnancy that monitors the health of both the mother and the fetus (Figure 2). According to the National Institutes of Health

([NIH], 2013), routine prenatal care is important because it can reduce the risk of complications to the mother and fetus during pregnancy. In fact, women who are trying to become pregnant or who may become pregnant should discuss pregnancy planning with their doctor. They may be advised, for example, to take a vitamin containing folic acid, which helps prevent certain birth defects, or to monitor aspects of their diet or exercise routines.

Recall that when the zygote attaches to the wall of the mother's uterus, the placenta is formed. The placenta provides nourishment and oxygen to the fetus. Most everything the mother ingests, including food, liquid, and even medication, travels through the placenta to the fetus, hence the common phrase "eating for two." Anything the mother is exposed to in the environment affects the fetus; if the mother is exposed to something harmful, the child can show life-long effects.

A **teratogen** is any environmental agent—biological, chemical, or physical—that causes damage to the developing embryo or fetus. There are different types of terato-

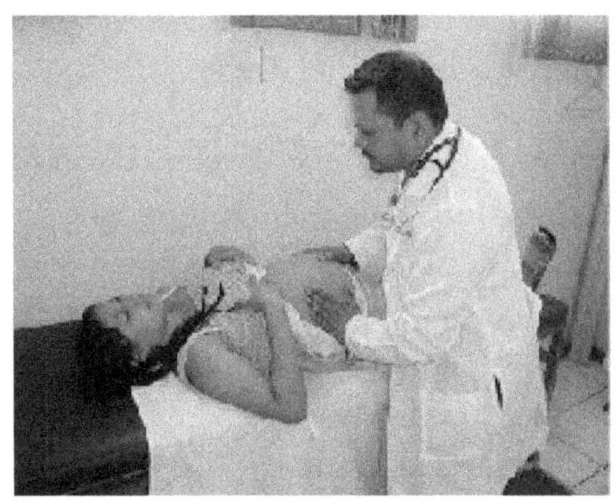

Figure 2. A pregnant woman receives an ultrasound as part of her prenatal care. (credit: United States Agency for International Development)

gens. Alcohol and most drugs cross the placenta and affect the fetus. Alcohol is not safe to drink in any amount during pregnancy. Alcohol use during pregnancy has been found to be the leading preventable cause of mental retardation in children in the United States (Maier & West, 2001). Excessive maternal drinking while pregnant can cause fetal alcohol spectrum disorders with life-long consequences for the child ranging in severity from minor to major (Table 1). Fetal alcohol spectrum disorders (FASD) are a collection of birth defects associated with heavy consumption of alcohol during pregnancy. Physically, children with FASD may have a small head size and abnormal facial features. Cognitively, these children may have poor judgment, poor impulse control, higher rates of ADHD, learning issues, and lower IQ scores. These developmental problems and delays persist into adulthood (Streissguth et al., 2004). Based on studies conducted on animals, it also has been suggested that a mother's alcohol consumption during pregnancy may predispose her child to like alcohol (Youngentob et al., 2007).

Table 1. Fetal Alcohol Syndrome Facial Features

Facial Feature	Potential Effect of Fetal Alcohol Syndrome
Head size	Below-average head circumference
Eyes	Smaller than average eye opening, skin folds at corners of eyes
Nose	Low nasal bridge, short nose
Midface	Smaller than average midface size
Lip and philtrum	Thin upper lip, indistinct philtrum

Smoking is also considered a teratogen because nicotine travels through the placenta to the fetus. When the mother smokes, the developing baby experiences a reduction in blood oxygen levels. According to the Centers for Disease Control and Prevention (2013), smoking while pregnant can result in premature birth, low-birth-weight infants, stillbirth, and sudden infant death syndrome (SIDS).

Heroin, cocaine, methamphetamine, almost all prescription medicines, and most over-the counter medications are also considered teratogens. Babies born with a heroin addiction need heroin just like an adult addict. The child will need to be gradually weaned from the heroin under medical supervision; otherwise, the child could have seizures and die. Other teratogens include radiation, viruses such as HIV and herpes, and rubella (German measles). Women in the United States are much less likely to be afflicted with rubella because most women received childhood immunizations or vaccinations that protect the body from disease.

Each organ of the fetus develops during a specific period in the pregnancy, called the **critical or sensitive period** (Figure 2). For example, research with primate models of FASD has demonstrated that the time during which a developing fetus is exposed to alcohol can dramatically affect the appearance of facial characteristics associated with fetal alcohol syndrome. Specifically, this research suggests that alcohol exposure that is limited to day 19 or 20 of gestation can lead to significant facial abnormalities in the offspring (Ashley, Magnuson, Omnell, & Clarren, 1999). Given regions of the brain also show sensitive periods during which they are most susceptible to the teratogenic effects of alcohol (Tran & Kelly, 2003).

> ### What Do You Think? Should Women Who Use Drugs During Pregnancy Be Arrested and Jailed?
>
> As you now know, women who use drugs or alcohol during pregnancy can cause serious lifelong harm to their child. Some people have advocated mandatory screenings for women who are pregnant and have a history of drug abuse, and if the women continue using, to arrest, prosecute, and incarcerate them (Figdor & Kaeser, 1998). This policy was tried in Charleston, South Carolina, as recently as 20 years ago. The policy was called the Interagency Policy on Management of Substance Abuse During Pregnancy, and had disastrous results.
>
> > The Interagency Policy applied to patients attending the obstetrics clinic at MUSC, which primarily serves patients who are indigent or on Medicaid. It did not apply to private obstetrical patients. The policy required patient education about the harmful effects of substance abuse during pregnancy. . . . [A] statement also warned patients that protection of unborn and newborn children from the harms of illegal drug abuse could involve the Charleston police, the Solicitor of the Ninth Judicial Court, and the Protective Services Division of the Department of Social Services (DSS). (Jos, Marshall, & Perlmutter, 1995, pp. 120–121)
>
> This policy seemed to deter women from seeking prenatal care, deterred them from seeking other social services, and was applied solely to low-income women, resulting in lawsuits. The program was canceled after 5 years, during which 42 women were arrested. A federal agency later determined that the program involved human experimentation without the approval and oversight of an institutional review board (IRB). What were the flaws in the program and how would you correct them? What are the ethical implications of charging pregnant women with child abuse?

Infancy

The average newborn weighs approximately 7.5 pounds. Although small, a newborn is not completely helpless because his reflexes and sensory capacities help him interact with the environment from the moment of birth. All healthy babies are born with **newborn reflexes**: inborn automatic responses to particular forms of stimulation. Reflexes help the newborn survive until it is capable of more complex behaviors—these reflexes are crucial to survival. They are present in babies whose brains are developing normally and usually disappear around 4–5 months old. Let's take a look at some of these newborn reflexes. The *rooting reflex* is the newborn's response to anything that touches her cheek: When you stroke a baby's cheek, she naturally turns her head in that direction and begins to suck. The *sucking reflex* is the automatic, unlearned, sucking motions that infants do with their mouths. Several other interesting newborn reflexes can be observed. For instance, if you put your finger into a newborn's hand, you will witness the *grasping reflex*, in which a baby automatically grasps anything that touches his palms. The *Moro reflex* is the newborn's response when she feels like she is falling. The baby spreads her arms, pulls them back in, and then (usually) cries. How do you think these reflexes promote survival in the first months of life?

Link to Learning

Take a few minutes to view this brief video clip illustrating several newborn reflexes.

* https://www.youtube.com/watch?v=Sv5SsLH70mY

If you are interested in learning more about human development in babies, watch this TED talk by Alison Gopnik. Recent discoveries reveal that babies are probably smarter than we think.

* http://www.ted.com/talks/
  alison_gopnik_what_do_babies_think?language=en#t-551802

What can young infants see, hear, and smell? Newborn infants' sensory abilities are significant, but their senses are not yet fully developed. Many of a newborn's innate preferences facilitate interaction with caregivers and other humans. Although vision is their least developed sense, newborns already show a preference for faces. Babies who are just a few days old also prefer human voices, they will listen to voices longer than sounds that do not involve speech (Vouloumanos & Werker, 2004), and they seem to prefer their mother's voice over a stranger's voice (Mills & Melhuish, 1974). In an interesting experiment, 3-week-old babies were given pacifiers that played a recording of the infant's mother's voice and of a stranger's voice. When the infants heard their mother's voice, they sucked more strongly at the pacifier (Mills & Melhuish, 1974). Newborns also have a strong sense of smell. For instance, newborn babies can distinguish the smell of their own mother from that of others. In a study by MacFarlane (1978), 1-week-old babies who were being breastfed were placed between two gauze pads. One gauze pad was from the bra of a nursing mother who was a stranger, and the other gauze pad was from the bra of the infant's own mother. More than two-thirds of the week-old babies turned toward the gauze pad with their mother's scent.

Glossary

conception: when a sperm fertilizes an egg and forms a zygote

critical (sensitive) period: time during fetal growth when specific parts or organs develop

embryo: multi-cellular organism in its early stages of development

mitosis: process of cell division

newborn reflexes: inborn automatic response to a particular form of stimulation that all healthy babies are born with

placenta: structure connected to the uterus that provides nourishment and oxygen to the developing baby

prenatal care: medical care during pregnancy that monitors the health of both the mother and the fetus

teratogen: biological, chemical, or physical environmental agent that causes damage to the developing embryo or fetus

zygote: structure created when a sperm and egg merge at conception; begins as a single cell and rapidly divides to form the embryo and placenta

Attributions

CC licensed content, Original

- Modification and adaptation, addition of TED talk. **Provided by:** Lumen Learning. **License:** *CC BY: Attribution*

CC licensed content, Shared previously

- Stages of Development. **Authored by:** OpenStax College. **Located at:** http://cnx.org/contents/Sr8Ev5Og@5.52:b7opmCF3@6/Stages-of-Development#Figure_09_02_Stages. **License:** *CC BY: Attribution*. **License Terms:** Download for free at http://cnx.org/content/col11629/latest/.

All rights reserved content

- Monkeys and Morality: Crash Course Psychology #19. **Provided by:** CrashCourse. **Located at:** https://youtu.be/YcQg1EshflE?list=PL8dPuuaLjXtOPRKzVLY0jJY-uHOH9KVU6. **License:** *All Rights Reserved*. **License Terms:** Standard YouTube License

Putting It Together: Lifespan Development

In this module, you learned to

- compare and contrast theories lifespan development theories
- explain the physical, cognitive, and emotional development that occurs from infancy through childhood
- describe physical, cognitive, and emotional development in adolescence and adulthood

Our understanding of human nature has come a long way since the belief that children were just little adults in need of instruction. Through ongoing research, we now know that children hit certain milestones that enable them to take another viewpoint or understand the law of conservation, that babies can understand enough about the world around them to make moral judgments, and that issues of physical, social, and cognitive importance change across the lifespan.

Adolescence is one of the time periods of interest to psychologists, especially due to the focus on identity formation, which often involves a period of exploration followed by commitments to particular identities. Adolescence is characterized by risky behavior, which is made more likely by changes in the brain in which reward-processing centers develop more rapidly than cognitive control systems, making adolescents more sensitive to rewards than to possible negative consequences.

Marcia (1966) described identify formation during adolescence as involving both decision points and commitments with respect to ideologies (e.g., religion, politics) and occupations. He described four identity statuses: foreclosure, identity diffusion, moratorium, and identity achievement.

- Foreclosure occurs when an individual commits to an identity without exploring options.
- Identity diffusion occurs when adolescents neither explore nor commit to any identities.
- Moratorium is a state in which adolescents are actively exploring options but have not yet made commitments.

- Identity achievement occurs when individuals have explored different options and then made identity commitments.

Think about your own adolescent experience (you may consider yourself still in this life stage). Which identity status best fits with your own experience? Do you feel committed to your current identity, or do you feel as though you are still developing? Regardless of your answer, you can rest assured that human development does not end with adolescence, and research proves that people can continue to learn, grow, and even change as long as they would like.

Attributions

CC licensed content, Shared previously

- Putting It Together: Lifespan Development. **Provided by:** Lumen Learning. **License:** *CC BY: Attribution*

- Section on Adolescent Development. **Authored by:** Jennifer Lansford . **Provided by:** Duke University. **Located at:** http://nobaproject.com/modules/adolescent-development?r=MTc0ODYsMzIxMDM%3D. **Project:** The Noba Project. **License:** *CC BY-NC-SA: Attribution-NonCommercial-ShareAlike*

- Youth Interacting in Oslo, Norway. **Authored by:** Leifern. **Provided by:** Wikipedia. **Located at:** https://chr.wikipedia.org/wiki/%E1%8E%BE%E1%8E%A5_%E1%8F%84%E1%8E%BE%E1%8F%93%E1%8E%B8#/media/File:Diversity_of_youth_in_Oslo_Norway.jpg. **License:** *CC BY-SA: Attribution-ShareAlike*

Module 4: Biopsychology

Why It Matters: Biospychology

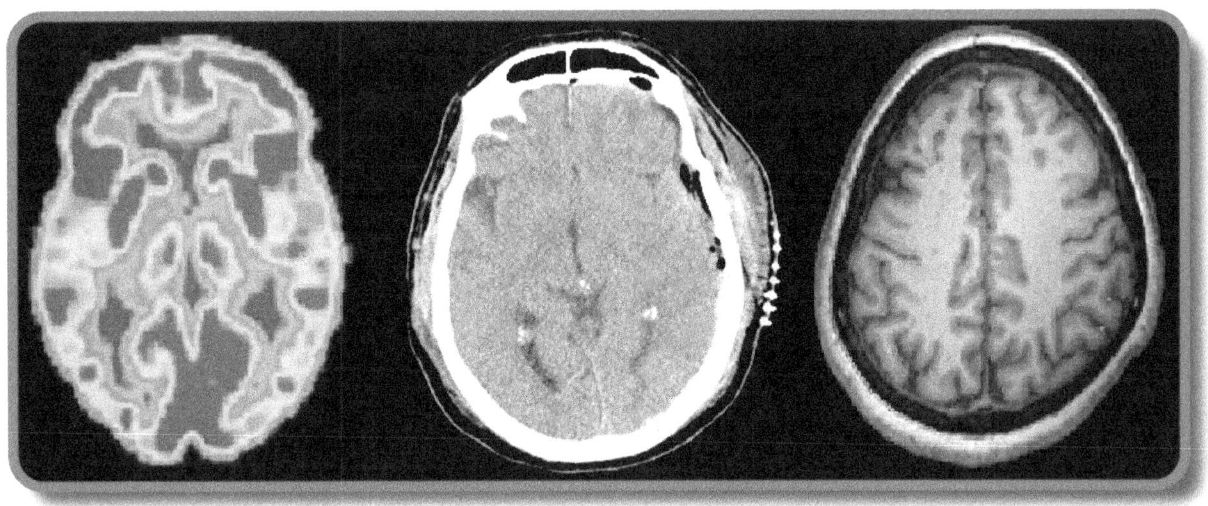

Different brain imaging techniques provide scientists with insight into different aspects of how the human brain functions. Left to right, PET scan (positron emission tomography), CT scan (computed tomography), and fMRI (functional magnetic resonance imaging) are three types of scans. (credit "left": modification of work by Health and Human Services Department, National Institutes of Health; credit "center": modification of work by "Aceofhearts1968"/Wikimedia Commons; credit "right": modification of work by Kim J, Matthews NL, Park S.)

Have you ever taken a device apart to find out how it works? Many of us have done so, whether to attempt a repair or simply to satisfy our curiosity. A device's internal workings are often distinct from its user interface on the outside. For example, we don't think about microchips and circuits when we turn up the volume on a mobile phone; instead, we think about getting the volume just right. Similarly, the inner workings of the human body are often distinct from the external expression of those workings. It is the job of psychologists to find the connection between these—for example, to figure out how the firings of millions of neurons become a thought.

This module strives to explain the biological mechanisms that underlie behavior. These physiological and anatomical foundations are the basis for many areas of psychology. In this module, you will learn how genetics influence both physiological and psychological traits. You will become familiar with the structure and function of the nervous system, learn how the nervous system interacts with the endocrine system, and understand the nature vs. nurture debate.

Module References

Arnst, C. (2003, November). Commentary: Getting rational about health-care rationing. *Bloomberg Businessweek Magazine*. Retrieved from http://www.businessweek.com/stories/2003-11-16/commentary-getting-rational-about-health-care-rationing

Berridge, K. C., & Robinson, T. E. (1998). What is the role of dopamine in reward: Hedonic impact, reward learning, or incentive salience? *Brain Research Reviews, 28*, 309–369.

Chandola, T., Brunner, E., & Marmot, M. (2006). Chronic stress at work and the metabolic syndrome: A prospective study. *BMJ, 332*, 521–524.

Comings, D. E., Gonzales, N., Saucier, G., Johnson, J. P., & MacMurray, J. P. (2000). The DRD4 gene and the spiritual transcendence scale of the character temperament index. *Psychiatric Genetics, 10*, 185–189.

Confer, J. C., Easton, J. A., Fleischman, D. S., Goetz, C. D., Lewis, D. M. G, Perilloux, C., & Buss, D. M. (2010). Evolutionary psychology: Controversies, questions, prospects, and limitations. *American Psychologist, 65*, 110–126.

Gaines, C. (2013, August). An A-Rod suspension would save the Yankees as much as $37.5 million in 2014 alone. *Business Insider*. Retrieved from http://www.businessinsider.com/an-a-rod-suspension-would-save-the-yankees-as-much-as-375-million-in-2014-2013-8

Gardner, E. L. (2011). Addiction and brain reward and antireward pathways. *Advances in Psychosomatic Medicine, 30*, 22–60.

George, O., Le Moal, M., & Koob, G. F. (2012). Allostasis and addiction: Role of the dopamine and corticotropin-releasing factor systems. *Physiology & Behavior, 106*, 58–64.

Glaser, R., & Kiecolt-Glaser, J. K. (2005). Stress-induced immune dysfunction: Implications for health. *Nature Reviews Immunology, 5*, 243–251.

Gong, L., Parikh, S., Rosenthal, P. J., & Greenhouse, B. (2013). Biochemical and immunological mechanisms by which sickle cell trait protects against malaria. *Malaria Journal*. Advance online publication. doi:10.1186/1475-2875-12-317

Hardt, O., Einarsson, E. Ö., & Nader, K. (2010). A bridge over troubled water: Reconsolidation as a link between cognitive and neuroscientific memory research traditions. *Annual Review of Psychology, 61*, 141–167.

Macmillan, M. (1999). The Phineas Gage Information Page. Retrieved from http://www.uakron.edu/gage

March, J. S., Silva, S., Petrycki, S., Curry, J., Wells, K., Fairbank, J., … Severe, J. (2007). The treatment for adolescents with depression study (TADS): Long-term effectiveness and safety outcomes. *Arch Gen Psychiatry, 64*, 1132–1143.

Mustanski, B. S., DuPree, M. G., Nievergelt, C. M., Bocklandt, S., Schork, N. J., & Hamer, D. H. (2005). A genome wide scan of male sexual orientation. *Human Genetics, 116*, 272–278.

National Institute on Drug Abuse. (2001, July). Anabolic steroid abuse: What are the health consequences of steroid abuse? *National Institutes of Health*. Retrieved from http://www.drugabuse.gov/publications/research-reports/anabolic-steroid-abuse/what-are-health-consequences-steroid-abuse

Squire, L. R. (2009). The legacy of patient H. M. for neuroscience. *Neuron, 61*, 6–9.

Tienari, P., Wynne, L. C., Sorri, A., et al. (2004). Genotype–environment interaction in schizophrenia spectrum disorder: long-term follow-up study of Finnish adoptees. *British Journal of Psychiatry, 184*, 216–222.

University of Utah Genetic Science Learning Center. (n.d.). What are genetic disorders? Retrieved from http://learn.genetics.utah.edu/content/disorders/whataregd/

Attributions

CC licensed content, Shared previously

- Psychology. **Authored by:** OpenStax College. **Located at:** http://cnx.org/contents/
  4abf04bf-93a0-45c3-9cbc-2cefd46e68cc@4.100:1/Psychology. **License:** *CC BY: Attribution.* **License Terms:** Download
  for free at http://cnx.org/content/col11629/latest/.

Neural Communication

What you'll learn to do: identify the basic structures of a neuron, the function of each structure, and how messages travel through the neuron

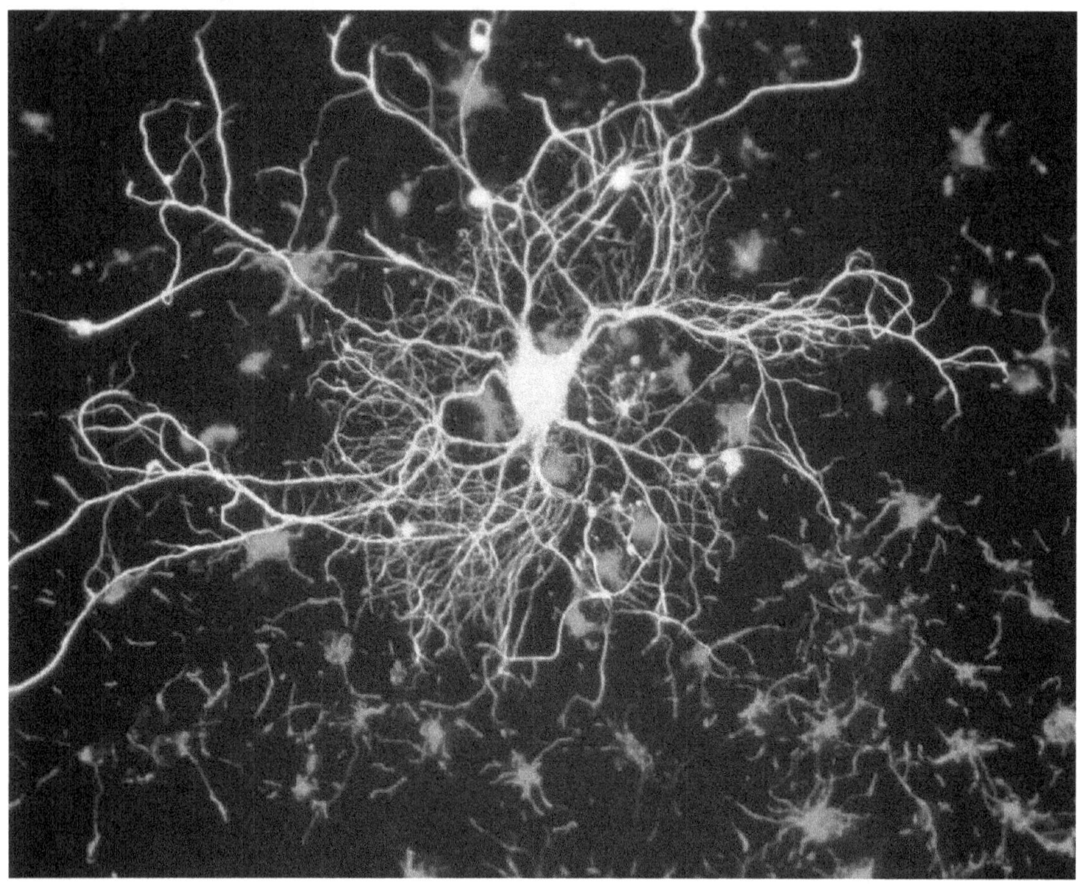

Neuron in tissue culture.

Ever wonder how your brain actually works? What exactly is going on inside of your small, wrinkly mass while you read this text? In this section, you'll learn about the basics of neural communication in the brain, which is the brain's way of sending messages to and from different regions in order to relay critical information about your body and its surroundings.

Glia and neurons are the two cell types that make up the nervous system. While glia generally play supporting roles, the communication between neurons is fundamental to all of the functions associated with the nervous system. Neuronal communication is made possible by the neuron's specialized structures, like the soma, dendrites, axons, terminal buttons, and synaptic vesicles.

Neuronal communication is an electrochemical event. The dendrites contain receptors for neurotransmitters released by nearby neurons. If the signals received from other neurons are sufficiently strong, an action potential will travel down the length of the axon to the terminal buttons, resulting in the release of neurotransmitters into the synapse.

Different neurotransmitters are associated with different functions. Often, psychological disorders involve imbalances in a given neurotransmitter system. Therefore, psychotropic drugs are prescribed in an attempt to bring the neurotransmitters back into balance. Drugs can act either as agonists or as antagonists for a given neurotransmitter system.

Learning Objectives

- Explain the role and function of the basic structures of a neuron
- Describe how neurons communicate with each other
- Explain how drugs act as agonists or antagonists for a given neurotransmitter system

---

Neurons

Psychologists striving to understand the human mind may study the **nervous system.** Learning how the cells and organs (like the brain) function, help us understand the biological basis behind human psychology. The nervous system is composed of two basic cell types: glial cells (also known as glia) and neurons. **Glial cells**, which outnumber neurons ten to one, are traditionally thought to play a supportive role to neurons, both physically and metabolically. Glial cells provide scaffolding on which the nervous system is built, help neurons line up closely with each other to allow neuronal communication, provide insulation to neurons, transport nutrients and waste products, and mediate immune responses. **Neurons**, on the other hand, serve as interconnected information processors that are essential for all of the tasks of the nervous system. This section briefly describes the structure and function of neurons.

Neuron Structure

Neurons are the central building blocks of the nervous system, 100 billion strong at birth. Like all cells, neurons consist of several different parts, each serving a specialized function (Figure 1). A neuron's outer surface is made up of a **semipermeable membrane.** This membrane allows smaller molecules and molecules without an electrical charge to pass through it, while stopping larger or highly charged molecules.

The nucleus of the neuron is located in the soma, or cell body. The **soma** has branching extensions known as **dendrites.** The neuron is a small information processor, and dendrites serve as input sites where signals are received from other neurons. These signals are transmitted electrically across the soma and down a major extension from the soma known as the **axon**, which ends at multiple **terminal buttons.** The terminal buttons contain **synaptic vesicles** that house **neurotransmitters**, the chemical messengers of the nervous system.

Axons range in length from a fraction of an inch to several feet. In some axons, glial cells form a fatty substance known as the **myelin sheath**, which coats the axon and acts as an insulator, increasing the speed at which the signal travels. The myelin sheath is crucial for the normal operation of the neurons within the nervous system: the loss of the insulation it provides can be detrimental to normal function. To understand how this works, let's consider an example. Multiple sclerosis (MS), an autoimmune dis-

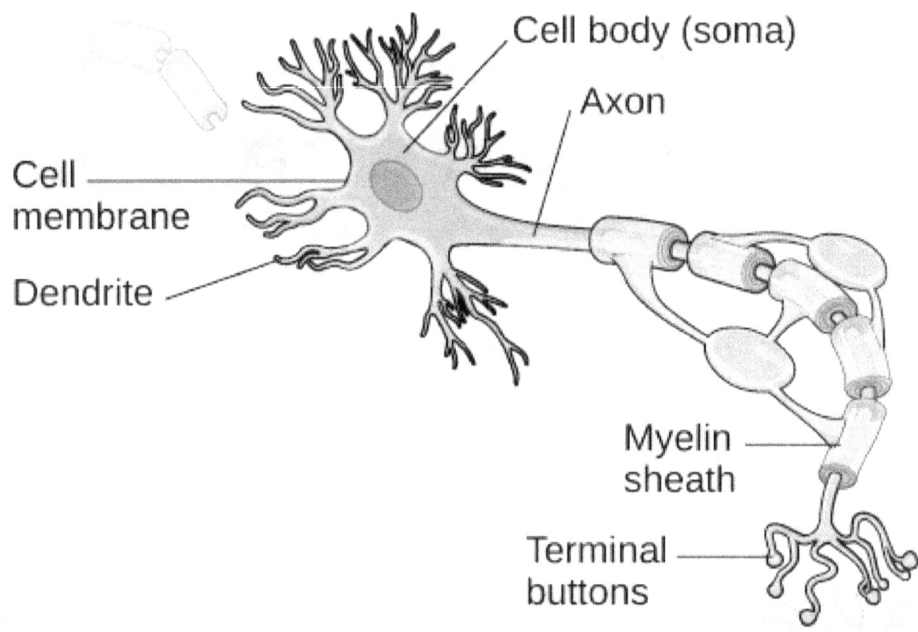

Figure 1. This illustration shows a prototypical neuron, which is being myelinated.

order, involves a large-scale loss of the myelin sheath on axons throughout the nervous system. The resulting interference in the electrical signal prevents the quick transmittal of information by neurons and can lead to a number of symptoms, such as dizziness, fatigue, loss of motor control, and sexual dysfunction. While some treatments may help to modify the course of the disease and manage certain symptoms, there is currently no known cure for multiple sclerosis.

In healthy individuals, the neuronal signal moves rapidly down the axon to the terminal buttons, where synaptic vesicles release neurotransmitters into the synapse (Figure 2). The **synapse** is a very small space between two neurons and is an important site where communication between neurons occurs. Once neurotransmitters are released into the synapse, they travel across the small space and bind with corresponding receptors on the dendrite of an adjacent neuron. **Receptors**, proteins on the cell surface where neurotransmitters attach, vary in shape, with different shapes "matching" different neurotransmitters.

How does a neurotransmitter "know" which receptor to bind to? The neurotransmitter and the receptor have what is referred to as a lock-and-key relationship—specific neurotransmitters fit specific receptors similar to how a key fits a lock. The neurotransmitter binds to any receptor that it fits.

Link to Learning

Click through the links at the top of this interactive simulation to review the parts of a nerve cell and to take a closer look at how neurons communicate.

- https://apps.childrenshospital.org/clinical/animation/neuron/

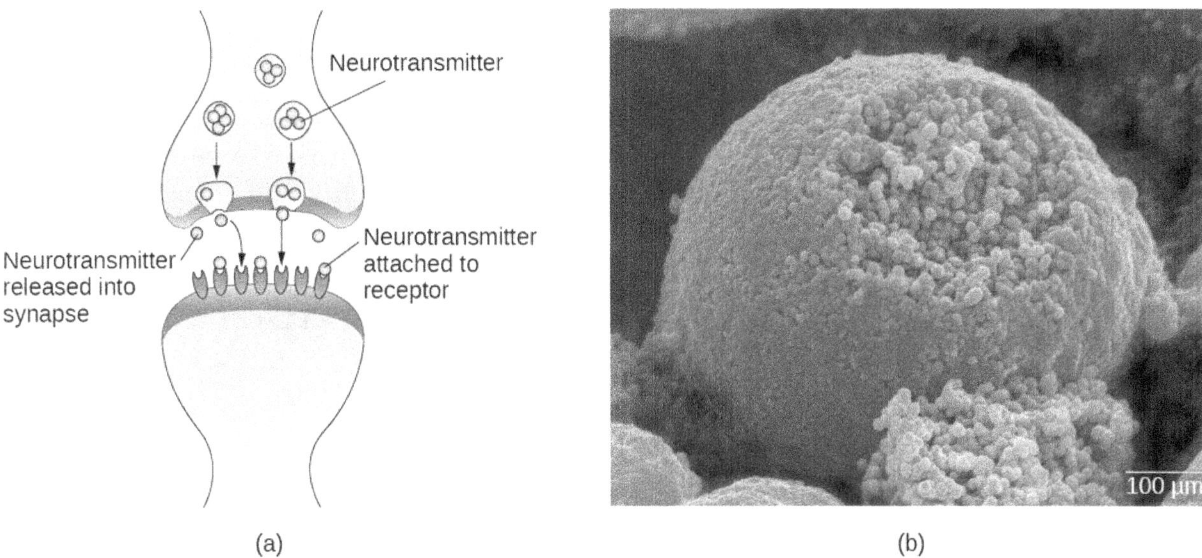

Figure 2. (a) The synapse is the space between the terminal button of one neuron and the dendrite of another neuron. (b) In this pseudo-colored image from a scanning electron microscope, a terminal button (green) has been opened to reveal the synaptic vesicles (orange and blue) inside. Each vesicle contains about 10,000 neurotransmitter molecules. (credit b: modification of work by Tina Carvalho, NIH-NIGMS; scale-bar data from Matt Russell)

Glossary

axon: major extension of the soma

dendrite: branch-like extension of the soma that receives incoming signals from other neurons

glial cell: nervous system cell that provides physical and metabolic support to neurons, including neuronal insulation and communication, and nutrient and waste transport

myelin sheath: fatty substance that insulates axons

neuron: cells in the nervous system that act as interconnected information processors, which are essential for all of the tasks of the nervous system

neurotransmitter: chemical messenger of the nervous system

receptor: protein on the cell surface where neurotransmitters attach

semipermeable membrane: cell membrane that allows smaller molecules or molecules without an electrical charge to pass through it, while stopping larger or highly charged molecules

soma: cell body

synapse: small gap between two neurons where communication occurs

synaptic vesicle: storage site for neurotransmitters

CC licensed content, Shared previously

- Neuron in tissue culture. **Located at:** https://commons.wikimedia.org/wiki/File:Neuron_in_tissue_culture.jpg. **License:** *CC BY-SA: Attribution-ShareAlike*
- Cells of the Nervous System. **Authored by:** OpenStax College. **Located at:** http://cnx.org/contents/Sr8Ev5Og@5.52:SO2ufnKm@7/Cells-of-the-Nervous-System. **License:** *CC BY: Attribution.* **License Terms:** Download for free at http://cnx.org/contents/4abf04bf-93a0-45c3-9cbc-2cefd46e68cc@5.48

All rights reserved content

- 2-Minute Neuroscience: The Neuron. **Authored by:** Neuroscientifically Challenged. **Located at:** https://www.youtube.com/watch?v=6qS83wD29PY. **License:** *Other.* **License Terms:** Standard YouTube License

The Nervous System and Endocrine System

What you'll learn to do: describe the role of the nervous system and endocrine systems

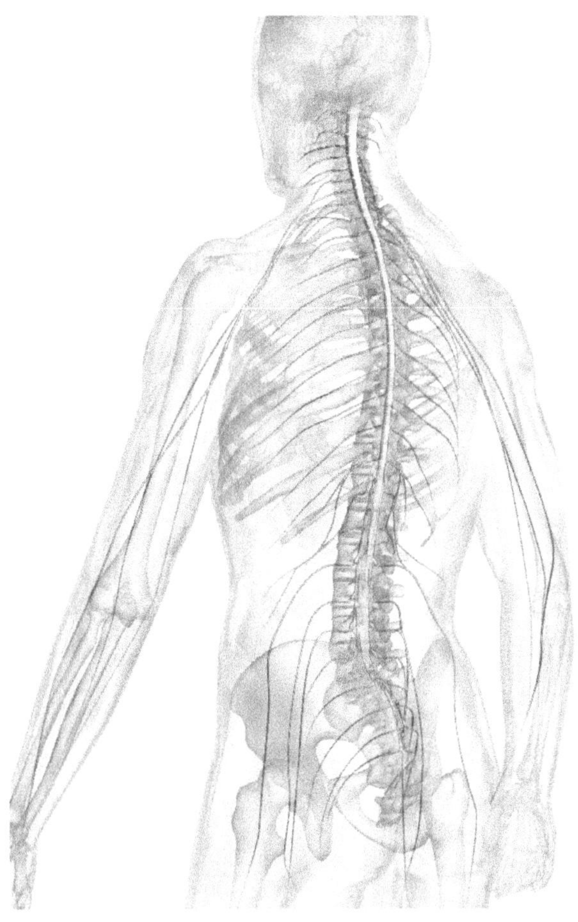

In this section, you'll learn about the basics of the central nervous system, which consists of the brain and spinal cord, as well as the peripheral nervous system. The **peripheral nervous system** is comprised of the somatic and autonomic nervous systems. The **somatic nervous system** transmits sensory and motor signals to and from the central nervous system. The **autonomic nervous system** controls the function of our organs and glands, and can be divided into the sympathetic and parasympathetic divisions. **Sympathetic** activation prepares us for fight or flight, while **parasympathetic** activation is associated with normal functioning under relaxed conditions. The **endocrine system** consists of a series of glands that produce chemical substances known as hormones, which produce widespread effects on the body. Got all that? We'll review each of these systems in the coming pages.

- Describe the difference between the central and peripheral nervous systems and the somatic and autonomic nervous systems
- Differentiate between the sympathetic and parasympathetic divisions of the autonomic nervous system
- Describe the endocrine system and explain its primary responsibilities within the body

The Central Nervous System and the Peripheral Nervous System

The **nervous system** can be divided into two major subdivisions: the **central nervous system (CNS)** and the **peripheral nervous system (PNS)**, shown in Figure 1. The CNS is comprised of the brain and spinal cord; the PNS connects the CNS to the rest of the body. In this section, we focus on the peripheral nervous system; later, we look at the brain and spinal cord.

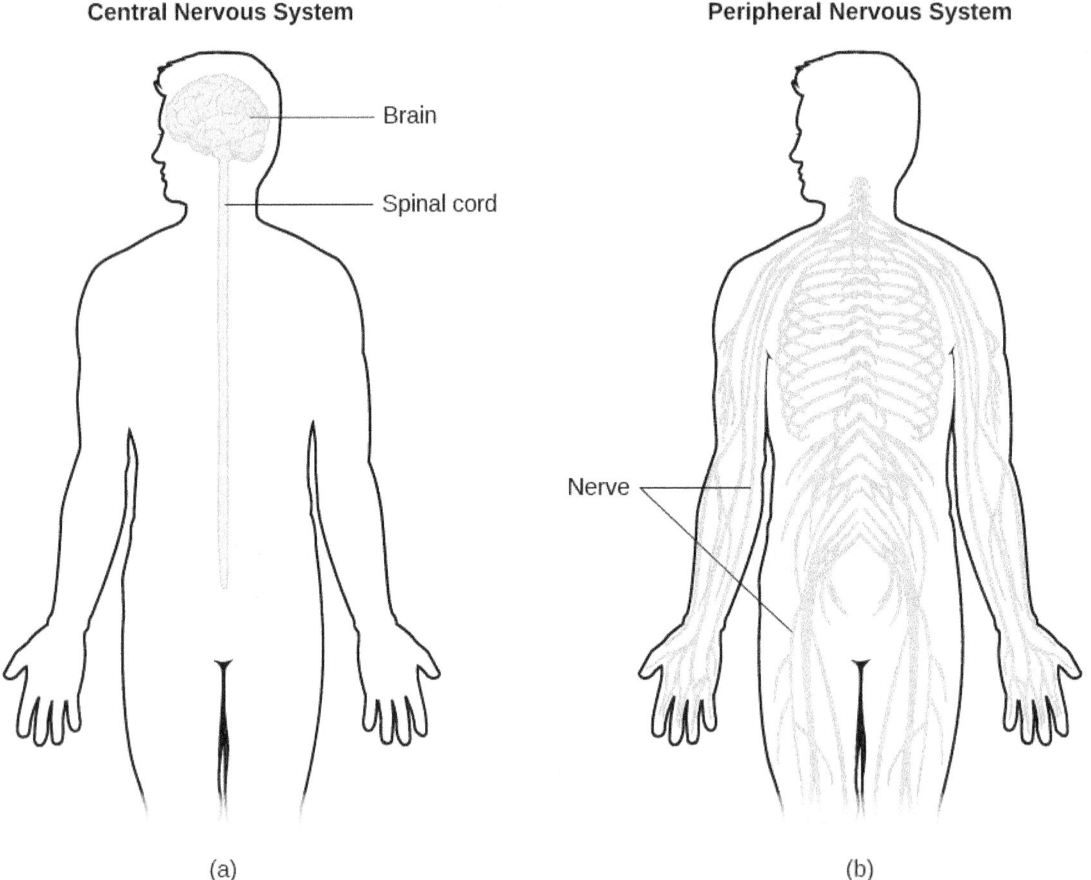

Figure 1. The nervous system is divided into two major parts: (a) the Central Nervous System and (b) the Peripheral Nervous System.

Peripheral Nervous System

The peripheral nervous system is made up of thick bundles of axons, called nerves, carrying messages back and forth between the CNS and the muscles, organs, and senses in the periphery of the body (i.e., everything outside the CNS). The PNS has two major subdivisions: the somatic nervous system and the autonomic nervous system.

The **somatic nervous system** is associated with activities traditionally thought of as conscious or voluntary. It is involved in the relay of sensory and motor information to and from the CNS; therefore, it consists of motor neurons and sensory neurons. Motor neurons, carrying instructions from the CNS to the muscles, are efferent fibers (efferent means "moving away from"). Sensory neurons, carrying sensory information to the CNS, are afferent fibers (afferent means "moving toward"). Each nerve is basically a two-way superhighway, containing thousands of axons, both efferent and afferent.

The **autonomic nervous system** controls our internal organs and glands and is generally considered to be outside the realm of voluntary control. It can be further subdivided into the sympathetic and parasympathetic divisions (Figure 2). The **sympathetic nervous system** is involved in preparing the body for stress-related activities; the **parasympathetic nervous system** is associated with returning the body to routine, day-to-day operations. The two systems have complementary functions, operating in tandem to maintain the body's homeostasis. **Homeostasis** is a state of equilibrium, in which biological conditions (such as body temperature) are maintained at optimal levels.

The sympathetic nervous system is activated when we are faced with stressful or high-arousal situations. The activity of this system was adaptive for our ancestors, increasing their chances of survival. Imagine, for example, that one of our early ancestors, out hunting small game, suddenly disturbs a large bear with her cubs. At that moment, his body undergoes a series of changes—a direct function of sympathetic activation—preparing him to face the threat. His pupils dilate, his heart rate and blood pressure increase, his bladder relaxes, his liver releases glucose, and adrenaline surges into his bloodstream. This constellation of physiological changes, known as the **fight or flight response**, allows the body access to energy reserves and heightened sensory capacity so that it might fight off a threat or run away to safety.

Link to Learning

Reinforce what you've learned about the nervous system by playing this BBC-produced interactive game about the nervous system.

- https://www.bbc.co.uk/science/humanbody/body/interactives/3djigsaw_02/index.shtml?nervous

While it is clear that such a response would be critical for survival for our ancestors, who lived in a world full of real physical threats, many of the high-arousal situations we face in the modern world are more psychological in nature. For example, think about how you feel when you have to stand up and give a presentation in front of a roomful of people, or right before taking a big test. You are in no real physical danger in those situations, and yet you have evolved to respond to any perceived threat

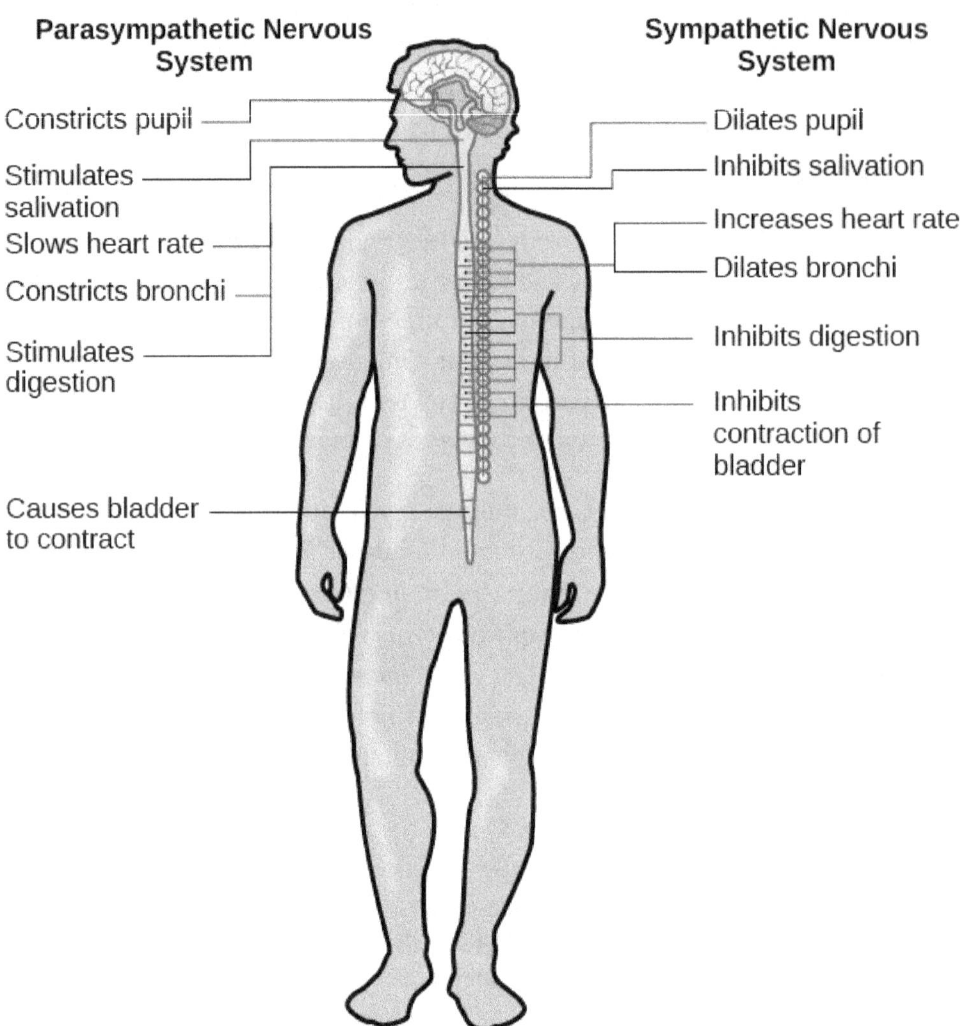

Figure 2. The sympathetic and parasympathetic divisions of the autonomic nervous system have the opposite effects on various systems.

with the fight or flight response. This kind of response is not nearly as adaptive in the modern world; in fact, we suffer negative health consequences when faced constantly with psychological threats that we can neither fight nor flee. Recent research suggests that an increase in susceptibility to heart disease (Chandola, Brunner, & Marmot, 2006) and impaired function of the immune system (Glaser & Kiecolt-Glaser, 2005) are among the many negative consequences of persistent and repeated exposure to stressful situations.

Once the threat has been resolved, the parasympathetic nervous system takes over and returns bodily functions to a relaxed state. Our hunter's heart rate and blood pressure return to normal, his pupils constrict, he regains control of his bladder, and the liver begins to store glucose in the form of glycogen for future use. These processes are associated with activation of the parasympathetic nervous system.

The Endocrine System

The **endocrine system** consists of a series of glands that produce chemical substances known as **hormones** (Figure 1). Like neurotransmitters, hormones are chemical messengers that must bind to a receptor in order to send their signal. However, unlike neurotransmitters, which are released in close proximity to cells with their receptors, hormones are secreted into the bloodstream and travel throughout the body, affecting any cells that contain receptors for them. Thus, whereas neurotransmitters' effects are localized, the effects of hormones are widespread. Also, hormones are slower to take effect, and tend to be longer lasting.

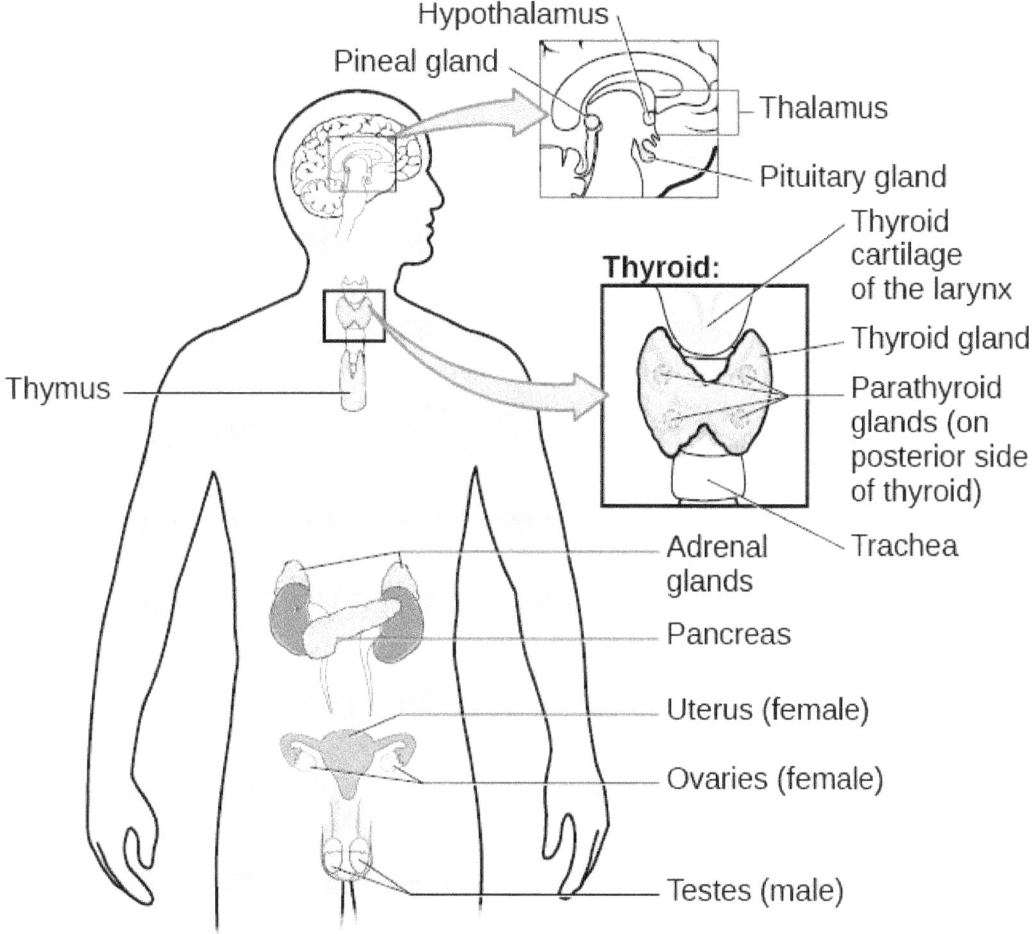

Figure 3. The major glands of the endocrine system are shown.

The study of psychology and the endocrine system is called behavioral endocrinology, which is the scientific study of the interaction between hormones and behavior. This interaction is bidirectional: hormones can influence behavior, and behavior can sometimes influence hormone concentrations. Hormones regulate behaviors such as aggression, mating, and parenting of individuals. Hormones are involved in regulating all sorts of bodily functions, and they are ultimately controlled through interactions between the hypothalamus (in the central nervous system) and the pituitary gland (in the endocrine system). Imbalances in hormones are related to a number of disorders. This section explores some of the major glands that make up the endocrine system and the hormones secreted by these glands.

Major Glands

The **pituitary gland** descends from the hypothalamus at the base of the brain, and acts in close association with it. The pituitary is often referred to as the "master gland" because its messenger hormones control all the other glands in the endocrine system, although it mostly carries out instructions from the hypothalamus. In addition to messenger hormones, the pituitary also secretes growth hormone, endorphins for pain relief, and a number of key hormones that regulate fluid levels in the body.

Located in the neck, the **thyroid gland** releases hormones that regulate growth, metabolism, and appetite. In hyperthyroidism, or Grave's disease, the thyroid secretes too much of the hormone thyroxine, causing agitation, bulging eyes, and weight loss. In hypothyroidism, reduced hormone levels cause sufferers to experience tiredness, and they often complain of feeling cold. Fortunately, thyroid disorders are often treatable with medications that help reestablish a balance in the hormones secreted by the thyroid.

The **adrenal glands** sit atop our kidneys and secrete hormones involved in the stress response, such as epinephrine (adrenaline) and norepinephrine (noradrenaline). The **pancreas** is an internal organ that secretes hormones that regulate blood sugar levels: insulin and glucagon. These pancreatic hormones are essential for maintaining stable levels of blood sugar throughout the day by lowering blood glucose levels (insulin) or raising them (glucagon). People who suffer from **diabetes** do not produce enough insulin; therefore, they must take medications that stimulate or replace insulin production, and they must closely control the amount of sugars and carbohydrates they consume.

The **gonads** secrete sexual hormones, which are important in reproduction, and mediate both sexual motivation and behavior. The female gonads are the ovaries; the male gonads are the testis. Ovaries secrete estrogens and progesterone, and the testes secrete androgens, such as testosterone.

Although it is against most laws to do so, many professional athletes and body builders use anabolic steroid drugs to improve their athletic performance and physique. Anabolic steroid drugs mimic the effects of the body's own steroid hormones, like testosterone and its derivatives. These drugs have the potential to provide a competitive edge by increasing muscle mass, strength, and endurance, although not all users may experience these results. Moreover, use of performance-enhancing drugs (PEDs) does not come without risks. Anabolic steroid use has been linked with a wide variety of potentially negative outcomes, ranging in severity from largely cosmetic (acne) to life threatening (heart attack). Furthermore, use of these substances can result in profound changes in mood and can increase aggressive behavior (National Institute on Drug Abuse, 2001).

Baseball player Alex Rodriguez (A-Rod) has been at the center of a media storm regarding his use of illegal PEDs. Rodriguez's performance on the field was unparalleled while using the drugs; his success played a large role in negotiating a contract that made him the highest paid player in professional baseball. Although Rodriguez maintains that he has not used PEDs for the several years, he received a substantial suspension in 2013 that, if upheld, will cost him more than 20 million dollars in earnings (Gaines, 2013). What are your thoughts on athletes and doping? Why or why not should the use of PEDs be banned? What advice would you give an athlete who was considering using PEDs?

Hormones and Behavior

How might behaviors affect hormones? Extensive studies on male zebra finches and their singing (only males finches sing) demonstrate that the hormones testosterone and estradiol affect their singing, but the reciprocal relation also occurs; that is, behavior can affect hormone concentrations. For example, the sight of a territorial intruder may elevate blood testosterone concentrations in resident male birds and thereby stimulate singing or fighting behavior. Similarly, male mice or rhesus monkeys that lose a fight decrease circulating testosterone concentrations for several days or even weeks afterward. Comparable results have also been reported in humans. Testosterone concentrations are affected not only in humans involved in physical combat, but also in those involved in simulated battles. For example, testosterone concentrations were elevated in winners and reduced in losers of regional chess tournaments.

People do not have to be directly involved in a contest to have their hormones affected by the outcome of the contest. Male fans of both the Brazilian and Italian teams were recruited to provide saliva samples to be assayed for testosterone before and after the final game of the World Cup soccer match in 1994. Brazil and Italy were tied going into the final game, but Brazil won on a penalty kick at the last possible moment. The Brazilian fans were elated and the Italian fans were crestfallen. When the samples were assayed, 11 of 12 Brazilian fans who were sampled had increased testosterone concentrations, and 9 of 9 Italian fans had decreased testosterone concentrations, compared with pre-game baseline values (Dabbs, 2000).

In some cases, hormones can be affected by anticipation of behavior. For example, testosterone concentrations also influence sexual motivation and behavior in women. In one study, the interaction between sexual intercourse and testosterone was compared with other activities (cuddling or exercise) in women (van Anders, Hamilton, Schmidt, & Watson, 2007). On three separate occasions, women provided a pre-activity, post-activity, and next-morning saliva sample. After analysis, the women's testosterone was determined to be elevated prior to intercourse as compared to other times. Thus, an anticipatory relationship exists between sexual behavior and testosterone. Testosterone values were higher post-intercourse compared to exercise, suggesting that engaging in sexual behavior may also influence hormone concentrations in women.

Link to Learning

Learn more about endocrinology from *The Noba Psychology* article, "Hormones and Behavior."

- http://nobaproject.com/textbooks/wendy-king-introduction-to-psychology-the-full-noba-collection/modules/hormones-behavior

Glossary

adrenal gland: sits atop our kidneys and secretes hormones involved in the stress response

autonomic nervous system: controls our internal organs and glands

central nervous system (CNS): brain and spinal cord

diabetes: disease related to insufficient insulin production

endocrine system: series of glands that produce chemical substances known as hormones

fight or flight response: activation of the sympathetic division of the autonomic nervous system, allowing access to energy reserves and heightened sensory capacity so that we might fight off a given threat or run away to safety

gonad: secretes sexual hormones, which are important for successful reproduction, and mediate both sexual motivation and behavior

homeostasis: state of equilibrium—biological conditions, such as body temperature, are maintained at optimal levels

hormone: chemical messenger released by endocrine glands

pancreas: secretes hormones that regulate blood sugar

parasympathetic nervous system: associated with routine, day-to-day operations of the body

peripheral nervous system (PNS): connects the brain and spinal cord to the muscles, organs and senses in the periphery of the body

pituitary gland: secretes a number of key hormones, which regulate fluid levels in the body, and a number of messenger hormones, which direct the activity of other glands in the endocrine system

thyroid: secretes hormones that regulate growth, metabolism, and appetite

somatic nervous system: relays sensory and motor information to and from the CNS

sympathetic nervous system: involved in stress-related activities and functions

https://assessments.lumenlearning.com/assessments/4813

Attributions

CC licensed content, Original

- Modification, adaptation, and original content. **Provided by:** Lumen Learning. **License:** *CC BY: Attribution*

CC licensed content, Shared previously

- The Endocrine System. **Authored by:** OpenStax College. **Located at:** http://cnx.org/contents/Sr8Ev5Og@5.49:34oFmAxl@6/The-Endocrine-System. **License:** *CC BY: Attribution.* **License Terms:** Download for free at http://cnx.org/content/col11629/latest/.

- Hormones and Behavior and introductory section and part on endocrinology. **Authored by:** Randy J. Nelson. **Provided by:** The Ohio State University. **Located at:** http://nobaproject.com/textbooks/wendy-king-introduction-to-psychology-the-full-noba-collection/modules/hormones-behavior. **Project:** The Noba Project. **License:** *CC BY-NC-SA: Attribution-NonCommercial-ShareAlike*

- Parts of the Nervous System. **Authored by:** OpenStax College. **Located at:** http://cnx.org/contents/Sr8Ev5Og@5.52:-xs7Ve8V@6/Parts-of-the-Nervous-System. **License:** *CC BY: Attribution.* **License Terms:** Download for free at http://cnx.org/contents/4abf04bf-93a0-45c3-9cbc-2cefd46e68cc@5.48

Public domain content

This is a modified version of OpenStax Psychology. Download the original text for free at https://openstax.org/details/books/psychology

- Spinal Cord. **Authored by:** BruceBlaus. **Provided by:** Wikimedia. **Located at:** https://en.wikipedia.org/wiki/Surfer%27s_myelopathy#/media/File:Blausen_0822_SpinalCord.png. **License:** *CC BY: Attribution*

Parts of the Brain

What you'll learn to do: identify and describe the parts of the brain

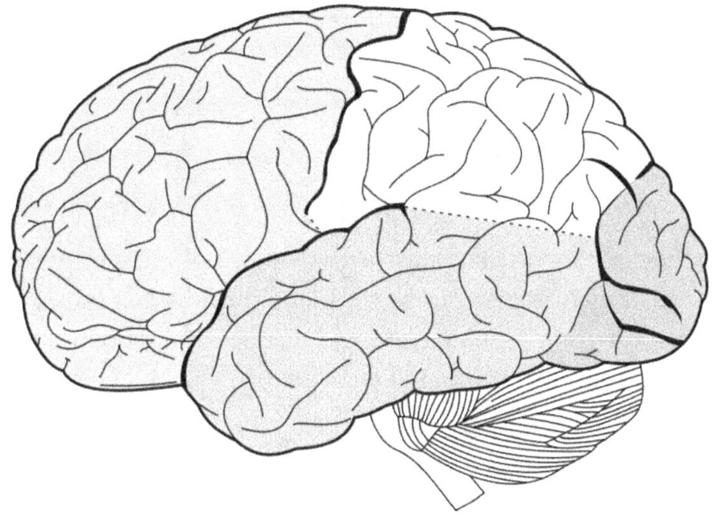

In this section, you'll learn about the specific parts of the brain and their roles and functions. While this is not an anatomy class, you'll see how important it is to understand the parts of the brain and what they do so that we can understand mental processes and behavior. Watch this CrashCourse Psychology video for an overview on the brain and the interesting topics we'll cover:

Learning Objectives

- Explain the two hemispheres of the brain, lateralization and plasticity
- Identify the location and function of the lobes of the brain

The Central Nervous System

The central nervous system (CNS), consists of the brain and the spinal cord.

The Brain

The brain is a remarkably complex organ comprised of billions of interconnected neurons and glia. It is a bilateral, or two-sided, structure that can be separated into distinct lobes. Each lobe is associated with certain types of functions, but, ultimately, all of the areas of the brain interact with one another to provide the foundation for our thoughts and behaviors.

The Spinal Cord

It can be said that the spinal cord is what connects the brain to the outside world. Because of it, the brain can act. The spinal cord is like a relay station, but a very smart one. It not only routes messages to and from the brain, but it also has its own system of automatic processes, called reflexes.

The top of the spinal cord merges with the brain stem, where the basic processes of life are controlled, such as breathing and digestion. In the opposite direction, the spinal cord ends just below the ribs—contrary to what we might expect, it does not extend all the way to the base of the spine.

The spinal cord is functionally organized in 30 segments, corresponding with the vertebrae. Each segment is connected to a specific part of the body through the peripheral nervous system. Nerves branch out from the spine at each vertebra. Sensory nerves bring messages in; motor nerves send messages out to the muscles and organs. Messages travel to and from the brain through every segment.

Some sensory messages are immediately acted on by the spinal cord, without any input from the brain. Withdrawal from heat and knee jerk are two examples. When a sensory message meets certain parameters, the spinal cord initiates an automatic reflex. The signal passes from the sensory nerve to a simple processing center, which initiates a motor command. Seconds are saved, because messages don't have to go the brain, be processed, and get sent back. In matters of survival, the spinal reflexes allow the body to react extraordinarily fast.

The spinal cord is protected by bony vertebrae and cushioned in cerebrospinal fluid, but injuries still occur. When the spinal cord is damaged in a particular segment, all lower segments are cut off from the brain, causing paralysis. Therefore, the lower on the spine damage is, the fewer functions an injured individual loses.

The Two Hemispheres

The surface of the brain, known as the **cerebral cortex**, is very uneven, characterized by a distinctive pattern of folds or bumps, known as **gyri** (singular: gyrus), and grooves, known as **sulci** (singular: sulcus), shown in Figure 1. These gyri and sulci form important landmarks that allow us to separate the brain into functional centers. The most prominent sulcus, known as the longitudinal fissure, is the deep groove that separates the brain into two halves or hemispheres: the left hemisphere and the right hemisphere.

There is evidence of some specialization of function—referred to as **lateralization**—in each hemisphere, mainly regarding differences in language ability. Beyond that, however, the differences that have been found have been minor. What we do know is that the left hemisphere controls the right half of the body, and the right hemisphere controls the left half of the body.

The two hemispheres are connected by a thick band of neural fibers known as the **corpus callosum**, consisting of about 200 million axons. The corpus callosum allows the two hemispheres to communicate with each other and allows for information being processed on one side of the brain to be shared with the other side.

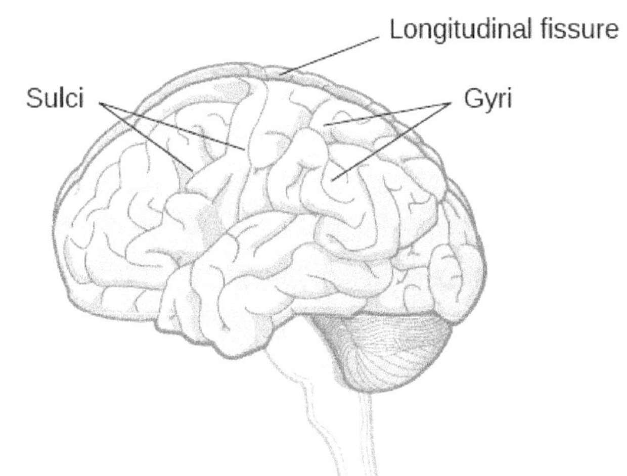

Figure 1. The surface of the brain is covered with gyri and sulci. A deep sulcus is called a fissure, such as the longitudinal fissure that divides the brain into left and right hemispheres. (credit: modification of work by Bruce Blaus)

Normally, we are not aware of the different roles that our two hemispheres play in day-to-day functions, but there are people who come to know the capabilities and functions of their two hemispheres quite well. In some cases of severe epilepsy, doctors elect to sever the corpus callosum as a means of controlling the spread of seizures (Figure 2). While this is an effective treatment option, it results in individuals who have split brains. After surgery, these split-brain patients show a variety of interesting behaviors. For instance, a split-brain patient is unable to name a picture that is shown in the patient's left visual field because the information is only available in the largely nonverbal right hemisphere. However, they are able to recreate the picture with their left hand, which is also controlled by the right hemisphere. When the more verbal left hemisphere sees the picture that the hand drew, the patient is able to name it (assuming the left hemisphere can interpret what was drawn by the left hand).

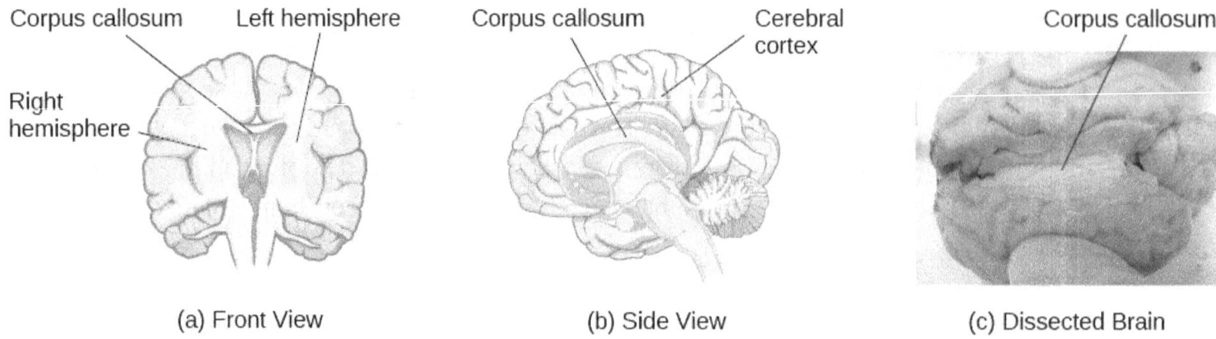

Figure 2. (a, b) The corpus callosum connects the left and right hemispheres of the brain. (c) A scientist spreads this dissected sheep brain apart to show the corpus callosum between the hemispheres. (credit c: modification of work by Aaron Bornstein)

Link to Learning

This interactive animation from the Nobel Prize website walks users through the hemispheres of the brain.

- http://www.nobelprize.org/educational/medicine/split-brain/splitbrainexp.html

---

Much of what we know about the functions of different areas of the brain comes from studying changes in the behavior and ability of individuals who have suffered damage to the brain. For example, researchers study the behavioral changes caused by strokes to learn about the functions of specific brain areas. A stroke, caused by an interruption of blood flow to a region in the brain, causes a loss of brain function in the affected region. The damage can be in a small area, and, if it is, this gives researchers the opportunity to link any resulting behavioral changes to a specific area. The types of deficits displayed after a stroke will be largely dependent on where in the brain the damage occurred.

Consider Theona, an intelligent, self-sufficient woman, who is 62 years old. Recently, she suffered a stroke in the front portion of her right hemisphere. As a result, she has great difficulty moving her left leg. (As you learned earlier, the right hemisphere controls the left side of the body; also, the brain's main motor centers are located at the front of the head, in the frontal lobe.) Theona has also experienced behavioral changes. For example, while in the produce section of the grocery store, she sometimes eats grapes, strawberries, and apples directly from their bins before paying for them. This behavior—which would have been very embarrassing to her before the stroke—is consistent with damage in another region in the frontal lobe—the prefrontal cortex, which is associated with judgment, reasoning, and impulse control.

Watch this video to see an incredible example of the challenges facing a split-brain patient shortly following the surgery to sever her corpus callosum.

Watch this second about another patient who underwent a dramatic surgery to prevent her seizures. You'll learn more about the brain's ability to change, adapt, and reorganize itself, also known as brain **plasticity**.

Forebrain Structures

The two hemispheres of the cerebral cortex are part of the **forebrain** (Figure 3), which is the largest part of the brain. The forebrain contains the cerebral cortex and a number of other structures that lie beneath the cortex (called subcortical structures): thalamus, hypothalamus, pituitary gland, and the limbic system (collection of structures). The cerebral cortex, which is the outer surface of the brain, is associated with higher level processes such as consciousness, thought, emotion, reasoning, language, and memory. Each cerebral hemisphere can be subdivided into four lobes, each associated with different functions.

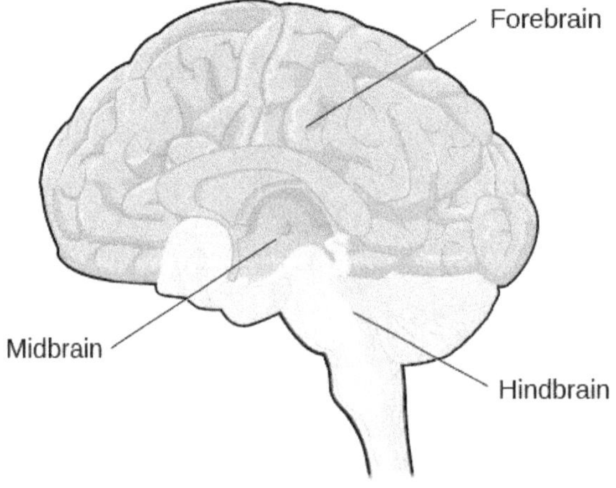

Figure 3. The brain and its parts can be divided into three main categories: the forebrain, midbrain, and hindbrain.

Lobes of the Brain

The four lobes of the brain are the frontal, parietal, temporal, and occipital lobes (Figure 4). The **frontal lobe** is located in the forward part of the brain, extending back to a fissure known as the central sulcus. The frontal lobe is involved in reasoning, motor control, emotion, and language. It contains the **motor cortex**, which is involved in planning and coordinating movement; the **prefrontal cortex**, which is responsible for higher-level cognitive functioning; and **Broca's area**, which is essential for language production.

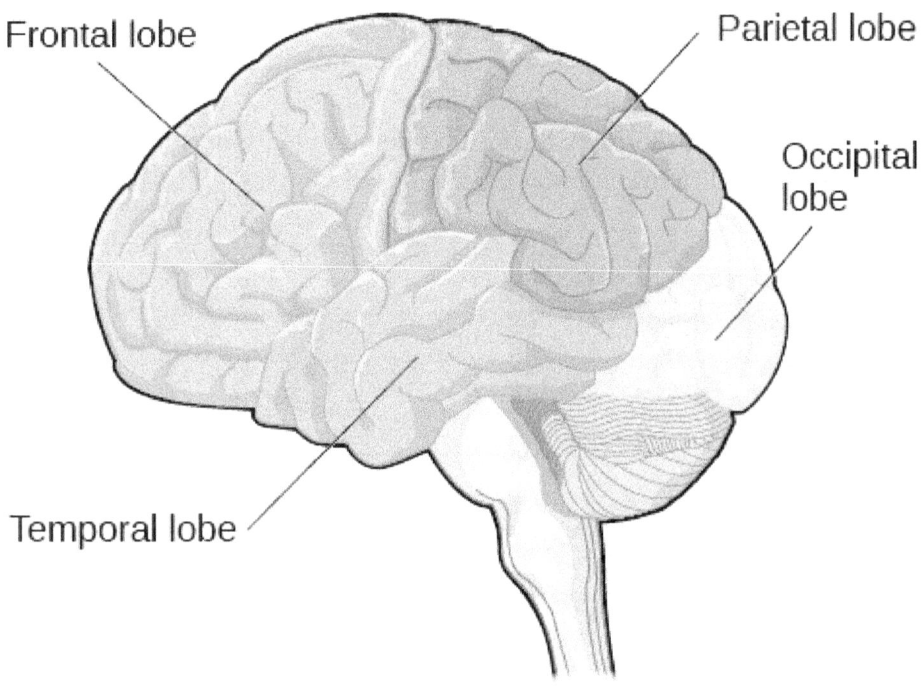

Figure 4. The lobes of the brain are shown.

People who suffer damage to Broca's area have great difficulty producing language of any form. For example, Padma was an electrical engineer who was socially active and a caring, involved mother. About twenty years ago, she was in a car accident and suffered damage to her Broca's area. She completely lost the ability to speak and form any kind of meaningful language. There is nothing wrong with her mouth or her vocal cords, but she is unable to produce words. She can follow directions but can't respond verbally, and she can read but no longer write. She can do routine tasks like running to the market to buy milk, but she could not communicate verbally if a situation called for it.

Probably the most famous case of frontal lobe damage is that of a man by the name of Phineas Gage. On September 13, 1848, Gage (age 25) was working as a railroad foreman in Vermont. He and his crew were using an iron rod to tamp explosives down into a blasting hole to remove rock along the railway's path. Unfortunately, the iron rod created a spark and caused the rod to explode out of the blasting hole, into Gage's face, and through his skull (Figure 5). Although lying in a pool of his own blood with brain matter emerging from his head, Gage was conscious and able to get up, walk, and speak. But in the months following his accident, people noticed that his personality had changed. Many of his friends described him as no longer being himself. Before the accident, it was said that

Gage was a well-mannered, soft-spoken man, but he began to behave in odd and inappropriate ways after the accident. Such changes in personality would be consistent with loss of impulse control—a frontal lobe function.

Beyond the damage to the frontal lobe itself, subsequent investigations into the rod's path also identified probable damage to pathways between the frontal lobe and other brain structures, including the limbic system. With connections between the planning functions of the frontal lobe and the emotional processes of the limbic system severed, Gage had difficulty controlling his emotional impulses.

However, there is some evidence suggesting that the dramatic changes in Gage's personality were exaggerated and embellished. Gage's case occurred in the midst of a 19th century debate over localization—regarding whether certain areas of the brain are associated with particular functions. On the basis of extremely limited information about Gage, the extent of his injury, and his life before and after the accident, scientists tended to find support for their own views, on whichever side of the debate they fell (Macmillan, 1999).

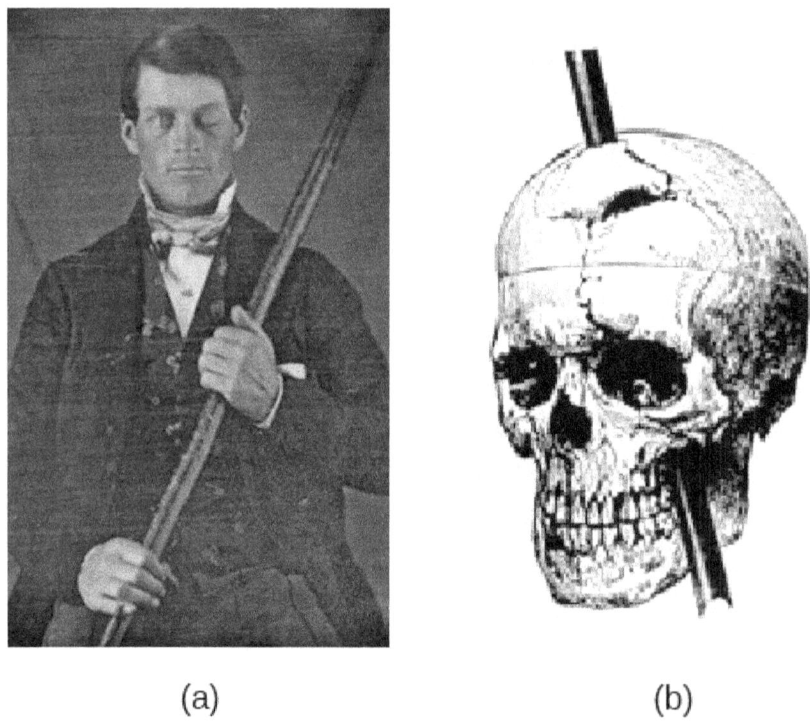

(a)   (b)

Figure 5. (a) Phineas Gage holds the iron rod that penetrated his skull in an 1848 railroad construction accident. (b) Gage's prefrontal cortex was severely damaged in the left hemisphere. The rod entered Gage's face on the left side, passed behind his eye, and exited through the top of his skull, before landing about 80 feet away. (credit a: modification of work by Jack and Beverly Wilgus)

Watch this clip about Phineas Gage to learn more about his accident and injury.

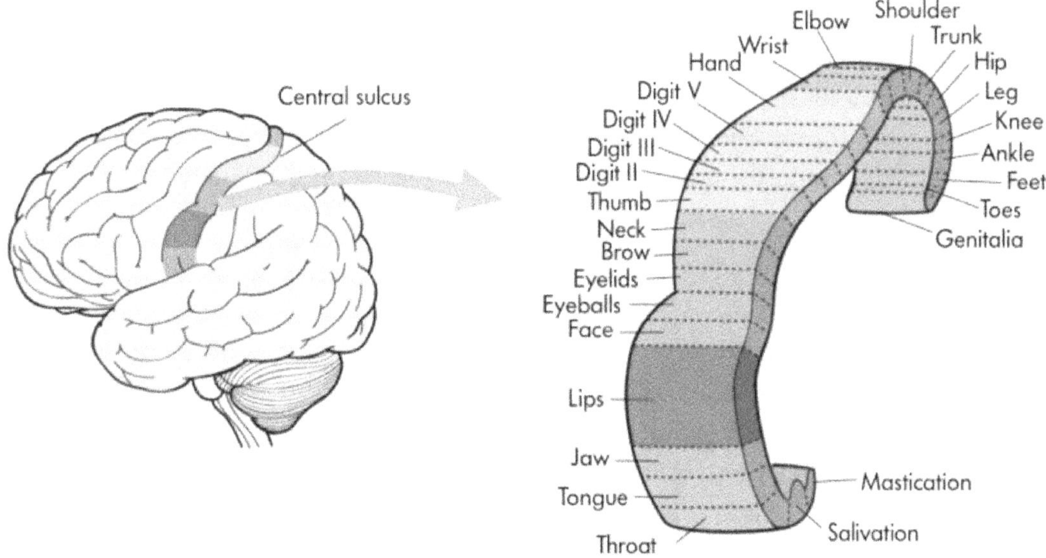

Figure 6: Specific body parts like the tongue or fingers are mapped onto certain areas of the brain including the primary motor cortex.

One particularly fascinating area in the frontal lobe is called the "primary motor cortex". This strip running along the side of the brain is in charge of voluntary movements like waving goodbye, wiggling your eyebrows, and kissing. It is an excellent example of the way that the various regions of the brain are highly specialized. Interestingly, each of our various body parts has a unique portion of the primary motor cortex devoted to it (see Figure 6). Each individual finger has about as much dedicated brain space as your entire leg. Your lips, in turn, require about as much dedicated brain processing as all of your fingers and your hand combined!

Because the cerebral cortex in general, and the frontal lobe in particular, are associated with such sophisticated functions as planning and being self-aware they are often thought of as a higher, less primal portion of the brain. Indeed, other animals such as rats and kangaroos while they do have frontal regions of their brain do not have the same level of development in the cerebral cortices. The closer an animal is to humans on the evolutionary tree—think chimpanzees and gorillas, the more developed is this portion of their brain.

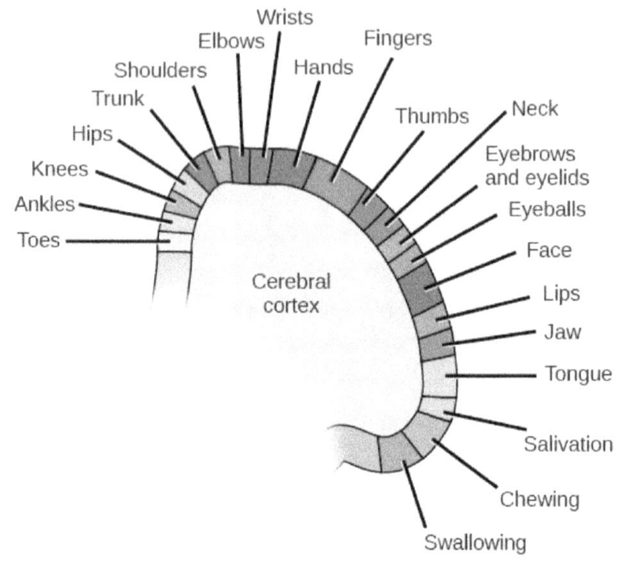

Figure 7. Spatial relationships in the body are mirrored in the organization of the somatosensory cortex.

The brain's **parietal lobe** is located immediately behind the frontal lobe, and is involved in processing information from the body's senses. It contains the **somatosensory cortex**, which is essential for processing sensory information from across the body, such as touch, temperature, and pain. The somatosensory cortex is organized topographically, which means that spatial relationships that exist in the body are maintained on the surface of the somatosensory cortex. For example, the portion of the cortex that processes sensory information from the hand is adjacent to the portion that processes information from the wrist.

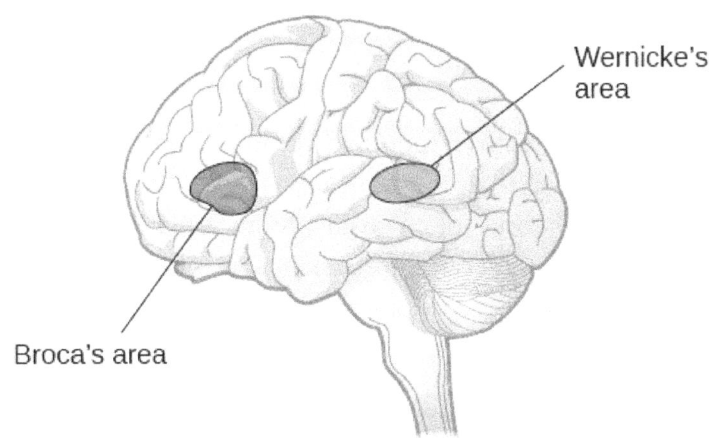

Figure 8. Damage to either Broca's area or Wernicke's area can result in language deficits. The types of deficits are very different, however, depending on which area is affected.

The **temporal lobe** is located on the side of the head (temporal means "near the temples"), and is associated with hearing, memory, emotion, and some aspects of language. The **auditory cortex**, the main area responsible for processing auditory information, is located within the temporal lobe. **Wernicke's area**, important for speech comprehension, is also located here. Whereas individuals with damage to Broca's area have difficulty producing language, those with damage to Wernicke's area can produce sensible language, but they are unable to understand it (Figure 8).

The **occipital lobe** is located at the very back of the brain, and contains the primary visual cortex, which is responsible for interpreting incoming visual information. The occipital cortex is organized retinotopically, which means there is a close relationship between the position of an object in a person's visual field and the position of that object's representation on the cortex. You will learn much more about how visual information is processed in the occipital lobe when you study sensation and perception.

Food for Thought

Consider the following advice from Joseph LeDoux, a professor of neuroscience and psychology at New York University, as you learn about the specific parts of the brain:

Be suspicious of any statement that says a brain area is a center responsible for some function. The notion of functions being products of brain areas or centers is left over from the days when most evidence about brain function was based on the effects of brain lesions localized to specific areas. Today, we think of functions as products of systems rather than of areas. Neurons in areas contribute because they are part of a system. The amygdala, for example, contributes to threat detection because it is part of a threat detection system. And just because the amygdala contributes to threat detection does not mean that threat detection is the only function to which it contributes. Amygdala neurons, for example, are also components of systems that process the significance of stimuli related to eating, drinking, sex, and addictive drugs.

Glossary

auditory cortex: strip of cortex in the temporal lobe that is responsible for processing auditory information

Broca's area: region in the left hemisphere that is essential for language production

cerebral cortex: surface of the brain that is associated with our highest mental capabilities

corpus callosum: thick band of neural fibers connecting the brain's two hemispheres

forebrain: largest part of the brain, containing the cerebral cortex, the thalamus, and the limbic system, among other structures

frontal lobe: part of the cerebral cortex involved in reasoning, motor control, emotion, and language; contains motor cortex

gyrus (plural: gyri): bump or ridge on the cerebral cortex

hemisphere: left or right half of the brain

lateralization: concept that each hemisphere of the brain is associated with specialized functions

longitudinal fissure: deep groove in the brain's cortex

motor cortex: strip of cortex involved in planning and coordinating movement

occipital lobe: part of the cerebral cortex associated with visual processing; contains the primary visual cortex

parietal lobe: part of the cerebral cortex involved in processing various sensory and perceptual information; contains the primary somatosensory cortex

prefrontal cortex: area in the frontal lobe responsible for higher-level cognitive functioning

somatosensory cortex: essential for processing sensory information from across the body, such as touch, temperature, and pain

sulcus (plural: sulci): depressions or grooves in the cerebral cortex

temporal lobe: part of cerebral cortex associated with hearing, memory, emotion, and some aspects of language; contains primary auditory cortex

Wernicke's area: important for speech comprehension

Attributions

CC licensed content, Original

- Introduction. **Provided by:** Lumen Learning. **License:** *CC BY: Attribution*

CC licensed content, Shared previously

- The Brain and Spinal Cord. **Authored by:** OpenStax College. **Located at:** http://cnx.org/contents/Sr8Ev5Og@5.49:_Io4zP0c@7/The-Brain-and-Spinal-Cord. **License:** *CC BY: Attribution.* **License Terms:** Download for free at http://cnx.org/content/col11629/latest/.

- Modification, adaptation, and original content. **Provided by:** Lumen Learning. **License:** *CC BY: Attribution*

- The Amygdala Is Not The Brains Fear Center. **Authored by:** Joseph LeDoux. **Located at:** http://thepsychreport.com/science/the-amygdala-is-not-the-brains-fear-center/. **Project:** The Psych Report. **License:** *CC BY-NC-SA: Attribution-NonCommercial-ShareAlike*

- Motor cortex paragraphs and image. **Authored by:** Robert Biswas-Diener. **Provided by:** Portland State University. **Located at:** http://nobaproject.com/modules/the-brain-and-nervous-system. **Project:** The Noba Project. **License:** *CC BY-NC-SA: Attribution-NonCommercial-ShareAlike*

This is a modified version of OpenStax Psychology. Download the original text for free at https://openstax.org/details/books/psychology

- Meet Your Master: Getting to Know Your Brain – Crash Course Psychology #4. **Provided by:** CrashCourse . **Located at:** https://www.youtube.com/watch?v=vHrmiy4W9C0. **License:** *Other*. **License Terms:** Standard YouTube License

- Split Brain mpeg1video. **Authored by:** mrsrooboy. **Located at:** https://www.youtube.com/watch?v=8C8qu8FnuAo&feature=youtu.be. **License:** *Other*. **License Terms:** Standard YouTube License

- Brain Plasticity – the story of Jody. **Authored by:** Streetwisdom Billy. **Located at:** https://www.youtube.com/watch?v=VaDlLD97CLM&feature=youtu.be. **License:** *Other*. **License Terms:** Standard YouTube License

- Phineas Gage (LEGO Stop-Motion Music Video). **Authored by:** Brad Wray. **Located at:** https://www.youtube.com/watch?v=_nikOxNfjqs. **License:** *Other*. **License Terms:** Standard YouTube License

- brain image. **Authored by:** Henry Gray. **Provided by:** Wikimedia. **Located at:** https://commons.wikimedia.org/wiki/File:Lobes_of_the_brain_NL.svg. **License:** *Public Domain: No Known Copyright*

Nature and Nurture

What you'll learn to do: explain how nature, nurture, and epigenetics influence personality and behavior

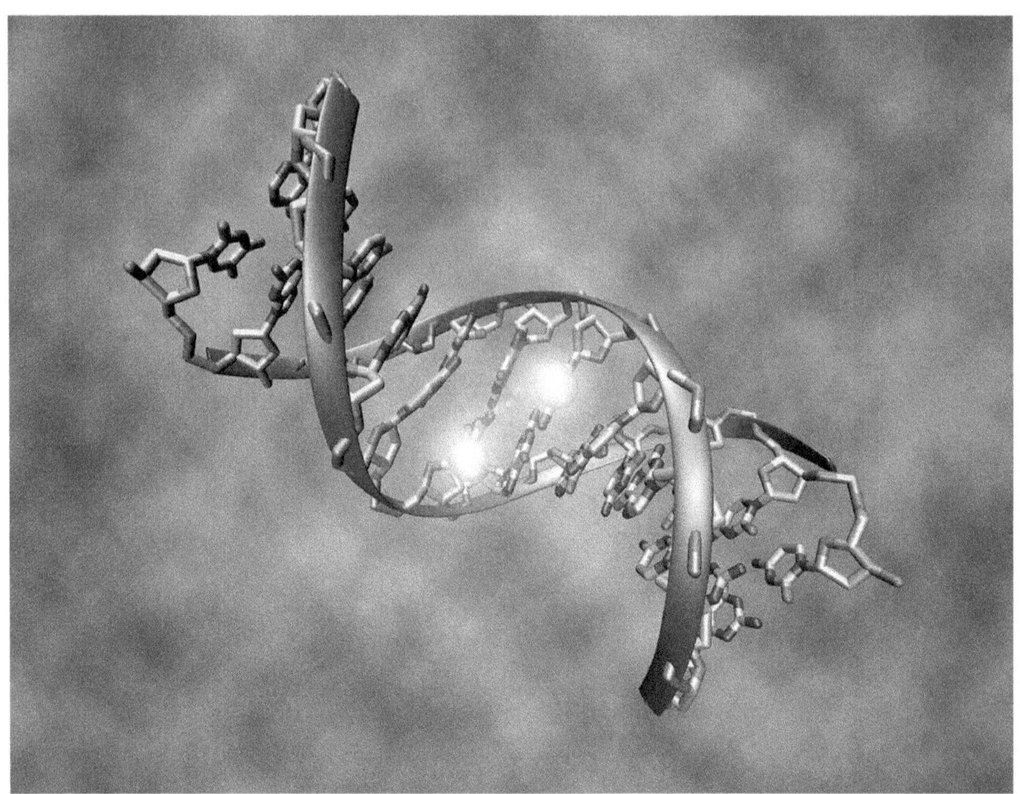

How do we become who we are? Traditionally, people's answers have placed them in one of two camps: nature or nurture. The one says genes determine an individual while the other claims the environment is the linchpin for development. Since the 16th century, when the terms "nature" and "nurture" first came into use, many people have spent ample time debating which is more important, but these discussions have more often led to ideological cul-de-sacs rather than pinnacles of insight.

New research into epigenetics—the science of how the environment influences genetic expression—is changing the conversation. As psychologist David S. Moore explains in his newest book, *The Developing Genome*, this burgeoning field reveals that what counts is not what genes you *have* so much as what your genes are *doing*. And what your genes are doing is influenced by the ever-changing environment they're in. Factors like stress, nutrition, and exposure to toxins all play a role in how genes are expressed—essentially which genes are turned on or off. Unlike the static conception of nature or nurture, epigenetic research demonstrates how genes and environments continuously interact to produce characteristics throughout a lifetime.

- Investigate the historic nature vs. nurture debate and describe techniques psychologists use to learn about the origin of traits
- Explain the basic principles of the theory of evolution by natural selection, genetic variation, and mutation

The Nature vs. Nurture Debate

Are you the way you are because you were born that way, or because of the way you were raised? Do your genetics and biology dictate your personality and behavior, or is it your environment and how you were raised? These questions are central to the age-old **nature–nurture** debate. In the history of psychology, no other question has caused so much controversy and offense: We are so concerned with nature–nurture because our very sense of moral character seems to depend on it. While we may admire the athletic skills of a great basketball player, we think of his height as simply a gift, a payoff in the "genetic lottery." For the same reason, no one blames a short person for his height or someone's congenital disability on poor decisions: To state the obvious, it's "not their fault." But we do praise the concert violinist (and perhaps her parents and teachers as well) for her dedication, just as we condemn cheaters, slackers, and bullies for their bad behavior. The problem is, most human characteristics aren't usually as clear-cut as height or instrument-mastery, affirming our nature–nurture expectations strongly one way or the other. In fact, even the great violinist might have some inborn qualities—perfect pitch, or long, nimble fingers—that support and reward her hard work. And the basketball player might have eaten a diet while growing up that promoted his genetic tendency for being tall. When we think about our own qualities, they seem under our control in some respects, yet beyond our control in others. And often the traits that don't seem to have an obvious cause are the ones that concern us the most and are far more personally significant. What about how much we drink or worry? What about our honesty, or religiosity, or sexual orientation? They all come from that uncertain zone, neither fixed by nature nor totally under our own control.

Figure 1. Researchers have learned a great deal about the nature-nurture dynamic by working with animals. But of course many of the techniques used to study animals cannot be applied to people. Separating these two influences in human subjects is a greater research challenge. [Photo: mharrsch]

One major problem with answering nature-nurture questions about people is, how do you set up an experiment? In nonhuman animals, there are relatively straightforward experiments for tackling nature-nurture questions. Say, for example, you are interested in aggressiveness in dogs. You want to test for the more important determinant of aggression: being born to aggressive dogs or being raised by them. You could mate two aggressive dogs—angry Chihuahuas—together, and mate two nonaggressive dogs—happy beagles—together, then switch half the puppies from each litter between the different sets of parents to raise. You would then have puppies born to aggressive parents (the Chihuahuas) but being raised by nonaggressive parents (the Beagles), and vice versa, in litters that mirror each other in puppy distribution. The big questions are: Would the Chihuahua parents raise aggressive beagle puppies? Would the beagle parents raise *non*aggressive Chihuahua puppies? Would the puppies' *nature* win out, regardless of who raised them? Or… would the result be a combination of nature *and* nurture? Much of the most significant nature-nurture research has been done in this way (Scott & Fuller, 1998), and animal breeders have been doing it successfully for thousands of years. In fact, it is fairly easy to breed animals for behavioral traits.

With people, however, we can't assign babies to parents at random, or select parents with certain behavioral characteristics to mate, merely in the interest of science (though history does include horrific examples of such practices, in misguided attempts at "eugenics," the shaping of human characteristics through intentional breeding). In typical human families, children's biological parents raise them, so it is very difficult to know whether children act like their parents due to genetic (nature) or environmental (nurture) reasons. Nevertheless, despite our restrictions on setting up human-based experiments, we do see real-world examples of nature-nurture at work in the human sphere—though they only provide partial answers to our many questions. The science of how genes and environments work together to influence behavior is called **behavioral genetics**. The easiest opportunity we have to observe this is the **adoption study**. When children are put up for adoption, the parents who give birth to them are no longer the parents who raise them. This setup isn't quite the same as the experiments with dogs (children aren't assigned to random adoptive parents in order to suit the particular interests of a scientist) but adoption still tells us some interesting things, or at least confirms some basic expectations. For instance, if the biological child of tall parents were adopted into a family of short people, do you suppose the child's growth would be affected? What about the biological child of a Spanish-speaking family adopted at birth into an English-speaking family? What language would you expect the child to speak? And what might these outcomes tell you about the difference between height and language in terms of nature-nurture?

Another option for observing nature-nurture in humans involves **twin studies**. There are two types of twins: monozygotic (MZ) and dizygotic (DZ). Monozygotic twins, also called "identical" twins, result from a single zygote (fertilized egg) and have the same DNA. They are essentially clones. Dizygotic twins, also known as "fraternal" twins, develop from two zygotes and share 50% of their DNA. Fraternal twins are ordinary siblings who happen to have been born at the same time. To analyze nature–nurture using twins, we compare

Figure 2. Studies focused on twins have lead to important insights about the biological origins of many personality characteristics. [Photo: ethermoon]

the similarity of MZ and DZ pairs. Sticking with the features of height and spoken language, let's take a look at how nature and nurture apply: Identical twins, unsurprisingly, are almost perfectly similar for height. The heights of fraternal twins, however, are like any other sibling pairs: more similar to each other than to people from other families, but hardly identical. This contrast between twin types gives us a clue about the role genetics plays in determining height.

Now consider spoken language. If one identical twin speaks Spanish at home, the co-twin with whom she is raised almost certainly does too. But the same would be true for a pair of fraternal twins raised together. In terms of spoken language, fraternal twins are just as similar as identical twins, so it appears that the genetic match of identical twins doesn't make much difference. Twin and adoption studies are two instances of a much broader class of methods for observing nature-nurture called **quantitative genetics**, the scientific discipline in which similarities among individuals are analyzed based on how biologically related they are. We can do these studies with siblings and half-siblings, cousins, twins who have been separated at birth and raised separately (Bouchard, Lykken, McGue, & Segal, 1990; such twins are very rare and play a smaller role than is commonly believed in the science of nature–nurture), or with entire extended families (see Plomin, DeFries, Knopik, & Neiderhiser, 2012, for a complete introduction to research methods relevant to nature–nurture).

For better or for worse, contentions about nature–nurture have intensified because quantitative genetics produces a number called a **heritability coefficient**, varying from 0 to 1, that is meant to provide a single measure of genetics' influence of a trait. In a general way, a heritability coefficient measures how strongly differences among individuals are related to differences among their genes. But beware: Heritability coefficients, although simple to compute, are deceptively difficult to interpret. Nevertheless, numbers that provide simple answers to complicated questions tend to have a strong influence on the human imagination, and a great deal of time has been spent discussing whether the heritability of intelligence or personality or depression is equal to one number or another.

One reason nature–nurture continues to fascinate us so much is that we live in an era of great scientific discovery in genetics, comparable to the times of Copernicus, Galileo, and Newton, with regard to astronomy and physics. Every day, it seems, new discoveries are made, new possibilities proposed. When Francis Galton first started thinking about nature–nurture in the late-19th century he was very influenced by his cousin, Charles Darwin, but genetics *per se* was unknown. Mendel's famous work with peas, conducted at about the same time, went undiscovered for 20 years; quantitative genetics was developed in the 1920s; DNA was discovered by Watson and Crick in the 1950s; the human genome was completely sequenced at the turn of the 21st century; and we are now on the verge of being able to obtain the specific DNA sequence of anyone at a relatively low cost. No one knows what this new genetic knowledge will mean for the study of nature–nurture, but as we will see in the next section, answers to nature–nurture questions have turned out to be far more difficult and mysterious than anyone imagined.

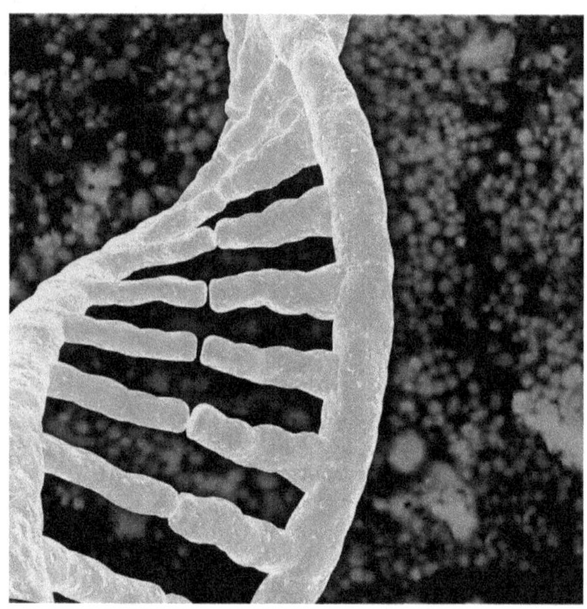

Figure 3. Quantitative genetics uses statistical methods to study the effects that both heredity and environment have on test subjects. These methods have provided us with the heritability coefficient which measures how strongly differences among individuals for a trait are related to differences among their genes. [Image: EMSL]

What Have We Learned About Nature–Nurture?

It would be satisfying to be able to say that nature–nurture studies have given us conclusive and complete evidence about where traits come from, with some traits clearly resulting from genetics and others almost entirely from environmental factors, such as childrearing practices and personal will; but that is not the case. Instead, *everything* has turned out to have some footing in genetics. The more genetically-related people are, the more similar they are—for *everything*: height, weight, intelligence, personality, mental illness, etc. Sure, it seems like common sense that some traits have a genetic bias. For example, adopted children resemble their biological parents even if they have never met them, and identical twins are more similar to each other than are fraternal twins. And while certain psychological traits, such as personality or mental illness (e.g., schizophrenia), seem reasonably influenced by genetics, it turns out that the same is true for political attitudes, how much television people watch (Plomin, Corley, DeFries, & Fulker, 1990), and whether or not they get divorced (McGue & Lykken, 1992).

Figure 4. Research over the last half century has revealed how central genetics are to behavior. The more genetically related people are the more similar they are not just physically but also in terms of personality and behavior. [Photo: ??? aikawake]

It may seem surprising, but genetic influence on behavior is a relatively recent discovery. In the middle of the 20th century, psychology was dominated by the doctrine of behaviorism, which held that behavior could only be explained in terms of environmental factors. Psychiatry concentrated on psychoanalysis, which probed for roots of behavior in individuals' early life-histories. The truth is, neither behaviorism nor psychoanalysis is incompatible with genetic influences on behavior, and neither Freud nor Skinner was naive about the importance of organic processes in behavior. Nevertheless, in their day it was widely thought that children's personalities were shaped entirely by imitating their parents' behavior, and that schizophrenia was caused by certain kinds of "pathological mothering."

Whatever the outcome of our broader discussion of nature–nurture, the basic fact that the best predictors of an adopted child's personality or mental health are found in the biological parents he or she has never met, rather than in the adoptive parents who raised him or her, presents a significant challenge to purely environmental explanations of personality or psychopathology. The message is clear: You can't leave genes out of the equation. But keep in mind, no behavioral traits are completely inherited, so you can't leave the environment out altogether, either. Trying to untangle the various ways nature-nurture influences human behavior can be messy, and often common-sense notions can get in the way of good science. One very significant contribution of behavioral genetics that has changed psychology for good can be very helpful to keep in mind: When your subjects are biologically-related, no matter how clearly a situation may seem to point to environmental influence, it is never safe to interpret a behavior as wholly the result of nurture without further evidence. For example, when presented with data showing that children whose mothers read to them often are likely to have better reading scores in third grade, it is tempting to conclude that reading to your kids out loud is important to success in school; this may well be true, but the study as described is inconclusive, because there are genetic *as well as* environmental pathways between the parenting practices of mothers and the abilities of their children. This is a case where "correlation does not imply causation," as they say. To establish that reading aloud causes success, a scientist can either study the problem in adoptive families (in which the genetic pathway is absent) or by finding a way to randomly assign children to oral reading conditions.

Psychological researchers study genetics in order to better understand the biological basis that contributes to certain behaviors. While all humans share certain biological mechanisms, we are each unique. And while our bodies have many of the same parts—brains and hormones and cells with genetic codes—these are expressed in a wide variety of behaviors, thoughts, and reactions.

Why do two people infected by the same disease have different outcomes: one surviving and one succumbing to the ailment? How are genetic diseases passed through family lines? Are there genetic components to psychological disorders, such as depression or schizophrenia? To what extent might there be a psychological basis to health conditions such as childhood obesity?

To explore these questions, let's start by focusing on a specific disease, sickle-cell anemia, and how it might affect two infected sisters. **Sickle-cell anemia** is a genetic condition in which red blood cells, which are normally round, take on a crescent-like shape (Figure 5). The changed shape of these cells affects how they function: sickle-shaped cells can clog blood vessels and block blood flow, leading to high fever, severe pain, swelling, and tissue damage.

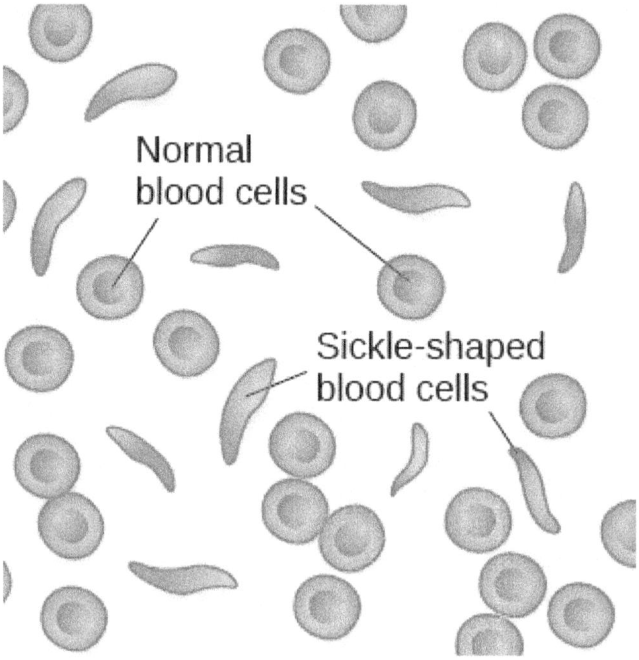

Many people with sickle-cell anemia—and the particular genetic mutation that causes it—die at an early age. While the notion of "survival of the fittest" may suggest that people suffering from this disease have a low survival rate and therefore the disease will become less common, this is not the case. Despite the negative evolutionary effects associated with this genetic mutation, the sickle-cell gene remains relatively common among people of African descent. Why is this? The explanation is illustrated with the following scenario.

Imagine two young women—Luwi and Sena—sisters in rural Zambia, Africa. Luwi carries the gene for sickle-cell anemia; Sena does not carry the gene. Sickle-cell carriers have one copy of the sickle-cell gene but do

Figure 5. *Normal blood cells travel freely through the blood vessels, while sickle-shaped cells form blockages preventing blood flow.*

not have full-blown sickle-cell anemia. They experience symptoms only if they are severely dehydrated or are deprived of oxygen (as in mountain climbing). Carriers are thought to be immune from malaria (an often deadly disease that is widespread in tropical climates) because changes in their blood chemistry and immune functioning prevent the malaria parasite from having its effects (Gong, Parikh, Rosenthal, & Greenhouse, 2013). However, full-blown sickle-cell anemia, with two copies of the sickle-cell gene, does not provide immunity to malaria.

While walking home from school, both sisters are bitten by mosquitos carrying the malaria parasite. Luwi does not get malaria because she carries the sickle-cell mutation. Sena, on the other hand, develops malaria and dies just two weeks later. Luwi survives and eventually has children, to whom she may pass on the sickle-cell mutation.

Malaria is rare in the United States, so the sickle-cell gene benefits nobody: the gene manifests primarily in health problems—minor in carriers, severe in the full-blown disease—with no health benefits for carriers. However, the situation is quite different in other parts of the world. In parts of Africa where malaria is prevalent, having the sickle-cell mutation does provide health benefits for carriers (protection from malaria).

This is precisely the situation that Charles Darwin describes in the **theory of evolution by natural selection** (Figure 6). In simple terms, the theory states that organisms that are better suited for their environment will survive and reproduce, while those that are poorly suited for their environment will die off. In our example, we can see that as a carrier, Luwi's mutation is highly adaptive in her African homeland; however, if she resided in the United States (where malaria is much less common), her mutation could prove costly—with a high probability of the disease in her descendants and minor health problems of her own.

(a)

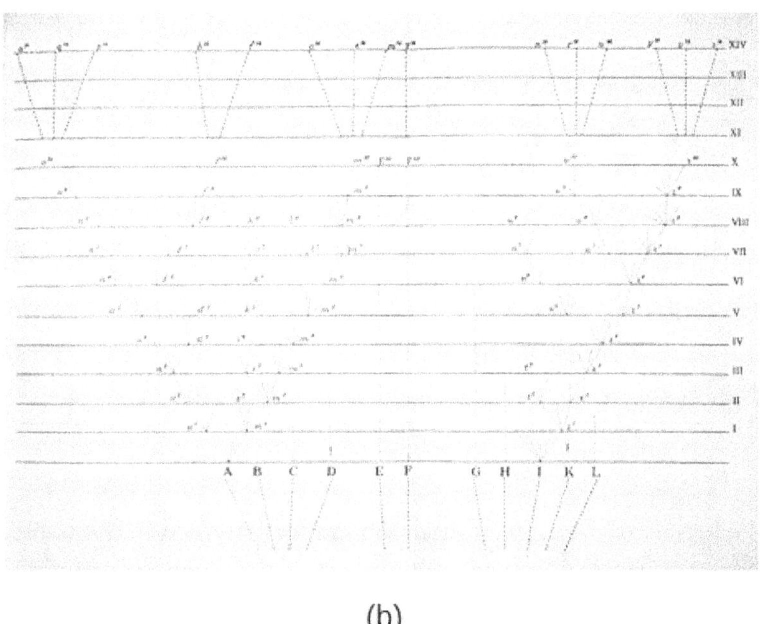

(b)

Figure 6. (a) In 1859, Charles Darwin proposed his theory of evolution by natural selection in his book, On the Origin of Species. (b) The book contains just one illustration: this diagram that shows how species evolve over time through natural selection.

Dig Deeper: Two Perspectives on Genetics and Behavior

It's easy to get confused about two fields that study the interaction of genes and the environment, such as the fields of **evolutionary psychology** and **behavioral genetics.** How can we tell them apart?

In both fields, it is understood that genes not only code for particular traits, but also contribute to certain patterns of cognition and behavior. Evolutionary psychology focuses on how universal patterns of behavior and cognitive processes have evolved over time. Therefore, variations in cognition and behavior would make individuals more or less successful in reproducing and passing those genes to their offspring. Evolutionary psychologists study a variety of psychological phenomena that may have evolved as adaptations, including fear response, food preferences, mate selection, and cooperative behaviors (Confer et al., 2010).

Whereas evolutionary psychologists focus on universal patterns that evolved over millions of years, behavioral geneticists study how individual differences arise, in the present, through the interaction of genes and the environment. When studying human behavior, behavioral geneticists often employ twin and adoption studies to research questions of interest. Twin studies compare the rates that a given behavioral trait is shared among identical and fraternal twins; adoption studies compare those rates among biologically related relatives and adopted relatives. Both approaches provide some insight into the relative importance of genes and environment for the expression of a given trait.

Link to Learning

Watch this interview with renowned evolutionary psychologist Davis Buss for an explanation of how a psychologist approaches evolution and how this approach fits within the field of social science.

- https://youtu.be/xbRCFuet0Nk

Genetic Variation

Genetic variation, the genetic difference between individuals, is what contributes to a species' adaptation to its environment. In humans, genetic variation begins with an egg, about 100 million sperm, and fertilization. Fertile women ovulate roughly once per month, releasing an egg from follicles in the ovary. The egg travels, via the fallopian tube, from the ovary to the uterus, where it may be fertilized by a sperm.

The egg and the sperm each contain 23 chromosomes. **Chromosomes** are long strings of genetic material known as **deoxyribonucleic acid (DNA).** DNA is a helix-shaped molecule made up of nucleotide base pairs. In each chromosome, sequences of DNA make up **genes** that control or partially control a number of visible characteristics, known as traits, such as eye color, hair color, and so on. A single gene may have multiple possible variations, or alleles. An **allele** is a specific version of a gene. So, a given gene may code for the trait of hair color, and the different alleles of that gene affect which hair color an individual has.

When a sperm and egg fuse, their 23 chromosomes pair up and create a zygote with 23 pairs of chromosomes. Therefore, each parent contributes half the genetic information carried by the offspring; the resulting physical characteristics of the offspring (called the phenotype) are determined by the interaction of genetic material supplied by the parents (called the genotype). A person's **genotype** is the genetic makeup of that individual. **Phenotype,** on the other hand, refers to the individual's inherited physical characteristics (Figure 7).

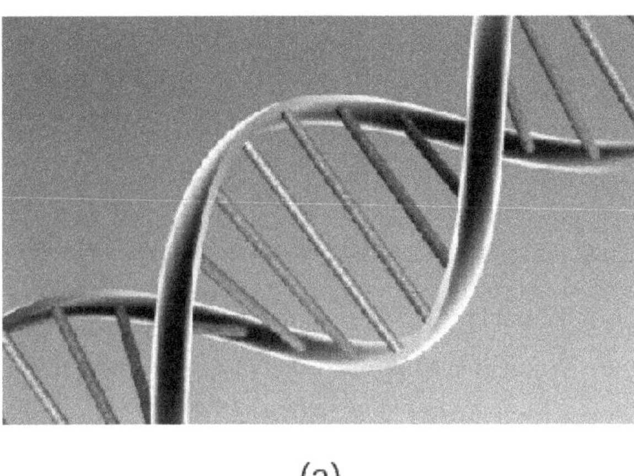

(a)

(b)

Figure 7. (a) Genotype refers to the genetic makeup of an individual based on the genetic material (DNA) inherited from one's parents. (b) Phenotype describes an individual's observable characteristics, such as hair color, skin color, height, and build. (credit a: modification of work by Caroline Davis; credit b: modification of work by Cory Zanker)

Most traits are controlled by multiple genes, but some traits are controlled by one gene. A characteristic like **cleft chin**, for example, is influenced by a single gene from each parent. In this example, we will call the gene for cleft chin "B," and the gene for smooth chin "b." Cleft chin is a dominant trait, which means that having the **dominant allele** either from one parent (Bb) or both parents (BB) will always result in the phenotype associated with the dominant allele. When someone has two copies of the same allele, they are said to be **homozygous** for that allele. When someone has a combination of alleles for a given gene, they are said to be **heterozygous.** For example, smooth chin is a recessive trait, which means that an individual will only display the smooth chin phenotype if they are homozygous for that **recessive allele** (bb).

Imagine that a woman with a cleft chin has a child with a man with a smooth chin. What type of chin will their child have? The answer to that depends on which alleles each parent carries. If the woman is homozygous for cleft chin (BB), her offspring will always have cleft chin. It gets a little more complicated, however, if the mother is heterozygous for this gene (Bb). Since the father has a smooth chin—therefore homozygous for the recessive allele (bb)—we can expect the offspring to have a 50% chance of having a cleft chin and a 50% chance of having a smooth chin (Figure 8).

Sickle-cell anemia is just one of many genetic disorders caused by the pairing of two recessive genes. For example, **phenylketonuria (PKU)** is a condition in which individuals lack an enzyme that normally converts harmful amino acids into harmless byproducts. If someone with this condition goes

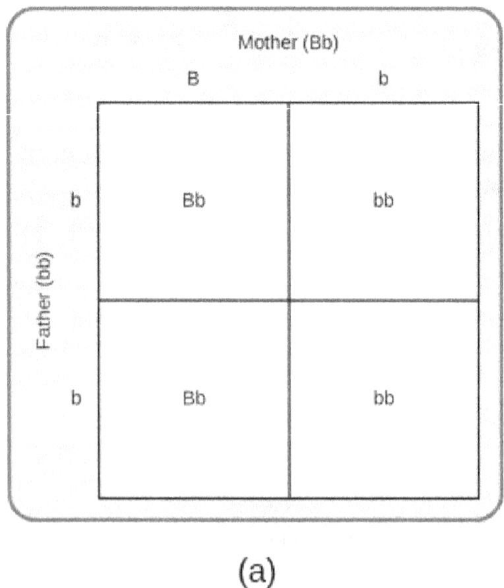

(a)

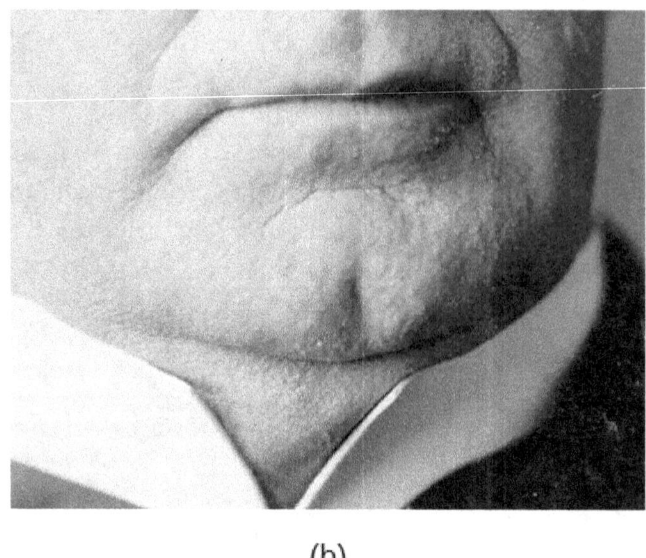

(b)

Figure 8. (a) A Punnett square is a tool used to predict how genes will interact in the production of offspring. The capital B represents the dominant allele, and the lowercase b represents the recessive allele. In the example of the cleft chin, where B is cleft chin (dominant allele), wherever a pair contains the dominant allele, B, you can expect a cleft chin phenotype. You can expect a smooth chin phenotype only when there are two copies of the recessive allele, bb. (b) A cleft chin, shown here, is an inherited trait.

untreated, he or she will experience significant deficits in cognitive function, seizures, and increased risk of various psychiatric disorders. Because PKU is a recessive trait, each parent must have at least one copy of the recessive allele in order to produce a child with the condition (Figure 9).

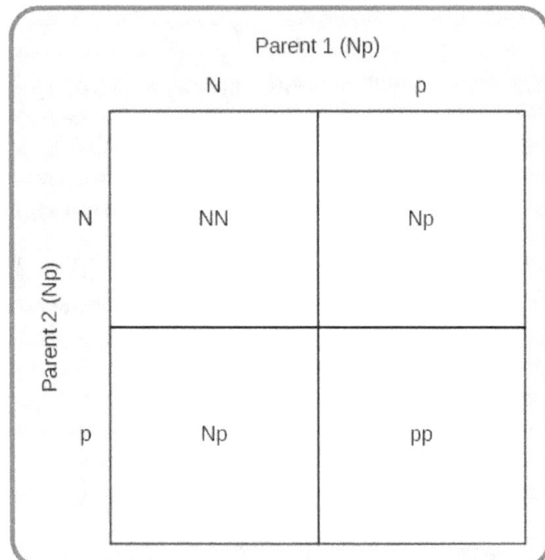

Figure 9. In this Punnett square, N represents the normal allele, and p represents the recessive allele that is associated with PKU. If two individuals mate who are both heterozygous for the allele associated with PKU, their offspring have a 25% chance of expressing the PKU phenotype.

So far, we have discussed traits that involve just one gene, but few human characteristics are controlled by a single gene. Most traits are **polygenic**: controlled by more than one gene. Height is one example of a polygenic trait, as are skin color and weight.

Where do harmful genes that contribute to diseases like PKU come from? Gene mutations provide one source of harmful genes. A **mutation** is a sudden, permanent change in a gene. While many mutations can be harmful or lethal, once in a while, a mutation benefits an individual by giving that person an advantage over those who do not have the mutation. Recall that the theory of evolution asserts that individuals best adapted to their particular environments are more likely to reproduce and pass on their genes to future generations. In order for this process to occur, there must be competition—more technically, there must be variability in genes (and resultant traits) that allow for variation in adaptability to the environment. If a population consisted of identical individuals, then any dramatic changes in the environment would affect everyone in the same way, and there would be no variation in selection. In contrast, diversity in genes and associated traits allows some individuals to perform slightly better than others when faced with environmental change. This creates a distinct advantage for individuals best suited for their environments in terms of successful reproduction and genetic transmission.

Glossary

adoption study: a behavior genetic research method that involves comparison of adopted children to their adoptive and biological parents

allele: specific version of a gene

behavioral genetics: the empirical science of how genes and environments combine to generate behavior

chromosome: long strand of genetic information

deoxyribonucleic acid (DNA): helix-shaped molecule made of nucleotide base pairs

dominant allele: allele whose phenotype will be expressed in an individual that possesses that allele

genetic environmental correlation: view of gene-environment interaction that asserts our genes affect our environment, and our environment influences the expression of our genes

genotype: genetic makeup of an individual

heterozygous: consisting of two different alleles

heritability coefficient: an easily misinterpreted statistical construct that purports to measure the role of genetics in the explanation of differences among individuals

homozygous: consisting of two identical alleles

mutation: sudden, permanent change in a gene

phenotype: individual's inheritable physical characteristics

polygenic: multiple genes affecting a given trait

quantitative genetics: scientific and mathematical methods for inferring genetic and environmental processes based on the degree of genetic and environmental similarity among organisms

recessive allele: allele whose phenotype will be expressed only if an individual is homozygous for that allele

theory of evolution by natural selection: states that organisms that are better suited for their environments will survive and reproduce compared to those that are poorly suited for their environments

twin studies: a behavior genetic research method that involves comparison of the similarity of identical (monozygotic; MZ) and fraternal (dizygotic; DZ) twins

Attributions

CC licensed content, Original

- Modification, adaptation, and original content. **Provided by:** Lumen Learning. **License:** *CC BY-NC-SA: Attribution-NonCommercial-ShareAlike*

CC licensed content, Shared previously

This is a modified version of OpenStax Psychology. Download the original text for free at https://openstax.org/details/books/psychology

Gene-Environment Interactions

Learning Objectives

- Describe epigenetics and examine how gene-environment interactions are critical for expression of physical and psychological characteristics

Genes do not exist in a vacuum. Although we are all biological organisms, we also exist in an environment that is incredibly important in determining not only when and how our genes express themselves, but also in what combination. Each of us represents a unique interaction between our genetic makeup and our environment; range of reaction is one way to describe this interaction. **Range of reaction** asserts that our genes set the boundaries within which we can operate, and our environment interacts with the genes to determine where in that range we will fall. For example, if an individual's genetic makeup predisposes her to high levels of intellectual potential and she is reared in a rich, stimulating environment, then she will be more likely to achieve her full potential than if she were raised under conditions of significant deprivation. According to the concept of range of reaction, genes set definite limits on potential, and environment determines how much of that potential is achieved.

Another perspective on the interaction between genes and the environment is the concept of **genetic environmental correlation**. Stated simply, our genes influence our environment, and our environment influences the expression of our genes (Figure 1). Not only do our genes and environment interact, as in range of reaction, but they also influence one another bidirectionally. For example, the child of an NBA player would probably be exposed to basketball from an early age. Such exposure might allow the child to realize his or her full genetic, athletic potential. Thus, the parents' genes, which the child shares, influence the child's environment, and that environment, in turn, is well suited to support the child's genetic potential.

In another approach to gene-environment interactions, the field of **epigenetics** looks beyond the genotype itself and studies how the same genotype can be expressed in different ways. In other words, researchers study how the same genotype can lead to very different phenotypes. As mentioned earlier, gene expression is often influenced by environmental context in ways that are not entirely obvious. For instance, identical twins share the same genetic information

Figure 1. Nature and nurture work together like complex pieces of a human puzzle. The interaction of our environment and genes makes us the individuals we are. (credit "puzzle": modification of work by Cory Zanker; credit "houses": modification of work by Ben Salter; credit "DNA": modification of work by NHGRI)

(**identical twins** develop from a single fertilized egg that split, so the genetic material is exactly the same in each; in contrast, **fraternal twins** develop from two different eggs fertilized by different sperm, so the genetic material varies as with non-twin siblings). But even with identical genes, there remains an incredible amount of variability in how gene expression can unfold over the course of each twin's life. Sometimes, one twin will develop a disease and the other will not. In one example, Tiffany, an identical twin, died from cancer at age 7, but her twin, now 19 years old, has never had cancer. Although these individuals share an identical genotype, their phenotypes differ as a result of how that genetic information is expressed over time. The epigenetic perspective is very different from range of reaction, because here the genotype is not fixed and limited.

Link to Learning

Visit this site for an engaging video primer on the epigenetics of twin studies.

- http://learn.genetics.utah.edu/content/epigenetics/twins/

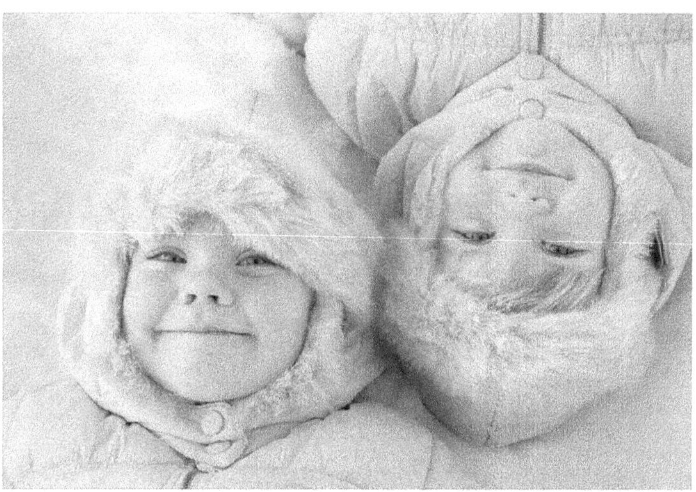

Figure 2. *Identical twins are the perfect example of epigenetics. Although they share exactly the same DNA, their unique experiences in life will cause some genes (and not others) to express themselves. This is why, over time, identical twins come to look and behave differently. [Image: Inese Dunajeva]*

Genes affect more than our physical characteristics. Indeed, scientists have found genetic linkages to a number of behavioral characteristics, ranging from basic personality traits to sexual orientation to spirituality (for examples, see Mustanski et al., 2005; Comings, Gonzales, Saucier, Johnson, & MacMurray, 2000). Genes are also associated with temperament and a number of psychological disorders, such as depression and schizophrenia. So while it is true that genes provide the biological blueprints for our cells, tissues, organs, and body, they also have significant impact on our experiences and our behaviors.

Let's look at the following findings regarding schizophrenia in light of our three views of gene-environment interactions. Which view do you think best explains this evidence?

In a study of people who were given up for adoption, adoptees whose biological mothers had schizophrenia *and* who had been raised in a disturbed family environment were much more likely to develop schizophrenia or another psychotic disorder than were any of the other groups in the study:

- Of adoptees whose biological mothers had schizophrenia (high genetic risk) and who were raised in disturbed family environments, 36.8% were likely to develop schizophrenia.

- Of adoptees whose biological mothers had schizophrenia (high genetic risk) and who were raised in healthy family environments, 5.8% were likely to develop schizophrenia.

- Of adoptees with a low genetic risk (whose mothers did not have schizophrenia) and who were raised in disturbed family environments, 5.3% were likely to develop schizophrenia.

- Of adoptees with a low genetic risk (whose mothers did not have schizophrenia) and who were raised in healthy family environments, 4.8% were likely to develop schizophrenia (Tienari et al., 2004).

The study shows that adoptees with high genetic risk were especially likely to develop schizophrenia only if they were raised in disturbed home environments. This research lends credibility to the notion that both genetic vulnerability and environmental stress are necessary for schizophrenia to develop, and that genes alone do not tell the full tale.

The most comprehensive study to date of variations in parental investment and epigenetic inheritance in mammals is that of the maternally transmitted responses to stress in rats. In rat pups, maternal nurturing (licking and grooming) during the first week of life is associated with long-term programming of individual differences in stress responsiveness, emotionality, cognitive performance, and reproductive behavior (Caldji et al., 1998; Francis, Diorio, Liu, & Meaney, 1999; Liu et al., 1997; Myers, Brunelli, Shair, Squire, & Hofer, 1989; Stern, 1997). In adulthood, the offspring of mothers that exhibit increased levels of pup licking and grooming over the first week of life show increased expression of the glucocorticoid receptor in the hippocampus (a brain structure associated with stress responsivity as well as learning and memory) and a lower hormonal response to stress compared with adult animals reared by low licking and grooming mothers (Francis et al., 1999; Liu et al., 1997). Moreover, rat pups that received low levels of maternal licking and grooming during the first week of life showed decreased histone acetylation and increased DNA methylation of a neuron-specific promoter of the glucocorticoid receptor gene (Weaver et al., 2004). The expression of this gene is then reduced, the number of glucocorticoid receptors in the brain is decreased, and the animals show a higher hormonal response to stress throughout their life.

The effects of maternal care on stress hormone responses and behavior in the offspring can be eliminated in adulthood by pharmacological treatment (HDAC inhibitor trichostatin A, TSA) or dietary amino acid supplementation (methyl donor L-methionine), treatments that influence histone acetylation, DNA methylation, and expression of the glucocorticoid receptor gene (Weaver et al., 2004;Weaver et al., 2005). This series of experiments shows that histone acetylation and DNA methylation of the glucocorticoid receptor gene promoter is a necessary link in the process leading to the long-term physiological and behavioral sequelae of poor maternal care. This points to a possible molecular target for treatments that may reverse or ameliorate the traces of childhood maltreatment.

Several studies have attempted to determine to what extent the findings from model animals are transferable to humans. Examination of post-mortem brain tissue from healthy human subjects found that the human equivalent of the glucocorticoid receptor gene promoter (NR3C1 exon 1F promoter) is also unique to the individual (Turner, Pelascini, Macedo, & Muller, 2008). A similar study examining newborns showed that methylation of the glucocorticoid receptor gene promoter maybe an early epigenetic marker of maternal mood and risk of increased hormonal responses to stress in infants 3 months of age (Oberlander et al., 2008).

Although further studies are required to examine the functional consequence of this DNA methylation, these findings are consistent with our studies in the neonate and adult offspring of low licking and grooming mothers that show increased DNA methylation of the promoter of the glucocorticoid receptor gene, decreased glucocorticoid receptor gene expression, and increased hormonal responses to stress (Weaver et al., 2004).

Examination of brain tissue from suicide victims found that the human glucocorticoid receptor gene promoter is also more methylated in the brains of individuals who had experienced maltreatment during childhood (McGowan et al., 2009). Examination of blood samples from adult patients with bipolar disorder, who also retrospectively reported on their experiences of childhood abuse and neglect, found that the degree of DNA methylation of the human glucocorticoid receptor gene promoter was strongly positively related to the reported experience of childhood maltreatment decades earlier.

Watch this video to see another example of how diet can alter the phenotype of genetically identical mice.

- https://www.youtube.com/watch?v=YfAV4poRkJ4

Glossary

epigenome: a dynamic layer of information associated with DNA that differs between individuals and can be altered through various experiences and environments

epigenetics: study of gene-environment interactions, such as how the same genotype leads to different phenotypes

fraternal twins: twins who develop from two different eggs fertilized by different sperm, so their genetic material varies the same as in non-twin siblings

gene: sequence of DNA that controls or partially controls physical characteristics

identical twins: twins that develop from the same sperm and egg

range of reaction: asserts our genes set the boundaries within which we can operate, and our environment interacts with the genes to determine where in that range we will fall

https://assessments.lumenlearning.com/assessments/4815

Attributions

CC licensed content, Shared previously

- Human Genetics. **Authored by:** OpenStax College. **Located at:** http://cnx.org/contents/Sr8Ev5Og@5.49:vQpw884b@8/Human-Genetics. **License:** *CC BY: Attribution.* **License Terms:** Download for free at http://cnx.org/contents/4abf04bf-93a0-45c3-9cbc-2cefd46e68cc@5.48
- Epigenetics in Psychology (Dig Deeper activity and image of twins). **Authored by:** Ian Weaver. **Provided by:** Dalhousie University. **Located at:** http://nobaproject.com/modules/epigenetics-in-psychology?r=LDExNDY3. **Project:** The Noba Project. **License:** *CC BY-NC-SA: Attribution-NonCommercial-ShareAlike*

All rights reserved content

- Introducing epigenetics - Intro to Psychology. **Authored by:** Udacity. **Located at:** https://www.youtube.com/watch?v=JCZ-flJ-QxA. **License:** *Other.* **License Terms:** Download for free at http://cnx.org/contents/4abf04bf-93a0-45c3-9cbc-2cefd46e68cc@5.48

Putting It Together: Biopsychology

Read this abstract from Lane Beckes, James A. Coan, and Karen Hasselmo's 2012 study, "Familiarity promotes the blurring of self and other in the neural representation of threat."

Neurobiological investigations of empathy often support an embodied simulation account. Using functional magnetic resonance imaging (fMRI), we monitored statistical associations between brain activations indicating self-focused threat to those indicating threats to a familiar friend or an unfamiliar stranger. Results in regions such as the anterior insula, putamen and supramarginal gyrus indicate that self-focused threat activations are robustly correlated with friend-focused threat activations but not stranger-focused threat activations. These results suggest that one of the defining features of human social bonding may be increasing levels of overlap between neural representations of self and other. This article presents a novel and important methodological approach to fMRI empathy studies, which informs how differences in brain activation can be detected in such studies and how covariate approaches can provide novel and important information regarding the brain and empathy.

Did you recognize any of the concepts discussed in this module? This study used fMRI to examine the brain activation of people as they looked at cues and received, or were threatened with receiving, mild electric shocks while holding hands with either a friend or a stranger. The results showed the expected response—brain activation in the anterior insula, putamen, and supramarginal gyrus when a person was threatened with a shock. What was remarkable, however, was that people showed nearly the same brain activation when a friend was threatened with the shock, but not a stranger. This provides insight into studies on empathy, and the idea that the concept of "self" can expand to include others as well.

As you can see, there is a limitless amount of information that could be studied on the brain. Neuroscience is a relatively new field, but the more research that is done, the more it appears that much of human behavior and mental processes—the key interests for psychological study—are intimately intertwined with activity in the brain. Understanding the brain is important no matter what type of psychology you will be involved with, because its effects permeate all human behavior.

The more we learn about the brain and its functioning, the better able we are to work towards repairing the brain or mimicking its capabilities. These advances in research lead to medical discoveries and breakthroughs, such as the one explained in the following video:

Attributions

CC licensed content, Original

- Modification, adaptation, and original content. **Provided by:** Lumen Learning. **License:** *CC BY-SA: Attribution-ShareAlike*

CC licensed content, Shared previously

- Familiarity promotes the blurring of self and other in the neural representation of threat. **Authored by:** Lane Beckes, James A. Coan, and Karen Hasselmo. **Provided by:** Oxford Academic. **Located at:** https://academic.oup.com/scan/article/8/6/670/1611749/Familiarity-promotes-the-blurring-of-self-and. **Project:** Social Cognitive and Affective Neuroscience (2012) 8 (6): 670-677. **License:** *CC BY-NC: Attribution-NonCommercial*
- Psychology and the Brain. **Provided by:** Boundless. **Located at:** https://www.boundless.com/psychology/textbooks/boundless-psychology-textbook/biological-foundations-of-psychology-3/psychology-and-the-brain-406/studying-the-brain-149-12684/. **Project:** Boundless Psychology. **License:** *CC BY-SA: Attribution-ShareAlike*

All rights reserved content

- The nerve bypass: how to move a paralysed hand. **Provided by:** Nature. **Located at:** https://www.youtube.com/watch?v=60fAjaRfwnU. **License:** *Other*. **License Terms:** Standard YouTube License

Module 5: Body Rhythms

Why It Matters: States of Consciousness

Sleep, which we all experience, is a quiet and mysterious pause in our daily lives. Two sleeping children are depicted in this 1895 oil painting titled Zwei schlafende Mädchen auf der Ofenbank, which translates as "two sleeping girls on the stove," by Swiss painter Albert Anker.

Our lives involve regular, dramatic changes in the degree to which we are aware of our surroundings and our internal states. While awake, we feel alert and aware of the many important things going on around us. Our experiences change dramatically while we are in deep sleep and once again when we are dreaming. Sometimes, we seek to alter our awareness and experience by using psychoactive drugs; that is, drugs that alter the central nervous system and produce a change of consciousness or a deep meditative state. Consciousness is an awareness of external and internal stimuli. As discussed in the module on the biology of psychology, the brain activity during different phases of consciousness produces characteristic brain waves, which can be observed by electroencephalography (EEG) and other types of analysis.

This module will discuss states of consciousness with a particular emphasis on sleep. You'll learn about the different stages of sleep, sleep disorders as well as the altered states of consciousness produced by psychoactive drugs, hypnosis, and meditation.

Module References

Aggarwal, S. K., Carter, G. T., Sullivan, M. D., ZumBrunnen, C., Morrill, R., & Mayer, J. D. (2009). Medicinal use of cannabis in the United States: Historical perspectives, current trends, and future directions. *Journal of Opioid Management, 5*, 153–168.

Alhola, P. & Polo-Kantola, P. (2007). Sleep Deprivation: Impact on cognitive performance. *Neuropsychiatric Disease and Treatment, 3*, 553–557.

Alladin, A. (2012). Cognitive hypnotherapy for major depressive disorder. *The American Journal of Clinical Hypnosis, 54*, 275–293.

American Psychiatric Association. (2013). *Diagnostic and statistical manual of mental disorders* (5th ed.). Arlington, VA: Author.

Aquina, C. T., Marques-Baptista, A., Bridgeman, P., & Merlin, M. A. (2009). Oxycontin abuse and overdose. *Postgraduate Medicine, 121*, 163–167.

Arnulf, I. (2012). REM sleep behavior disorder: Motor manifestations and pathophysiology. *Movement Disorders, 27*, 677–689.

Augustinova, M., & Ferrand, L. (2012). Suggestion does not de-automatize word reading: Evidence from the semantically based Stroop task. *Psychonomic Bulletin & Review, 19*, 521–527.

Banks, S., & Dinges, D. F. (2007). Behavioral and physiological consequences of sleep restriction. *Journal of Clinical Sleep Medicine, 3*, 519–528.

Bartke, A., Sun, L. Y., & Longo, V. (2013). Somatotropic signaling: Trade-offs between growth, reproductive development, and longevity. *Physiological Reviews, 93*, 571–598.

Berkowitz, C. D. (2012). Sudden infant death syndrome, sudden unexpected infant death, and apparent life-threatening events. *Advances in Pediatrics, 59*, 183–208.

Berry, R. B., Kryger, M. H., & Massie, C. A. (2011). A novel nasal excitatory positive airway pressure (EPAP) device for the treatment of obstructive sleep apnea: A randomized controlled trial. *Sleep, 34*, 479–485.

Bixler, E. O., Kales, A., Soldatos, C. R., Kales, J. D., & Healey, S. (1979). Prevalence of sleep disorders in the Los Angeles metropolitan area. *American Journal of Psychiatry, 136*, 1257–1262.

Bostwick, J. M. (2012). Blurred boundaries: The therapeutics and politics of medical marijuana. *Mayo Clinic Proceedings, 87*, 172–186.

Brook, R. D., Appel, L. J., Rubenfire, M., Ogedegbe, G., Bisognano, J. D., Elliott, W. K., . . . Rajagopalan, S. (2013). Beyond medications and diet: Alternative approaches to lowering blood pressure: A scientific statement from the American Heart Association. *Hypertension, 61*, 1360–1383.

Broughton, R., Billings, R., Cartwright, R., Doucette, D., Edmeads, J., Edwardh, M., . . . Turrell, G. (1994). Homicidal somnambulism: A case report. *Sleep, 17*, 253–264.

Brown, L. K. (2012). Can sleep deprivation studies explain why human adults sleep? *Current Opinion in Pulmonary Medicine, 18*, 541–545.

Burgess, C. R., & Scammell, T. E. (2012). Narcolepsy: Neural mechanisms of sleepiness and cataplexy. *Journal of Neuroscience, 32*, 12305–12311.

Cai, D. J., Mednick, S. A., Harrison, E. M., Kanady, J. C., & Mednick, S. C. (2009). REM, not incubation, improves creativity by priming associative networks. *Proceedings of the National Academy of Sciences, USA, 106*, 10130–10134.

Caldwell, K., Harrison, M., Adams, M., Quin, R. H., & Greeson, J. (2010). Developing mindfulness in college students through movement based courses: Effects on self-regulatory self-efficacy, mood, stress, and sleep quality. *Journal of American College Health, 58*, 433–442.

Capellini, I., Barton, R. A., McNamara, P., Preston, B. T., & Nunn, C. L. (2008). Phylogenetic analysis of the ecology and evolution of mammalian sleep. *Evolution, 62*, 1764–1776.

Cartwright, R. (2004). Sleepwalking violence: A sleep disorder, a legal dilemma, and a psychological challenge. *American Journal of Psychiatry, 161*, 1149–1158.

Cartwright, R., Agargun, M. Y., Kirkby, J., & Friedman, J. K. (2006). Relation of dreams to waking concerns. *Psychiatry Research, 141*, 261–270.

Casati, A., Sedefov, R., & Pfeiffer-Gerschel, T. (2012). Misuse of medications in the European Union: A systematic review of the literature. *European Addiction Research, 18*, 228–245.

Chen, K. W., Berger, C. C., Manheimer, E., Forde, D., Magidson, J., Dachman, L., & Lejuez, C. W. (2013). Meditative therapies for reducing anxiety: A systematic review and meta-analysis of randomized controlled trials. *Depression and Anxiety, 29*, 545–562.

Chokroverty, S. (2010). Overview of sleep & sleep disorders. *Indian Journal of Medical Research, 131*, 126–140.

Christensen, A., Bentley, G. E., Cabrera, R., Ortega, H. H., Perfito, N., Wu, T. J., & Micevych, P. (2012). Hormonal regulation of female reproduction. *Hormone and Metabolic Research, 44*, 587–591.

CNN. (1999, June 25). 'Sleepwalker' convicted of murder. Retrieved from http://www.cnn.com/US/9906/25/sleepwalker.01/

Cropley, M., Theadom, A., Pravettoni, G., & Webb, G. (2008). The effectiveness of smoking cessation interventions prior to surgery: A systematic review. *Nicotine and Tobacco Research, 10*, 407–412.

De la Herrán-Arita, A. K., & Drucker-Colín, R. (2012). Models for narcolepsy with cataplexy drug discovery. *Expert Opinion on Drug Discovery, 7*, 155–164.

Del Casale, A., Ferracuti, S., Rapinesi, C., Serata, D., Sani, G., Savoja, V., . . . Girardi, P. (2012). Neurocognition under hypnosis: Findings from recent functional neuroimaging studies. *International Journal of Clinical and Experimental Hypnosis, 60*, 286–317.

Elkins, G., Johnson, A., & Fisher, W. (2012). Cognitive hypnotherapy for pain management. *The American Journal of Clinical Hypnosis, 54*, 294–310.

Ellenbogen, J. M., Hu, P. T., Payne, J. D., Titone, D., & Walker, M. P. (2007). Human relational memory requires time and sleep. *Proceedings of the National Academy of Sciences, USA, 104*, 7723–7728.

Fell, J., Axmacher, N., & Haupt, S. (2010). From alpha to gamma: Electrophysiological correlates meditation-related states of consciousness. *Medical Hypotheses, 75*, 218–224.

Fenn, K. M., Nusbaum, H. C., & Margoliash, D. (2003). Consolidation during sleep of perceptual learning of spoken language. *Nature, 425*, 614–616.

Ferini-Strambi, L. (2011). Does idiopathic REM sleep behavior disorder (iRBD) really exist? What are the potential markers of neurodegeneration in iRBD [Supplemental material]? *Sleep Medicine, 12*(2 Suppl.), S43–S49.

Fiorentini, A., Volonteri, L.S., Dragogna, F., Rovera, C., Maffini, M., Mauri, M. C., & Altamura, C. A. (2011). Substance-induced psychoses: A critical review of the literature. *Current Drug Abuse Reviews, 4*, 228–240.

Fogel, S. M., & Smith, C. T. (2011). The function of the sleep spindle: A physiological index of intelligence and a mechanism for sleep-dependent memory consolidation. *Neuroscience and Biobehavioral Reviews, 35*, 1154–1165.

Frank, M. G. (2006). The mystery of sleep function: Current perspectives and future directions. *Reviews in the Neurosciences, 17*, 375–392.

Freeman, M. P., Fava, M., Lake, J., Trivedi, M. H., Wisner, K. L., & Mischoulon, D. (2010). Complementary and alternative medicine in major depressive disorder: The American Psychiatric Association task force report. *The Journal of Clinical Psychiatry, 71*, 669–681.

Giedke, H., & Schwärzler, F. (2002). Therapeutic use of sleep deprivation in depression. *Sleep Medicine Reviews, 6*, 361–377.

Gold, D. R., Rogacz, S. R., Bock, N., Tosteson, T. D., Baum, T. M., Speizer, F. M., & Czeisler, C. A. (1992). Rotating shift work, sleep, and accidents related to sleepiness in hospital nurses. *American Journal of Public Health, 82*, 1011–1014.

Golden, W. L. (2012). Cognitive hypnotherapy for anxiety disorders. *The American Journal of Clinical Hypnosis, 54*, 263–274.

Gómez, R. L., Bootzin, R. R., & Nadel, L. (2006). Naps promote abstraction in language-learning infants. *Psychological Science, 17*, 670–674.

Guilleminault, C., Kirisoglu, C., Bao, G., Arias, V., Chan, A., & Li, K. K. (2005). Adult chronic sleepwalking and its treatment based on polysomnography. *Brain, 128*, 1062–1069.

Gujar, N., Yoo, S., Hu, P., & Walker, M. P. (2011). Sleep deprivation amplifies reactivity of brain reward networks, biasing the appraisal of positive emotional experiences. *The Journal of Neuroscience, 31*, 4466–4474.

Guldenmund, P., Vanhaudenhuyse, A., Boly, M., Laureys, S., & Soddu, A. (2012). A default mode of brain function in altered states of consciousness. *Archives Italiennes de Biologie, 150*, 107–121.

Halász, P. (1993). Arousals without awakening—Dynamic aspect of sleep. *Physiology and Behavior, 54*, 795–802.

Han, F. (2012). Sleepiness that cannot be overcome: Narcolepsy and cataplexy. *Respirology, 17*, 1157–1165.

Hardeland, R., Pandi-Perumal, S. R., & Cardinali, D. P. (2006). Melatonin. *International Journal of Biochemistry & Cell Biology, 38*, 313–316.

Haasen, C., & Krausz, M. (2001). Myths versus experience with respect to cocaine and crack: Learning from the US experience. *European Addiction Research, 7*, 159–160.

Henry, D., & Rosenthal, L. (2013). "Listening for his breath:" The significance of gender and partner reporting on the diagnosis, management, and treatment of obstructive sleep apnea. *Social Science & Medicine, 79*, 48–56.

Hicks, R. A., Fernandez, C., & Pelligrini, R. J. (2001). The changing sleep habits of university students: An update. *Perceptual and Motor Skills, 93*, 648.

Hicks, R. A., Johnson, C., & Pelligrini, R. J. (1992). Changes in the self-reported consistency of normal habitual sleep duration of college students (1978 and 1992). *Perceptual and Motor Skills, 75*, 1168–1170.

Hilgard, E. R., & Hilgard, J. R. (1994). *Hypnosis in the Relief of Pain.* New York: Brunner/Mazel.

Hishikawa, Y., & Shimizu, T. (1995). Physiology of REM sleep, cataplexy, and sleep paralysis. *Advances in Neurology, 67*, 245–271.

Herman, A., & Herman, A. P. (2013). Caffeine's mechanism of action and its cosmetic use. *Skin Pharmacology and Physiology, 26*, 8–14.

Hobson, J. A. (2009). REM sleep and dreaming: Towards a theory of protoconsciousness. *Nature Reviews Neuroscience, 10*, 803–814.

Horikawa,T., Tamaki, M., Miyawaki, Y. & Kamitani, Y. (2013). Neural Decoding of Visual Imagery During Sleep. *Science, 340*(6132), 639–642. doi:10.1126/science.1234330

Hossain, J. L., & Shapiro, C. M. (2002). The prevalence, cost implications, and management of sleep disorders: An overview. *Sleep and Breathing, 6*, 85–102.

Huang, L. B., Tsai, M. C., Chen, C. Y., & Hsu, S. C. (2013). The effectiveness of light/dark exposure to treat insomnia in female nurses undertaking shift work during the evening/night shift. *Journal of Clinical Sleep Medicine, 9*, 641–646.

Huber, R., Ghilardi, M. F., Massimini, M., & Tononi, G. (2004). Local sleep and learning. *Nature, 430*, 78–81.

Jayanthi, L. D., & Ramamoorthy, S. (2005). Regulation of monoamine transporters: Influence of psychostimulants and therapeutic antidepressants. *The AAPS Journal, 7*, E728–738.

Julien, R. M. (2005). Opioid analgesics. In *A primer of drug action: A comprehensive guide to the actions, uses, and side effects of psychoactive drugs* (pp. 461–500). Portland, OR: Worth.

Kihlstrom, J. F. (2013). Neuro-hypnotism: Prospects for hypnosis and neuroscience. *Cortex, 49*, 365–374.

Klein, D. C., Moore, R. Y., & Reppert, S. M. (Eds.). (1991). *Suprachiasmatic nucleus: The mind's clock.* New York, NY: Oxford University Press.

Kogan, N. M., & Mechoulam, R. (2007). Cannabinoids in health and disease. *Dialogues in Clinical Neuroscience, 9*, 413–430.

Kromann, C. B., & Nielson, C. T. (2012). A case of cola dependency in a woman with recurrent depression. *BMC Research Notes, 5*, 692.

Lang, A. J., Strauss, J. L., Bomeya, J., Bormann, J. E., Hickman, S. D., Good, R. C., & Essex, M. (2012). The theoretical and empirical basis for meditation as an intervention for PTSD. *Behavior Modification, 36*, 759–786.

LaBerge, S. (1990). Lucid dreaming: Psychophysiological studies of consciousness during REM sleep. In R. R. Bootzen, J. F. Kihlstrom, & D. L. Schacter (Eds.), *Sleep and cognition* (pp. 109–126). Washington, DC: American Psychological Association.

Lesku, J. A., Roth, T. C., 2nd, Amlaner, C. J., & Lima, S. L. (2006). A phylogenetic analysis of sleep architecture in mammals: The integration of anatomy, physiology, and ecology. *The American Naturalist, 168*, 441–453.

Levitt, C., Shaw, E., Wong, S., & Kaczorowski, J. (2007). Systematic review of the literature on postpartum care: Effectiveness of interventions for smoking relapse prevention, cessation, and reduction in postpartum women. *Birth, 34*, 341–347.

Lifshitz, M., Aubert Bonn, N., Fischer, A., Kashem, I. F., & Raz, A. (2013). Using suggestion to modulate automatic processes: From Stroop to McGurk and beyond. *Cortex, 49*, 463–473.

Luppi, P. H., Clément, O., Sapin, E., Gervasoni, D., Peyron, C., Léger, L., . . . Fort, P. (2011). The neuronal network responsible for paradoxical sleep and its dysfunctions causing narcolepsy and rapid eye movement (REM) behavior disorder. *Sleep Medicine Reviews, 15*, 153–163.

Mage, D. T., & Donner, M. (2006). Female resistance to hypoxia: Does it explain the sex difference in mortality rates? *Journal of Women's Health, 15*, 786–794.

Mahowald, M. W., & Schenck, C. H. (2000). Diagnosis and management of parasomnias. *Clinical Cornerstone, 2*, 48–54.

Mahowald, M. W., Schenck, C. H., & Cramer Bornemann, M. A. (2005). Sleep-related violence. *Current Neurology and Neuroscience Reports, 5*, 153–158.

Mayo Clinic. (n.d.). *Sleep terrors (night terrors)*. Retrieved from http://www.mayoclinic.org/diseases-conditions/night-terrors/basics/treatment/con-20032552

Mather, L. E., Rauwendaal, E. R., Moxham-Hall, V. L., & Wodak, A. D. (2013). (Re)introducing medical cannabis. *The Medical Journal of Australia, 199*, 759–761.

Maxwell, J. C. (2006). *Trends in the abuse of prescription drugs. Gulf Coast Addiction Technology Transfer Center*. Retrieved from http://asi.nattc.org/userfiles/file/GulfCoast/PrescriptionTrends_Web.pdf

McCarty, D. E. (2010). A case of narcolepsy with strictly unilateral cataplexy. *Journal of Clinical Sleep Medicine, 15*, 75–76.

McDaid, C., Durée, K. H., Griffin, S. C., Weatherly, H. L., Stradling, J. R., Davies, R. J., . . . Westwood, M. E. (2009). A systematic review of continuous positive airway pressure for obstructive sleep apnoea-hypopnoea syndrome. *Sleep Medicine Reviews, 13*, 427–436.

McKim, W. A., & Hancock, S. D. (2013). *Drugs and behavior: An introduction to behavioral pharmacology, 7th edition*. Boston, MA: Pearson.

Mignot, E. J. M. (2012). A practical guide to the therapy of narcolepsy and hypersomnia syndromes. *Neurotherapeutics, 9*, 739–752.

Miller, N. L., Shattuck, L. G., & Matsangas, P. (2010). Longitudinal study of sleep patterns of United States Military Academy cadets. *Sleep, 33*, 1623–1631.

Mitchell, E. A. (2009). SIDS: Past, present and future. *Acta Paediatrica, 98*, 1712–1719.

Montgomery, G. H., Schnur, J. B., & Kravits, K. (2012). Hypnosis for cancer care: Over 200 years young. *CA: A Cancer Journal for Clinicians, 63*, 31–44.

National Institutes of Health. (n.d.). *Information about sleep*. Retrieved from http://science.education.nih.gov/supplements/nih3/sleep/guide/info-sleep.htm

National Research Council. (1994). *Learning, remembering, believing: Enhancing human performance*. Washington, DC: The National Academies Press.

National Sleep Foundation. (n.d.). *How much sleep do we really need?* Retrieved from http://sleepfoundation.org/how-sleep-works/how-much-sleep-do-we-really-need

Ohayon, M. M. (1997). Prevalence of DSM-IV diagnostic criteria of insomnia: Distinguishing insomnia related to mental disorders from sleep disorders. *Journal of Psychiatric Research, 31,* 333–346.

Ohayon, M. M. (2002). Epidemiology of insomnia: What we know and what we still need to learn. *Sleep Medicine Reviews, 6,* 97–111.

Ohayon, M. M., Carskadon, M. A., Guilleminault, C., & Vitiello, M. V. (2004). Meta-analysis of quantitative sleep parameters from childhood to old age in healthy individuals: Developing normative sleep values across the human lifespan. *Sleep, 27,* 1255–1273.

Ohayon, M. M., & Roth, T. (2002). Prevalence of restless legs syndrome and periodic limb movement disorder in the general population. *Journal of Psychosomatic Research, 53,* 547–554.

Poe, G. R., Walsh, C. M., & Bjorness, T. E. (2010). Cognitive neuroscience of sleep. *Progress in Brain Research, 185,* 1–19.

Porkka-Heiskanen, T. (2011). Methylxanthines and sleep. *Handbook of Experimental Pharmacology, 200,* 331–348.

Presser, H. B. (1995). Job, family, and gender: Determinants of nonstandard work schedules among employed Americans in 1991. *Demography, 32,* 577–598.

Pressman, M. R. (2007). Disorders of arousal from sleep and violent behavior: The role of physical contact and proximity. *Sleep, 30,* 1039–1047.

Provini, F., Tinuper, P., Bisulli, F., & Lagaresi, E. (2011). Arousal disorders [Supplemental material]. *Sleep Medicine, 12*(2 Suppl.), S22–S26.

Rattenborg, N. C., Lesku, J. A., Martinez-Gonzalez, D., & Lima, S. L. (2007). The non-trivial functions of sleep. *Sleep Medicine Reviews, 11,* 405–409.

Raz, A. (2011). Hypnosis: A twilight zone of the top-down variety: Few have never heard of hypnosis but most know little about the potential of this mind-body regulation technique for advancing science. *Trends in Cognitive Sciences, 15,* 555–557.

Raz, A., Shapiro, T., Fan, J., & Posner, M. I. (2002). Hypnotic suggestion and the modulation of Stroop interference. *Archives of General Psychiatry, 59,* 1151–1161.

Reiner, K., Tibi, L., & Lipsitz, J. D. (2013). Do mindfulness-based interventions reduce pain intensity? A critical review of the literature. *Pain Medicine, 14,* 230–242.

Restless Legs Syndrome Foundation. (n.d.). *Restless legs syndrome: Causes, diagnosis, and treatment for the patient living with Restless legs syndrome (RSL).* Retrieved from www.rls.org

Rial, R. V., Nicolau, M. C., Gamundí, A., Akaârir, M., Aparicio, S., Garau, C., . . . Esteban, S. (2007). The trivial function of sleep. *Sleep Medicine Reviews, 11,* 311–325.

Riemann, D., Berger, M., & Volderholzer, U. (2001). Sleep and depression—Results from psychobiological studies: An overview. *Biological Psychology, 57*, 67–103.

Reinerman, C. (2007, October 14). 5 myths about that demon crack. *Washington Post.* Retrieved from http://www.washingtonpost.com/wp-dyn/content/article/2007/10/09/AR2007100900751.html

Reissig, C. J., Strain, E. C., & Griffiths, R. R. (2009). Caffeinated energy drinks—A growing problem. *Drug and Alcohol Dependence, 99*, 1–10.

Robson, P. J. (2014). Therapeutic potential of cannabinoid medicines. *Drug Testing and Analysis, 6*, 24–30.

Roth, T. (2007). Insomnia: Definition, prevalence, etiology, and consequences [Supplemental material]. *Journal of Clinical Sleep Medicine, 3*(5 Suppl.), S7–S10.

Rothman, R. B., Blough, B. E., & Baumann, M. H. (2007). Dual dopamine/serotonin releasers as potential medications for stimulant and alcohol addictions. *The AAPS Journal, 9*, E1–10.

Sánchez-de-la-Torre, M., Campos-Rodriguez, F., & Barbé, F. (2012). Obstructive sleep apnoea and cardiovascular disease. *The Lancet Respiratory Medicine, 1*, 31–72.

Savard, J., Simard, S., Ivers, H., & Morin, C. M. (2005). Randomized study on the efficacy of cognitive-behavioral therapy for insomnia secondary to breast cancer, part I: Sleep and psychological effects. *Journal of Clinical Oncology, 23*, 6083–6096.

Schicho, R., & Storr, M. (2014). Cannabis finds its way into treatment of Crohn's disease. *Pharmacology, 93*, 1–3.

Shukla, R. K, Crump, J. L., & Chrisco, E. S. (2012). An evolving problem: Methamphetamine production and trafficking in the United States. *International Journal of Drug Policy, 23*, 426–435.

Siegel, J. M. (2008). Do all animals sleep? *Trends in Neuroscience, 31*, 208–213.

Siegel, J. M. (2001). The REM sleep-memory consolidation hypothesis. *Science, 294*, 1058–1063.

Singh, G. K., & Siahpush, M. (2006). Widening socioeconomic inequalities in US life expectancy, 1980–2000. *International Journal of Epidemiology, 35*, 969–979.

Smedslund, G., Fisher, K. J., Boles, S. M., & Lichtenstein, E. (2004). The effectiveness of workplace smoking cessation programmes: A meta-analysis of recent studies. *Tobacco Control, 13*, 197–204.

Sofikitis, N., Giotitsas, N., Tsounapi, P., Baltogiannis, D., Giannakis, D., & Pardalidis, N. (2008). Hormonal regulation of spermatogenesis and spermiogenesis. *Journal of Steroid Biochemistry and Molecular Biology, 109*, 323–330.

Steriade, M., & Amzica, F. (1998). Slow sleep oscillation, rhythmic K-complexes, and their paroxysmal developments [Supplemental material]. *Journal of Sleep Research, 7*(1 Suppl.), 30–35.

Stickgold, R. (2005). Sleep-dependent memory consolidation. *Nature, 437*, 1272–1278.

Stone, K. C., Taylor, D. J., McCrae, C. S., Kalsekar, A., & Lichstein, K. L. (2008). Nonrestorative sleep. *Sleep Medicine Reviews, 12*, 275–288.

Suchecki, D., Tiba, P. A., & Machado, R. B. (2012). REM sleep rebound as an adaptive response to stressful situations. Frontiers in Neuroscience, 3. doi: 10.3389/fneur.2012.00041

Task Force on Sudden Infant Death Syndrome. (2011). SIDS and other sleep-related infant deaths: Expansion of recommendations for a safe infant sleeping environment. *Pediatrics, 128*, 1030–1039.

Taillard, J., Philip, P., Coste, O., Sagaspe, P., & Bioulac, B. (2003). The circadian and homeostatic modulation of sleep pressure during wakefulness differs between morning and evening chrono-types. *Journal of Sleep Research, 12*, 275–282.

Thach, B. T. (2005). The role of respiratory control disorders in SIDS. *Respiratory Physiology & Neurobiology, 149*, 343–353.

U.S. Food and Drug Administration. (2013, October 24). *Statement on Proposed Hydrocodone Reclassification from Janet Woodcock, M.D., Director, Center for Drug Evaluation and Research.* Retrieved from http://www.fda.gov/drugs/drugsafety/ucm372089.htm

Vogel, G. W. (1975). A review of REM sleep deprivation. *Archives of General Psychiatry, 32*, 749–761.

Vøllestad, J., Nielsen, M. B., & Nielsen, G. H. (2012). Mindfulness- and acceptance-based interventions for anxiety disorders: A systematic review and meta-analysis. *The British Journal of Clinical Psychology, 51*, 239–260.

Wagner, U., Gais, S., & Born, J. (2001). Emotional memory formation is enhanced across sleep intervals with high amounts of rapid eye movement sleep. *Learning & Memory, 8*, 112–119.

Wagner, U., Gais, S., Haider, H., Verleger, R., & Born, J. (2004). Sleep improves insight. *Nature, 427*, 352–355.

Walker, M. P. (2009). The role of sleep in cognition and emotion. *Annals of the New York Academy of Sciences, 1156*, 168–197.

Wark, D. M. (2011). Traditional and alert hypnosis for education: A literature review. *The American Journal of Clinical Hypnosis, 54*(2), 96–106.

Waterhouse. J., Fukuda, Y., & Morita, T. (2012). Daily rhythms of the sleep-wake cycle [Special issue]. *Journal of Physiological Anthropology, 31*(5). doi:10.1186/1880-6805-31-5

Welsh, D. K. Takahashi, J. S., & Kay, S. A. (2010). Suprachiasmatic nucleus: Cell autonomy and network properties. *Annual Review of Physiology, 72*, 551–577.

West, S., Boughton, M., & Byrnes, M. (2009). Juggling multiple temporalities: The shift work story of mid-life nurses. *Journal of Nursing Management, 17*, 110–119.

White, D. P. (2005). Pathogenesis of obstructive and central sleep apnea. *American Journal of Respiratory and Critical Care Medicine, 172*, 1363–1370.

Williams, J., Roth, A., Vatthauer, K., & McCrae, C. S. (2013). Cognitive behavioral treatment of insomnia. *Chest, 143*, 554–565.

Williamson, A. M., & Feyer, A. M. (2000). Moderate sleep deprivation produces impairments in cognitive and motor performance equivalent to legally prescribed levels of alcohol intoxication. *Occupational and Environmental Medicine, 57*, 649–655.

Wolt, B. J., Ganetsky, M., & Babu, K. M. (2012). Toxicity of energy drinks. *Current Opinion in Pediatrics, 24*, 243–251.

Zangini, S., Calandra-Buonaura, G., Grimaldi, D., & Cortelli, P. (2011). REM behaviour disorder and neurodegenerative diseases [Supplemental material]. *Sleep Medicine, 12*(2 Suppl.), S54–S58.

Zeidan, F., Grant, J. A., Brown, C. A., McHaffie, J. G., & Coghill, R. C. (2012). Mindfulness meditation-related pain relief: Evidence for unique brain mechanisms in the regulation of pain. *Neuroscience Letters, 520*, 165–173.

Attributions

CC licensed content, Original

- Modification, adaptation, and original content. **Provided by:** Lumen Learning. **License:** *CC BY: Attribution*

CC licensed content, Shared previously

- Introduction to States of Consciousness. **Authored by:** OpenStax College. **Located at:** http://cnx.org/contents/Sr8Ev5Og@5.48:zywvQOJS@5/Introduction. **License:** *CC BY: Attribution*. **License Terms:** Download for free at http://cnx.org/content/col11629/latest/.

Consciousness and Biological Rhythms

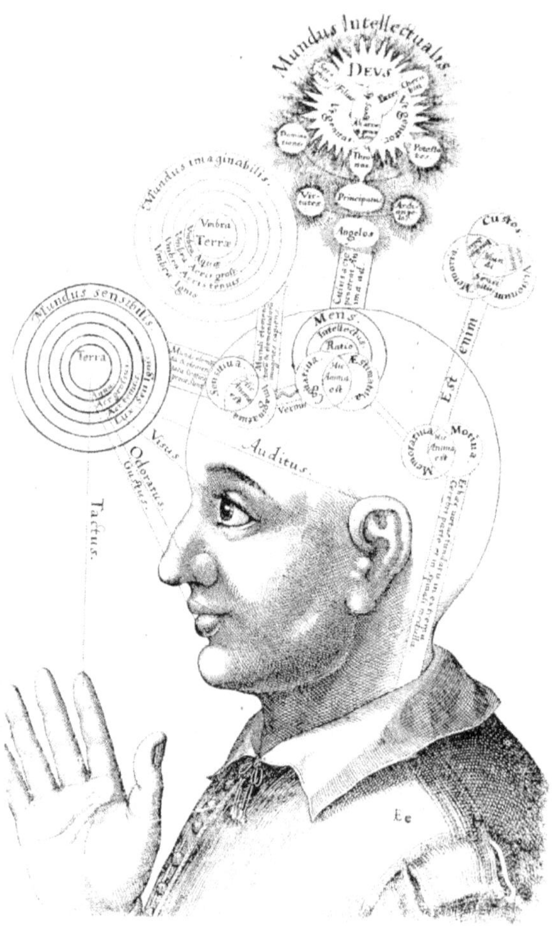

Are you tired? Have you ever pulled an all-nighter? How did you feel the next day? Do you think your lack of sleep impacted your behavior? Chances are, you could answer that question with a resounding, "yes!". Because psychologists are interested in mental processes and behavior, it's essential to study consciousness, or our awareness, as humans. States of consciousness vary over the course of the day and throughout our lives, and sleep plays a major role in alertness levels. Important factors in daily changes in consciousness are biological rhythms, and, more specifically, the circadian rhythms generated by the suprachiasmatic nucleus. Typically, our biological clocks are aligned with our external environment, and light tends to be an important cue in setting this clock. When people travel across multiple time zones or work rotating shifts, they can experience disruptions of their circadian cycles that can lead to insomnia, sleepiness, and decreased alertness. If people go extended periods of time without sleep, they will accrue a sleep debt and potentially experience a number of adverse psychological and physiological consequences.

Learning Objectives

- Describe consciousness and circadian rhythms
- Explain disruptions in biological rhythms, including sleep debt

Consciousness

Consciousness describes our awareness of internal and external stimuli. Awareness of internal stimuli includes feeling pain, hunger, thirst, sleepiness, and being aware of our thoughts and emotions. Awareness of external stimuli includes seeing the light from the sun, feeling the warmth of a room, and hearing the voice of a friend.

We experience different states of consciousness and different levels of awareness on a regular basis. We might even describe consciousness as a continuum that ranges from full awareness to a deep sleep. **Sleep** is a state marked by relatively low levels of physical activity and reduced sensory awareness that is distinct from periods of rest that occur during wakefulness. **Wakefulness** is characterized by high levels of sensory awareness, thought, and behavior. In between these extremes are states of consciousness related to daydreaming, intoxication as a result of alcohol or other drug use, meditative states, hypnotic states, and altered states of consciousness following sleep deprivation. We might also experience unconscious states of being via drug-induced anesthesia for medical purposes. Often, we are not completely aware of our surroundings, even when we are fully awake. For instance, have you ever daydreamed while driving home from work or school without really thinking about the drive itself? You were capable of engaging in the all of the complex tasks involved with operating a motor vehicle even though you were not aware of doing so. Many of these processes, like much of psychological behavior, are rooted in our biology.

Biological Rhythms

Biological rhythms are internal rhythms of biological activity. A woman's menstrual cycle is an example of a biological rhythm—a recurring, cyclical pattern of bodily changes. One complete menstrual cycle takes about 28 days—a lunar month—but many biological cycles are much shorter. For example, body temperature fluctuates cyclically over a 24-hour period (Figure 1). Alertness is associated with higher body temperatures, and sleepiness with lower body temperatures.

This pattern of temperature fluctuation, which repeats every day, is one example of a circadian rhythm. A **circadian rhythm** is a biological rhythm that takes place over a period of about 24 hours. Our sleep-wake cycle, which is linked to our environment's natural light-dark cycle, is perhaps the most obvious example of a circadian rhythm, but we also have daily fluctuations in heart rate, blood pressure, blood sugar, and body temperature. Some circadian rhythms play a role in changes in our state of consciousness.

If we have biological rhythms, then is there some sort of **biological clock**? In the brain, the hypothalamus, which lies above the pituitary gland, is a main center of homeostasis. **Homeostasis** is the tendency to maintain a balance, or optimal level, within a biological system.

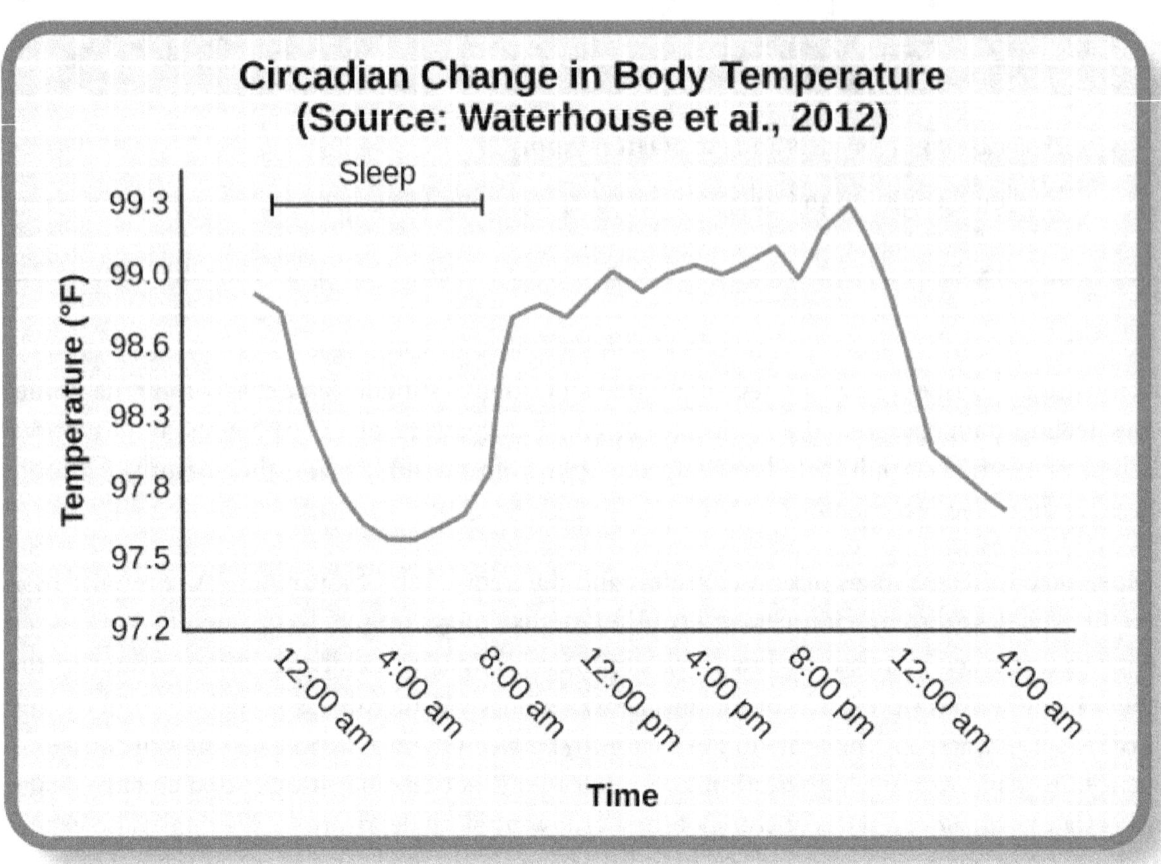

Figure 1. This chart illustrates the circadian change in body temperature over 28 hours in a group of eight young men. Body temperature rises throughout the waking day, peaking in the afternoon, and falls during sleep with the lowest point occurring during the very early morning hours.

The brain's clock mechanism is located in an area of the hypothalamus known as the **suprachiasmatic nucleus (SCN)**. The axons of light-sensitive neurons in the retina provide information to the SCN based on the amount of light present, allowing this internal clock to be synchronized with the outside world (Klein, Moore, & Reppert, 1991; Welsh, Takahashi, & Kay, 2010) (Figure 2).

Problems with Circadian Rhythms

Generally, and for most people, our circadian cycles are aligned with the outside world. For example, most people sleep during the night and are awake during the day. One important regulator of sleep-wake cycles is the hormone **melatonin**. The **pineal gland**, an endocrine structure located inside the brain that releases melatonin, is thought to be involved in the regulation of various biological rhythms and of the immune system during sleep (Hardeland, Pandi-Perumal, & Cardinali, 2006). Melatonin release is stimulated by darkness and inhibited by light.

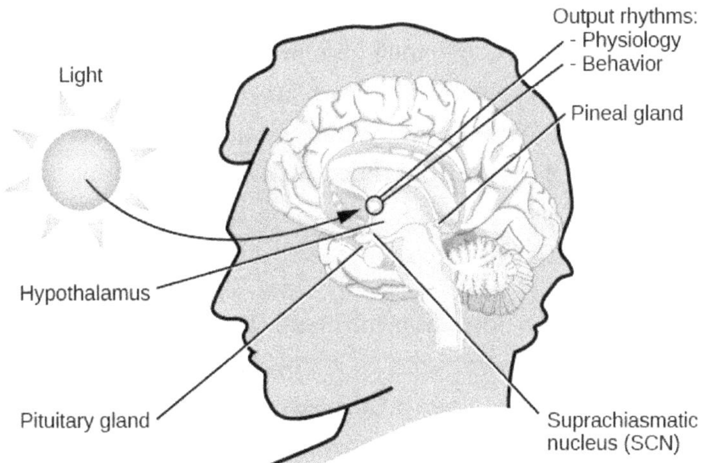

Figure 2. The suprachiasmatic nucleus (SCN) serves as the brain's clock mechanism. The clock sets itself with light information received through projections from the retina.

There are individual differences with regards to our sleep-wake cycle. For instance, some people would say they are morning people, while others would consider themselves to be night owls. These individual differences in circadian patterns of activity are known as a person's chronotype, and research demonstrates that morning larks and night owls differ with regard to sleep regulation (Taillard, Philip, Coste, Sagaspe, & Bioulac, 2003). **Sleep regulation** refers to the brain's control of switching between sleep and wakefulness as well as coordinating this cycle with the outside world.

Link to Learning

Watch this brief video describing circadian rhythms and how they affect sleep.

Disruptions of Normal Sleep

Whether lark, owl, or somewhere in between, there are situations in which a person's circadian clock gets out of synchrony with the external environment. One way that this happens involves traveling across multiple time zones. When we do this, we often experience jet lag. **Jet lag** is a collection of symptoms that results from the mismatch between our internal circadian cycles and our environment. These symptoms include fatigue, sluggishness, irritability, and **insomnia** (i.e., a consistent difficulty in falling or staying asleep for at least three nights a week over a month's time) (Roth, 2007).

Individuals who do rotating shift work are also likely to experience disruptions in circadian cycles. **Rotating shift work** refers to a work schedule that changes from early to late on a daily or weekly basis. For example, a person may work from 7:00 a.m. to 3:00 p.m. on Monday, 3:00 a.m. to 11:00 a.m. on Tuesday, and 11:00 a.m. to 7:00 p.m. on Wednesday. In such instances, the individual's schedule changes so frequently that it becomes difficult for a normal circadian rhythm to be maintained. This often results in sleeping problems, and it can lead to signs of depression and anxiety. These kinds of schedules are common for individuals working in health care professions and service industries, and they are associated with persistent feelings of exhaustion and agitation that can make someone more prone to making mistakes on the job (Gold et al., 1992; Presser, 1995).

Rotating shift work has pervasive effects on the lives and experiences of individuals engaged in that kind of work, which is clearly illustrated in stories reported in a qualitative study that researched the experiences of middle-aged nurses who worked rotating shifts (West, Boughton & Byrnes, 2009). Several of the nurses interviewed commented that their work schedules affected their relationships with their family. One of the nurses said,

> If you've had a partner who does work regular job 9 to 5 office hours . . . the ability to spend time, good time with them when you're not feeling absolutely exhausted . . . that would be one of the problems that I've encountered. (West et al., 2009, p. 114)

While disruptions in circadian rhythms can have negative consequences, there are things we can do to help us realign our biological clocks with the external environment. Some of these approaches, such as using a bright light as shown in Figure 1, have been shown to alleviate some of the problems experienced by individuals suffering from jet lag or from the consequences of rotating shift work. Because the biological clock is driven by light, exposure to bright light during working shifts and dark exposure when not working can help combat insomnia and symptoms of anxiety and depression (Huang, Tsai, Chen, & Hsu, 2013).

Insufficient Sleep

When people have difficulty getting sleep due to their work or the demands of day-to-day life, they accumulate a sleep debt. A person with a **sleep debt** does not get sufficient sleep on a chronic basis. The consequences of sleep debt include decreased levels of alertness and mental efficiency. Interestingly, since the advent of electric light, the amount of sleep that people get has declined. While we certainly welcome the convenience of having the darkness lit up, we also suffer the consequences of reduced amounts of sleep because we are more active during the nighttime hours than our ancestors were. As a result, many of us sleep less than 7–8 hours a night and accrue a sleep debt. While

Figure 1. Devices like this are designed to provide exposure to bright light to help people maintain a regular circadian cycle. They can be helpful for people working night shifts or for people affected by seasonal variations in light.

there is tremendous variation in any given individual's sleep needs, the National Sleep Foundation (n.d.) cites research to estimate that newborns require the most sleep (between 12 and 18 hours a night) and that this amount declines to just 7–9 hours by the time we are adults.

If you lie down to take a nap and fall asleep very easily, chances are you may have sleep debt. Given that college students are notorious for suffering from significant sleep debt (Hicks, Fernandez, & Pelligrini, 2001; Hicks, Johnson, & Pelligrini, 1992; Miller, Shattuck, & Matsangas, 2010), chances are you and your classmates deal with sleep debt-related issues on a regular basis. The table below shows recommended amounts of sleep at different ages.

Sleep Needs at Different Ages

Age	Nightly Sleep Needs
0–3 months	12–18 hours
3 months–1 year	14–15 hours
1–3 years	12–14 hours
3–5 years	11–13 hours
5–10 years	10–11 hours
10–18 years	8–10 hours
18 and older	7–9 hours

Sleep debt and sleep deprivation have significant negative psychological and physiological consequences. As mentioned earlier, lack of sleep can result in decreased mental alertness and cognitive function. In addition, sleep deprivation often results in depression-like symptoms. These effects can occur as a function of accumulated sleep debt or in response to more acute periods of sleep deprivation. It may surprise you to know that sleep deprivation is associated with obesity, increased blood pressure, increased levels of stress hormones, and reduced immune functioning (Banks & Dinges, 2007). Furthermore, individuals suffering from sleep deprivation can also put themselves and others at risk when they put themselves behind the wheel of a car or work with dangerous machinery. Some research suggests that sleep deprivation affects cognitive and motor function as much as, if not more than, alcohol intoxication (Williamson & Feyer, 2000).

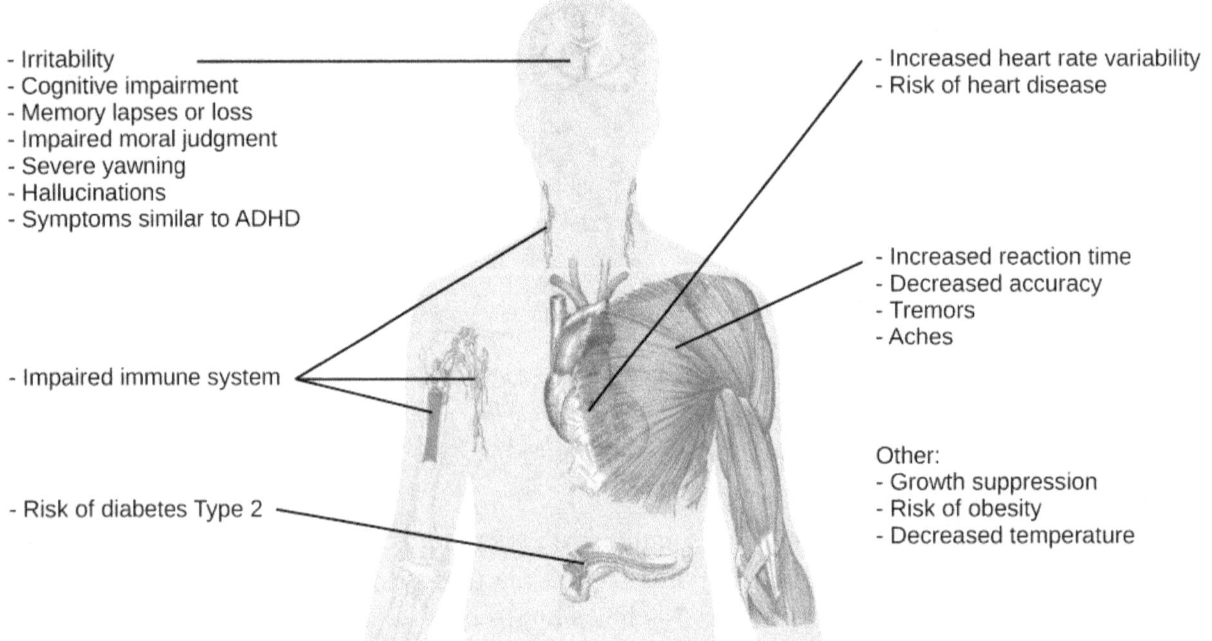

Figure 2. This figure illustrates some of the negative consequences of sleep deprivation. While cognitive deficits may be the most obvious, many body systems are negatively impacted by lack of sleep. (credit: modification of work by Mikael Häggström)

Link to Learning

To assess your own sleeping habits, read this article about sleep needs.

- https://sleepfoundation.org/how-sleep-works/how-much-sleep-do-we-really-need

The amount of sleep we get varies across the lifespan. When we are very young, we spend up to 16 hours a day sleeping. As we grow older, we sleep less. In fact, a **meta-analysis**, which is a study that combines the results of many related studies, conducted within the last decade indicates that by the time we are 65 years old, we average fewer than 7 hours of sleep per day (Ohayon, Carskadon, Guilleminault, & Vitiello, 2004). As the amount of time we sleep varies over our lifespan, presumably the sleep debt would adjust accordingly.

Glossary

biological rhythm: internal cycle of biological activity

circadian rhythm: biological rhythm that occurs over approximately 24 hours

consciousness: awareness of internal and external stimuli

homeostasis: tendency to maintain a balance, or optimal level, within a biological system

insomnia: consistent difficulty in falling or staying asleep for at least three nights a week over a month's time

jet lag: collection of symptoms brought on by travel from one time zone to another that results from the mismatch between our internal circadian cycles and our environment

melatonin: hormone secreted by the endocrine gland that serves as an important regulator of the sleep-wake cycle

meta-analysis: study that combines the results of several related studies

pineal gland: endocrine structure located inside the brain that releases melatonin

rotating shift work: work schedule that changes from early to late on a daily or weekly basis

sleep: state marked by relatively low levels of physical activity and reduced sensory awareness that is distinct from periods of rest that occur during wakefulness

sleep debt: result of insufficient sleep on a chronic basis

sleep regulation: brain's control of switching between sleep and wakefulness as well as coordinating this cycle with the outside world

suprachiasmatic nucleus (SCN): area of the hypothalamus in which the body's biological clock is located

wakefulness: characterized by high levels of sensory awareness, thought, and behavior

https://assessments.lumenlearning.com/assessments/4818

Attributions

CC licensed content, Original

- Modification, adaptation, and original content. **Provided by:** Lumen Learning. **License:** *CC BY: Attribution*

CC licensed content, Shared previously

- What is Consciousness?. **Authored by:** OpenStax College. **Located at:** http://cnx.org/contents/Sr8Ev5Og@5.52:tefy7E6c@6/What-Is-Consciousness. **License:** *CC BY: Attribution.* **License Terms:** Download for free at http://cnx.org/contents/4abf04bf-93a0-45c3-9cbc-2cefd46e68cc@5.48

- **Authored by:** Robert Fludd. **Provided by:** Wikipedia. **Located at:** https://en.wikipedia.org/wiki/Consciousness#/media/File:RobertFuddBewusstsein17Jh.png. **License:** *Public Domain: No Known Copyright*

- Reprogramming Our Circadian Rhythms for the Modern World. **Authored by:** Big Think. **Located at:** https://www.youtube.com/watch?v=rtCQ9jzC-Ek. **License:** *Other.* **License Terms:** Standard YouTube License

Sleep and Sleep Stages

What you'll learn to do: describe what happens to the brain and body during sleep

We devote a very large portion of time to sleep, and our brains have complex systems that control various aspects of sleep. Several hormones important for physical growth and maturation are secreted during sleep. While the reason we sleep remains something of a mystery, there is some evidence to suggest that sleep is very important to learning and memory.

You may not feel particularly busy while you sleep, but you'll learn in this section that your brain and body are quite active. You pass through four different stages of sleep. In this section, you'll learn more about these sleep stages, dreaming, and sleep disorders.

Learning Objectives

- Describe areas of the brain and hormone secretions involved in sleep
- Describe several theories (adaptive and cognitive) aimed at explaining the function of sleep
- Differentiate between REM and non–REM sleep
- Describe the stages of sleep

We spend approximately one-third of our lives sleeping. Given the average life expectancy for U.S. citizens falls between 73 and 79 years old (Singh & Siahpush, 2006), we can expect to spend approximately 25 years of our lives sleeping. Some animals never sleep (e.g., several fish and amphibian species); other animals can go extended periods of time without sleep and without apparent negative consequences (e.g., dolphins); yet some animals (e.g., rats) die after two weeks of sleep deprivation (Siegel, 2008). Why do we devote so much time to sleeping? Is it absolutely essential that we sleep? This section will consider these questions and explore various explanations for why we sleep.

What is Sleep?

You have read that sleep is distinguished by low levels of physical activity and reduced sensory awareness. As discussed by Siegel (2008), a definition of sleep must also include mention of the interplay of the circadian and homeostatic mechanisms that regulate sleep. Homeostatic regulation of sleep is evidenced by sleep rebound following sleep deprivation. Sleep rebound refers to the fact that a sleep-deprived individual will tend to take longer falling asleep during subsequent opportunities for sleep. Sleep is characterized by certain patterns of activity of the brain that can be visualized using electroencephalography (EEG), and different phases of sleep can be differentiated using EEG as well (Figure 1).

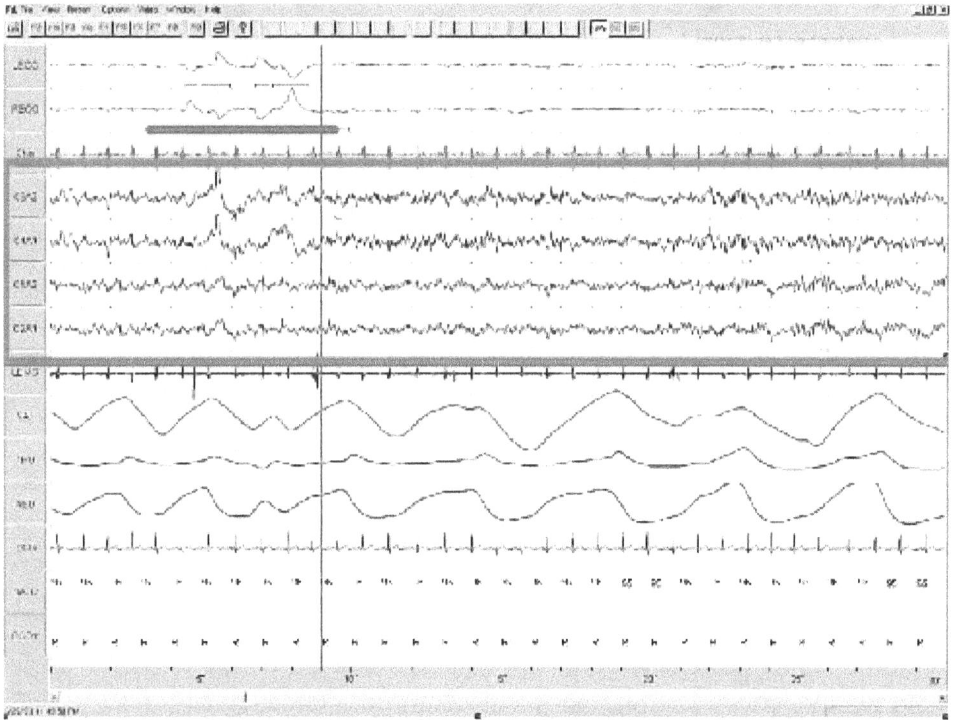

Figure 1. This is a segment of a polysonograph (PSG), a recording of several physical variables during sleep. The x-axis shows passage of time in seconds; this record includes 30 seconds of data. The location of the sets of electrode that produced each signal is labeled on the y-axis. The red box encompasses EEG output, and the waveforms are characteristic of a specific stage of sleep. Other curves show other sleep-related data, such as body temperature, muscle activity, and heartbeat.

Sleep-wake cycles seem to be controlled by multiple brain areas acting in conjunction with one another. Some of these areas include the thalamus, the hypothalamus, and the pons. As already mentioned, the hypothalamus contains the SCN—the biological clock of the body—in addition to other nuclei that, in conjunction with the thalamus, regulate slow-wave sleep. The pons is important for regulating rapid eye movement (REM) sleep (National Institutes of Health, n.d.).

Sleep is also associated with the secretion and regulation of a number of hormones from several endocrine glands including: melatonin, follicle stimulating hormone (FSH), luteinizing hormone (LH), and growth hormone (National Institutes of Health, n.d.). You have read that the pineal gland releases melatonin during sleep (Figure 2). Melatonin is thought to be involved in the regulation of various biological rhythms and the immune system (Hardeland et al., 2006). During sleep, the pituitary gland secretes both FSH and LH which are important in regulating the reproductive system (Christensen et al., 2012; Sofikitis et al., 2008). The pituitary gland also secretes growth hormone, during sleep, which plays a role in physical growth and maturation as well as other metabolic processes (Bartke, Sun, & Longo, 2013).

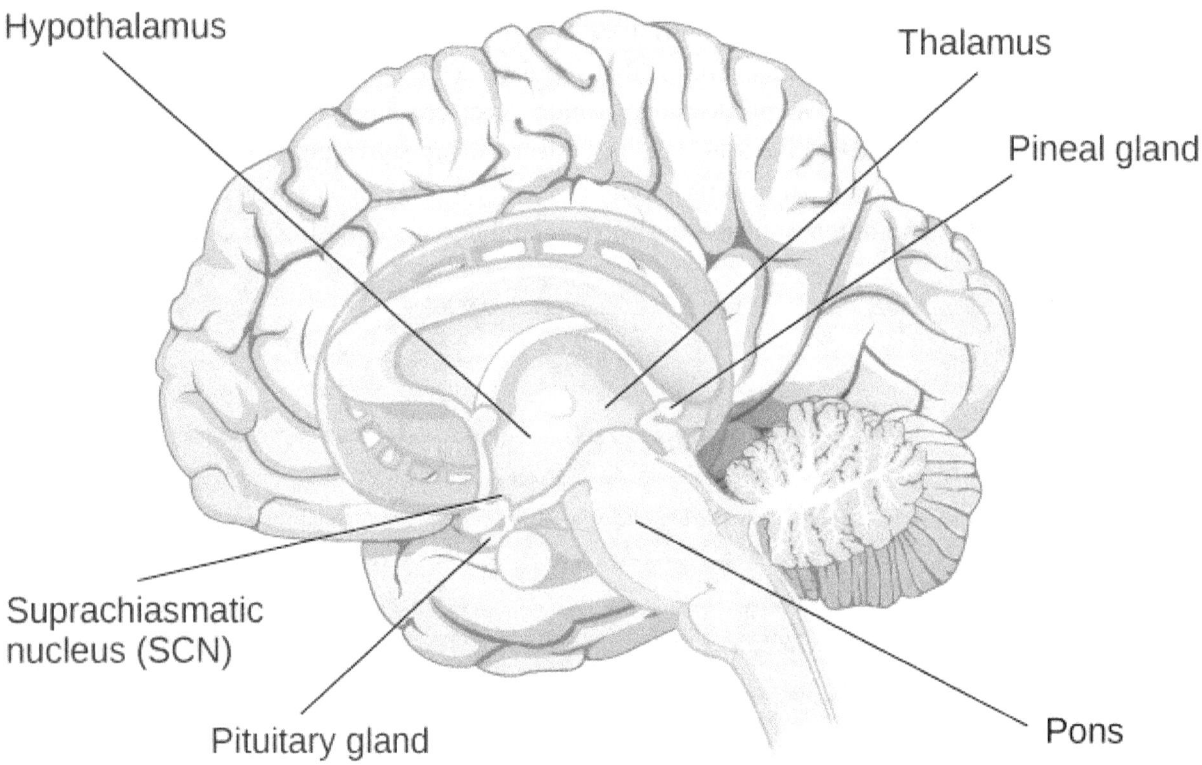

Figure 2. The pineal and pituitary glands secrete a number of hormones during sleep.

Why Do We Sleep?

Given the central role that sleep plays in our lives and the number of adverse consequences that have been associated with sleep deprivation, one would think that we would have a clear understanding of why it is that we sleep. Unfortunately, this is not the case; however, several hypotheses have been proposed to explain the function of sleep.

Adaptive Function of Sleep

One popular hypothesis of sleep incorporates the perspective of evolutionary psychology. Evolutionary psychology is a discipline that studies how universal patterns of behavior and cognitive processes have evolved over time as a result of natural selection. Variations and adaptations in cognition and behavior make individuals more or less successful in reproducing and passing their genes to their offspring. One hypothesis from this perspective might argue that sleep is essential to restore resources that are expended during the day. Just as bears hibernate in the winter when resources are scarce, perhaps people sleep at night to reduce their energy expenditures. While this is an intuitive explanation of sleep, there is little research that supports this explanation. In fact, it has been suggested that there is no reason to think that energetic demands could not be addressed with periods of rest and inactivity (Frank, 2006; Rial et al., 2007), and some research has actually found a negative correlation between energetic demands and the amount of time spent sleeping (Capellini, Barton, McNamara, Preston, & Nunn, 2008).

Another evolutionary hypothesis of sleep holds that our sleep patterns evolved as an adaptive response to predatory risks, which increase in darkness. Thus we sleep in safe areas to reduce the chance of harm. Again, this is an intuitive and appealing explanation for why we sleep. Perhaps our ancestors spent extended periods of time asleep to reduce attention to themselves from potential predators. Comparative research indicates, however, that the relationship that exists between predatory risk and sleep is very complex and equivocal. Some research suggests that species that face higher predatory risks sleep fewer hours than other species (Capellini et al., 2008), while other researchers suggest there is no relationship between the amount of time a given species spends in deep sleep and its predation risk (Lesku, Roth, Amlaner, & Lima, 2006).

It is quite possible that sleep serves no single universally adaptive function, and different species have evolved different patterns of sleep in response to their unique evolutionary pressures. While we have discussed the negative outcomes associated with sleep deprivation, it should be pointed out that there are many benefits that are associated with adequate amounts of sleep. A few such benefits listed by the National Sleep Foundation (n.d.) include maintaining healthy weight, lowering stress levels, improving mood, and increasing motor coordination, as well as a number of benefits related to cognition and memory formation.

Cognitive Function of Sleep

Another theory regarding why we sleep involves sleep's importance for cognitive function and memory formation (Rattenborg, Lesku, Martinez-Gonzalez, & Lima, 2007). Indeed, we know sleep deprivation results in disruptions in cognition and memory deficits (Brown, 2012), leading to impairments in our abilities to maintain attention, make decisions, and recall long-term memories. Moreover, these impairments become more severe as the amount of sleep deprivation increases (Alhola & Polo-Kantola, 2007). Furthermore, slow-wave sleep after learning a new task can improve resultant performance on that task (Huber, Ghilardi, Massimini, & Tononi, 2004) and seems essential for effective memory formation (Stickgold, 2005). Understanding the impact of sleep on cognitive function should help you understand that cramming all night for a test may be not effective and can even prove counterproductive.

Link to Learning

Watch this video to learn more about the function of sleep and the harmful effects of sleep deprivation.

Sleep has also been associated with other cognitive benefits. Research indicates that included among these possible benefits are increased capacities for creative thinking (Cai, Mednick, Harrison, Kanady, & Mednick, 2009; Wagner, Gais, Haider, Verleger, & Born, 2004), language learning (Fenn, Nusbaum, & Margoliash, 2003; Gómez, Bootzin, & Nadel, 2006), and inferential judgments (Ellenbogen, Hu, Payne, Titone, & Walker, 2007). It is possible that even the processing of emotional information is influenced by certain aspects of sleep (Walker, 2009).

Link to Learning

Learn about the connection between memory and sleep in the following clip:

- https://goo.gl/j4QmPF

Stages of Sleep

Sleep is not a uniform state of being. Instead, sleep is composed of several different stages that can be differentiated from one another by the patterns of brain wave activity that occur during each stage. These changes in brain wave activity can be visualized using EEG and are distinguished from one another by both the frequency and amplitude of brain waves (Figure 3). Sleep can be divided into two different general phases: REM sleep and non-REM (NREM) sleep. Rapid eye movement (REM) sleep is characterized by darting movements of the eyes under closed eyelids. Brain waves during REM sleep appear very similar to brain waves during wakefulness. In contrast, non-REM (NREM) sleep is subdivided into three stages distinguished from each other and from wakefulness by characteristic patterns of brain waves. The first three stages of sleep are NREM sleep, while the fourth and final stage of sleep is REM sleep. In this section, we will discuss each of these stages of sleep and their associated patterns of brain wave activity. [Note that psychologists originally identified four stages of non-REM sleep, but these were revised in 2008, resulting in just three distinct phases of NREM sleep. You will see that stage 3 of NREM sleep is sometimes presented as both stage 3 and stage 4 in various texts.]

NREM Stages of Sleep

The first stage of NREM sleep is known as stage 1 sleep. Stage 1 sleep is a transitional phase that occurs between wakefulness and sleep, the period during which we drift off to sleep. During this time, there is a slowdown in both the rates of respiration and heartbeat. In addition, stage 1 sleep involves a marked decrease in both overall muscle tension and core body temperature.

In terms of brain wave activity, stage 1 sleep is associated with both alpha and theta waves. The early portion of stage 1 sleep produces alpha waves, which are relatively low frequency (8–13Hz), high amplitude patterns of electrical activity (waves) that become synchronized (Figure 3). This pattern of brain wave activity resembles that of someone who is very relaxed, yet awake. As an individual continues through stage 1 sleep, there is an increase in theta wave activity. Theta waves are even lower frequency (4–7 Hz), higher amplitude brain waves than alpha waves. It is relatively easy to wake someone from stage 1 sleep; in fact, people often report that they have not been asleep if they are awoken during stage 1 sleep.

As we move into stage 2 sleep, the body goes into a state of deep relaxation. Theta waves still dominate the activity of the brain, but they are interrupted by brief bursts of activity known as sleep spindles (Figure 4). A sleep spindle is a rapid burst of higher frequency brain waves that may be important for learning and memory (Fogel & Smith, 2011; Poe, Walsh, & Bjorness, 2010). In addition, the appearance of K-complexes is often associated with stage 2 sleep. A K-complex is a very high amplitude pattern of brain activity that may in some cases occur in response to environmental stimuli. Thus, K-complexes might serve as a bridge to higher levels of arousal in response to what is going on in our environments (Halász, 1993; Steriade & Amzica, 1998).

Stage 3 of sleep is often referred to as deep sleep or slow-wave sleep because these stages are characterized by low frequency (up to 4 Hz), high amplitude delta waves (Figure 5). During this time, an individual's heart rate and respiration slow dramatically. It is much more difficult to awaken someone from sleep during stage 3 than during earlier stages. Interestingly, individuals who have increased levels of alpha brain wave activity (more often associated with wakefulness and transition into stage 1 sleep) during stage 3 often report that they do not feel refreshed upon waking, regardless of how long they slept (Stone, Taylor, McCrae, Kalsekar, & Lichstein, 2008).

REM Sleep

As mentioned earlier, REM sleep is marked by rapid movements of the eyes. The brain waves associated with this stage of sleep are very similar to those observed when a person is awake, as shown in Figure 6, and this is the period of sleep in which dreaming occurs. It is also associated with paralysis of muscle systems in the body with the exception of those that make circulation and respiration possible. Therefore, no movement of voluntary muscles occurs during REM sleep in a normal individual; REM sleep is often referred to as paradoxical sleep because of this combination of high brain activity and lack of muscle tone. Like NREM sleep, REM has been implicated in various aspects of learning and

EEG RECORDINGS DURING SLEEP

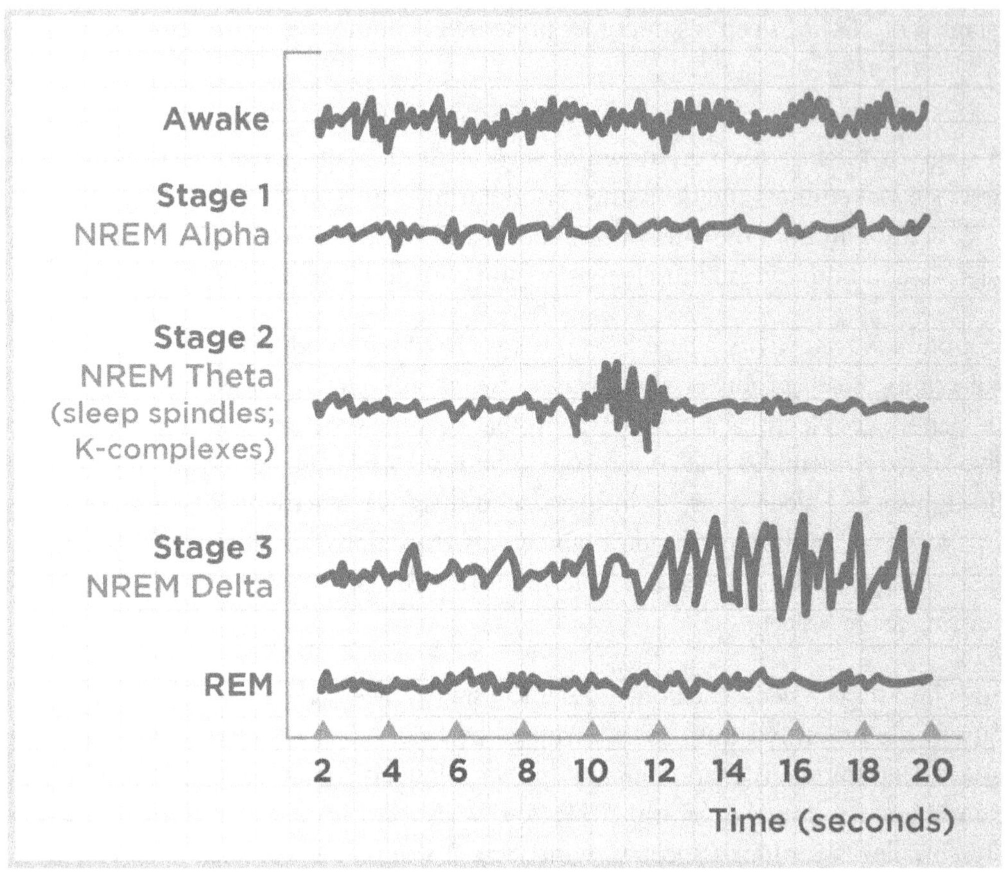

Figure 3. Brainwave activity changes dramatically across the different stages of sleep.

memory (Wagner, Gais, & Born, 2001), although there is disagreement within the scientific community about how important both NREM and REM sleep are for normal learning and memory (Siegel, 2001).

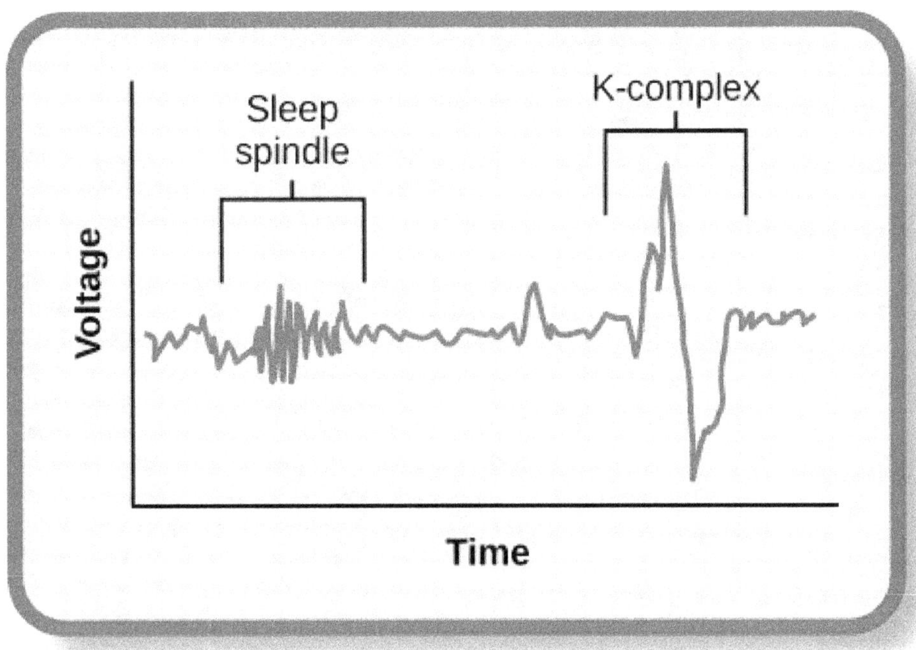

Figure 4. Stage 2 sleep is characterized by the appearance of both sleep spindles and K-complexes.

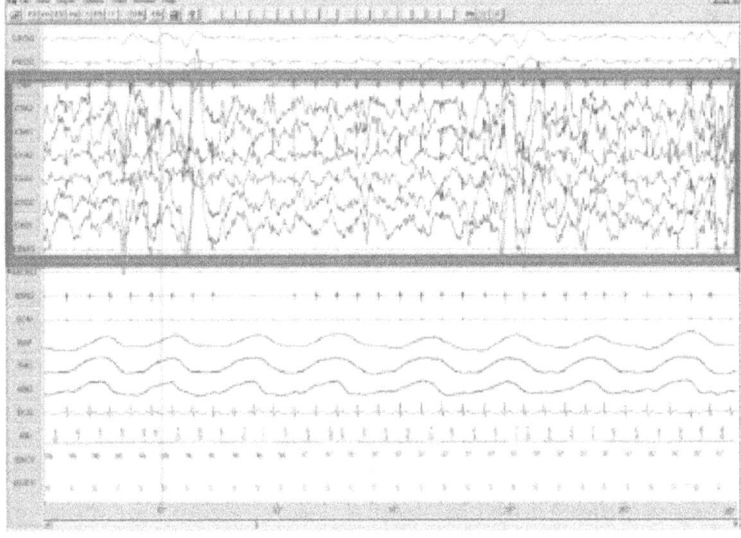

*Figure 5. Delta waves, which are low frequency and high amplitude, characterize
slow-wave stage 3 sleep.*

If people are deprived of REM sleep and then allowed to sleep without disturbance, they will spend more time in REM sleep in what would appear to be an effort to recoup the lost time in REM. This is known as the REM rebound, and it suggests that REM sleep is also homeostatically regulated. Aside from the role that REM sleep may play in processes related to learning and memory, REM sleep may also be involved in emotional processing and regulation. In such instances, REM

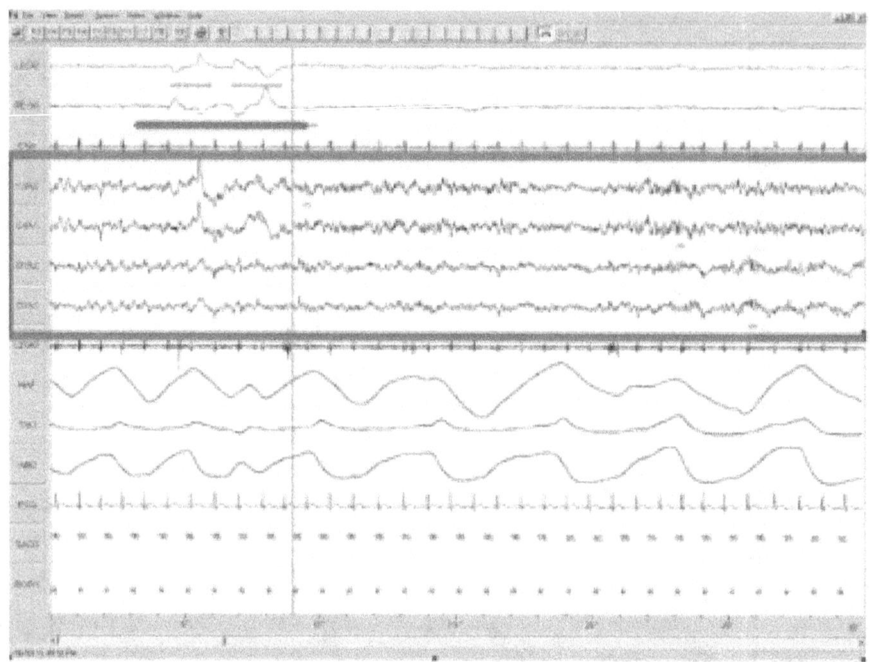

Figure 6. (a) A period of rapid eye movement is marked by the short red line segment. The brain waves associated with REM sleep, outlined in the red box, look very similar to those seen during wakefulness.

rebound may actually represent an adaptive response to stress in nondepressed individuals by suppressing the emotional salience of aversive events that occurred in wakefulness (Suchecki, Tiba, & Machado, 2012).

While sleep deprivation in general is associated with a number of negative consequences (Brown, 2012), the consequences of REM deprivation appear to be less profound (as discussed in Siegel, 2001). In fact, some have suggested that REM deprivation can actually be beneficial in some circumstances. For instance, REM sleep deprivation has been demonstrated to improve symptoms of people suffering from major depression, and many effective antidepressant medications suppress REM sleep (Riemann, Berger, & Volderholzer, 2001; Vogel, 1975).

It should be pointed out that some reviews of the literature challenge this finding, suggesting that sleep deprivation that is not limited to REM sleep is just as effective or more effective at alleviating depressive symptoms among some patients suffering from depression. In either case, why sleep deprivation improves the mood of some patients is not entirely understood (Giedke & Schwärzler, 2002). Recently, however, some have suggested that sleep deprivation might change emotional processing so that various stimuli are more likely to be perceived as positive in nature (Gujar, Yoo, Hu, & Walker, 2011). The hypnogram below (Figure 7) shows a person's passage through the stages of sleep.

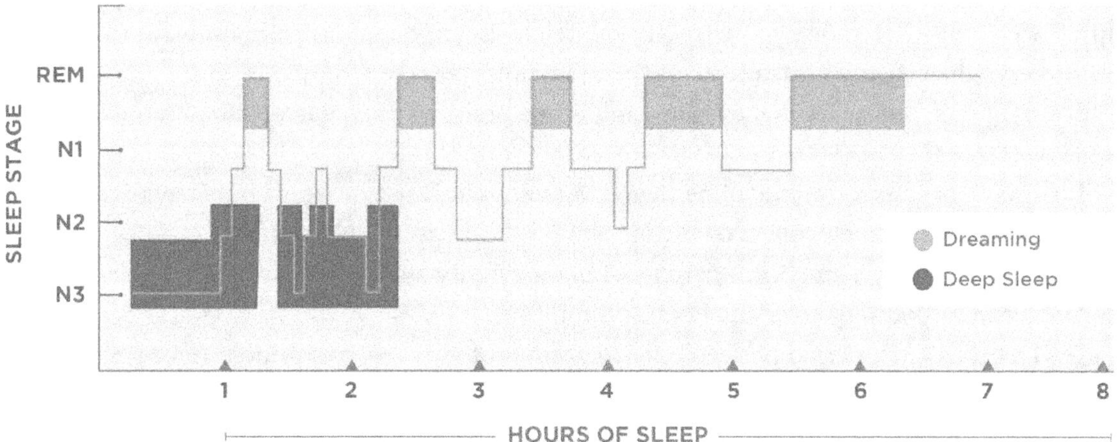

Figure 7. This hypnogram illustrates how an individual moves through the various stages of sleep. Deeper NREM sleep occurs early on in the night, while the duration of REM sleep increases as the night progresses.

Link to Learning

Read this article that describes the various stages of sleep.

- https://www.verywell.com/the-four-stages-of-sleep-2795920

Glossary

alpha wave: type of relatively low frequency, relatively high amplitude brain wave that becomes synchronized; characteristic of the beginning of stage 1 sleep

delta wave: type of low frequency, high amplitude brain wave characteristic of stage 3 and stage 4 sleep

evolutionary psychology: discipline that studies how universal patterns of behavior and cognitive processes have evolved over time as a result of natural selection

K-complex: very high amplitude pattern of brain activity associated with stage 2 sleep that may occur in response to environmental stimuli

non-REM (NREM): period of sleep outside periods of rapid eye movement (REM) sleep

rapid eye movement (REM) sleep: period of sleep characterized by brain waves very similar to those during wakefulness and by darting movements of the eyes under closed eyelids

sleep rebound: sleep-deprived individuals will experience longer sleep latencies during subsequent opportunities for sleep

sleep spindle: rapid burst of high frequency brain waves during stage 2 sleep that may be important for learning and memory

stage 1 sleep: first stage of sleep; transitional phase that occurs between wakefulness and sleep; the period during which a person drifts off to sleep

stage 2 sleep: second stage of sleep; the body goes into deep relaxation; characterized by the appearance of sleep spindles

stage 3 sleep: third stage of sleep; deep sleep characterized by low frequency, high amplitude delta waves

theta wave: type of low frequency, low amplitude brain wave characteristic of the end of stage 1 sleep

Attributions

CC licensed content, Original

- Modification, adaptation, and original content. **Provided by:** Lumen Learning. **License:** *CC BY-SA: Attribution-ShareAlike*

CC licensed content, Shared previously

- Sleep and Why We Sleep. **Authored by:** OpenStax College. **Located at:** http://cnx.org/contents/Sr8Ev5Og@5.52:HBTk06bf@7/Sleep-and-Why-We-Sleep. **License:** *CC BY: Attribution*. **License Terms:** Download for free at http://cnx.org/contents/4abf04bf-93a0-45c3-9cbc-2cefd46e68cc@5.48

- Image of sleeping girl. **Authored by:** College Degrees 360. **Provided by:** Flickr. **Located at:** https://www.flickr.com/photos/83633410@N07/7658254172. **License:** *CC BY-SA: Attribution-ShareAlike*

- What would happen if you didnt sleep? - Claudia Aguirre. **Authored by:** Ted-Ed. **Located at:** https://www.youtube.com/watch?v=dqONk48l5vY. **License:** *Other*. **License Terms:** Standard YouTube License

All rights reserved content

- The Connection Between Sleep and Memory . **Provided by:** Science360 Video. **Located at:** https://science360.gov/obj/video/1bdb1ef6-8a9c-4c06-b8f3-5f6045daf859/connection-between-sleep-memory. **License:** *All Rights Reserved*

Dreams and Dreaming

Dreams

The meaning of dreams varies across different cultures and periods of time. By the late 19th century, German psychiatrist Sigmund Freud had become convinced that dreams represented an opportunity to gain access to the unconscious. By analyzing dreams, Freud thought people could increase self-awareness and gain valuable insight to help them deal with the problems they faced in their lives. Freud made distinctions between the manifest content and the latent content of dreams.

Manifest content is the actual content, or storyline, of a dream. **Latent content**, on the other hand, refers to the hidden meaning of a dream. For instance, if a woman dreams about being chased by a snake, Freud might have argued that this represents the woman's fear of sexual intimacy, with the snake serving as a symbol of a man's penis.

Freud was not the only theorist to focus on the content of dreams. The 20th century Swiss psychiatrist Carl Jung believed that dreams allowed us to tap into the **collective unconscious**. The collective unconscious, as described by Jung, is a theoretical repository of information he believed to be shared by everyone. According to Jung, certain symbols in dreams reflected universal archetypes with meanings that are similar for all people regardless of culture or location.

The sleep and dreaming researcher Rosalind Cartwright, however, believes that dreams simply reflect life events that are important to the dreamer. Unlike Freud and Jung, Cartwright's ideas about dreaming have found empirical support. For example, she and her colleagues published a study in which women going through divorce were asked several times over a five month period to report the degree to which their former spouses were on their minds. These same women were awakened during REM sleep in order to provide a detailed account of their dream content. There was a significant positive correlation between the degree to which women thought about their former spouses during waking hours and the number of times their former spouses appeared as characters in their dreams (Cartwright, Agargun, Kirkby, & Friedman, 2006). Recent research (Horikawa, Tamaki, Miyawaki, & Kamitani, 2013) has uncovered new techniques by which researchers may effectively detect and classify the visual images that occur during dreaming by using fMRI for neural measurement of brain activity patterns, opening the way for additional research in this area.

Recently, neuroscientists have also become interested in understanding why we dream. For example, Hobson (2009) suggests that dreaming may represent a state of protoconsciousness. In other words, dreaming involves constructing a virtual reality in our heads that we might use to help us during wakefulness. Among a variety of neurobiological evidence, John Hobson cites research on lucid dreams as an opportunity to better understand dreaming in general. **Lucid dreams** are dreams in which certain aspects of wakefulness are maintained during a dream state. In a lucid dream, a person becomes aware of the fact that they are dreaming, and as such, they can control the dream's content (LaBerge, 1990).

Theories on Dreaming

While the Freudian theory of dreaming may be the most well known, and Cartwright's suggestions on dreaming the most plausible, there are several other theories about the purpose of dreaming. The **threat-simulation theory** suggests that dreaming should be seen as an ancient biological defense mechanism. Dreams are thought to provide an evolutionary advantage because of their capacity to repeatedly simulate potential threatening events. This process enhances the neurocognitive mechanisms required for efficient threat perception and avoidance.

The **expectation-fulfillment theory** posits that dreaming serves to discharge emotional arousals (however minor) that haven't been expressed during the day. This practice frees up space in the brain to deal with the emotional arousals of the next day and allows instinctive urges to stay intact. In effect, the expectation is fulfilled (the action is "completed") in a metaphorical form so that a false memory is not created. This theory explains why dreams are usually forgotten immediately afterwards.

One prominent neurobiological theory of dreaming is the **activation–synthesis theory**, which states that dreams don't actually mean anything. They are merely electrical brain impulses that pull random thoughts and imagery from our memories. The theory posits that humans construct dream stories after they wake up, in a natural attempt to make sense of the nonsensical. However, given the vast documentation of the realistic aspects of human dreaming, as well as indirect experimental evidence that other mammals such as cats also dream, evolutionary psychologists have theorized that dreaming does indeed serve a purpose.

The **continual-activation theory** proposes that dreaming is a result of brain activation and synthesis. Dreaming and REM sleep are simultaneously controlled by different brain mechanisms. The hypothesis states that the function of sleep is to process, encode, and transfer data from short-term memory to long-term memory through a process called consolidation. However, there is not much evidence to back this up. NREM sleep processes the conscious-related memory (declarative memory), and REM sleep processes the unconscious related memory (procedural memory).

The underlying assumption of continual-activation theory is that, during REM sleep, the unconscious part of the brain is busy processing procedural memory. Meanwhile, the level of activation in the conscious part of the brain descends to a very low level as the inputs from the senses are basically disconnected. This triggers the "continual-activation" mechanism to generate a data stream from the memory stores to flow through to the conscious part of the brain.

Review the purpose and stages of sleep as well as the reasons why we dream in the following CrashCourse video:

Glossary

activation-synthesis theory: states that dreams don't actually mean anything. Instead, dreams are merely electrical brain impulses that pull random thoughts and imagery from our memories.

collective unconscious: theoretical repository of information shared by all people across cultures, as described by Carl Jung

continual-activation theory: proposes that dreaming is a result of brain activation and synthesis; its assumption is that, during REM sleep, the unconscious part of the brain is busy processing procedural memory

latent content: hidden meaning of a dream, per Sigmund Freud's view of the function of dreams

lucid dream: people become aware that they are dreaming and can control the dream's content

manifest content: storyline of events that occur during a dream, per Sigmund Freud's view of the function of dreams

threat-simulation theory: suggests that dreaming should be seen as an ancient biological defense mechanism that provides an evolutionary advantage because of its capacity to repeatedly simulate potential threatening events, thus enhancing the mechanisms required for efficient threat avoidance.

Attributions

Drugs and Consciousness

What you'll learn to do: explain how drugs affect consciousness

While we all experience altered states of consciousness in the form of sleep on a regular basis, some people use drugs and other substances that result in altered states of consciousness as well. This section will present information relating to the use of various psychoactive drugs and problems associated with such use. You'll also learned about other altered states of consciousness like hypnosis and meditation. This CrashCourse video gives an excellent overview of these altered states:

Learning Objectives

- Describe how substance abuse disorders are diagnosed
- Explain how depressants impact nervous system activity
- Identify stimulants and describe how they affect the brain and body
- Identify opioids and describe how they impact the brain and behavior
- Describe hallucinogens and how they affect the brain and behavior
- Compare and contrast between depressants, stimulants, opioids, and hallucinogens

Substance Abuse Disorders

The fifth edition of the *Diagnostic and Statistical Manual of Mental Disorders, Fifth Edition* (**DSM-5**) is used by clinicians to diagnose individuals suffering from various psychological disorders. Drug use disorders are addictive disorders, and the criteria for specific substance (drug) use disorders are described in DSM-5. A person who has a substance use disorder often uses more of the substance than they originally intended to and continues to use that substance despite experiencing significant adverse consequences. In individuals diagnosed with a substance use disorder, there is a compulsive pattern of drug use that is often associated with both physical and psychological dependence.

Physical dependence involves changes in normal bodily functions—the user will experience withdrawal from the drug upon cessation of use. In contrast, a person who has **psychological dependence** has an emotional, rather than physical, need for the drug and may use the drug to relieve psychological distress. **Tolerance** is linked to physiological dependence, and it occurs when a person requires more and more drug to achieve effects previously experienced at lower doses. Tolerance can cause the user to increase the amount of drug used to a dangerous level—even to the point of overdose and death.

Drug **withdrawal** includes a variety of negative symptoms experienced when drug use is discontinued. These symptoms usually are opposite of the effects of the drug. For example, withdrawal from sedative drugs often produces unpleasant arousal and agitation. In addition to withdrawal, many individuals who are diagnosed with substance use disorders will also develop tolerance to these substances. Psychological dependence, or drug craving, is a recent addition to the diagnostic criteria for substance use disorder in DSM-5. This is an important factor because we can develop tolerance and experience withdrawal from any number of drugs that we do not abuse. In other words, physical dependence in and of itself is of limited utility in determining whether or not someone has a substance use disorder.

Read through this fascinating comic created by Stuart McMillen about psychologist's Bruce Alexander's Rat Park study on addiction, found here.

- http://www.stuartmcmillen.com/comics_en/rat-park/

For more information on Bruce Alexander's study and a better understanding of addiction, listen to Johann Hari's TED Talk, "Everything you think you know about addiction is wrong."

- https://www.ted.com/talks/
  johann_hari_everything_you_think_you_know_about_addiction_is_wrong

Drug Categories

The effects of all psychoactive drugs occur through their interactions with our endogenous neurotransmitter systems. Many of these drugs, and their relationships, are shown in Figure 1. As you have learned, drugs can act as agonists or antagonists of a given neurotransmitter system. An agonist facilitates the activity of a neurotransmitter system, and antagonists impede neurotransmitter activity.

The main categories of drugs are **depressants**, **stimulants**, and **hallucinogens**. You'll learn more about these types drugs in the coming pages.

Depressants

Ethanol, which we commonly refer to as alcohol, is in a class of psychoactive drugs known as depressants (Figure 1). A **depressant** is a drug that tends to suppress central nervous system activity. Other depressants include barbiturates and benzodiazepines. These drugs share in common their ability to serve as agonists of the gamma-Aminobutyric acid (GABA) neurotransmitter system. Because GABA has a quieting effect on the brain, GABA agonists also have a quieting effect; these types of drugs are often prescribed to treat both anxiety and insomnia.

Acute alcohol administration results in a variety of changes to consciousness. At rather low doses, alcohol use is associated with feelings of euphoria. As the dose increases, people report feeling sedated. Generally, alcohol is associated with decreases in reaction time and visual acuity, lowered levels of alertness, and reduction in behavioral control. With excessive alcohol use, a person might experience a complete loss of consciousness and/or difficulty remembering events that occurred during a period of intoxication (McKim & Hancock, 2013). In addition, if a pregnant woman consumes alcohol, her infant may be born with a cluster of birth defects and symptoms collectively called fetal alcohol spectrum disorder (FASD) or fetal alcohol syndrome (FAS).

With repeated use of many central nervous system depressants, such as alcohol, a person becomes physically dependent upon the substance and will exhibit signs of both tolerance and withdrawal. Psychological dependence on these drugs is also possible. Therefore, the abuse potential of central nervous system depressants is relatively high.

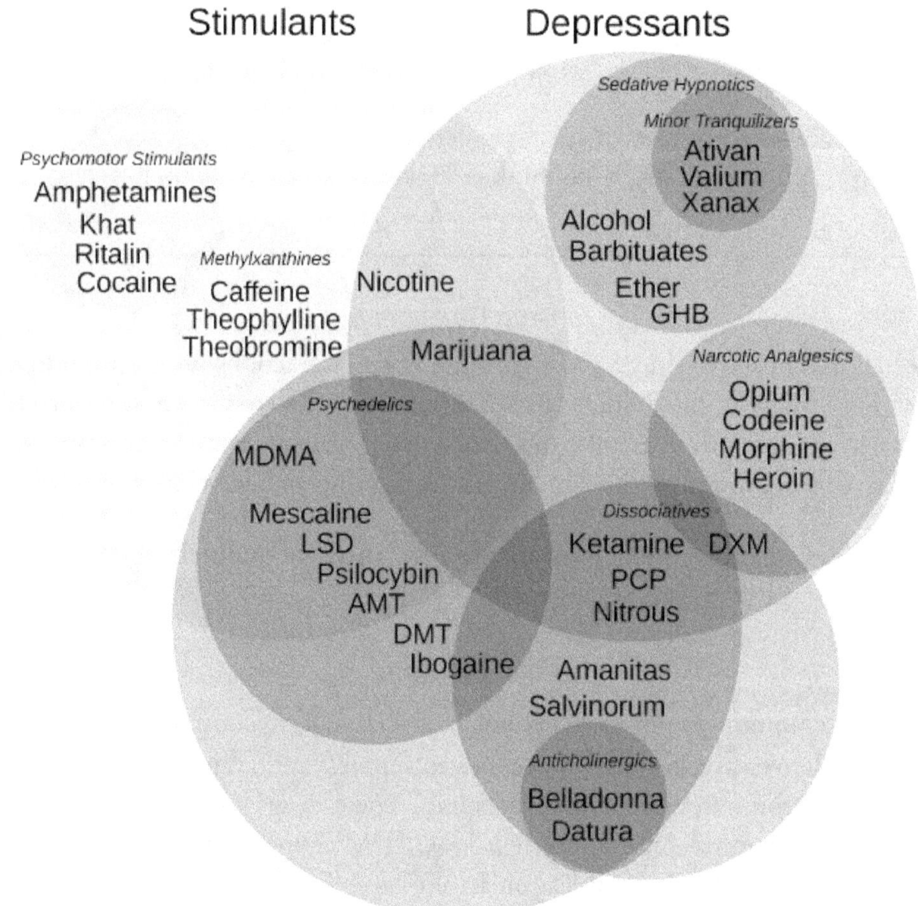

Figure 1. This figure illustrates various drug categories and overlap among them. (credit: modification of work by Derrick Snider)

Drug withdrawal is usually an aversive experience, and it can be a life-threatening process in individuals who have a long history of very high doses of alcohol and/or barbiturates. This is of such concern that people who are trying to overcome addiction to these substances should only do so under medical supervision.

Stimulants

Stimulants are drugs that tend to increase overall levels of neural activity. Many of these drugs act as agonists of the dopamine neurotransmitter system. Dopamine activity is often associated with reward and craving; therefore, drugs that affect dopamine neurotransmission often have abuse liability. Drugs in this category include cocaine, amphetamines (including methamphetamine), cathinones (i.e., bath salts), MDMA (ecstasy), nicotine, and caffeine.

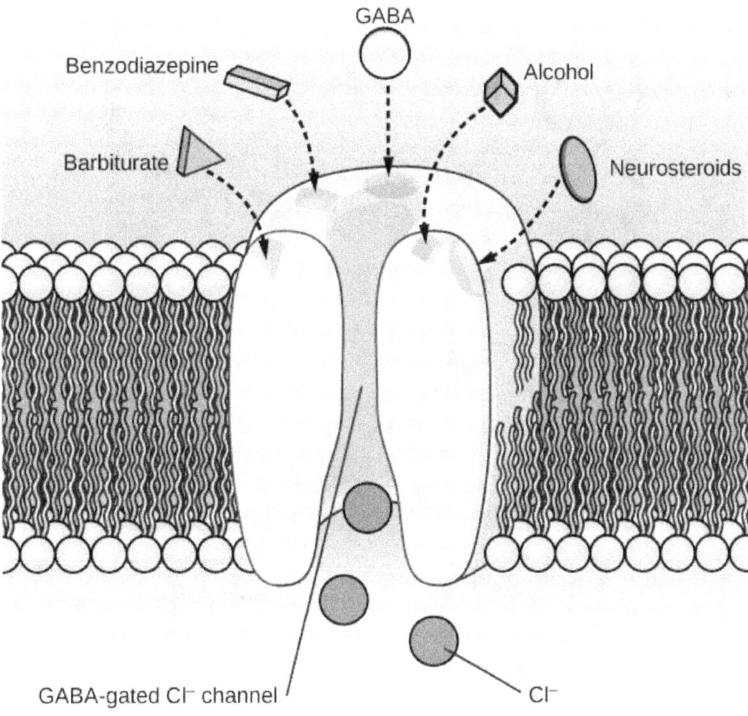

Figure 2. The GABA-gated chloride (Cl-) channel is embedded in the cell membrane of certain neurons. The channel has multiple receptor sites where alcohol, barbiturates, and benzodiazepines bind to exert their effects. The binding of these molecules opens the chloride channel, allowing negatively-charged chloride ions (Cl-) into the neuron's cell body. Changing its charge in a negative direction pushes the neuron away from firing; thus, activating a GABA neuron has a quieting effect on the brain.

Cocaine can be taken in multiple ways. While many users snort cocaine, intravenous injection and ingestion are also common. The freebase version of cocaine, known as crack, is a potent, smokable version of the drug. Like many other stimulants, cocaine agonizes the dopamine neurotransmitter system by blocking the reuptake of dopamine in the neuronal synapse.

Dig Deeper: Crack Cocaine

Crack (Figure 3) is often considered to be more addictive than cocaine itself because it is smokable and reaches the brain very quickly. Crack is often less expensive than other forms of cocaine; therefore, it tends to be a more accessible drug for individuals from impoverished segments of society. During the 1980s, many drug laws were rewritten to punish crack users more severely than cocaine users. This led to discriminatory sentencing with low-income, inner-city minority populations receiving the harshest punishments. The wisdom of these laws has recently been called into question, especially given research that suggests crack may not be more addictive than other forms of cocaine, as previously thought (Haasen & Krausz, 2001; Reinerman, 2007).

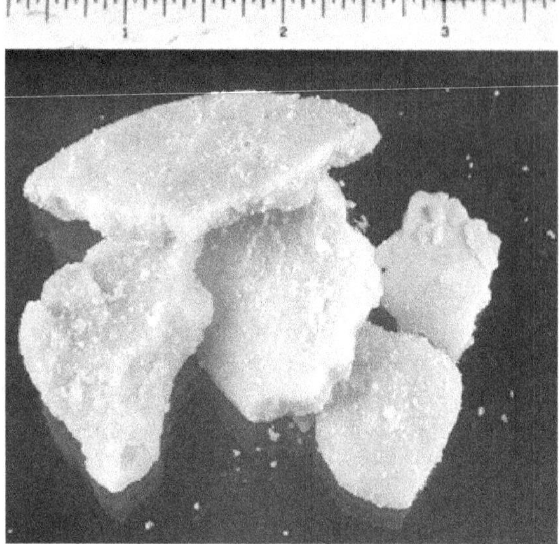

Figure 3. Crack rocks like these are smoked to achieve a high. Compared with other routes of administration, smoking a drug allows it to enter the brain more rapidly, which can often enhance the user's experience. (credit: modification of work by U.S. Department of Justice)

Amphetamines have a mechanism of action quite similar to cocaine in that they block the reuptake of dopamine in addition to stimulating its release (Figure 4). While amphetamines are often abused, they are also commonly prescribed to children diagnosed with attention deficit hyperactivity disorder (ADHD). It may seem counterintuitive that stimulant medications are prescribed to treat a disorder that involves hyperactivity, but the therapeutic effect comes from increases in neurotransmitter activity within certain areas of the brain associated with impulse control.

In recent years, methamphetamine (meth) use has become increasingly widespread. **Methamphetamine** is a type of amphetamine that can be made from ingredients that are readily available (e.g., medications containing pseudoephedrine, a compound found in many over-the-counter cold and flu remedies). Despite recent changes in laws designed to make obtaining pseudoephedrine more difficult, methamphetamine continues to be an easily accessible and relatively inexpensive drug option (Shukla, Crump, & Chrisco, 2012).

The cocaine, amphetamine, cathinones, and MDMA users seek a **euphoric high,** feelings of intense elation and pleasure,

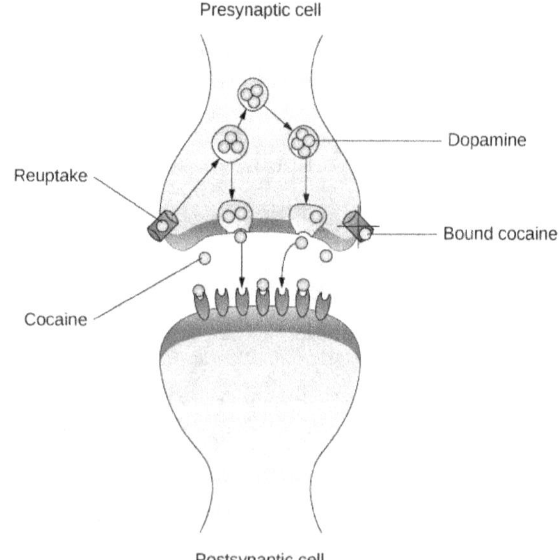

Figure 4. As one of their mechanisms of action, cocaine and amphetamines block the reuptake of dopamine from the synapse into the presynaptic cell.

especially in those users who take the drug via intravenous injection or smoking. Repeated use of these stimulants can have significant adverse consequences. Users can experience physical symptoms that include nausea, elevated blood pressure, and increased heart rate. In addition, these drugs can cause feelings of anxiety, hallucinations, and paranoia (Fiorentini et al., 2011). Normal brain functioning is altered after repeated use of these drugs. For example, repeated use can lead to overall depletion among the monoamine neurotransmitters (dopamine, norepinephrine, and serotonin). People may engage in compulsive use of these stimulant substances in part to try to reestablish normal levels of these neurotransmitters (Jayanthi & Ramamoorthy, 2005; Rothman, Blough, & Baumann, 2007).

Caffeine is another stimulant drug. While it is probably the most commonly used drug in the world, the potency of this particular drug pales in comparison to the other stimulant drugs described in this section. Generally, people use caffeine to maintain increased levels of alertness and arousal. Caffeine is found in many common medicines (such as weight loss drugs), beverages, foods, and even cosmetics (Herman & Herman, 2013). While caffeine may have some indirect effects on dopamine neurotransmission, its primary mechanism of action involves antagonizing adenosine activity (Porkka-Heiskanen, 2011).

While caffeine is generally considered a relatively safe drug, high blood levels of caffeine can result in insomnia, agitation, muscle twitching, nausea, irregular heartbeat, and even death (Reissig, Strain, & Griffiths, 2009; Wolt, Ganetsky, & Babu, 2012). In 2012, Kromann and Nielson reported on a case study of a 40-year-old woman who suffered significant ill effects from her use of caffeine. The woman used caffeine in the past to boost her mood and to provide energy, but over the course of several years, she increased her caffeine consumption to the point that she was consuming three liters of soda each day. Although she had been taking a prescription antidepressant, her symptoms of depression continued to worsen and she began to suffer physically, displaying significant warning signs of cardiovascular disease and diabetes. Upon admission to an outpatient clinic for treatment of mood disorders, she met all of the diagnostic criteria for substance dependence and was advised to dramatically limit her caffeine intake. Once she was able to limit her use to less than 12 ounces of soda a day, both her mental and physical health gradually improved. Despite the prevalence of caffeine use and the large number of people who confess to suffering from caffeine addiction, this was the first published description of soda dependence appearing in scientific literature.

Nicotine is highly addictive, and the use of tobacco products is associated with increased risks of heart disease, stroke, and a variety of cancers. Nicotine exerts its effects through its interaction with acetylcholine receptors. Acetylcholine functions as a neurotransmitter in motor neurons. In the central nervous system, it plays a role in arousal and reward mechanisms. Nicotine is most commonly used in the form of tobacco products like cigarettes or chewing tobacco; therefore, there is a tremendous interest in developing effective smoking cessation techniques. To date, people have used a variety of nicotine replacement therapies in addition to various psychotherapeutic options in an attempt to discontinue their use of tobacco products. In general, smoking cessation programs may be effective in the short term, but it is unclear whether these effects persist (Cropley, Theadom, Pravettoni, & Webb, 2008; Levitt, Shaw, Wong, & Kaczorowski, 2007; Smedslund, Fisher, Boles, & Lichtenstein, 2004).

Opioids

An **opioid** is one of a category of drugs that includes heroin, morphine, methadone, and codeine. Opioids have analgesic properties; that is, they decrease pain. Humans have an endogenous opioid neurotransmitter system—the body makes small quantities of opioid compounds that bind to opioid receptors reducing pain and producing euphoria. Thus, opioid drugs, which mimic this endogenous painkilling mechanism, have an extremely high potential for abuse. Natural opioids, called opiates, are derivatives of opium, which is a naturally occurring compound found in the poppy plant. There are now several synthetic versions of opiate drugs (correctly called opioids) that have very potent painkilling effects, and they are often abused. For example, the National Institutes of Drug Abuse has sponsored research that suggests the misuse and abuse of the prescription pain killers hydrocodone and oxycodone are significant public health concerns (Maxwell, 2006). In 2013, the U.S. Food and Drug Administration recommended tighter controls on their medical use.

Historically, heroin has been a major opioid drug of abuse (Figure 5). Heroin can be snorted, smoked, or injected intravenously. Like the stimulants described earlier, the use of heroin is associated with an initial feeling of euphoria followed by periods of agitation. Because heroin is often administered via intravenous injection, users often bear needle track marks on their arms and, like all abusers of intravenous drugs, have an increased risk for contraction of both tuberculosis and HIV.

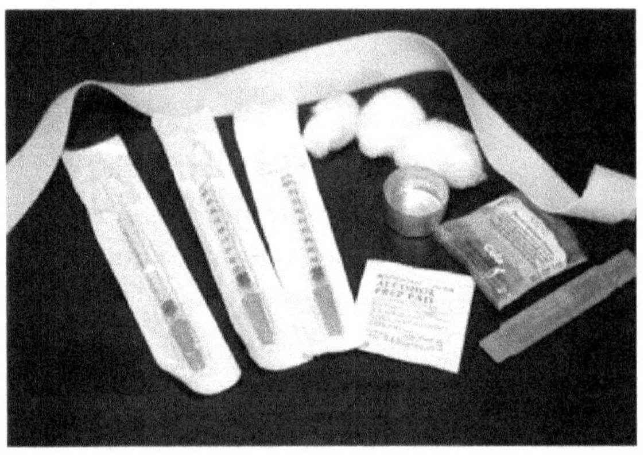

(a)

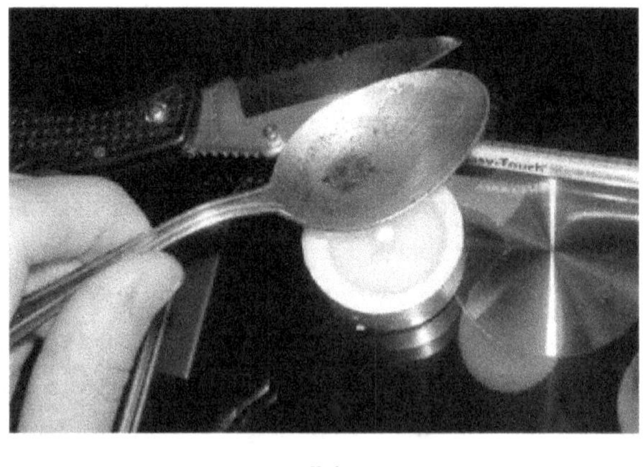

(b)

Figure 5. (a) Common paraphernalia for heroin preparation and use are shown here in a needle exchange kit. (b) Heroin is cooked on a spoon over a candle. (credit a: modification of work by Todd Huffman)

Aside from their utility as analgesic drugs, opioid-like compounds are often found in cough suppressants, anti-nausea, and anti-diarrhea medications. Given that withdrawal from a drug often involves an experience opposite to the effect of the drug, it should be no surprise that opioid withdrawal resembles a severe case of the flu. While opioid withdrawal can be extremely unpleasant, it is not life-threatening (Julien, 2005). Still, people experiencing opioid withdrawal may be given **methadone** to make withdrawal from the drug less difficult. Methadone is a synthetic opioid that is less euphorigenic than heroin and similar drugs. **Methadone clinics** help people who previously struggled with opioid addiction manage withdrawal symptoms through the use of methadone. Other drugs, including the opioid buprenorphine, have also been used to alleviate symptoms of opiate withdrawal.

Codeine is an opioid with relatively low potency. It is often prescribed for minor pain, and it is available over-the-counter in some other countries. Like all opioids, codeine does have abuse potential. In fact, abuse of prescription opioid medications is becoming a major concern worldwide (Aquina, Marques-Baptista, Bridgeman, & Merlin, 2009; Casati, Sedefov, & Pfeiffer-Gerschel, 2012).

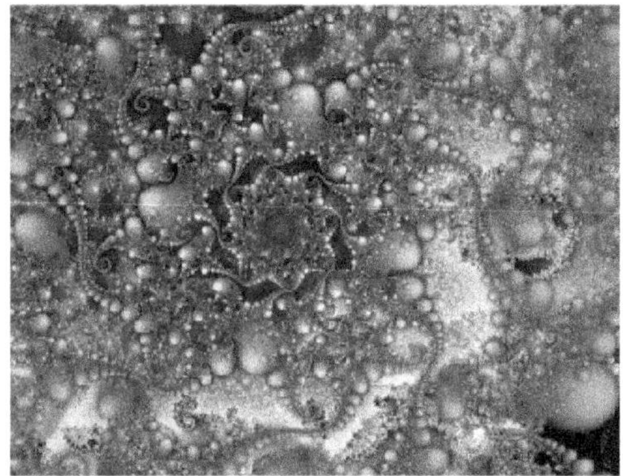

Figure 6. Psychedelic images like this are often associated with hallucinogenic compounds. (credit: modification of work by "new 1lluminati"/Flickr)

Hallucinogens

A **hallucinogen** is one of a class of drugs that results in profound alterations in sensory and perceptual experiences (Figure 6). In some cases, users experience vivid visual hallucinations. Common hallucinogens include marijuana, psilocybin (shrooms), mescaline (peyote), and LSD. It is also common for these types of drugs to cause hallucinations of body sensations (e.g., feeling as if you are a giant) and a skewed perception of the passage of time.

As a group, hallucinogens are incredibly varied in terms of the neurotransmitter systems they affect. Mescaline and LSD are serotonin agonists, and PCP (angel dust) and ketamine (an animal anesthetic) act as antagonists of the NMDA glutamate receptor. In general, these drugs are not thought to possess the same sort of abuse potential as other classes of drugs discussed in this section.

Dig Deeper: Medical Marijuana

While the possession and use of marijuana is illegal in most states, it is now legal in Washington, Colorado, Oregon, and Alaska to possess limited quantities of marijuana for recreational use. In contrast, medical marijuana use is now legal in nearly half of the United States. Medical marijuana is marijuana that is prescribed by a doctor for the treatment of a health condition. For example, people who undergo chemotherapy will often be prescribed marijuana to stimulate their appetites and prevent excessive weight loss resulting from the side effects of chemotherapy treatment. Marijuana may also have some promise in the treatment of a variety of medical conditions (Mather, Rauwendaal, Moxham-Hall, & Wodak, 2013; Robson, 2014; Schicho & Storr, 2014).

While medical marijuana laws have been passed on a state-by-state basis, federal laws still classify this as an illicit substance, making conducting research on the potentially beneficial medicinal uses of marijuana problematic. There is quite a bit of controversy within the scientific community as to the extent to which marijuana might have medicinal benefits due to a lack of large-scale, controlled research (Bostwick, 2012). As a result, many

Figure 7. Medical marijuana shops are becoming more and more common in the United States. (credit: Laurie Avocado)

scientists have urged the federal government to allow for relaxation of current marijuana laws and classifications in order to facilitate a more widespread study of the drug's effects (Aggarwal et al., 2009; Bostwick, 2012; Kogan & Mechoulam, 2007).

Until recently, the United States Department of Justice routinely arrested people involved and seized marijuana used in medicinal settings. In the latter part of 2013, however, the United States Department of Justice issued statements indicating that they would not continue to challenge state medical marijuana laws. This shift in policy may be in response to the scientific community's recommendations and/or reflect changing public opinion regarding marijuana.

Summary of Psychoactive Drugs

Substance use disorder is defined in DSM-5 as a compulsive pattern of drug use despite negative consequences. Both physical and psychological dependence are important parts of this disorder. Alcohol, barbiturates, and benzodiazepines are central nervous system depressants that affect GABA neurotransmission. Cocaine, amphetamine, cathinones, and MDMA are all central nervous stimulants that agonize dopamine neurotransmission, while nicotine and caffeine affect acetylcholine and adenosine, respectively. Opiate drugs serve as powerful analgesics through their effects on the endogenous opioid neurotransmitter system, and hallucinogenic drugs cause pronounced changes in sensory and perceptual experiences. The hallucinogens are variable with regards to the specific neurotransmitter systems they affect.

Practice your understanding of how drugs affect neurotransmitters in the brain in the the PsychSim Tutorial "Your Mind on Drugs."

- http://bcs.worthpublishers.com/webpub/Ektron/Myers_Psychology%2010e/PsychSim5_Tutorials/Your_Mind_On_Drugs/your_mind_on_drugs.htm

Then visit the Mouse Party website to see a visual example of how drugs alter the chemicals in the brain.

- http://learn.genetics.utah.edu/content/addiction/mouse/

Glossary

codeine: opiate with relatively low potency often prescribed for minor pain

depressant: drug that tends to suppress central nervous system activity

euphoric high: feelings of intense elation and pleasure from drug use

hallucinogen: one of a class of drugs that results in profound alterations in sensory and perceptual experiences, often with vivid hallucinations

methadone: synthetic opioid that is less euphorogenic than heroin and similar drugs; used to manage withdrawal symptoms in opiate users

methadone clinic: uses methadone to treat withdrawal symptoms in opiate users

methamphetamine: type of amphetamine that can be made from pseudoephedrine, an over-the-counter drug; widely manufactured and abused**opiate/opioid:** one of a category of drugs that has strong analgesic properties; opiates are produced from the resin of the opium poppy; includes heroin, morphine, methadone, and codeine

opiate/opioid: one of a category of drugs that has strong analgesic properties; opiates are produced from the resin of the opium poppy; includes heroin, morphine, methadone, and codeine

physical dependence: changes in normal bodily functions that cause a drug user to experience withdrawal symptoms upon cessation of use

psychological dependence: emotional, rather than a physical, need for a drug which may be used to relieve psychological distress

stimulant: drug that tends to increase overall levels of neural activity; includes caffeine, nicotine, amphetamines, and cocaine

tolerance: state of requiring increasing quantities of the drug to gain the desired effect

withdrawal: variety of negative symptoms experienced when drug use is discontinued

Attributions

CC licensed content, Original

- Modification, adaptation, and original content. **Provided by:** Lumen Learning. **License:** *CC BY: Attribution*

- Psychology. **Authored by:** OpenStax College. **Located at:** http://cnx.org/contents/Sr8Ev5Og@5.52:fOU1RGxh@6/Substance-Use-and-Abuse. **License:** *CC BY: Attribution*. **License Terms:** Download for free at http://cnx.org/contents/4abf04bf-93a0-45c3-9cbc-2cefd46e68cc@5.48
- Mandelbrot Islands of Consciousness image. **Authored by:** David R. Ingham. **Provided by:** Wikipedia. **Located at:** https://commons.wikimedia.org/wiki/File:Mandelbrot_Islands_of_Consciousness.jpg. **License:** *CC BY-SA: Attribution-ShareAlike*
- **License:** *Public Domain: No Known Copyright*

- Altered States – Crash Course Psychology #10. **Provided by:** CrashCourse. **Located at:** https://youtu.be/9PW1fwKjo-Y?list=PL8dPuuaLjXtOPRKzVLY0jJY-uHOH9KVU6. **License:** *Other*. **License Terms:** Standard YouTube License

Putting It Together: States of Consciousness

In this module, you learned to:

- describe consciousness and biological rhythms

- describe what happens to the brain and body during sleep

- explain how drugs affect consciousness

Remember that psychology is the study of the mind and behavior. Consider how your behavior is affected by varying states of consciousness—what happens if you don't get enough sleep? How does your concentration and mood change? What happens to your conscious awareness when you take strong medications or drugs? In this module, you learned that varying states of consciousness, whether it be tiredness from jet lag, deep sleep, daydreaming, alcohol or drug use, hypnosis, or meditation, can all change physiological components in the mind as well as behavior. While we have control over some of these altered states, like meditation, there are sometimes variables outside of our control that lead to things like sleep disorders. Drug use often begins as a personal choice or something prescribed by a doctor, but many drugs have addictive qualities that make them hard to put down.

Substance abuse disorders can develop out of drug use, and those with drug addictions struggle with physical and psychological dependence on the drug. This is an especially important issue for us today because death by drug overdoses has been dramatically increasing over the past few years. Take a look at the interactive below to see the increasing prevalence of drug overdoses.

Visit the NYTimes article, "You Draw It: Just How Bad Is the Drug Overdose Epidemic?" to take a look at current trends and the alarming amount of deaths caused by drug overdoses.

- https://www.nytimes.com/interactive/2017/04/14/upshot/drug-overdose-epidemic-you-draw-it.html

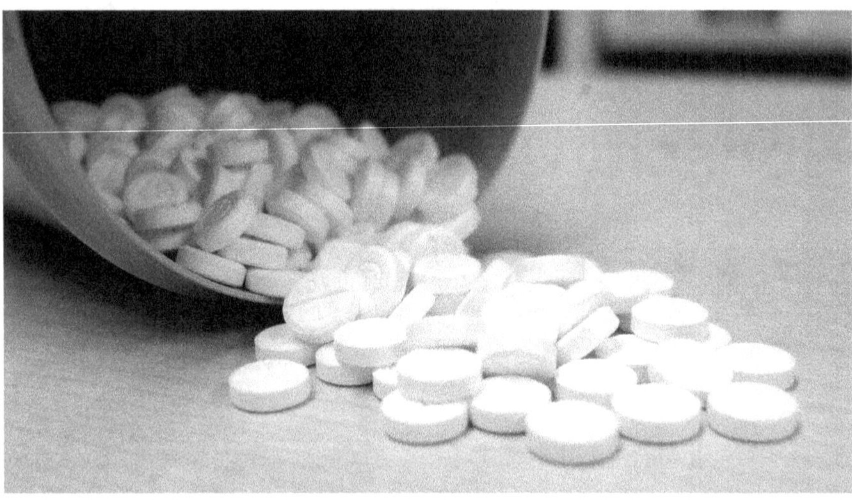

A 2017 survey in Utah found that about 80 percent of heroin users started with prescription drugs.

As you read in the article above, in 2015 there were 52,000 American deaths from all drug overdoses. Two thirds of them, 33,000, were from opioids, compared to 16,000 in 2010 and 4,000 in 1999. Death from opioid drug overdoses were nearly equal to the number of deaths from car crashes, with deaths from heroin alone accounting for more deaths than from gun violence. In 2016, deaths from overdoses increased over the previous year by 26% in Connecticut, 35% in Delaware, 39% in Maine, and 62% in Maryland. Nearly half of all opioid overdose deaths involve a prescription opioid.

The governor of Maryland declared a State of Emergency in March 2017 to combat the epidemic and CDC director Thomas Frieden has said that "America is awash in opioids; urgent action is critical."

With this sudden, extreme increase in drug overdoses, psychologists and psychiatrists will continue to play an important role in researching, educating, and preventing substance abuse disorders. You can read more about what researchers are doing at the Addiction Connection or even find some practical tips on ways to prevent a drug overdose in this article from Psychology Today.

- https://www.psychologytoday.com/blog/the-addiction-connection/201407/how-prevent-drug-overdose

Attributions

CC licensed content, Original

- **Provided by:** Lumen Learning. **License:** *CC BY: Attribution*

CC licensed content, Shared previously

- Opioid Epidemic. **Provided by:** Wikipedia. **Located at:** https://en.wikipedia.org/wiki/Opioid_epidemic. **License:** *CC BY-SA: Attribution-ShareAlike*
- Generic temazepam 10 mg tablets. **Provided by:** Wikipedia. **Located at:** https://en.wikipedia.org/wiki/Temazepam#/media/File:Temazepam_10mg_tablets-1.jpg. **License:** *CC BY-SA: Attribution-ShareAlike*

Module 6: Sensation and Perception

Why It Matters: Sensation and Perception

If you were standing in the midst of this street scene, you would be absorbing and processing numerous pieces of sensory input. (credit: modification of work by Cory Zanker)

Imagine standing on a city street corner. You might be struck by movement everywhere as cars and people go about their business, by the sound of a street musician's melody or a horn honking in the distance, by the smell of exhaust fumes or of food being sold by a nearby vendor, and by the sensation of hard pavement under your feet.

We rely on our sensory systems to provide important information about our surroundings. We use this information to successfully navigate and interact with our environment so that we can find nourishment, seek shelter, maintain social relationships, and avoid potentially dangerous situations. But while sensory information is critical to our survival, there is so much information available at any given time that we would be overwhelmed if we were forced to attend to all of it. In fact, we are aware of only a fraction of the sensory information taken in by our sensory systems at any given time.

This module will provide an overview of how sensory information is received and processed by the nervous system and how that affects our conscious experience of the world. We begin by learning the distinction between sensation and perception. Then we consider the physical properties of light and sound stimuli, along with an overview of the basic structure and function of the major sensory systems. The module will close with a discussion of a historically important theory of perception called the Gestalt theory. This theory attempts to explain some underlying principles of perception.

Module References

Aaron, J. I., Mela, D. J., & Evans, R. E. (1994). The influences of attitudes, beliefs, and label information on perceptions of reduced-fat spread. *Appetite, 22,* 25–37.

Abraira, V. E., & Ginty, D. D. (2013). The sensory neurons of touch. *Neuron, 79,* 618–639.

Ayabe-Kanamura, S., Saito, S., Distel, H., Martínez-Gómez, M., & Hudson, R. (1998). Differences and similarities in the perception of everyday odors: A Japanese-German cross-cultural study. *Annals of the New York Academy of Sciences, 855,* 694–700.

Chen, Q., Deng, H., Brauth, S. E., Ding, L., & Tang, Y. (2012). Reduced performance of prey targeting in pit vipers with contralaterally occluded infrared and visual senses. *PloS ONE, 7*(5), e34989. doi:10.1371/journal.pone.0034989

Comfort, A. (1971). Likelihood of human pheromones. *Nature, 230,* 432–479.

Correll, J., Park, B., Judd, C. M., & Wittenbrink, B. (2002). The police officer's dilemma: Using ethnicity to disambiguate potentially threatening individuals. *Journal of Personality and Social Psychology, 83,* 1314–1329.

Correll, J., Urland, G. R., & Ito, T. A. (2006). Event-related potentials and the decision to shoot: The role of threat perception and cognitive control. *The Journal of Experimental Social Psychology, 42,* 120–128.

Dunkle T. (1982). The sound of silence. *Science, 82,* 30–33.

Fawcett, S. L., Wang, Y., & Birch, E. E. (2005). The critical period for susceptibility of human stereopsis. *Investigative Ophthalmology and Visual Science, 46,* 521–525.

Furlow, F. B. (1996, 2012). The smell of love. Retrieved from http://www.psychologytoday.com/articles/200910/the-smell-love

Galanter, E. (1962). Contemporary Psychophysics. In R. Brown, E.Galanter, E. H. Hess, & G. Mandler (Eds.), New directions in psychology. New York, NY: Holt, Rinehart & Winston.

Garland, E. L. (2012). Pain processing in the human nervous system: A selective review of nociceptive and biobehavioral pathways. *Primary Care, 39,* 561–571.

Goolkasian, P. & Woodbury, C. (2010). Priming effects with ambiguous figures. *Attention, Perception & Psychophysics, 72,* 168–178.

Grothe, B., Pecka, M., & McAlpine, D. (2010). Mechanisms of sound localization in mammals. *Physiological Reviews, 90,* 983–1012.

Hartline, P. H., Kass, L., & Loop, M. S. (1978). Merging of modalities in the optic tectum: Infrared and visual integration in rattlesnakes. *Science, 199,* 1225–1229.

Kaiser, P. K. (1997). *The joy of visual perception: A web book.* Retrieved from http://www.yorku.ca/eye/noframes.htm

Khan, S., & Chang, R. (2013). Anatomy of the vestibular system: A review. *NeuroRehabilitation, 32,* 437–443.

Kinnamon, S. C., & Vandenbeuch, A. (2009). Receptors and transduction of umami taste stimuli. *Annals of the New York Academy of Sciences, 1170,* 55–59.

Kunst-Wilson, W. R., & Zajonc, R. B. (1980). Affective discrimination of stimuli that cannot be recognized. *Science, 207,* 557–558.

Lackner, J. R., & DiZio, P. (2005). Vestibular, proprioceptive, and haptic contributions to spatial orientation. *Annual Review of Psychology, 56,* 115–147.

Land, E. H. (1959). Color vision and the natural image. Part 1. *Proceedings of the National Academy of Science, 45*(1), 115–129.

Liem, D. G., Westerbeek, A., Wolterink, S., Kok, F. J., & de Graaf, C. (2004). Sour taste preferences of children relate to preference for novel and intense stimuli. *Chemical Senses, 29,* 713–720.

Lodovichi, C., & Belluscio, L. (2012). Odorant receptors in the formation of olfactory bulb circuitry. *Physiology, 27,* 200–212.

Loersch, C., Durso, G. R. O., & Petty, R. E. (2013). Vicissitudes of desire: A matching mechanism for subliminal persuasion. *Social Psychological and Personality Science, 4*(5), 624–631.

Maffei, A., Haley, M., & Fontanini, A. (2012). Neural processing of gustatory information in insular circuits. *Current Opinion in Neurobiology, 22,* 709–716.

Milner, A. D., & Goodale, M. A. (2008). Two visual systems re-viewed. *Neuropsychological, 46,* 774–785.

Mizushige, T., Inoue, K., Fushiki, T. (2007). Why is fat so tasty? Chemical reception of fatty acid on the tongue. *Journal of Nutritional Science and Vitaminology, 53,* 1–4.

Most, S. B., Simons, D. J., Scholl, B. J., & Chabris, C. F. (2000). Sustained inattentional blindness: The role of location in the detection of unexpected dynamic events. *PSYCHE, 6*(14).

Nelson, M. R. (2008). The hidden persuaders: Then and now. *Journal of Advertising, 37*(1), 113–126.

Niimura, Y., & Nei, M. (2007). Extensive gains and losses of olfactory receptor genes in mammalian evolution. *PLoS ONE, 2,* e708.

Okawa, H., & Sampath, A. P. (2007). Optimization of single-photon response transmission at the rod-to-rod bipolar synapse. *Physiology, 22,* 279–286.

Payne, B. K. (2001). Prejudice and perception: The role of automatic and controlled processes in misperceiving a weapon. *Journal of Personality and Social Psychology, 81,* 181–192.

Payne, B. K., Shimizu, Y., & Jacoby, L. L. (2005). Mental control and visual illusions: Toward explaining race-biased weapon misidentifications. *Journal of Experimental Social Psychology, 41,* 36–47.

Peck, M. (2012, July 19). *How a movie changed one man's vision forever.* Retrieved from http://www.bbc.com/future/story/20120719-awoken-from-a-2d-world

Peterson, M. A., & Gibson, B. S. (1994). Must figure-ground organization precede object recognition? An assumption in peril. *Psychological Science, 5,* 253–259.

Petho, G., & Reeh, P. W. (2012). Sensory and signaling mechanisms of bradykinin, eicosanoids, platelet-activating factor, and nitric oxide in peripheral nociceptors. *Physiological Reviews, 92,* 1699–1775.

Proske, U. (2006). Kinesthesia: The role of muscle receptors. *Muscle & Nerve, 34,* 545–558.

Proske, U., & Gandevia, S. C. (2012). The proprioceptive senses: Their roles in signaling body shape, body position and movement, and muscle force. *Physiological Reviews, 92,* 1651–1697.

Purvis, K., & Haynes, N. B. (1972). The effect of female rat proximity on the reproductive system of male rats. *Physiology & Behavior, 9,* 401–407.

Radel, R., Sarrazin, P., Legrain, P., & Gobancé, L. (2009). Subliminal priming of motivational orientation in educational settings: Effect on academic performance moderated by mindfulness. *Journal of Research in Personality, 43*(4), 1–18.

Rauschecker, J. P., & Tian, B. (2000). Mechanisms and streams for processing "what" and "where" in auditory cortex. *Proceedings of the National Academy of Sciences, USA, 97,* 11800–11806.

Renier, L. A., Anurova, I., De Volder, A. G., Carlson, S., VanMeter, J., & Rauschecker, J. P. (2009). Multisensory integration of sounds and vibrotactile stimuli in processing streams for "what" and "where." *Journal of Neuroscience, 29,* 10950–10960.

Rensink, R. A. (2004). Visual sensing without seeing. *Psychological Science, 15,* 27–32.

Rock, I., & Palmer, S. (1990). The legacy of Gestalt psychology. *Scientific American, 262,* 84–90.

Roper, S. D. (2013). Taste buds as peripheral chemosensory receptors. *Seminars in Cell & Developmental Biology, 24,* 71–79.

Russell, M. J. (1976). Human olfactory communication. *Nature, 260,* 520–522.

Sachs, B. D. (1997). Erection evoked in male rats by airborne scent from estrous females. *Physiology & Behavior, 62,* 921–924.

Segall, M. H., Campbell, D. T., & Herskovits, M. J. (1963). Cultural differences in the perception of geometric illusions. *Science, 139,* 769–771.

Segall, M. H., Campbell, D. T., & Herskovits, M. J. (1966). *The influence of culture on visual perception.* Indianapolis: Bobbs-Merrill.

Segall, M. H., Dasen, P. P., Berry, J. W., & Poortinga, Y. H. (1999). *Human behavior in global perspective* (2nd ed.). Boston: Allyn & Bacon.

Semaan, M. T., & Megerian, C. A. (2010). Contemporary perspectives on the pathophysiology of Meniere's disease: implications for treatment. *Current opinion in Otolaryngology & Head and Neck Surgery, 18*(5), 392–398.

Shamma, S. (2001). On the role of space and time in auditory processing. *Trends in Cognitive Sciences, 5,* 340–348.

Simons, D. J., & Chabris, C. F. (1999). Gorillas in our midst: Sustained inattentional blindness for dynamic events. *Perception, 28,* 1059–1074.

Spors, H., Albeanu, D. F., Murthy, V. N., Rinberg, D., Uchida, N., Wachowiak, M., & Friedrich, R. W. (2013). Illuminating vertebrate olfactory processing. *Journal of Neuroscience, 32,* 14102–14108.

Spray, D. C. (1986). Cutaneous temperature receptors. *Annual Review of Physiology, 48,* 625–638.

Strain, G. M. (2003). *How well do dogs and other animals hear?* Retrieved from http://www.lsu.edu/deafness/HearingRange.html

Swets, J. A. (1964). Signal detection and recognition by human observers. *Psychological Bulletin, 60,* 429–441.

Ungerleider, L. G., & Haxby, J. V. (1994). 'What' and 'where' in the human brain. *Current Opinion in Neurobiology, 4,* 157–165.

U.S. National Library of Medicine. (2013). Genetics home reference: Congenital insensitivity to pain. Retrieved from http://ghr.nlm.nih.gov/condition/congenital-insensitivity-to-pain

Vecera, S. P., & O'Reilly, R. C. (1998). Figure-ground organization and object recognition processes: An interactive account. *Journal of Experimental Psychology-Human Perception and Performance, 24,* 441–462.

Wakakuwa, M., Stavenga, D. G., & Arikawa, K. (2007). Spectral organization of ommatidia in flower-visiting insects. *Photochemistry and Photobiology, 83,* 27–34.

Weller, A. (1998). Human pheromones: Communication through body odour. *Nature, 392,* 126–127.

Wells, D. L. (2010). Domestic dogs and human health: An overview. *British Journal of Health Psychology, 12,* 145–156.

Wolfgang-Kimball, D. (1992). Pheromones in humans: myth or reality?. Retrieved from http://www.anapsid.org/pheromones.html

Wysocki, C. J., & Preti, G. (2004). Facts, fallacies, fears, and frustrations with human pheromones. *The Anatomical Record Part A: Discoveries in Molecular, Cellular, and Evolutionary Biology, 281,* 1201–1211.

Attributions

CC licensed content, Shared previously

- Introduction to Sensation and Perception. **Authored by:** OpenStax College. **Located at:** http://cnx.org/contents/ Sr8Ev5Og@5.49:SPm67RdT@6/Introduction. **License:** *CC BY: Attribution.* **License Terms:** Download for free at http://cnx.org/content/col11629/latest/.

Sensation and Perception

What you'll learn to do: differentiate between sensation and perception

Sensation and perception are two separate processes that are very closely related. Sensation is input about the physical world obtained by our sensory receptors, and perception is the process by which the brain selects, organizes, and interprets these sensations. In other words, senses are the physiological basis of perception. Perception of the same senses may vary from one person to another because each person's brain interprets stimuli differently based on that individual's learning, memory, emotions, and expectations.

- Define sensation and explain its connection to the concepts of absolute threshold, difference threshold, and subliminal messages
- Discuss the roles attention, motivation, and sensory adaptation play in perception

Sensation

What does it mean to sense something? Sensory receptors are specialized neurons that respond to specific types of stimuli. When sensory information is detected by a sensory receptor, **sensation** has occurred. For example, light that enters the eye causes chemical changes in cells that line the back of the eye. These cells relay messages, in the form of action potentials (as you learned when studying biopsychology), to the central nervous system. The conversion from sensory stimulus energy to action potential is known as **transduction.**

You have probably known since elementary school that we have five senses: vision, hearing (audition), smell (olfaction), taste (gustation), and touch (somatosensation). It turns out that this notion of five senses is oversimplified. We also have sensory systems that provide information about balance (the vestibular sense), body position and movement (proprioception and kinesthesia), pain (nociception), and temperature (thermoception).

Figure 1. The absolute threshold for detecting light is greater than you probably imagined—the human eye can see a candle on a clear night up to 30 miles away!

The sensitivity of a given sensory system to the relevant stimuli can be expressed as an absolute threshold. **Absolute threshold** refers to the minimum amount of stimulus energy that must be present for the stimulus to be detected 50% of the time. Another way to think about this is by asking how dim can a light be or how soft can a sound be and still be detected half of the time. The sensitivity of our sensory receptors can be quite amazing. It has been estimated that on a clear night, the most sensitive sensory cells in the back of the eye can detect a candle flame 30 miles away (Okawa & Sampath, 2007). Under quiet conditions, the hair cells (the receptor cells of the inner ear) can detect the tick of a clock 20 feet away (Galanter, 1962).

It is also possible for us to get messages that are presented below the threshold for conscious awareness—these are called **subliminal messages.** A stimulus reaches a physiological threshold when it is strong enough to excite sensory receptors and send nerve impulses to the brain: This is an absolute threshold. A message below that threshold is said to be subliminal: We receive it, but we are not consciously aware of it. Over the years there has been a great deal of speculation about the use of subliminal messages in advertising, rock music, and self-help audio programs. Research evidence shows that in laboratory settings, people can process and respond to information outside of awareness. But this does not mean that we obey these messages like zombies; in fact, hidden messages have little effect on behavior outside the laboratory (Kunst-Wilson & Zajonc, 1980; Rensink, 2004; Nelson, 2008; Radel, Sarrazin, Legrain, & Gobancé, 2009; Loersch, Durso, & Petty, 2013).

Dig Deeper: Unconscious Perception

These days, most scientific research on unconscious processes is aimed at showing that people do not need consciousness for certain psychological processes or behaviors. One such example is attitude formation. The most basic process of attitude formation is through mere exposure (Zajonc, 1968). Merely perceiving a stimulus repeatedly, such as a brand on a billboard one passes every day or a song that is played on the radio frequently, renders it more positive. Interestingly, mere exposure does not require conscious awareness of the object of an attitude. In fact, **mere-exposure effects** occur even when novel stimuli are presented subliminally for extremely brief durations (e.g., Kunst-Wilson & Zajonc, 1980). Intriguingly, in such subliminal mere-exposure experiments, participants indicate a preference for, or a positive attitude towards, stimuli they do not consciously remember being exposed to.

Another example of modern research on unconscious processes is research on **priming**. In a well-known experiment by a research team led by the American psychologist John Bargh (Bargh, Chen, & Burrows, 1996), half the participants were primed with the stereotype of the elderly by doing a language task (they had to make sentences on the basis of lists of words). These lists contained words commonly associated with the elderly (e.g., "old," "bingo," "walking stick," "Florida"). The remaining participants received a language task in which the critical words were replaced by words not related to the elderly. After participants had finished they were told the experiment was over, but they were

Figure 2. *Priming can be used to improve intellectual test performance. Research subjects primed with the stereotype of a professor – a sort of intellectual role model – outperformed those primed with an anti-intellectual stereotype. [Photo: Jeremy Wilburn]*

secretly monitored to see how long they took to walk to the nearest elevator. The primed participants took significantly longer. That is, after being exposed to words typically associated with being old, they behaved in line with the stereotype of old people: being slow. Such priming effects have been shown in many different domains. For example, Dijksterhuis and van Knippenberg (1998) demonstrated that priming can improve intellectual performance. They asked their participants to answer 42 general knowledge questions taken from the game Trivial Pursuit. Under normal conditions, participants answered about 50% of the questions correctly. However, participants primed with the stereotype of professors—who are by most people seen as intelligent—managed to answer 60% of the questions correctly. Conversely, performance of participants primed with the "dumb" stereotype of hooligans dropped to 40%.

Absolute thresholds are generally measured under incredibly controlled conditions in situations that are optimal for sensitivity. Sometimes, we are more interested in how much difference in stimuli is required to detect a difference between them. This is known as the **just noticeable difference (jnd)** or **difference threshold**. Unlike the absolute threshold, the difference threshold changes depending on the stimulus intensity. As an example, imagine yourself in a very dark movie theater. If an audience member were to receive a text message on her cell phone which caused her screen to light up, chances are that many people would notice the change in illumination in the theater. However, if the same thing happened in a brightly lit arena during a basketball game, very few people would notice. The cell phone brightness does not change, but its ability to be detected as a change in illumination varies dramatically between the two contexts. Ernst Weber proposed this theory of change in difference threshold in the 1830s, and it has become known as **Weber's law**: The difference threshold is a constant fraction of the original stimulus, as the example illustrates. It is the idea that bigger stimuli require larger differences to be noticed. For example, it will be much harder for your friend to reliably tell the difference between 10 and 11 lbs. (or 5 versus 5.5 kg) than it is for 1 and 2 lbs.

Perception

While our sensory receptors are constantly collecting information from the environment, it is ultimately how we interpret that information that affects how we interact with the world. **Perception** refers to the way sensory information is organized, interpreted, and consciously experienced. Perception involves both bottom-up and top-down processing. **Bottom-up processing** refers to the fact that perceptions are built from sensory input. On the other hand, how we interpret those sensations is influenced by our available knowledge, our experiences, and our thoughts. This is called **top-down processing**.

Look at the shape in Figure 1 below. Seen alone, your brain engages in bottom-up processing. There are two thick vertical lines and three thin horizontal lines. There is no context to give it a specific meaning, so there is no top-down processing involved.

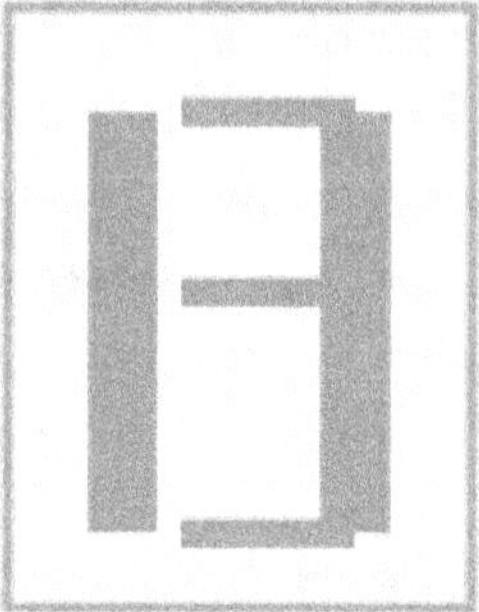

Figure 3.

Now, look at the same shape in two different contexts. Surrounded by sequential letters, your brain expects the shape to be a letter and to complete the sequence. In that context, you perceive the lines to form the shape of the letter "B."

Figure 4.

Surrounded by numbers, the same shape now looks like the number "13."

Figure 5.

When given a context, your perception is driven by your cognitive expectations. Now you are processing the shape in a top-down fashion.

One way to think of this concept is that sensation is a physical process, whereas perception is psychological. For example, upon walking into a kitchen and smelling the scent of baking cinnamon rolls, the *sensation* is the scent receptors detecting the odor of cinnamon, but the *perception* may be "Mmm, this smells like the bread Grandma used to bake when the family gathered for holidays."

Although our perceptions are built from sensations, not all sensations result in perception. In fact, we often don't perceive stimuli that remain relatively constant over prolonged periods of time. This is known as **sensory adaptation**. Imagine entering a classroom with an old analog clock. Upon first entering the room, you can hear the ticking of the clock; as you begin to engage in conversation with classmates or listen to your professor greet the class, you are no longer aware of the ticking. The clock is still ticking, and that information is still affecting sensory receptors of the auditory system. The fact that you no longer perceive the sound demonstrates sensory adaptation and shows that while closely associated, sensation and perception are different.

Attention and Perception

There is another factor that affects sensation and perception: attention. Attention plays a significant role in determining what is sensed versus what is perceived. Imagine you are at a party full of music, chatter, and laughter. You get involved in an interesting conversation with a friend, and you tune out all the background noise. If someone interrupted you to ask what song had just finished playing, you would probably be unable to answer that question.

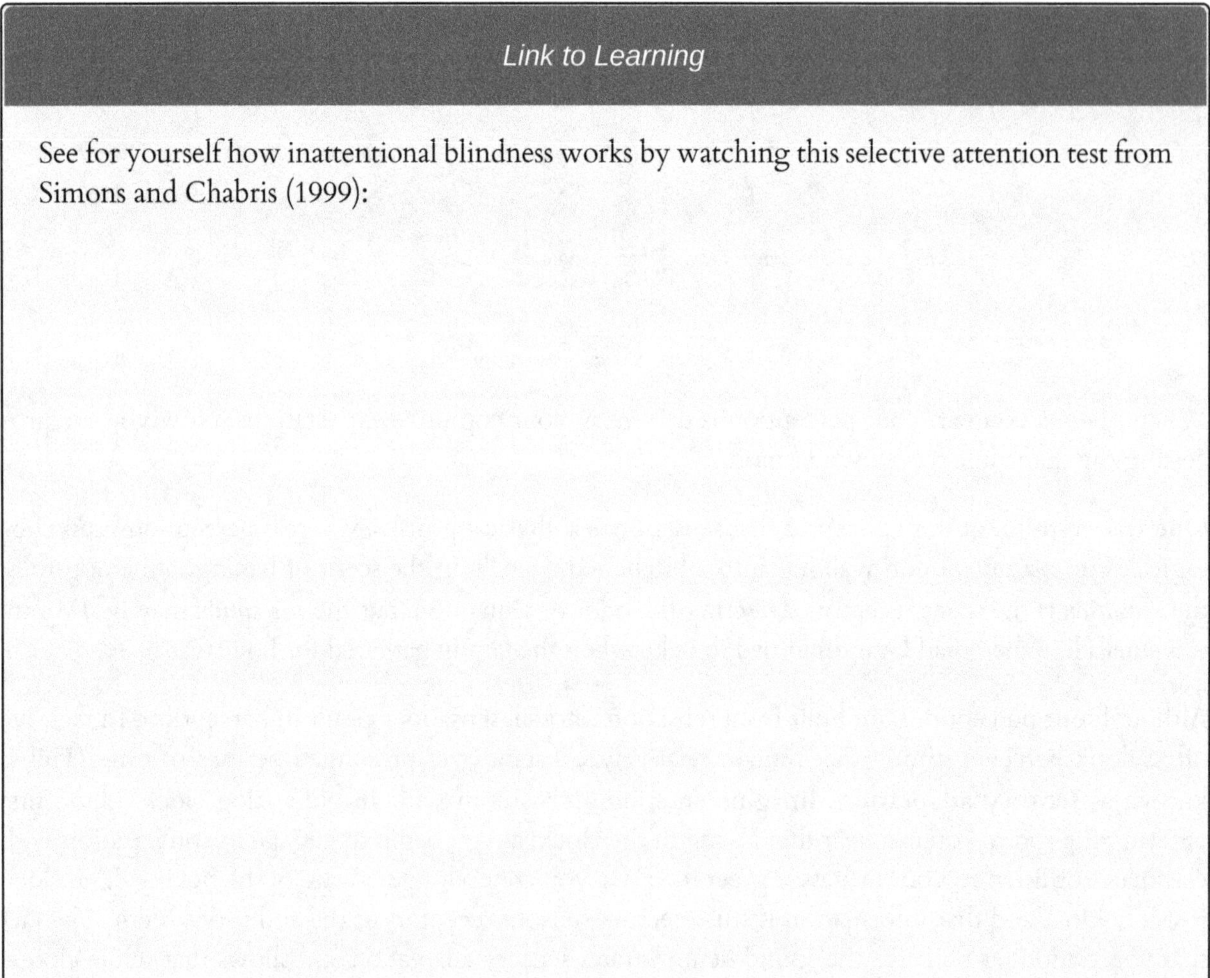

See for yourself how inattentional blindness works by watching this selective attention test from Simons and Chabris (1999):

One of the most interesting demonstrations of how important attention is in determining our perception of the environment occurred in a famous study conducted by Daniel Simons and Christopher Chabris (1999). In this study, participants watched a video of people dressed in black and white passing basketballs. Participants were asked to count the number of times the team in white passed the ball. During the video, a person dressed in a black gorilla costume walks among the two teams. You would think that someone would notice the gorilla, right? Nearly half of the people who watched the video didn't notice the gorilla at all, despite the fact that he was clearly visible for nine seconds. Because participants were so focused on the number of times the white team was passing the ball, they completely tuned out other visual information. Failure to notice something that is completely visible because of a lack of attention is called **inattentional blindness**.

In a similar experiment, researchers tested inattentional blindness by asking participants to observe images moving across a computer screen. They were instructed to focus on either white or black objects, disregarding the other color. When a red cross passed across the screen, about one third of subjects did not notice it (Figure 4) (Most, Simons, Scholl, & Chabris, 2000).

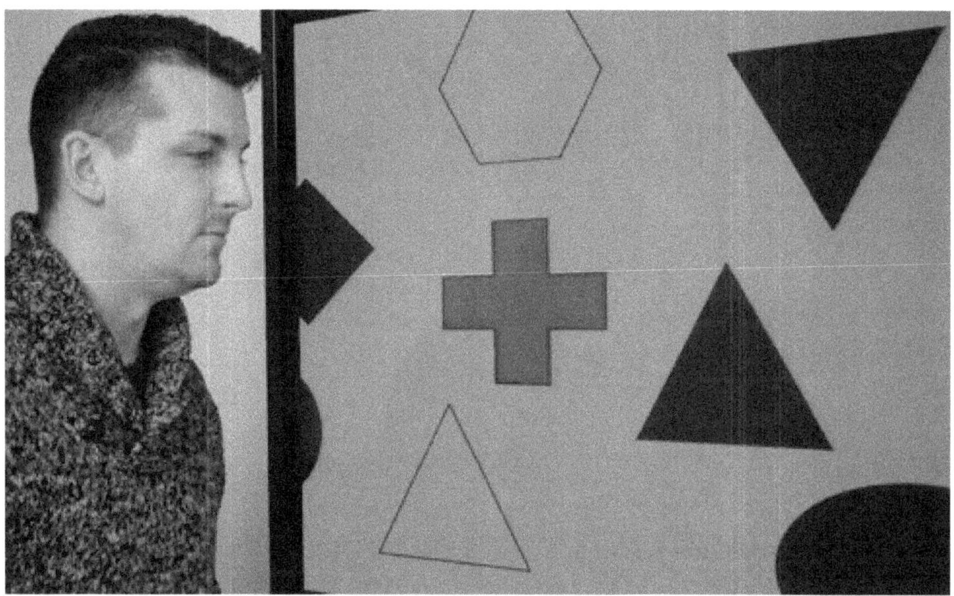

Figure 6. Nearly one third of participants in a study did not notice that a red cross passed on the screen because their attention was focused on the black or white figures. (credit: Cory Zanker)

Motivations, Expectations, and Perception

Motivation can also affect perception. Have you ever been expecting a really important phone call and, while taking a shower, you think you hear the phone ringing, only to discover that it is not? If so, then you have experienced how motivation to detect a meaningful stimulus can shift our ability to discriminate between a true sensory stimulus and background noise. The ability to identify a stimulus when it is embedded in a distracting background is called **signal detection theory**. This might also explain why a mother is awakened by a quiet murmur from her baby but not by other sounds that occur while she is asleep. Signal detection theory has practical applications, such as increasing air traffic controller accuracy. Controllers need to be able to detect planes among many signals (blips) that appear on the radar screen and follow those planes as they move through the sky. In fact, the original work of the researcher who developed signal detection theory was focused on improving the sensitivity of air traffic controllers to plane blips (Swets, 1964).

Our perceptions can also be affected by our beliefs, values, prejudices, expectations, and life experiences. As you will see later in this module, individuals who are deprived of the experience of binocular vision during critical periods of development have trouble perceiving depth (Fawcett, Wang, & Birch, 2005). The shared experiences of people within a given cultural context can have pronounced effects on perception. For example, Marshall Segall, Donald Campbell, and Melville Herskovits (1963) published the results of a multinational study in which they demonstrated that individuals from Western cultures were more prone to experience certain types of visual illusions than individuals from non-Western cultures, and vice versa. One such illusion that Westerners were more likely to experience was the **Müller-Lyer illusion** (Figure 5): The lines appear to be different lengths, but they are actually the same length.

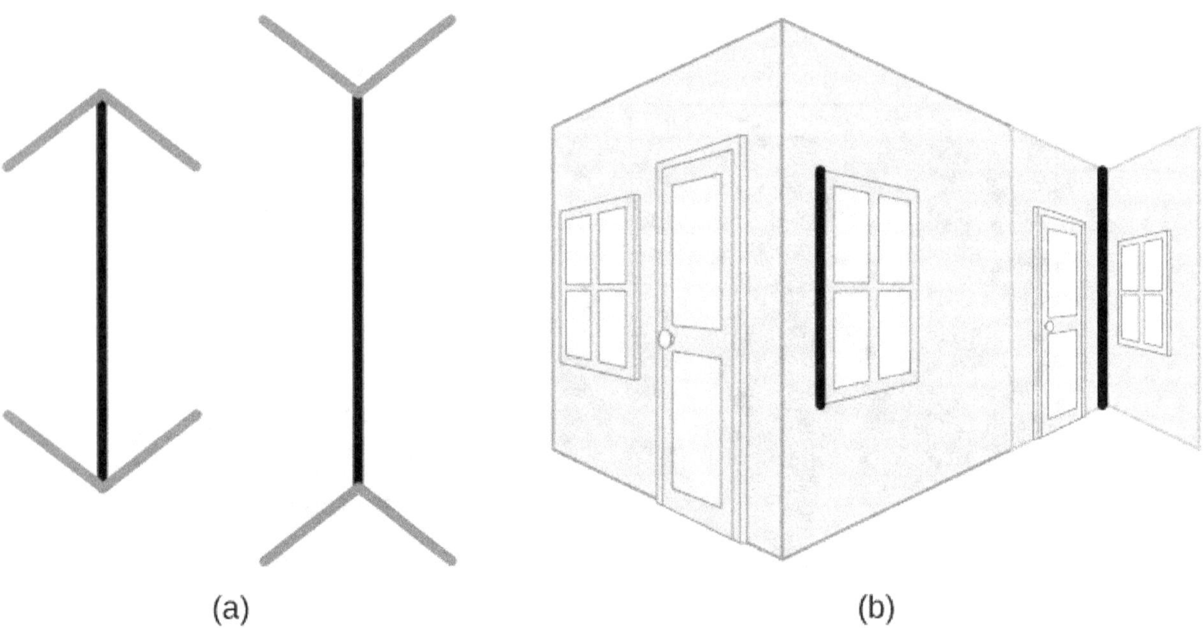

Figure 7. In the Müller-Lyer illusion, lines appear to be different lengths although they are identical. (a) Arrows at the ends of lines may make the line on the right appear longer, although the lines are the same length. (b) When applied to a three-dimensional image, the line on the right again may appear longer although both black lines are the same length.

These perceptual differences were consistent with differences in the types of environmental features experienced on a regular basis by people in a given cultural context. People in Western cultures, for example, have a perceptual context of buildings with straight lines, what Segall's study called a carpentered world (Segall et al., 1966). In contrast, people from certain non-Western cultures with an uncarpentered view, such as the Zulu of South Africa, whose villages are made up of round huts arranged in circles, are less susceptible to this illusion (Segall et al., 1999). It is not just vision that is affected by cultural factors. Indeed, research has demonstrated that the ability to identify an odor, and rate its pleasantness and its intensity, varies cross-culturally (Ayabe-Kanamura, Saito, Distel, Martínez-Gómez, & Hudson, 1998).

Children described as thrill seekers are more likely to show taste preferences for intense sour flavors (Liem, Westerbeek, Wolterink, Kok, & de Graaf, 2004), which suggests that basic aspects of personality might affect perception. Furthermore, individuals who hold positive attitudes toward reduced-fat foods are more likely to rate foods labeled as reduced fat as tasting better than people who have less positive attitudes about these products (Aaron, Mela, & Evans, 1994).

If you want to learn more about the differences between sensation and perception, you can review in this CrashCourse Psychology video:

Glossary

absolute threshold: minimum amount of stimulus energy that must be present for the stimulus to be detected 50% of the time

bottom-up processing: system in which perceptions are built from sensory input

inattentional blindness: failure to notice something that is completely visible because of a lack of attention

just noticeable difference: difference in stimuli required to detect a difference between the stimuli

mere-exposure effects: the result of developing a more positive attitude towards a stimulus after repeated instances of mere exposure to it.

perception: way that sensory information is interpreted and consciously experienced

priming: the process by which recent experiences increase a trait's accessibility.

sensation: what happens when sensory information is detected by a sensory receptor

signal detection theory: change in stimulus detection as a function of current mental state

subliminal message: message presented below the threshold of conscious awareness

top-down processing: interpretation of sensations is influenced by available knowledge, experiences, and thoughts

transduction: conversion from sensory stimulus energy to action potential

https://assessments.lumenlearning.com/assessments/4823
Attributions

CC licensed content, Original

- Modification, adaptation, and original content. **Provided by:** Lumen Learning. **License:** *CC BY: Attribution*

CC licensed content, Shared previously

- Sensation versus Perception. **Authored by:** OpenStax College. **Located at:** http://cnx.org/contents/Sr8Ev5Og@5.52:K-DZ-03P@5/Sensation-versus-Perception. **License:** *CC BY: Attribution*. **License Terms:** Download for free at http://cnx.org/contents/4abf04bf-93a0-45c3-9cbc-2cefd46e68cc@5.48

- Introduction to Sensation. **Provided by:** Boundless. **Located at:** https://www.boundless.com/psychology/textbooks/boundless-psychology-textbook/sensation-and-perception-5/introduction-to-sensation-37/introduction-to-sensation-157-12692/. **Project:** Boundless Psychology. **License:** *CC BY-SA: Attribution-ShareAlike*

- Dig Deeper on the Unconscious and image. **Authored by:** Ap Dijksterhuis Radboud. **Provided by:** University Nijmegen. **Located at:** http://nobaproject.com/modules/the-unconscious. **Project:** The Noba Project. **License:** *CC BY-NC-SA: Attribution-NonCommercial-ShareAlike*

- Sensation and Perception, last example on Weber's Law. **Authored by:** Adam John Privitera. **Provided by:** Chemeketa Community College. **Located at:** http://nobaproject.com/modules/sensation-and-perception. **Project:** The Noba Project. **License:** *CC BY-NC-SA: Attribution-NonCommercial-ShareAlike*

- Candle in the dark. **Authored by:** pratanti. **Provided by:** Flickr. **Located at:** https://www.flickr.com/photos/pratanti/3631956828. **License:** *CC BY: Attribution*

- Section on bottom-up versus top-down processing. **Authored by:** Dr. Scott Roberts, Dr. Ryan Curtis, Samantha Levy, and Dr. Dylan Selterman. **Provided by:** OpenPsyc. **Located at:** http://openpsyc.blogspot.com/2014/06/bottom-up-vs-top-down-processing.html. **License:** *CC BY-NC-SA: Attribution-NonCommercial-ShareAlike*

All rights reserved content

- Sensation & Perception - Crash Course Psychology #5. **Provided by:** CrashCourse. **Located at:** https://www.youtube.com/watch?v=unWnZvXJH2o. **License:** *Other*. **License Terms:** Standard YouTube License

Public domain content

- Painting. **Authored by:** Paul Signac. **Provided by:** Wikimedia. **Located at:** https://en.wikipedia.org/wiki/Soci%C3%A9t%C3%A9_des_Artistes_Ind%C3%A9pendants#/media/File:Signac_-_Portrait_de_F%C3%A9lix_F%C3%A9n%C3%A9on.jpg. **License:** *Public Domain: No Known Copyright*

Vision

Our eyes take in sensory information that helps us understand the world around us. (credit "top left": modification of work by "rajkumar1220"/Flickr; credit "top right": modification of work by Thomas Leuthard; credit "middle left": modification of work by Demietrich Baker; credit "middle right": modification of work by "kaybee07"/Flickr; credit "bottom left": modification of work by "Isengardt"/Flickr; credit "bottom right": modification of work by Willem Heerbaart)

The visual system constructs a mental representation of the world around us. This contributes to our ability to successfully navigate through physical space and interact with important individuals and objects in our environments. This section will provide an overview of the basic anatomy and function of the visual system. In addition, you'll explore our ability to perceive color and depth.

Learning Objectives

- Describe the basic anatomy of the visual system
- Describe how light waves enable vision
- Describe the trichromatic theory of color vision and the opponent-process theory
- Describe how monocular and binocular cues are used in the perception of depth

---

Anatomy of the Visual System

The eye is the major sensory organ involved in **vision** (Figure 1). Light waves are transmitted across the cornea and enter the eye through the pupil. The **cornea** is the transparent covering over the eye. It serves as a barrier between the inner eye and the outside world, and it is involved in focusing light waves that enter the eye. The **pupil** is the small opening in the eye through which light passes, and the size of the pupil can change as a function of light levels as well as emotional arousal. When light levels are low, the pupil will become dilated, or expanded, to allow more light to enter the eye. When light levels are high, the pupil will constrict, or become smaller, to reduce the amount of light that enters the eye. The pupil's size is controlled by muscles that are connected to the **iris**, which is the colored portion of the eye.

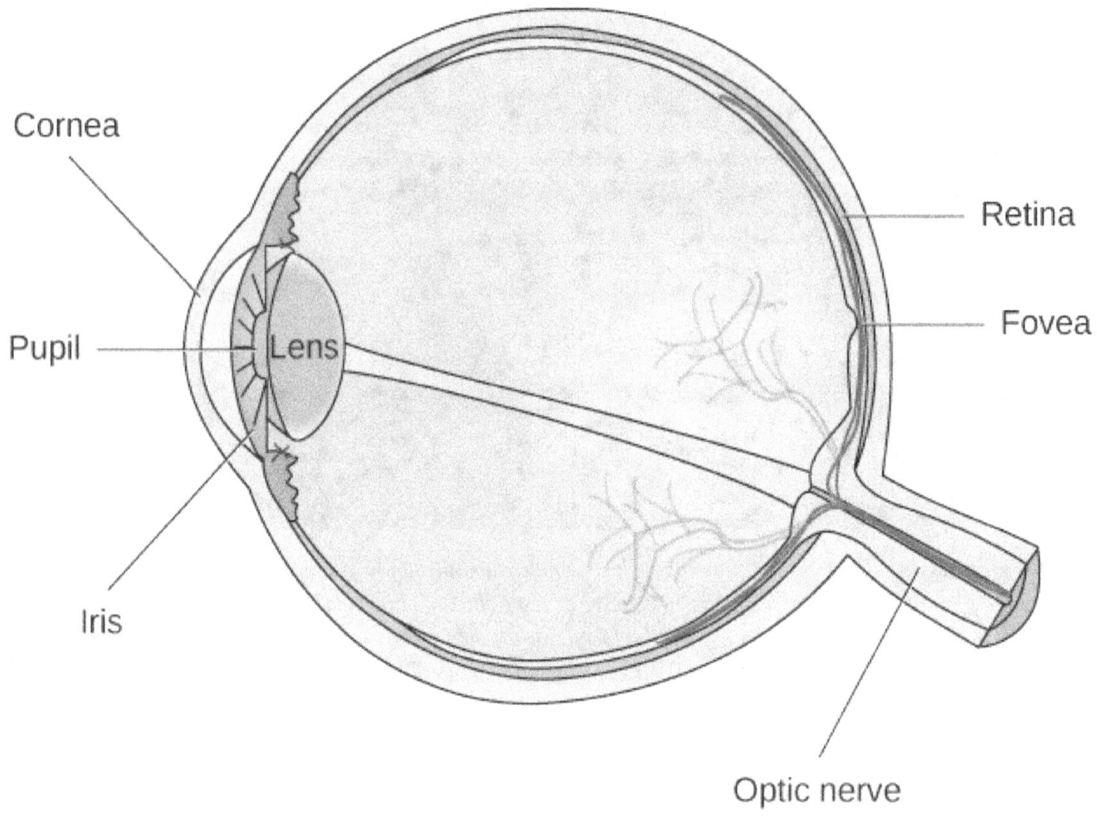

Figure 1. The anatomy of the eye is illustrated in this diagram.

After passing through the pupil, light crosses the **lens**, a curved, transparent structure that serves to provide additional focus. The lens is attached to muscles that can change its shape to aid in focusing light that is reflected from near or far objects. In a normal-sighted individual, the lens will focus images perfectly on a small indentation in the back of the eye known as the **fovea**, which is part of the **retina**, the light-sensitive lining of the eye. The fovea contains densely packed specialized photoreceptor cells (Figure 2). These **photoreceptor** cells, known as **cones**, are light-detecting cells. The cones are specialized types of photoreceptors that work best in bright light conditions. Cones are very sensitive to acute detail and provide tremendous spatial resolution. They also are directly involved in our ability to perceive color.

While cones are concentrated in the fovea, where images tend to be focused, rods, another type of photoreceptor, are located throughout the remainder of the retina. **Rods** are specialized photoreceptors that work well in low light conditions, and while they lack the spatial resolution and color function of the cones, they are involved in our vision in dimly lit environments as well as in our perception of movement on the periphery of our visual field.

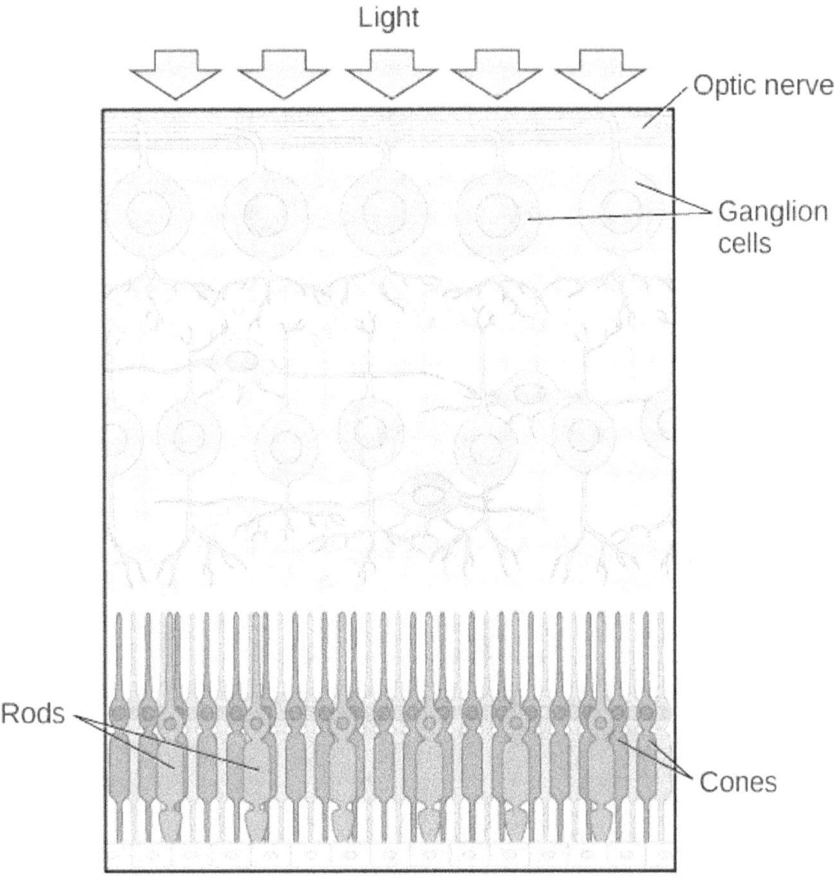

Figure 2. The two types of photoreceptors are shown in this image. Rods are colored green and cones are blue.

We have all experienced the different sensitivities of rods and cones when making the transition from a brightly lit environment to a dimly lit environment. Imagine going to see a blockbuster movie on a clear summer day. As you walk from the brightly lit lobby into the dark theater, you notice that you immediately have difficulty seeing much of anything. After a few minutes, you begin to adjust to the darkness and can see the interior of the theater. In the bright environment, your vision was dominated primarily by cone activity. As you move to the dark environment, rod activity dominates, but there is a delay in transitioning between the phases. If your rods do not transform light into nerve impulses as easily and efficiently as they should, you will have difficulty seeing in dim light, a condition known as night blindness.

Rods and cones are connected (via several interneurons) to retinal ganglion cells. Axons from the retinal ganglion cells converge and exit through the back of the eye to form the optic nerve. The **optic nerve** carries visual information from the retina to the brain. There is a point in the visual field called the **blind spot**: Even when light from a small object is focused on the blind spot, we do not see it. We are not consciously aware of our blind spots for two reasons: First, each eye gets a slightly different view of the visual field; therefore, the blind spots do not overlap. Second, our visual system fills in the blind spot so that although we cannot respond to visual information that occurs in that portion of the visual field, we are also not aware that information is missing.

The optic nerve from each eye merges just below the brain at a point called the **optic chiasm**. As Figure 3 shows, the optic chiasm is an X-shaped structure that sits just below the cerebral cortex at the front of the brain. At the point of the optic chiasm, information from the right visual field (which comes from both eyes) is sent to the left side of the brain, and information from the left visual field is sent to the right side of the brain.

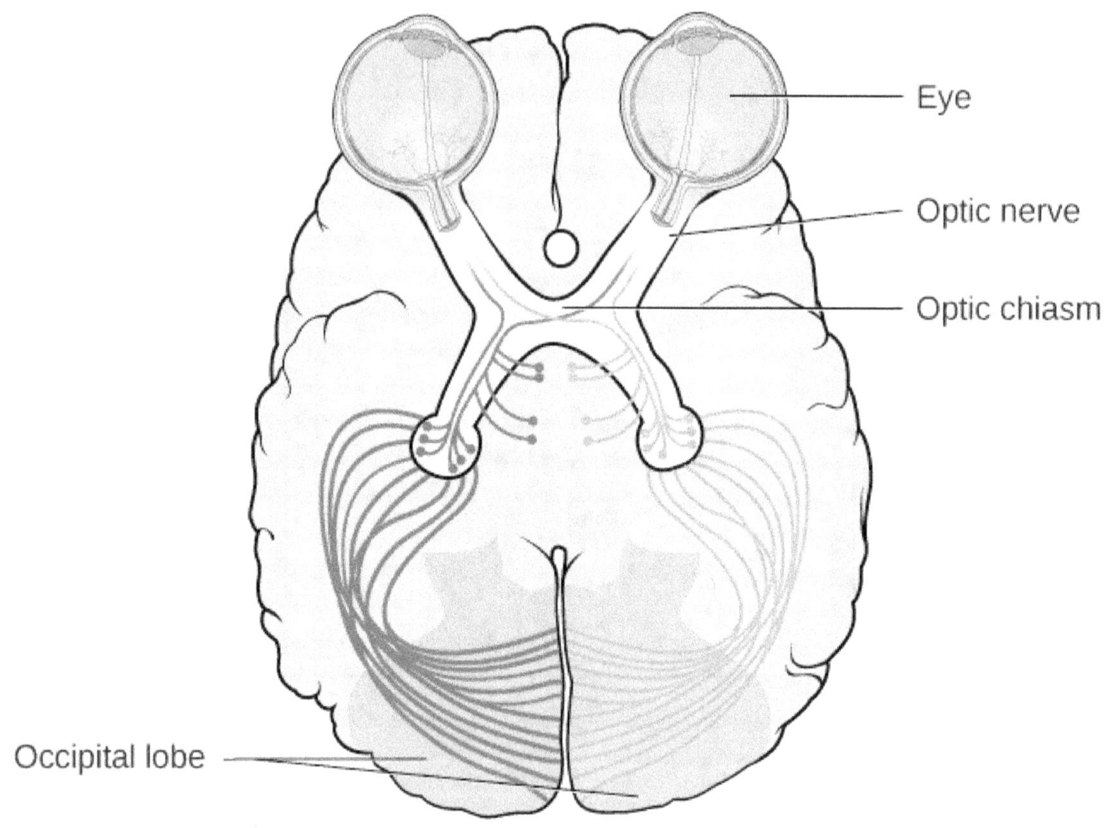

Figure 3. This illustration shows the optic chiasm at the front of the brain and the pathways to the occipital lobe at the back of the brain, where visual sensations are processed into meaningful perceptions.

Once inside the brain, visual information is sent via a number of structures to the occipital lobe at the back of the brain for processing. Visual information might be processed in parallel pathways which can generally be described as the "what pathway" (the ventral pathway) and the "where/how" pathway (the dorsal pathway). The "what pathway" is involved in object recognition and identification, while the "where/how pathway" is involved with location in space and how one might interact with a particular visual stimulus (Milner & Goodale, 2008; Ungerleider & Haxby, 1994). For example, when you see a ball rolling down the street, the "what pathway" identifies what the object is, and the "where/how pathway" identifies its location or movement in space.

Amplitude and Wavelength

As mentioned above, light enters your eyes as a wave. It is important to understand some basic properties of waves to see how they impact what we see. Two physical characteristics of a wave are **amplitude** and wavelength (Figure 5). The amplitude of a wave is the height of a wave as measured from the highest point on the **wave** (**peak** or **crest**) to the lowest point on the wave (trough). **Wavelength** refers to the length of a wave from one peak to the next.

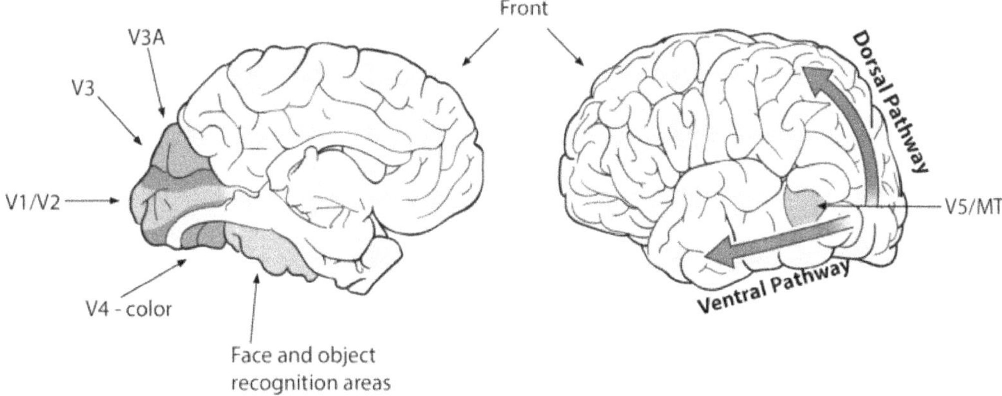

Figure 4. Visual areas in the brain.

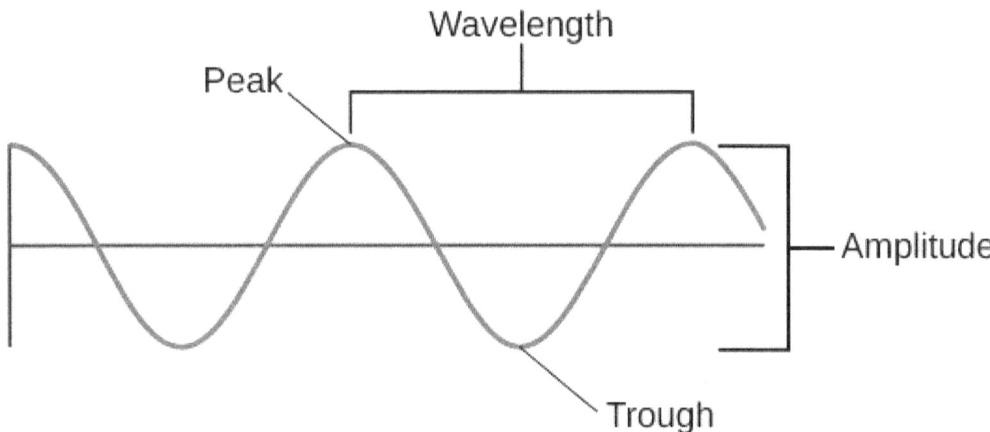

Figure 5. The amplitude or height of a wave is measured from the peak to the trough. The wavelength is measured from peak to peak.

Wavelength is directly related to the frequency of a given wave form. **Frequency** refers to the number of waves that pass a given point in a given time period and is often expressed in terms of **hertz (Hz)**, or cycles per second. Longer wavelengths will have lower frequencies, and shorter wavelengths will have higher frequencies (Figure 6).

Light Waves

The **visible spectrum** is the portion of the larger electromagnetic spectrum that we can see. As Figure 7 shows, the **electromagnetic spectrum** encompasses all of the electromagnetic radiation that occurs in our environment and includes gamma rays, x-rays, ultraviolet light, visible light, infrared light, microwaves, and radio waves. The visible spectrum in humans is associated with wavelengths that range from 380 to 740 nm—a very small distance, since a nanometer (nm) is one billionth of a meter. Other species can detect other portions of the electromagnetic spectrum. For instance, honeybees

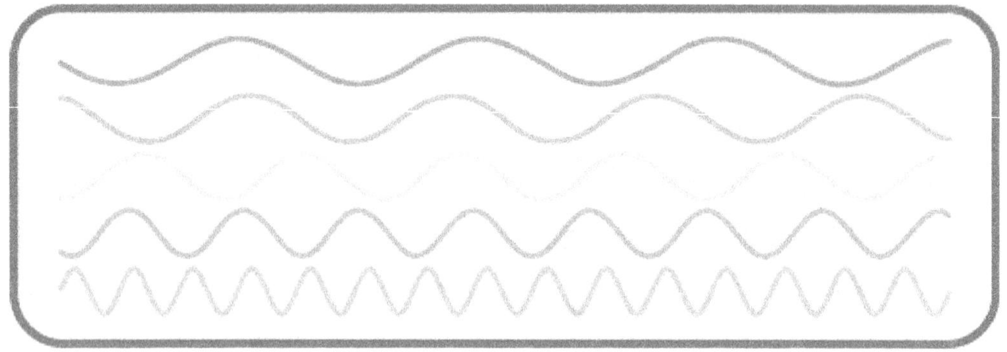

Figure 6. This figure illustrates waves of differing wavelengths/frequencies. At the top of the figure, the red wave has a long wavelength/short frequency. Moving from top to bottom, the wavelengths decrease and frequencies increase.

can see light in the ultraviolet range (Wakakuwa, Stavenga, & Arikawa, 2007), and some snakes can detect infrared radiation in addition to more traditional visual light cues (Chen, Deng, Brauth, Ding, & Tang, 2012; Hartline, Kass, & Loop, 1978).

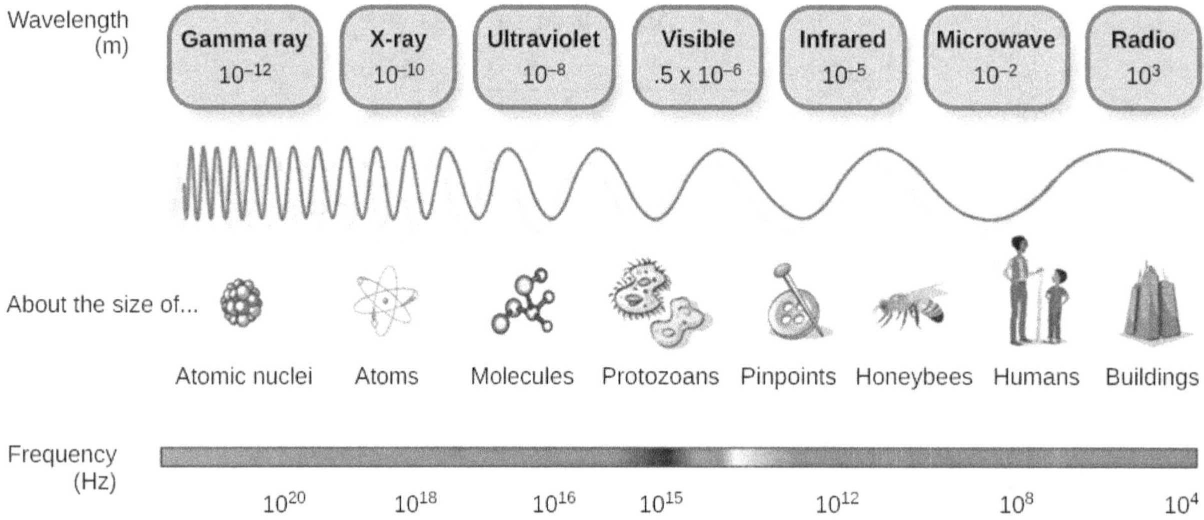

Figure 7. Light that is visible to humans makes up only a small portion of the electromagnetic spectrum.

In humans, light wavelength is associated with perception of color (Figure 8). Within the visible spectrum, our experience of red is associated with longer wavelengths, greens are intermediate, and blues and violets are shorter in wavelength. (An easy way to remember this is the mnemonic ROYGBIV: red, orange, yellow, green, blue, indigo, violet.) The amplitude of light waves is associated with our experience of brightness or intensity of color, with larger amplitudes appearing brighter.

We do not see the world in black and white; neither do we see it as two-dimensional (2-D) or flat (just height and width, no depth). Let's look at how color vision works and how we perceive three dimensions (height, width, and depth).

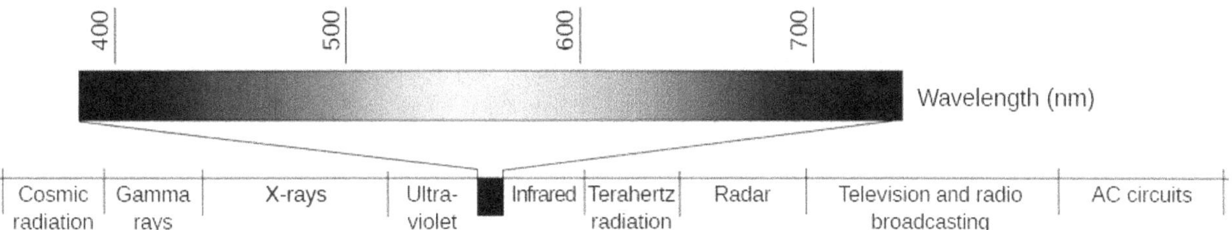

Figure 8. Different wavelengths of light are associated with our perception of different colors. (credit: modification of work by Johannes Ahlmann)

Color Vision

Normal-sighted individuals have three different types of cones that mediate **color vision**. Each of these cone types is maximally sensitive to a slightly different wavelength of light. According to the Young-Helmholtz **trichromatic theory of color vision**, shown in Figure 9, all colors in the spectrum can be produced by combining red, green, and blue. The three types of cones are each receptive to one of the colors.

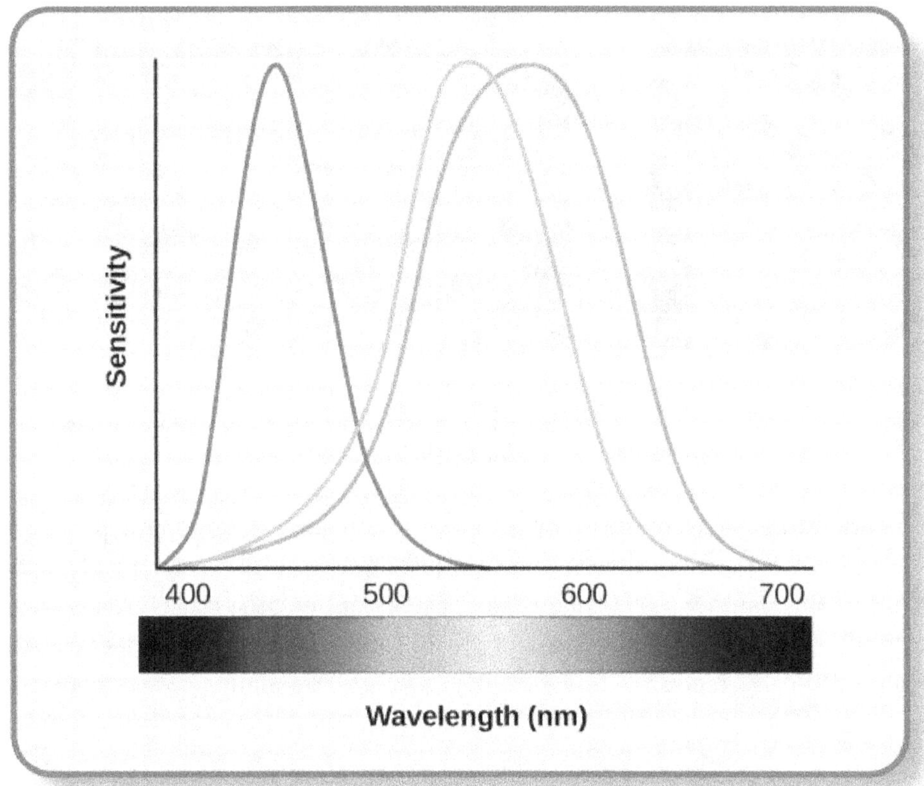

Figure 9. This figure illustrates the different sensitivities for the three cone types found in a normal-sighted individual. (credit: modification of work by Vanessa Ezekowitz)

The trichromatic theory of color vision is not the only theory—another major theory of color vision is known as the **opponent-process theory**. According to this theory, color is coded in opponent pairs: black-white, yellow-blue, and green-red. The basic idea is that some cells of the visual system are excited by one of the opponent colors and inhibited by the other. So, a cell that was excited by wavelengths associated with green would be inhibited by wavelengths associated with red, and vice versa. One of the implications of opponent processing is that we do not experience greenish-reds or yellowish-blues as colors. Another implication is that this leads to the experience of negative afterimages. An **afterimage** describes the continuation of a visual sensation after removal of the stimulus. For example, when you stare briefly at the sun and then look away from it, you may still perceive a spot of light although the stimulus (the sun) has been removed. When color is involved in the stimulus, the color pairings identified in the opponent-process theory lead to a negative afterimage. You can test this concept using the flag in Figure 10.

Figure 10. Stare at the white dot for 30–60 seconds and then move your eyes to a blank piece of white paper. What do you see? This is known as a negative afterimage, and it provides empirical support for the opponent-process theory of color vision.

But these two theories—the trichromatic theory of color vision and the opponent-process theory—are not mutually exclusive. Research has shown that they just apply to different levels of the nervous system. For visual processing on the retina, trichromatic theory applies: the cones are responsive to three different wavelengths that represent red, blue, and green. But once the signal moves past the retina on its way to the brain, the cells respond in a way consistent with opponent-process theory (Land, 1959; Kaiser, 1997).

Depth Perception

Our ability to perceive spatial relationships in three-dimensional (3-D) space is known as **depth perception**. With depth perception, we can describe things as being in front, behind, above, below, or to the side of other things.

Our world is three-dimensional, so it makes sense that our mental representation of the world has three-dimensional properties. We use a variety of cues in a visual scene to establish our sense of depth. Some of these are **binocular cues**, which means that they rely on the use of both eyes. One example of a binocular depth cue is **binocular disparity**, the slightly different view of the world that each of our eyes receives. To experience this slightly different view, do this simple exercise: extend your arm fully and extend one of your fingers and focus on that finger. Now, close your left eye without moving your head, then open your left eye and close your right eye without moving your head. You will notice that your finger seems to shift as you alternate between the two eyes because of the slightly different view each eye has of your finger.

A 3-D movie works on the same principle: the special glasses you wear allow the two slightly different images projected onto the screen to be seen separately by your left and your right eye. As your brain processes these images, you have the illusion that the leaping animal or running person is coming right toward you.

Although we rely on binocular cues to experience depth in our 3-D world, we can also perceive depth in 2-D arrays. Think about all the paintings and photographs you have seen. Generally, you pick up on depth in these images even though the visual stimulus is 2-D. When we do this, we are relying on a number of **monocular cues**, or cues that require only one eye. If you think you can't see depth with one eye, note that you don't bump into things when using only one eye while walking—and, in fact, we have more monocular cues than binocular cues. The following video of anamorphic art demonstrates how we rely on these monocular cues to see depth, even when the depth is only imagined.

An example of a monocular cue would be what is known as **linear perspective**. Linear perspective refers to the fact that we perceive depth when we see two parallel lines that seem to converge in an image (Figure 11). Some other monocular depth cues are interposition, the partial overlap of objects, the relative size and closeness of images to the horizon, relative size, and the variation between light and shadow.

Figure 11. We perceive depth in a two-dimensional figure like this one through the use of monocular cues like linear perspective, like the parallel lines converging as the road narrows in the distance. (credit: Marc Dalmulder)

Dig Deeper: Stereoblindness

Bruce Bridgeman was born with an extreme case of lazy eye that resulted in him being stereoblind, or unable to respond to binocular cues of depth. He relied heavily on monocular depth cues, but he never had a true appreciation of the 3-D nature of the world around him. This all changed one night in 2012 while Bruce was seeing a movie with his wife.

The movie the couple was going to see was shot in 3-D, and even though he thought it was a waste of money, Bruce paid for the 3-D glasses when he purchased his ticket. As soon as the film began, Bruce put on the glasses and experienced something completely new. For the first time in his life he appreciated the true depth of the world around him. Remarkably, his ability to perceive depth persisted outside of the movie theater.

There are cells in the nervous system that respond to binocular depth cues. Normally, these cells require activation during early development in order to persist, so experts familiar with Bruce's case (and others like his) assume that at some point in his development, Bruce must have experienced at least a fleeting moment of binocular vision. It was enough to ensure the survival of the cells in the visual system tuned to binocular cues. The mystery now is why it took Bruce nearly 70 years to have these cells activated (Peck, 2012).

Integration with Other Modalities

Vision is not an encapsulated system. It interacts with and depends on other sensory modalities. For example, when you move your head in one direction, your eyes reflexively move in the opposite direction to compensate, allowing you to maintain your gaze on the object that you are looking at. This reflex is called the **vestibulo-ocular reflex**. It is achieved by integrating information from both the visual and the vestibular system (which knows about body motion and position). You can experience this compensation quite simply. First, while you keep your head still and your gaze looking straight ahead, wave your finger in front of you from side to side. Notice how the image of the finger appears blurry. Now, keep your finger steady and look at it while you move your head from side to side. Notice how your eyes reflexively move to compensate the movement of your head and how the image of the finger stays sharp and stable. Vision also interacts with your proprioceptive system, to help you find where all your body parts are, and with your auditory system, to help you understand the sounds people make when they speak. You can learn more about this in the multimodal module.

Finally, vision is also often implicated in a blending-of-sensations phenomenon known as **synesthesia**. Synesthesia occurs when one sensory signal gives rise to two or more sensations. The most common type is *grapheme-color* synesthesia. About 1 in 200 individuals experience a sensation of color associated with specific letters, numbers, or words: the number 1 might always be seen as red, the number 2 as orange, etc. But the more fascinating forms of synesthesia blend sensations from entirely different sensory modalities, like taste and color or music and color: the taste of chicken might elicit a sensation of green, for example, and the timbre of violin a deep purple.

> ### Link to Learning
>
> All of this talk about vision may have you wondering what this has to do with psychology. Remember that sensation is input about the physical world obtained by our sensory receptors, and perception is the process by which the brain selects, organizes, and interprets these sensations. In other words, senses are the physiological basis of perception. Perception of the same senses may vary from one person to another because each person's brain interprets stimuli differently based on that individual's learning, memory, emotions, and expectations. It is for this reason that psychologists study sensation—in order to understand perception, which is clearly a component of behavior and mental processes (the definition of psychology).
> To see this all in action, visit the BBC website HERE to participate in the sensation lab. Complete the twenty exercises and click on the "explanation" after each question to learn about how our senses are easily fooled.
>
> - https://www.bbc.co.uk/science/humanbody/body/interactives/senseschallenge/senses.swf

Glossary

amplitude: height of a wave

afterimage: continuation of a visual sensation after removal of the stimulus

binocular cue: cue that relies on the use of both eyes

binocular disparity: slightly different view of the world that each eye receives

blind spot: point where we cannot respond to visual information in that portion of the visual field

cone: specialized photoreceptor that works best in bright light conditions and detects color

cornea: transparent covering over the eye

depth perception: ability to perceive depth

electromagnetic spectrum: all the electromagnetic radiation that occurs in our environment

fovea: small indentation in the retina that contains cones

frequency: number of waves that pass a given point in a given time period

hertz (Hz): cycles per second; measure of frequency

iris: colored portion of the eye

lens: curved, transparent structure that provides additional focus for light entering the eye

linear perspective: perceive depth in an image when two parallel lines seem to converge

monocular cue: cue that requires only one eye

opponent-process theory of color perception: color is coded in opponent pairs: black-white, yellow-blue, and red-green

optic chiasm: X-shaped structure that sits just below the brain's ventral surface; represents the merging of the optic nerves from the two eyes and the separation of information from the two sides of the visual field to the opposite side of the brain

optic nerve: carries visual information from the retina to the brain

peak: (also, crest) highest point of a wave

photoreceptor: light-detecting cell

pupil: small opening in the eye through which light passes

retina: light-sensitive lining of the eye

rod: specialized photoreceptor that works well in low light conditions

synesthesia: the blending of two or more sensory experiences, or the automatic activation of a secondary (indirect) sensory experience due to certain aspects of the primary (direct) sensory stimulation

trichromatic theory of color perception: color vision is mediated by the activity across the three groups of cones

trough: lowest point of a wave

vestibulo-ocular reflex: coordination of motion information with visual information that allows you to maintain your gaze on an object while you move

visible spectrum: portion of the electromagnetic spectrum that we can see

wavelength: length of a wave from one peak to the next peak

https://assessments.lumenlearning.com/assessments/4824

Attributions

This is a modified version of OpenStax Psychology. Download the original text for free at https://openstax.org/details/books/psychology

Hearing

What you'll learn to do: explain the basics of hearing

Our auditory system converts pressure waves into meaningful sounds. This translates into our ability to hear the sounds of nature, to appreciate the beauty of music, and to communicate with one another through spoken language. This section will provide an overview of the basic anatomy and function of the auditory system. It will include a discussion of how the sensory stimulus is translated into neural impulses, where in the brain that information is processed, how we perceive pitch, and how we know where sound is coming from.

Learning Objectives

- Describe the basic anatomy and function of the auditory system
- Show how physical properties of sound waves are associated with perceptual experience
- Explain how we encode and perceive pitch and localize sound
- Describe types of hearing loss

How We Hear

Our auditory system converts pressure waves into meaningful sounds. This translates into our ability to hear the sounds of nature, to appreciate the beauty of music, and to communicate with one another through spoken language. This section will provide an overview of the basic anatomy and function of the auditory system. It will include a discussion of how the sensory stimulus is translated into neural impulses, where in the brain that information is processed, how we perceive pitch, and how we know where sound is coming from.

Anatomy of the Auditory System

The ear can be separated into multiple sections. The outer ear includes the **pinna**, which is the visible part of the ear that protrudes from our heads, the auditory canal, and the **tympanic membrane**, or eardrum. The middle ear contains three tiny bones known as the **ossicles**, which are named the **malleus** (or hammer), **incus** (or anvil), and the **stapes** (or stirrup). The inner ear contains the semicircular canals, which are involved in balance and movement (the vestibular sense), and the cochlea. The **cochlea** is a fluid-filled, snail-shaped structure that contains the sensory receptor cells (hair cells) of the auditory system (Figure 1).

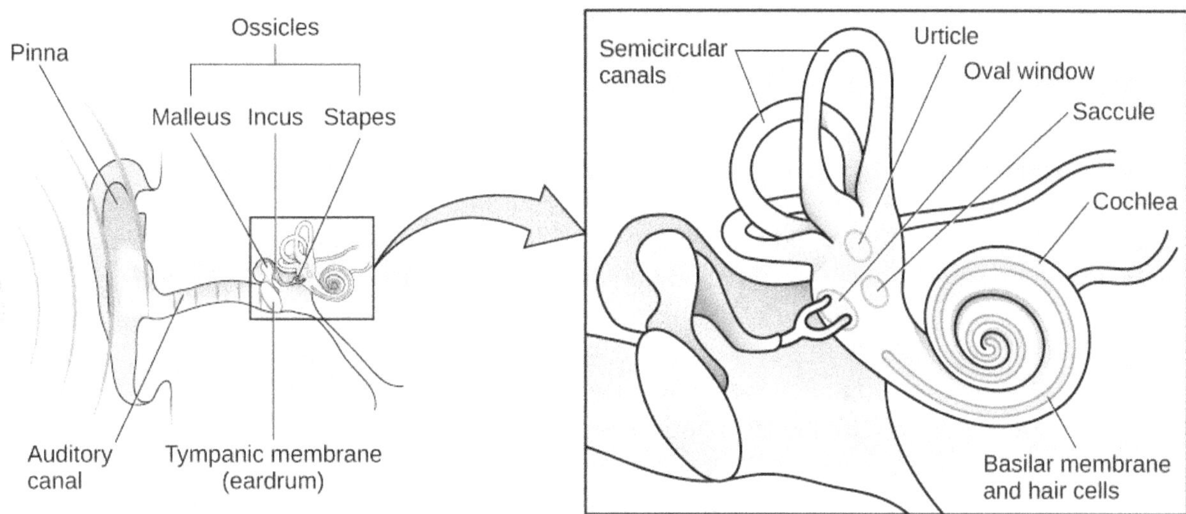

Figure 1. The ear is divided into outer (pinna and tympanic membrane), middle (the three ossicles: malleus, incus, and stapes), and inner (cochlea and basilar membrane) divisions.

Sound waves travel along the auditory canal and strike the tympanic membrane, causing it to vibrate. This vibration results in movement of the three ossicles. As the ossicles move, the stapes presses into a thin membrane of the cochlea known as the oval window. As the stapes presses into the oval window, the fluid inside the cochlea begins to move, which in turn stimulates **hair cells**, which are auditory receptor cells of the inner ear embedded in the basilar membrane. The **basilar membrane** is a thin strip of tissue within the cochlea. Sitting on the basilar membrane is the organ of Corti, which runs the entire length of the basilar membrane from the base (by the oval window) to the apex (the "tip" of the spiral). The organ of Corti includes three rows of outer hair cells and one row of inner hair cells. The hair cells sense the vibrations by way of their tiny hairs, or stereocillia. The outer hair cells seem to function to mechanically amplify the sound-induced vibrations, whereas the inner hair cells form synapses with the auditory nerve and transduce those vibrations into action potentials, or neural spikes, which are transmitted along the auditory nerve to higher centers of the auditory pathways.

The activation of hair cells is a mechanical process: the stimulation of the hair cell ultimately leads to activation of the cell. As hair cells become activated, they generate neural impulses that travel along the auditory nerve to the brain. Auditory information is shuttled to the inferior colliculus, the medial geniculate nucleus of the thalamus, and finally to the auditory cortex in the temporal lobe of the brain for processing. Like the visual system, there is also evidence suggesting that information about auditory recognition and localization is processed in parallel streams (Rauschecker & Tian, 2000; Renier et al., 2009).

Watch the process of audition in the following video:

Sound Waves

As mentioned above, the vibration of the tympanic membrane is what triggers the sequence of events that lead to our perception of sound. Sound waves travel into our ears at various speeds and amplitudes. Like light waves, the physical properties of sound waves are associated with various aspects of our perception of sound. The frequency of a sound wave is associated with our perception of that sound's **pitch**. High-frequency sound waves are perceived as high-pitched sounds, while low-frequency sound waves are perceived as low-pitched sounds. The audible range of sound frequencies is between 20 and 20000 Hz, with greatest sensitivity to those frequencies that fall in the middle of this range.

As was the case with the visible spectrum, other species show differences in their audible ranges. For instance, chickens have a very limited audible range, from 125 to 2000 Hz. Mice have an audible range from 1000 to 91000 Hz, and the beluga whale's audible range is from 1000 to 123000 Hz. Our pet dogs and cats have audible ranges of about 70–45000 Hz and 45–64000 Hz, respectively (Strain, 2003).

The loudness of a given sound is closely associated with the amplitude of the sound wave. Higher amplitudes are associated with louder sounds. Loudness is measured in terms of **decibels (dB)**, a logarithmic unit of sound intensity. A typical conversation would correlate with 60 dB; a rock concert might check in at 120 dB (Figure 2). A whisper 5 feet away or rustling leaves are at the low end of our hearing range; sounds like a window air conditioner, a normal conversation, and even heavy traffic or a vacuum cleaner are within a tolerable range. However, there is the potential for hearing damage from about 80 dB to 130 dB: These are sounds of a food processor, power lawnmower, heavy truck (25 feet away), subway train (20 feet away), live rock music, and a jackhammer. The threshold for pain is about 130 dB, a jet plane taking off or a revolver firing at close range (Dunkle, 1982).

Although wave amplitude is generally associated with loudness, there is some interaction between frequency and amplitude in our perception of loudness within the audible range. For example, a 10 Hz sound wave is inaudible no matter the amplitude of the wave. A 1000 Hz sound wave, on the other hand, would vary dramatically in terms of perceived loudness as the amplitude of the wave increased.

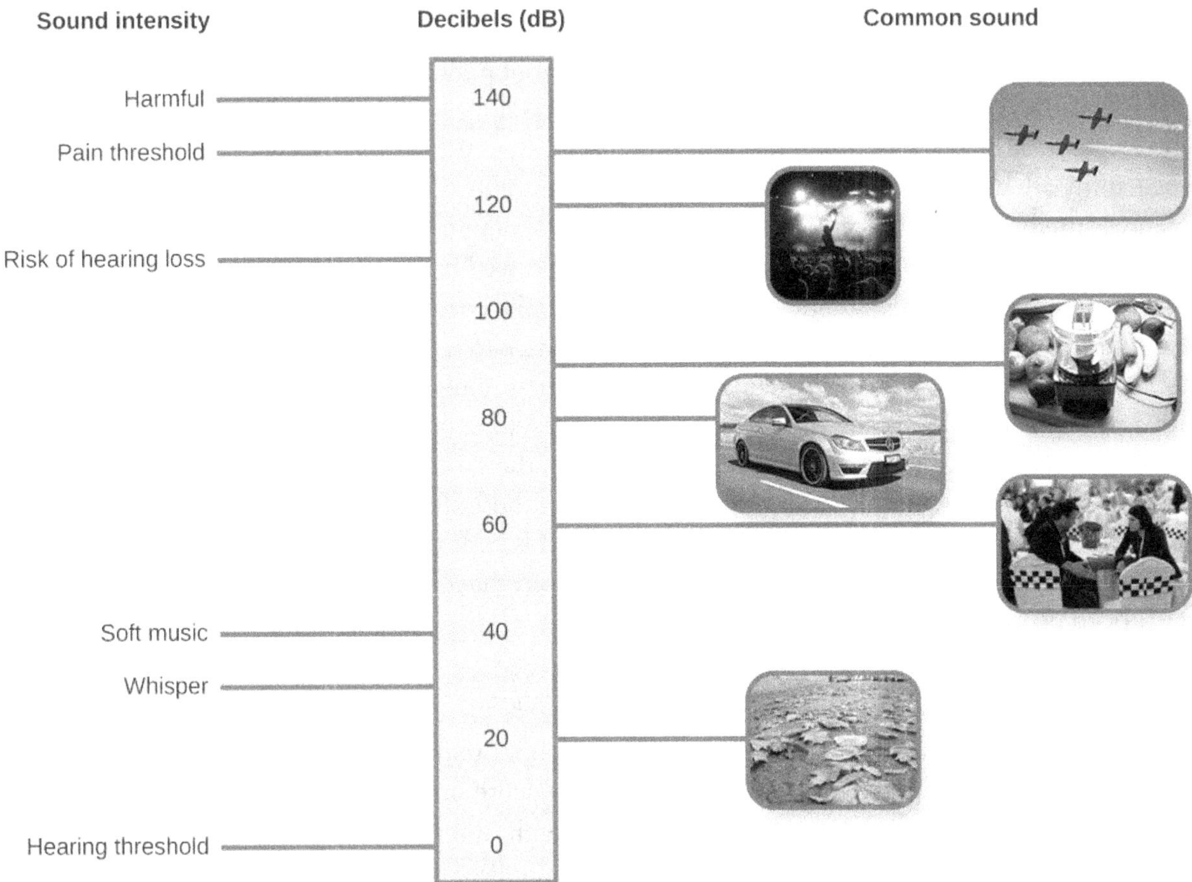

Figure 2. This figure illustrates the loudness of common sounds. (credit "planes": modification of work by Max Pfandl; credit "crowd": modification of work by Christian Holmér; credit "blender": modification of work by Jo Brodie; credit "car": modification of work by NRMA New Cars/Flickr; credit "talking": modification of work by Joi Ito; credit "leaves": modification of work by Aurelijus Valeiša)

Link to Learning

Watch this brief video demonstrating how frequency and amplitude interact in our perception of loudness.

- https://www.lynda.com/Logic-Pro-tutorials/perception-frequency-amplitude/86649/96460-4.html

---

Of course, different musical instruments can play the same musical note at the same level of loudness, yet they still sound quite different. This is known as the timbre of a sound. **Timbre** refers to a sound's purity, and it is affected by the complex interplay of frequency, amplitude, and timing of sound waves.

Pitch Perception

We know that different frequencies of sound waves are associated with differences in our perception of the pitch of those sounds. Low-frequency sounds are lower pitched, and high-frequency sounds are higher pitched. But how does the auditory system differentiate among various pitches? Several theories have been proposed to account for pitch perception. We'll discuss two of them here: temporal theory and place theory.The **temporal theory** of pitch perception asserts that frequency is coded by the activity level of a sensory neuron. This would mean that a given hair cell would fire action potentials related to the frequency of the sound wave. While this is a very intuitive explanation, we detect such a broad range of frequencies (20–20,000 Hz) that the frequency of action potentials fired by hair cells cannot account for the entire range. Because of properties related to sodium channels on the neuronal membrane that are involved in action potentials, there is a point at which a cell cannot fire any faster (Shamma, 2001).The **place theory** of pitch perception suggests that different portions of the basilar membrane are sensitive to sounds of different frequencies. More specifically, the base of the basilar membrane responds best to high frequencies and the tip of the basilar membrane responds best to low frequencies. Therefore, hair cells that are in the base portion would be labeled as high-pitch receptors, while those in the tip of basilar membrane would be labeled as low-pitch receptors (Shamma, 2001).In reality, both theories explain different aspects of pitch perception. At frequencies up to about 4000 Hz, it is clear that both the rate of action potentials and place contribute to our perception of pitch. However, much higher frequency sounds can only be encoded using place cues (Shamma, 2001).

Sound Localization

The ability to locate sound in our environments is an important part of **hearing**. Localizing sound could be considered similar to the way that we perceive depth in our visual fields. Like the monocular and binocular cues that provided information about depth, the auditory system uses both **monaural** (one-eared) and **binaural** (two-eared) cues to localize sound.

Each pinna interacts with incoming sound waves differently, depending on the sound's source relative to our bodies. This interaction provides a monaural cue that is helpful in locating sounds that occur above or below and in front or behind us. The sound waves received by your two ears from sounds that come from directly above, below, in front, or behind you would be identical; therefore, monaural cues are essential (Grothe, Pecka, & McAlpine, 2010).

Binaural cues, on the other hand, provide information on the location of a sound along a horizontal axis by relying on differences in patterns of vibration of the eardrum between our two ears. If a sound comes from an off-center location, it creates two types of binaural cues: interaural level differences and interaural timing differences. **Interaural level difference** refers to the fact that a sound coming from the right side of your body is more intense at your right ear than at your left ear because of the attenuation of the sound wave as it passes through your head. **Interaural timing difference** refers to the small difference in the time at which a given sound wave arrives at each ear (Figure 3). Certain brain areas monitor these differences to construct where along a horizontal axis a sound originates (Grothe et al., 2010).

Hearing Loss

Deafness is the partial or complete inability to hear. Some people are born deaf, which is known as **congenital deafness**. Many others begin to suffer from **conductive hearing loss** because of age, genetic predisposition, or environmental effects, including exposure to extreme noise (noise-induced

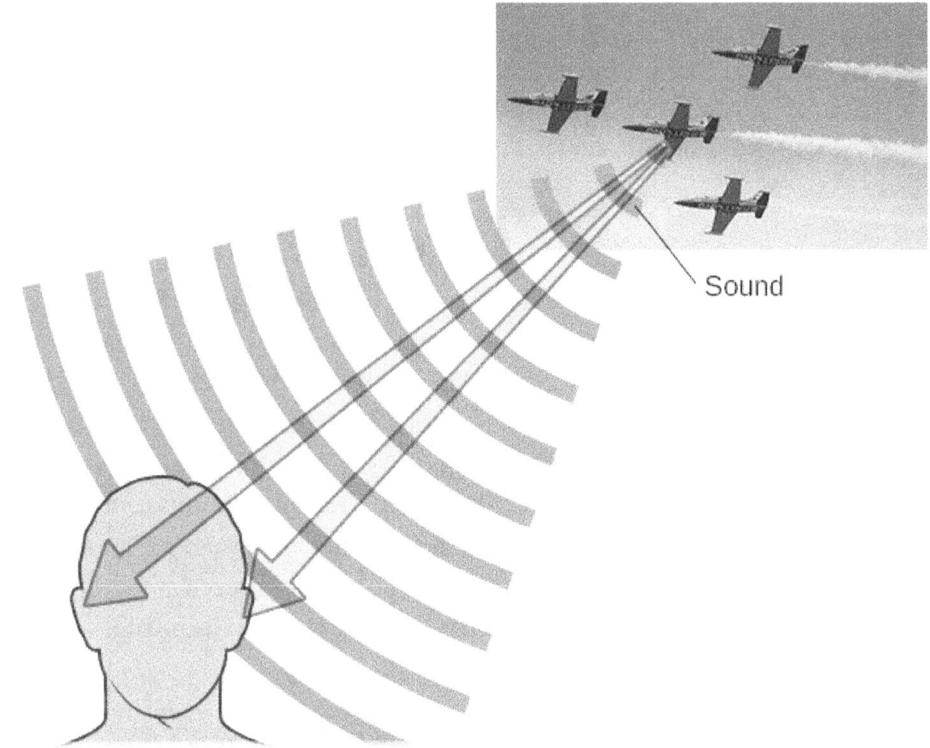

Figure 3. Localizing sound involves the use of both monaural and binaural cues. (credit "plane": modification of work by Max Pfandl)

hearing loss, as shown in Figure 4, certain illnesses (such as measles or mumps), or damage due to toxins (such as those found in certain solvents and metals). Conductive hearing loss involves structural damage to the ear such as failure in the vibration of the eardrum and/or movement of the ossicles.

(a)   (b)

Figure 4. Environmental factors that can lead to conductive hearing loss include regular exposure to loud music or construction equipment. (a) Rock musicians and (b) construction workers are at risk for this type of hearing loss. (credit a: modification of work by Kenny Sun; credit b: modification of work by Nick Allen)

Given the mechanical nature by which the sound wave stimulus is transmitted from the eardrum through the ossicles to the oval window of the cochlea, some degree of hearing loss is inevitable. With conductive hearing loss, hearing problems are associated with a failure in the vibration of the eardrum and/or movement of the ossicles. These problems are often dealt with through devices like hearing aids that amplify incoming sound waves to make vibration of the eardrum and movement of the ossicles more likely to occur.

When the hearing problem is associated with a failure to transmit neural signals from the cochlea to the brain, it is called **sensorineural hearing loss**. This type of loss accelerates with age and can be caused by prolonged exposure to loud noises, which causes damage to the hair cells within the cochlea. One disease that results in sensorineural hearing loss is **Ménière's disease**. Although not well understood, Ménière's disease results in a degeneration of inner ear structures that can lead to hearing loss, tinnitus (constant ringing or buzzing), **vertigo** (a sense of spinning), and an increase in pressure within the inner ear (Semaan & Megerian, 2011). This kind of loss cannot be treated with hearing aids, but some individuals might be candidates for a cochlear implant as a treatment option. **Cochlear implants** are electronic devices that consist of a microphone, a speech processor, and an electrode array. The device receives incoming sound information and directly stimulates the auditory nerve to transmit information to the brain.

What Do You Think?: Deaf Culture

In the United States and other places around the world, deaf people have their own language, schools, and customs. This is called deaf culture. In the United States, deaf individuals often communicate using American Sign Language (ASL); ASL has no verbal component and is based entirely on visual signs and gestures. The primary mode of communication is signing. One of the values of deaf culture is to continue traditions like using sign language rather than teaching deaf children to try to speak, read lips, or have cochlear implant surgery.

When a child is diagnosed as deaf, parents have difficult decisions to make. Should the child be enrolled in mainstream schools and taught to verbalize and read lips? Or should the child be sent to a school for deaf children to learn ASL and have significant exposure to deaf culture? Do you think there might be differences in the way that parents approach these decisions depending on whether or not they are also deaf?

Glossary

basilar membrane: thin strip of tissue within the cochlea that contains the hair cells which serve as the sensory receptors for the auditory system

binaural cue: two-eared cue to localize sound

cochlear implant: electronic device that consists of a microphone, a speech processor, and an electrode array to directly stimulate the auditory nerve to transmit information to the brain

conductive hearing loss: failure in the vibration of the eardrum and/or movement of the ossicles

congenital deafness: deafness from birth

deafness: partial or complete inability to hear

hair cell: auditory receptor cell of the inner ear

incus: middle ear ossicle; also known as the anvil

interaural: level difference sound coming from one side of the body is more intense at the closest ear because of the attenuation of the sound wave as it passes through the head

interaural timing difference: small difference in the time at which a given sound wave arrives at each ear

malleus: middle ear ossicle; also known as the hammer

Ménière's disease: results in a degeneration of inner ear structures that can lead to hearing loss, tinnitus, vertigo, and an increase in pressure within the inner ear

monaural cue: one-eared cue to localize sound

pinna: visible part of the ear that protrudes from the head

place theory of pitch perception: different portions of the basilar membrane are sensitive to sounds of different frequencies

sensorineural hearing loss: failure to transmit neural signals from the cochlea to the brain

stapes: middle ear ossicle; also known as the stirrup

temporal theory of pitch perception: sound's frequency is coded by the activity level of a sensory neuron

tympanic membrane: eardrum

vertigo: spinning sensation

https://assessments.lumenlearning.com/assessments/4825

Attributions

Taste and Smell

What you'll learn to do: describe the basic anatomy and functions of taste, smell, touch, pain, and the vestibular sense

Vision and hearing have received an incredible amount of attention from researchers over the years. While there is still much to be learned about how these sensory systems work, we have a much better understanding of them than of our other sensory modalities. In this section, we will explore our chemical senses (taste and smell) and our body senses (touch, temperature, pain, balance, and body position).

Learning Objectives

- Summarize the chemical process of taste and smell
- Explain the receptors that respond to touch

The Chemical Senses

Taste (gustation) and smell (olfaction) are called chemical senses because both have sensory receptors that respond to molecules in the food we eat or in the air we breathe. There is a pronounced interaction between our chemical senses. For example, when we describe the flavor of a given food, we are really referring to both gustatory and olfactory properties of the food working in combination.

Taste (Gustation)

You have learned since elementary school that there are four basic groupings of **taste**: sweet, salty, sour, and bitter. Research demonstrates, however, that we have at least six taste groupings. **Umami** is our fifth taste. Umami is actually a Japanese word that roughly translates to yummy, and it is associated with a taste for monosodium glutamate (Kinnamon & Vandenbeuch, 2009). There is also a growing body of experimental evidence suggesting that we possess a taste for the fatty content of a given food (Mizushige, Inoue, & Fushiki, 2007).

Molecules from the food and beverages we consume dissolve in our saliva and interact with taste receptors on our tongue and in our mouth and throat. **Taste buds** are formed by groupings of taste receptor cells with hair-like extensions that protrude into the central pore of the taste bud (Figure 1). Taste buds have a life cycle of ten days to two weeks, so even destroying some by burning your tongue won't have any long-term effect; they just grow right back. Taste molecules bind to receptors on this extension and cause chemical changes within the sensory cell that result in neural impulses being transmitted to the brain via different nerves, depending on where the receptor is located. Taste information is transmitted to the medulla, thalamus, and limbic system, and to the gustatory cortex, which is tucked underneath the overlap between the frontal and temporal lobes (Maffei, Haley, & Fontanini, 2012; Roper, 2013).

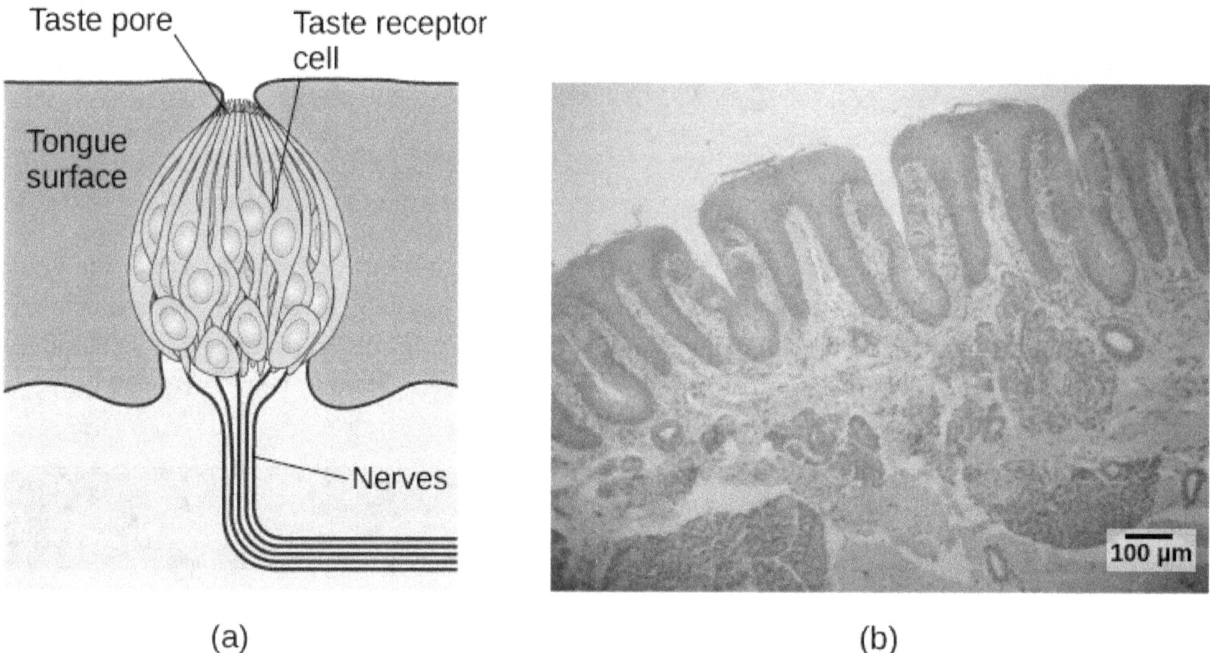

Figure 1. (a) Taste buds are composed of a number of individual taste receptors cells that transmit information to nerves. (b) This micrograph shows a close-up view of the tongue's surface. (credit a: modification of work by Jonas Töle; credit b: scale-bar data from Matt Russell)

Smell (Olfaction)

Olfactory receptor cells are located in a mucous membrane at the top of the nose. Small hair-like extensions from these receptors serve as the sites for odor molecules dissolved in the mucus to interact with chemical receptors located on these extensions (Figure 2). Once an odor molecule has bound a given receptor, chemical changes within the cell result in signals being sent to the **olfactory bulb**: a bulb-like structure at the tip of the frontal lobe where the olfactory nerves begin. From the olfactory bulb, information is sent to regions of the limbic system and to the primary olfactory cortex, which is located very near the gustatory cortex (Lodovichi & Belluscio, 2012; Spors et al., 2013).

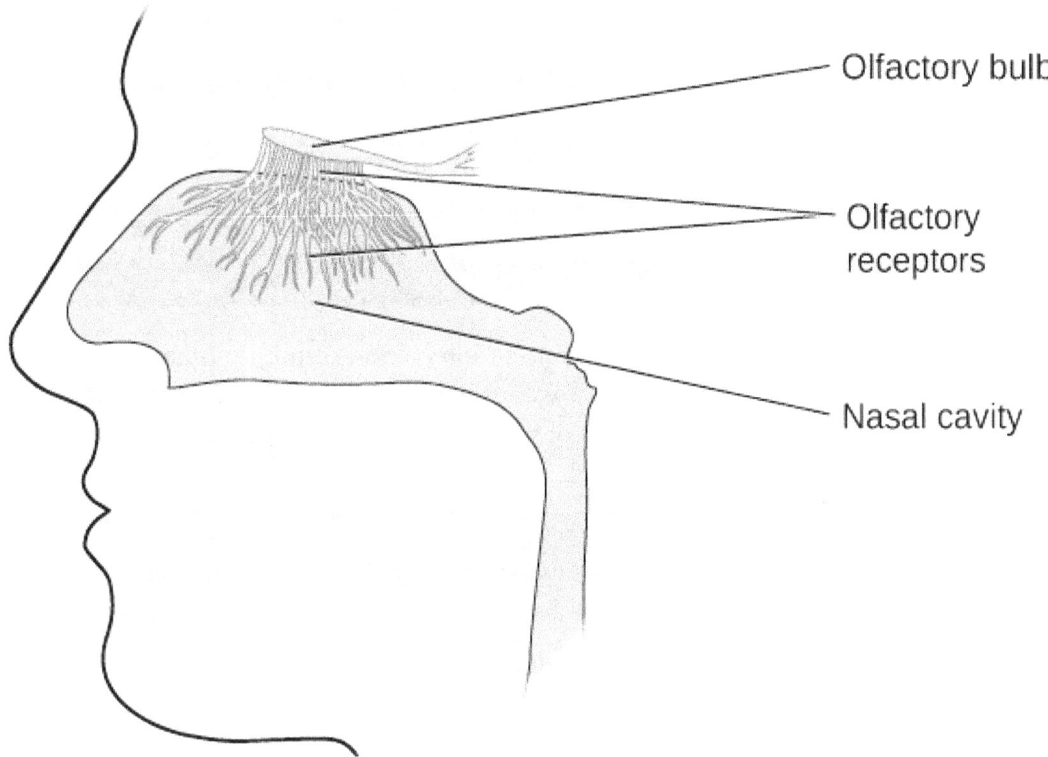

Figure 2. Olfactory receptors are the hair-like parts that extend from the olfactory bulb into the mucous membrane of the nasal cavity.

Olfactory receptors are complex proteins called G protein-coupled receptors (GPCRs). These structures are proteins that weave back and forth across the membranes of olfactory cells seven times, forming structures outside the cell that sense odorant molecules and structures inside the cell that activate the neural message ultimately conveyed to the brain by olfactory neurons. The structures that sense odorants can be thought of as tiny binding pockets with sites that respond to active parts of molecules (e.g., carbon chains). There are about 350 functional olfactory genes in humans; each gene expresses a particular kind of olfactory receptor. All olfactory receptors of a given kind project to structures called glomeruli (paired clusters of cells found on both sides of the brain). For a single molecule, the pattern of activation across the glomeruli paints a picture of the chemical structure of the molecule. Thus, the olfactory system can identify a vast array of chemicals present in the environment. Most of the odors we encounter are actually mixtures of chemicals (e.g., bacon odor). The olfactory system creates an image for the mixture and stores it in memory just as it does for the odor of a single molecule (Shepherd, 2005).

There is tremendous variation in the sensitivity of the olfactory systems of different species. We often think of dogs as having far superior olfactory systems than our own, and indeed, dogs can do some remarkable things with their noses. There is some evidence to suggest that dogs can "smell" dangerous drops in blood glucose levels as well as cancerous tumors (Wells, 2010). Dogs' extraordinary olfactory abilities may be due to the increased number of functional genes for olfactory receptors (between 800 and 1200), compared to the fewer than 400 observed in humans and other primates (Niimura & Nei, 2007).

Many species respond to chemical messages, known as **pheromones**, sent by another individual (Wysocki & Preti, 2004). Pheromonal communication often involves providing information about the reproductive status of a potential mate. So, for example, when a female rat is ready to mate, she secretes pheromonal signals that draw attention from nearby male rats. Pheromonal activation is actually an important component in eliciting sexual behavior in the male rat (Furlow, 1996, 2012; Purvis & Haynes, 1972; Sachs, 1997). There has also been a good deal of research (and controversy) about pheromones in humans (Comfort, 1971; Russell, 1976; Wolfgang-Kimball, 1992; Weller, 1998).

Learning Objectives

As mentioned earlier, a food's flavor represents an interaction of both gustatory and olfactory information. Think about the last time you were seriously congested due to a cold or the flu. What changes did you notice in the flavors of the foods that you ate during this time?

Glossary

olfactory bulb: bulb-like structure at the tip of the frontal lobe, where the olfactory nerves begin

olfactory receptor: sensory cell for the olfactory system

pheromone: chemical message sent by another individual

taste bud: grouping of taste receptor cells with hair-like extensions that protrude into the central pore of the taste bud

umami: taste for monosodium glutamate

Attributions

CC licensed content, Shared previously

- The Other Senses. **Authored by:** OpenStax College. **Located at:** http://cnx.org/contents/Sr8Ev5Og@5.49:Nw9FOKLs@6/The-Other-Senses. **License:** *CC BY: Attribution.* **License Terms:** Download for free at http://cnx.org/contents/4abf04bf-93a0-45c3-9cbc-2cefd46e68cc@5.48

- Paragraph on olfactory receptors. **Authored by:** Linda Bartoshuk and Derek Snyder . **Provided by:** University of Florida. **Located at:** http://nobaproject.com/modules/taste-and-smell?r=LDIzOTky. **Project:** The Noba Project. **License:** *CC BY-NC-SA: Attribution-NonCommercial-ShareAlike*

- Touch photo. **Authored by:** Wendy Longo. **Located at:** https://www.google.com/search?q=5+senses&rlz=1C5CHFA_enUS727US727&source=lnms&tbm=isch&sa=X&ved=0ahUKEwjCwNPv1-zRAhUJj1QKHdLfC-

Touch and Pain

- Explain the receptors that respond to touch
- Explain the importance of pain and give examples of how expectations and context affect pain and touch experiences.

Touch, Thermoception, and Noiception

A number of receptors are distributed throughout the skin to respond to various touch-related stimuli (Figure 1). These receptors include Meissner's corpuscles, Pacinian corpuscles, Merkel's disks, and Ruffini corpuscles. **Meissner's corpuscles** respond to pressure and lower frequency vibrations, and **Pacinian corpuscles** detect transient pressure and higher frequency vibrations. **Merkel's disks** respond to light pressure, while **Ruffini corpuscles** detect stretch (Abraira & Ginty, 2013).

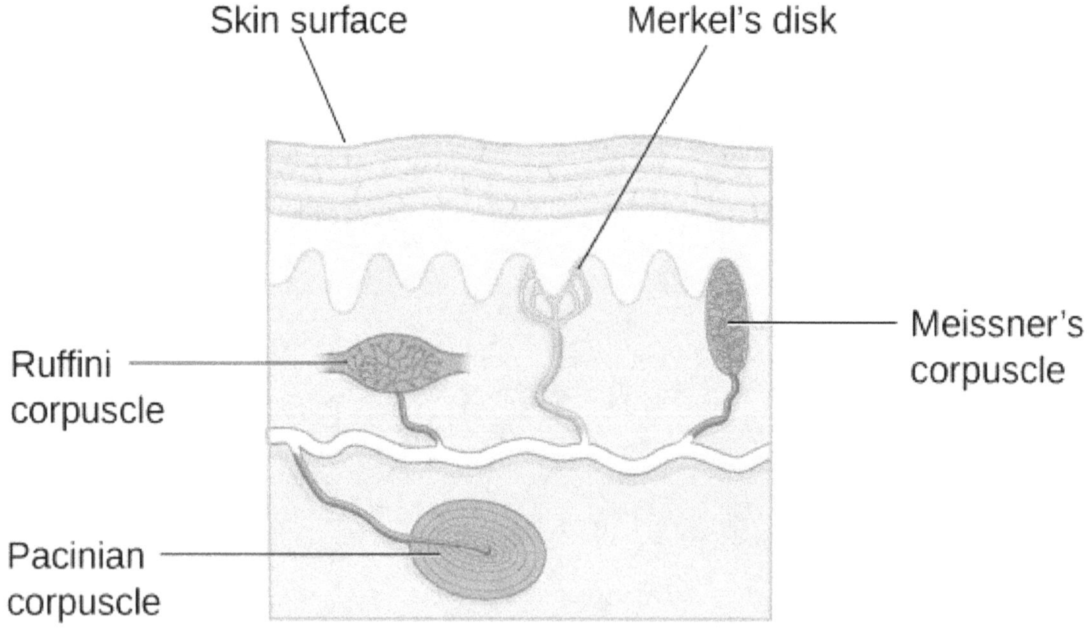

Figure 1. There are many types of sensory receptors located in the skin, each attuned to specific touch-related stimuli.

The skin can convey many sensations, such as the biting cold of a wind, the comfortable pressure of a hand holding yours, or the irritating itch from a woolen scarf. The different types of information activate specific receptors that convert the stimulation of the skin to electrical nerve impulses, a process called transduction. There are three main groups of receptors in our skin: *mechanoreceptors*, responding to mechanical stimuli, such as stroking, stretching, or vibration of the skin; *thermoreceptors*, responding to cold or hot temperatures; and *chemoreceptors*, responding to certain types of chemicals either applied externally or released within the skin (such as histamine from an inflammation). For an overview of the different receptor types and their properties, see Table 1. The experience of *pain* usually starts with activation of **nociceptors**—receptors that fire specifically to potentially tissue-damaging stimuli. Most of the nociceptors are subtypes of either chemoreceptors or mechanoreceptors. When tissue is damaged or inflamed, certain chemical substances are released from the cells, and these substances activate the chemosensitive nociceptors. Mechanoreceptive nociceptors have a high threshold for activation—they respond to mechanical stimulation that is so intense it might damage the tissue. Sensory information collected from the receptors and free nerve endings travels up the spinal cord and is transmitted to regions of the medulla, thalamus, and ultimately to somatosensory cortex, which is located in the postcentral gyrus of the parietal lobe.

Table 1. Categories of low-threshold mechanoreceptors*

Identity of receptor	Size of receptor*	Type of skin where found	Speed of adaptation*	Adequate stimulus*
Merkel's disks	small, sharp borders	glabrous*	slow	pressure
Meissner's corpusles	small, sharp borders	glabrous	rapid	indentation
Ruffini corpuscles	large, diffuse borders	hairy + glabrous	slow	stretching
Pacinian corpuscles	large, diffuse borders	hairy + glabrous	rapid	vibration

*Terms:
Adequate stimulus-the type of stimulus that the receptor is specialized to receive and respond to.

Glabrous skin-the hairless skin found on our palms and the soles of our feet. This skin has a higher density of receptors of a more complex range, which reflects the fact that we use these areas of our body to actively explore our surroundings and to discriminate tactile properties of objects we're interacting with.

Low-threshold mechanoreceptors-mechanoreceptors that respond to stimulus that is so light it doesn't threaten to damage the tissue around it. high-threshold mechanoreceptors respond to stimulation of higher intensity, and are a type of nociceptor.

Receptive field-the space of skin or tissue in which stimulation will elicit a response in the receptor. Smaller receptive fields make the receptor more sensitive to details.

Speed adaptation-slowly adapting mechanoreceptors continue to fire action potentials during sustained stimulation. Rapidly adapting mechanoreceptors continue to fire action potentials in response to stimulus onset and offset (i.e. to stimuli changes), and help detect stimulus movement on the skin.

Pain Perception

Life Without Pain?

Imagine a life free of pain. How would it be—calm, fearless, serene? Would you feel invulnerable, invincible? Getting rid of pain is a popular quest—a quick search for "pain-free life" on Google returns well over 4 million hits—including links to various bestselling self-help guides promising a pain-free life in only 7 steps, 6 weeks, or 3 minutes. Pain management is a billion-dollar market, and involves much more than just pharmaceuticals. Surely a life with no pain would be a better one?

Well, consider one of the "lucky few": 12-year-old "Thomas" has never felt deep pain. Not even when a fracture made him walk around with one leg shorter than the other, so that the bones of his healthy leg were slowly crushed to destruction underneath the knee joint. For Thomas and other members of a large Swedish family, life without pain is a harsh reality because of a mutated gene that affects the growth of the nerves conducting deep pain. Most of those affected suffer from joint damage and frequent fractures to bones in their feet and hands; some end up in wheelchairs even before they reach puberty (Minde et al., 2004). It turns out pain—generally—serves us well.

Living without a sense of touch sounds less attractive than being free of pain—touch is a source of pleasure and essential to how we feel. Losing the sense of touch has severe implications—something patient G. L. experienced when an antibiotics treatment damaged the type of nerves that signal touch from her skin and the position of her joints and muscles. She reported feeling like she'd lost her physical self from her nose down, making her "disembodied"—like she no longer had any connection to the body attached to her head. If she didn't look at her arms and legs they could just "wander off" without her knowing—initially she was unable to walk, and even after she relearned this skill she was so dependent on her visual attention that closing her eyes would cause her to land in a hopeless heap on the floor. Only light caresses like those from her children's hands can make her feel she has a body, but even these sensations remain vague and elusive (Olausson et al., 2002; Sacks, 1985).

Pain is an unpleasant experience that involves both physical and psychological components. Feeling pain is quite adaptive because it makes us aware of an injury, and it motivates us to remove ourselves from the cause of that injury. In addition, pain also makes us less likely to suffer additional injury because we will be gentler with our injured body parts.

Generally speaking, pain can be considered to be neuropathic or inflammatory in nature. Pain that signals some type of tissue damage is known as **inflammatory pain**. In some situations, pain results from damage to neurons of either the peripheral or central nervous system. As a result, pain signals that are sent to the brain get exaggerated. This type of pain is known as **neuropathic pain**. Multiple treatment options for pain relief range from relaxation therapy to the use of analgesic medications to deep brain stimulation. The most effective treatment option for a given individual will depend on a number of considerations, including the severity and persistence of the pain and any medical/psychological conditions.

Some individuals are born without the ability to feel pain. This very rare genetic disorder is known as **congenital insensitivity to pain** (or **congenital analgesia**). While those with congenital analgesia can detect differences in temperature and pressure, they cannot experience pain. As a result, they often suffer significant injuries. Young children have serious mouth and tongue injuries because they have bitten themselves repeatedly. Not surprisingly, individuals suffering from this disorder have much shorter life expectancies due to their injuries and secondary infections of injured sites (U.S. National Library of Medicine, 2013).

Link to Learning

Watch this video to learn more about congenital insensitivity to pain.

- https://www.youtube.com/watch?v=1vLsZ_dXFAg

Action Potentials in the Receptor Cells Travel as Nerve Impulses with Different Speeds

When you step on a pin, this activates a host of mechanoreceptors, many of which are nociceptors. You may have noticed that the sensation changes over time. First you feel a sharp stab that propels you to remove your foot, and only then you feel a wave of more aching pain. The sharp stab is signaled via fast-conducting A-fibers, which project to the somatosensory cortex. This part of the cortex is somatotopically organized—that is, the sensory signals are represented according to where in the body they stem from (see homunculus illustration, Figure 2). The unpleasant ache you feel after the sharp pin stab is a separate, simultaneous signal sent from the nociceptors in your foot via thin C-pain or Aδ-fibers to the insular cortex and other brain regions involved in processing of emotion and interoception (see Figure 3a for a schematic representation of this pathway). The experience of stepping on a pin is, in other words, composed by two separate signals: one discriminatory signal allowing us to localize the touch stimulus and distinguish whether it's a blunt or a sharp stab; and one affective signal that lets us know that stepping on the pin is bad. It is common to divide pain into sensory–discriminatory and affective–motivational aspects (Auvray, Myin, & Spence, 2010). This distinction corresponds, at least partly, to how this information travels from the peripheral to the central nervous system and how it is processed in the brain (Price, 2000).

Pain Is Necessary for Survival, but Our Brain Can Stop It if It Needs To

In April 2003, the climber Aron Ralston found himself at the floor of Blue John Canyon in Utah, forced to make an appalling choice: face a slow but certain death—or amputate his right arm. Five days earlier he fell down the canyon—since then he had been stuck with his right arm trapped between an 800-lb boulder and the steep sandstone wall. Weak from lack of food and water and close to giving up, it occurred to him like an epiphany that if he broke the two bones in his forearm he could manage to cut off the rest with his pocket knife. The thought of freeing himself and surviving made him so exited he spent the next 40 minutes completely engrossed in the task: first snapping his bones using his body as a lever, then sticking his fingers into the arm, pinching bundles of muscle fibers and severing them one by one, before cutting the blue arteries and the pale "noodle-like" nerves. The pain was unimportant. Only cutting through the thick white main nerve made him stop for a minute—the

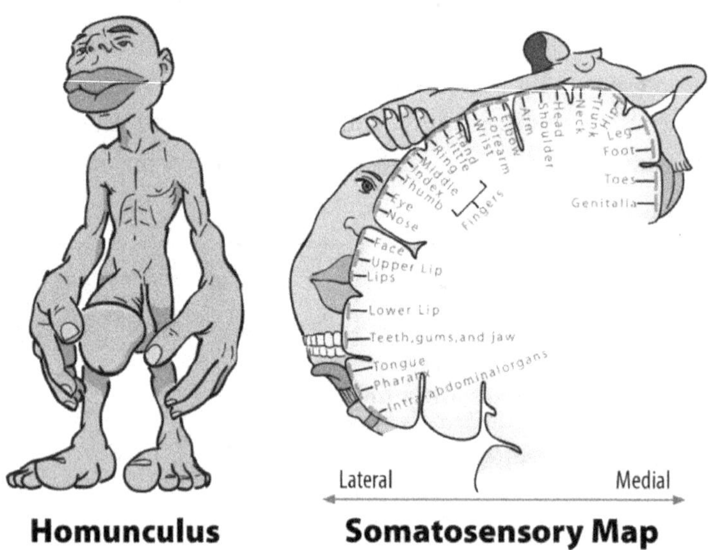

Figure 2a. The Homunculus: Homunculus means "little man", and here you see a scale model of the human body distorted to reflect the relative space that body parts occupy in the somatosensory cortex. As you can see, the lips, hands, feet and genitals send more somatosensory projections to the brain than do any other body parts. Figure 2b. Cortical mapping of the sensory homunculus: The body parts are represented in specific locations on the somatosensory cortex. Representations map out somatotopically, with the feet located medially and shoulders and arms laterally to the interhemispheric fissure. Facial structures are represented in a different location to the scalp and head; the face oriented «upside down» with the forehead pointing towards the shoulders.

flood of pain, he describes, was like thrusting his entire arm "into a cauldron of magma." Finally free, he rappelled down a cliff and walked another 7 miles until he was rescued by some hikers (Ralston, 2010).

How is it possible to do something so excruciatingly painful to yourself, as Aron Ralston did, and still manage to walk, talk, and think rationally afterwards? The answer lies within the brain, where signals from the body are interpreted. When we perceive somatosensory and nociceptive signals from the body, the experience is highly subjective and malleable by motivation, attention, emotion, and context.

The Motivation–Decision Model and Descending Modulation of Pain

According to *the motivation–decision model*, the brain automatically and continuously evaluates the pros and cons of any situation—weighing impending threats and available rewards (Fields, 2004, 2006). Anything more important for survival than avoiding the pain activates the brain's descending pain modulatory system—a top-down system involving several parts of the brain and brainstem, which inhibits nociceptive signaling so that the more important actions can be attended to.

In Aron's extreme case, his actions were likely based on such an unconscious decision process—taking into account his homeostatic state (his hunger, thirst, the inflammation and decay of his crushed hand slowly affecting the rest of his body), the sensory input available (the sweet smell of his dissolving

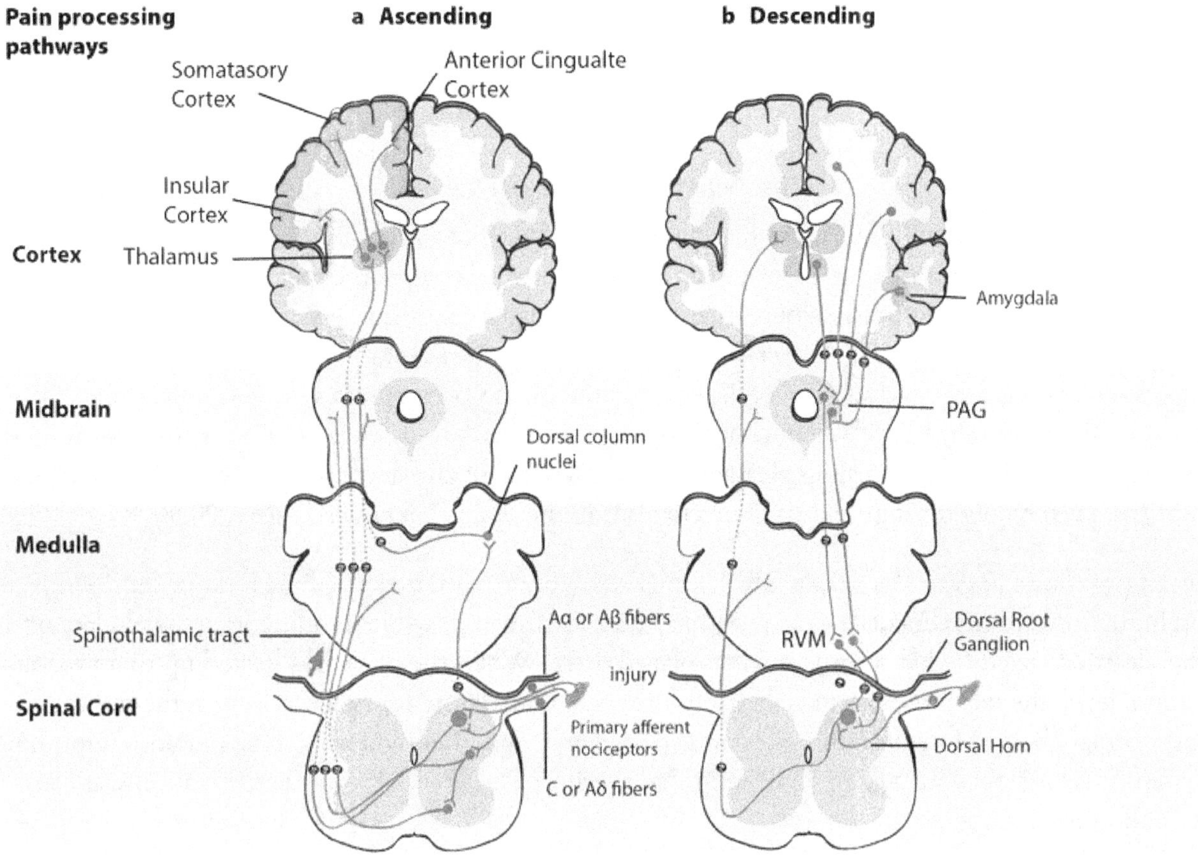

Figure 3: Pain processing pathways. Left – Ascending pain pathways: An injury is signaled simultaneously via fast-conducting Aα or Aβ-fibres and slow-conducting C-pain or Aδ-fibres. The fast A-fibres signal pressure, stretching and other tissue movements to the somatosensory cortex via the dorsal column nuclei. The C-pain and Aδ-fibres sends pain information from nociceptors in the tissue or skin, and transmits these signals to second order neurons in the dorsal horn of the spinal cord. The second order neurons then cross over to the opposite side, where they form the ascending spinothalamic tract. This tract projects signals to nuclei in the medulla and midbrain on the way up to the thalamus (T). The thalamus relays the information to the somatosensory and insular cortex, as well as cortical regions mediating different aspects of the pain experience such as affective responses in the cingulate cortex. Right – Descending pain modulation pathways: Information from the environment and certain motivational states can activate this top–down pathway. Several areas in the limbic forebrain including the anterior cingulate and insular cortex, nuclei in the amygdala and the hypothalamus (H), project to the midbrain periaqueductal grey (PAG), which then modulates ascending pain transmission from the afferent pain system indirectly through the rostral ventromedial medulla (RVM) in the brainstem. This modulating system produces analgesia by the release of endogenous opioids, and uses ON- and OFF-cells to exert either inhibitory (green) or facilitatory (red) control of nociceptive signals at the spinal dorsal horn.

skin, the silence around him indicating his solitude), and his knowledge about the threats facing him (death, or excruciating pain that won't kill him) versus the potential rewards (survival, seeing his family again). Aron's story illustrates the evolutionary advantage to being able to shut off pain: The descending pain modulatory system allows us to go through with potentially life-saving actions.

However, when one has reached safety or obtained the reward, healing is more important. The very same descending system can then "crank up" nociception from the body to promote healing and motivate us to avoid potentially painful actions. To facilitate or inhibit nociceptive signals from the body, the descending pain modulatory system uses a set of ON- or OFF-cells in the brainstem, which regulates how much of the nociceptive signal reaches the brain. The descending system is dependent on opioid signaling, and analgesics like morphine relieve pain via this circuit (Petrovic, Kalso, Petersson, & Ingvar, 2002).

The Analgesic Power of Reward

Thinking about the good things, like his loved ones and the life ahead of him, was probably pivotal to Aron's survival. The promise of a reward can be enough to relieve pain. Expecting pain relief (getting less pain is often the best possible outcome if you're in pain, i.e., it is a reward) from a medical treatment contributes to the placebo effect—where pain relief is due at least partly to your brain's descending modulation circuit, and such relief depends on the brain's own opioid system (Eippert et al., 2009; Eippert, Finsterbusch, Bingel, & Buchel, 2009; Levine, Gordon, & Fields, 1978). Eating tasty food, listening to good music, or feeling pleasant touch on your skin also decreases pain in both animals and humans, presumably through the same mechanism in the brain (Leknes & Tracey, 2008).

In a now classic experiment, Dum and Herz (1984) either fed rats normal rat food or let them feast on highly rewarding chocolate-covered candy (rats love sweets) while standing on a metal plate until they learned exactly what to expect when placed there. When the plate was heated up to a noxious/painful level, the rats that expected candy endured the temperature for twice as long as the rats expecting normal chow. Moreover, this effect was completely abolished when the rats' opioid (endorphin) system was blocked with a drug, indicating that the analgesic effect of reward anticipation was caused by endorphin release.

For Aron the climber, both the stress from knowing that death was impending and the anticipation of the reward it would be to survive probably flooded his brain with endorphins, contributing to the wave of excitement and euphoria he experienced while he carried out the amputation "like a five-year-old unleashed on his Christmas presents" (Ralston, 2010). This altered his experience of the pain from the extreme tissue damage he was causing and enabled him to focus on freeing himself. Our brain, it turns out, can modulate the perception of how unpleasant pain is, while still retaining the ability to experience the intensity of the sensation (Rainville, Duncan, Price, Carrier, & Bushnell, 1997; Rainville, Feine, Bushnell, & Duncan, 1992). Social rewards, like holding the hand of your boyfriend or girlfriend, have pain-reducing effects. Even looking at a picture of him/her can have similar effects—in fact, seeing a picture of a person we feel close to not only reduces subjective pain ratings, but also the activity in pain-related brain areas (Eisenberger et al., 2011). The most common things to do when wanting to help someone through a painful experience—being present and holding the person's hand—thus seems to have a measurably positive effect.

The Power of the Mind

The context of pain and touch has a great impact on how we interpret it. Just imagine how different it would feel to Aron if someone amputated his hand against his will and for no discernible reason. Prolonged pain from injuries can be easier to bear if the incident causing them provides a positive context—like a war wound that testifies to a soldier's courage and commitment—or phantom pain from a hand that was cut off to enable life to carry on.

The relative meaning of pain is illustrated by a recent experiment, where the same moderately painful heat was administered to participants in two different contexts—one control context where the alternative was a non-painful heat; and another where the alternative was an intensely painful heat. In the control context, where the moderate heat was the least preferable outcome, it was (unsurprisingly) rated as painful. In the other context it was the best possible outcome, and here the exact same moderately painful heat was actually rated as *pleasant*—because it meant the intensely painful heat had been avoided. This somewhat surprising change in perception—where pain becomes pleasant because it represents relief from something worse—highlights the importance of the meaning individuals ascribe to their pain, which can have decisive effects in pain treatment (Leknes et al., 2013). In the case of touch, knowing who or what is stroking your skin can make all the difference—try thinking about slugs the next time someone strokes your skin if you want an illustration of this point.

Pain and pleasure not only share modulatory systems—another common attribute is that we don't need to be on the receiving end of it ourselves in order to experience it. How did you feel when you read about Aron cutting through his own tissue, or "Thomas" destroying his own bones unknowingly? Did you cringe? It's quite likely that some of your brain areas processing affective aspects of pain were active even though the nociceptors in your skin and deep tissue were not firing. Pain can be experienced vicariously, as can itch, pleasurable touch, and other sensations. Tania Singer and her colleagues found in an fMRI study that some of the same brain areas that were active when participants felt pain on their own skin (anterior cingulate and insula) were also active when they were given a signal that a loved one was feeling the pain. Those who were most "empathetic" also showed the largest brain responses (Singer et al., 2004). A similar effect has been found for pleasurable touch: The posterior insula of participants watching videos of someone else's arm being gently stroked shows the same activation as if they were receiving the touch themselves (Morrison, Bjornsdotter, & Olausson, 2011).

Glossary

congenital insensitivity to pain (congenital analgesia): genetic disorder that results in the inability to experience pain

inflammatory pain: signal that some type of tissue damage has occurred

Meissner's corpuscle: touch receptor that responds to pressure and lower frequency vibrations

Merkel's disk: touch receptor that responds to light touch

neuropathic pain: pain from damage to neurons of either the peripheral or central nervous system

nociception: sensory signal indicating potential harm and maybe pain

Pacinian corpuscle: touch receptor that detects transient pressure and higher frequency vibrations

Ruffini corpuscle: touch receptor that detects stretch

vestibular sense: contributes to our ability to maintain balance and body posture

- Modification and adaptation, addition of Noba Link to Learning and CrashCourse video. **Provided by:** Lumen Learning. **License:** *CC BY: Attribution*

- The Other Senses. **Authored by:** OpenStax College. **Located at:** http://cnx.org/contents/Sr8Ev5Og@5.49:Nw9FOKLs@6/The-Other-Senses. **License:** *CC BY: Attribution*. **License Terms:** Download for free at http://cnx.org/contents/4abf04bf-93a0-45c3-9cbc-2cefd46e68cc@5.48

- Touch and Pain, information on mechanoreceptors through the power of the mind. **Authored by:** Guro E. Loseth, Dan-Mikael Ellingson, and Siri Leknes . **Provided by:** University of Oslo, University of Gothenburg. **Located at:** http://nobaproject.com/modules/touch-and-pain. **Project:** The Noba Project. **License:** *CC BY-NC-SA: Attribution-NonCommercial-ShareAlike*

The Vestibular Sense

- Describe the basic functions of the vestibular, proprioceptive, and kinesthetic sensory systems

The Vestibular Sense, Proprioception, and Kinesthesia

The **vestibular sense** contributes to our ability to maintain balance and body posture. As Figure 1 shows, the major sensory organs (utricle, saccule, and the three semicircular canals) of this system are located next to the cochlea in the inner ear. The vestibular organs are fluid-filled and have hair cells, similar to the ones found in the auditory system, which respond to movement of the head and gravitational forces. When these hair cells are stimulated, they send signals to the brain via the vestibular nerve. Although we may not be consciously aware of our vestibular system's sensory information under normal circumstances, its importance is apparent when we experience motion sickness and/or dizziness related to infections of the inner ear (Khan & Chang, 2013).

In addition to maintaining balance, the vestibular system collects information critical for controlling movement and the reflexes that move various parts of our bodies to compensate for changes in body position. Therefore, both **proprioception** (perception of body position) and **kinesthesia** (perception of the body's movement through space) interact with information provided by the vestibular system.

These sensory systems also gather information from receptors that respond to stretch and tension in muscles, joints, skin, and tendons (Lackner & DiZio, 2005; Proske, 2006; Proske & Gandevia, 2012). Proprioceptive and kinesthetic information travels to the brain via the spinal column. Several cortical regions in addition to the cerebellum receive information from and send information to the sensory organs of the proprioceptive and kinesthetic systems.

	Definition	Application
Vestibular Sense	Sensory system that contributes to balance and the sense of spatial orientation.	You have an ear infection and frequently feel dizzy. Or if you were to experience vertigo, you might feel like your entire body was spinning in space and be unable to walk.
Proprioception	The sense of the position of parts of the body, relative to other neighboring parts of the body. Focuses on the body's *cognitive awareness* of movement.	You step off a curb and know where to put your foot. You push an elevator button and control how hard you have to press down with your fingers.
Kinesthesia	Awareness of the position and movement of the parts of the body using sensory organs in joints and muscles. Kinesthesia is a key component in muscle memory and hand-eye coordination. It is more *behavioral* than proprioception.	You are aware of your arm movement while swinging a golf club. Focuses on the body's movements and not on equilibrium or balance.

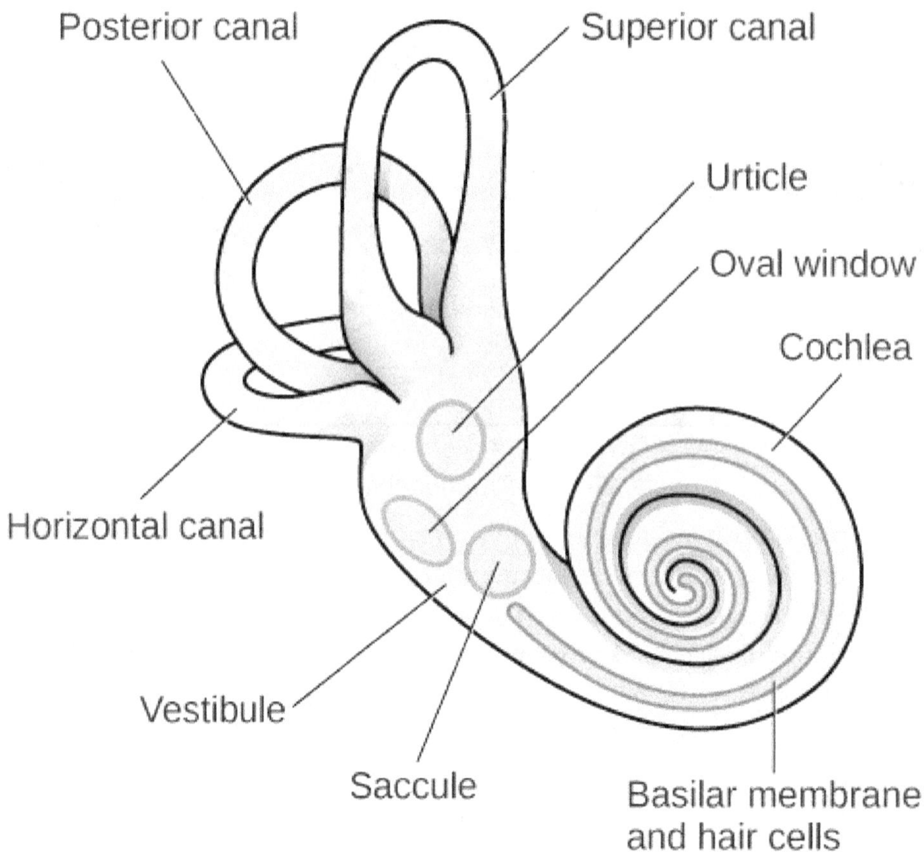

Figure 1. The major sensory organs of the vestibular system are located next to the cochlea in the inner ear. These include the utricle, saccule, and the three semicircular canals (posterior, superior, and horizontal).

Link to Learning

You can review the things you learned about the senses in the following CrashCourse video:

- https://youtu.be/fxZWtc0mYpQ

Glossary

kinesthesia: perception of the body's movement through space
proprioception: perception of body position
vestibular sense: contributes to our ability to maintain balance and body posture

---

https://assessments.lumenlearning.com/assessments/4826

Attributions

- Modification, adaptation, and original content. **Provided by:** Lumen Learning. **License:** *CC BY-SA: Attribution-ShareAlike*

- The Other Senses. **Authored by:** OpenStax College. **Located at:** http://cnx.org/contents/Sr8Ev5Og@5.49:Nw9FOKLs@6/The-Other-Senses. **License:** *CC BY: Attribution.* **License Terms:** Download for free at http://cnx.org/contents/4abf04bf-93a0-45c3-9cbc-2cefd46e68cc@5.48

- Homunculus - Crash Course Psychology #6. **Provided by:** CrashCourse. **Located at:** https://www.youtube.com/watch?v=fxZWtc0mYpQ. **License:** *Other.* **License Terms:** Standard YouTube License

- Additional Sensory Systems, information for chart. **Provided by:** Boundless. **Located at:** https://www.boundless.com/psychology/textbooks/boundless-psychology-textbook/sensation-and-perception-5/sensory-processes-38/additional-sensory-systems-166-12701/. **Project:** Boundless Psychology. **License:** *CC BY-SA: Attribution-ShareAlike*

Perception

What you'll learn to do: define perception and give examples of gestalt principles and multimodal perception

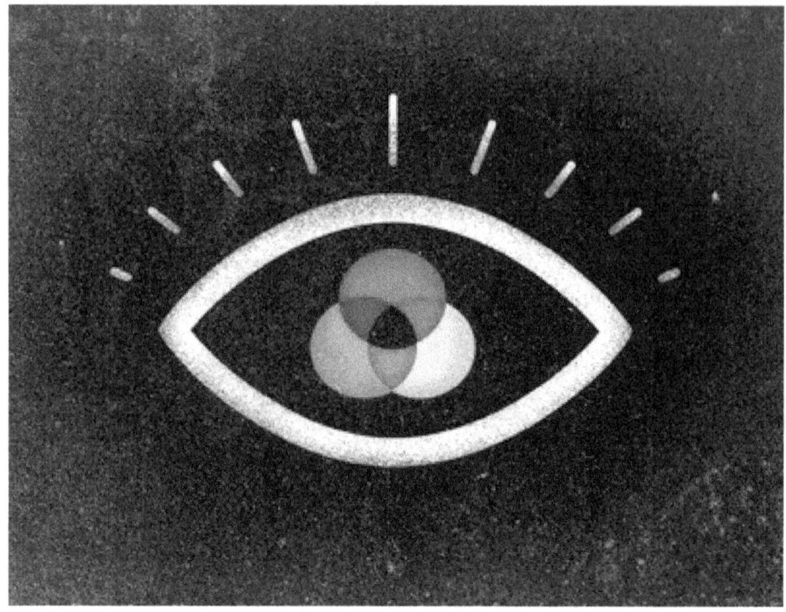

Seeing something is not the same thing as making sense of what you see. Why is it that our senses are so easily fooled? In this section, you will come to see how our perceptions are not infallible, and they can be influenced by bias, prejudice, and other factors. Psychologists are interested in how these false perceptions influence our thoughts and behavior.

Watch this CrashCourse video for a good overview of perception:

Gestalt Principles of Perception

In the early part of the 20th century, Max Wertheimer published a paper demonstrating that individuals perceived motion in rapidly flickering static images—an insight that came to him as he used a child's toy tachistoscope. Wertheimer, and his assistants Wolfgang Köhler and Kurt Koffka, who later became his partners, believed that perception involved more than simply combining sensory stimuli. This belief led to a new movement within the field of psychology known as **Gestalt psychology**. The word *gestalt* literally means form or pattern, but its use reflects the idea that the whole is different from the sum of its parts. In other words, the brain creates a perception that is more than simply the sum of available sensory inputs, and it does so in predictable ways. Gestalt psychologists translated these predictable ways into principles by which we organize sensory information. As a result, Gestalt psychology has been extremely influential in the area of sensation and perception (Rock & Palmer, 1990).

One Gestalt principle is the **figure-ground relationship**. According to this principle, we tend to segment our visual world into figure and ground. Figure is the object or person that is the focus of the visual field, while the ground is the background. As Figure 1 shows, our perception can vary tremendously, depending on what is perceived as figure and what is perceived as ground. Presumably, our ability to interpret sensory information depends on what we label as figure and what we label as ground in any particular case, although this assumption has been called into question (Peterson & Gibson, 1994; Vecera & O'Reilly, 1998).

Another Gestalt principle for organizing sensory stimuli into meaningful perception is **proximity**. This principle asserts that things that are close to one another tend to be grouped together, as Figure 2 illustrates.

How we read something provides another illustration of the proximity concept. For example, we read this sentence like this, notl iket hiso rt hat. We group the letters of a given word together because there are no spaces between the letters, and we perceive words because there are spaces between each word. Here are some more examples: Cany oum akes enseo ft hiss entence? What doth es e wor dsmea n?

We might also use the principle of **similarity** to group things in our visual fields. According to this principle, things that are alike tend to be grouped together (Figure 3). For example, when watching a football game, we tend to group individuals based on the colors of their uniforms. When watching an offensive drive, we can get a sense of the two teams simply by grouping along this dimension.

Figure 1. The concept of figure-ground relationship explains why this image can be perceived either as a vase or as a pair of faces.

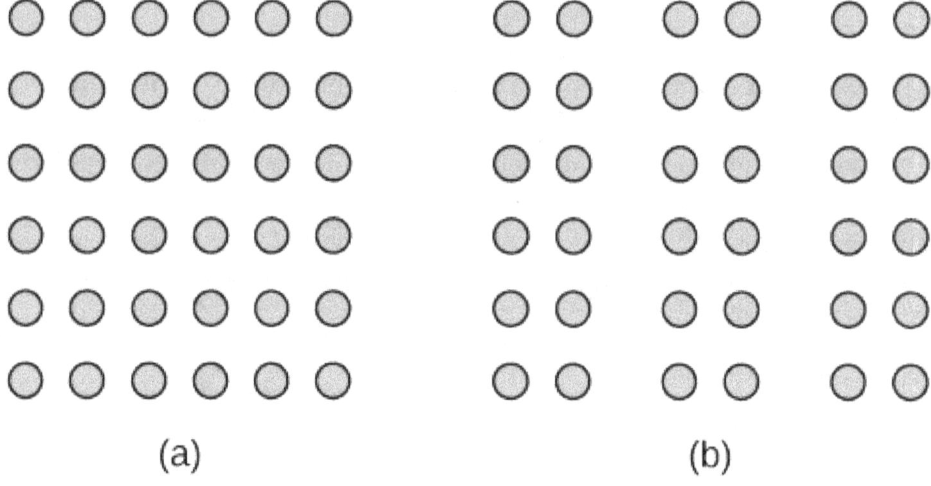

Figure 2. The Gestalt principle of proximity suggests that you see (a) one block of dots on the left side and (b) three columns on the right side.

Two additional Gestalt principles are the **law of continuity** (or good continuation) and **closure**. The law of continuity suggests that we are more likely to perceive continuous, smooth flowing lines rather than jagged, broken lines (Figure 4). The principle of closure states that we organize our perceptions into complete objects rather than as a series of parts (Figure 5).

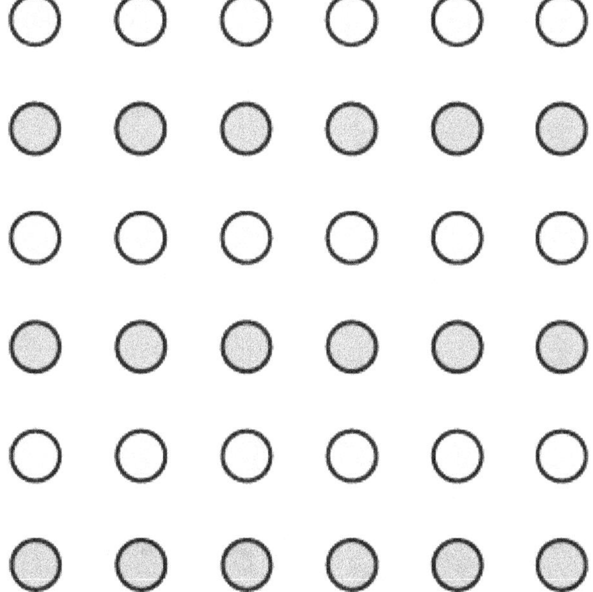

Figure 3. When looking at this array of dots, we likely perceive alternating rows of colors. We are grouping these dots according to the principle of similarity.

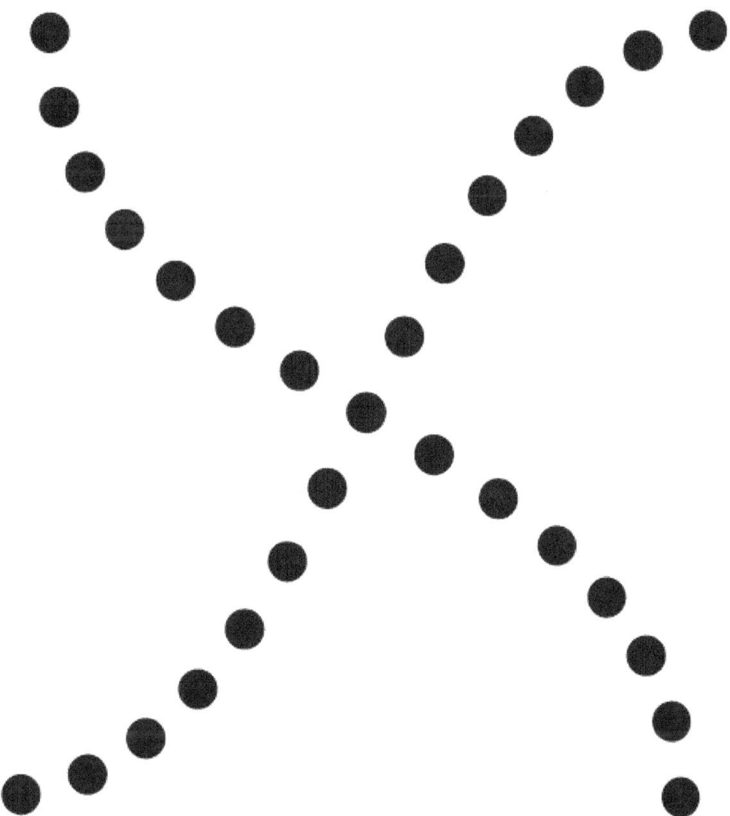

Figure 4. Good continuation would suggest that we are more likely to perceive this as two overlapping lines, rather than four lines meeting in the center.

Figure 5. Closure suggests that we will perceive a complete circle and rectangle rather than a series of segments.

> ### Link to Learning
>
> Watch this podcast showing real world illustrations of Gestalt principles.
>
> - https://secure-hwcdn.libsyn.com/p/e/c/0/ec024ff6bc3adce3/
>   TPF_031Gestalt_020709.m4v?c_id=1316744&expiration=1485984203&hwt=3dfc11440d95d651896

According to Gestalt theorists, **pattern perception**, or our ability to discriminate among different figures and shapes, occurs by following the principles described above. You probably feel fairly certain that your perception accurately matches the real world, but this is not always the case. Our perceptions are based on **perceptual hypotheses**: educated guesses that we make while interpreting sensory information. These hypotheses are informed by a number of factors, including our personalities, experiences, and expectations. We use these hypotheses to generate our perceptual set. For instance, research has demonstrated that those who are given verbal priming produce a biased interpretation of complex ambiguous figures (Goolkasian & Woodbury, 2010).

Dig Deeper: The Depths of Perception: Bias, Prejudice, and Cultural Factors

In this module, you have learned that perception is a complex process. Built from sensations, but influenced by our own experiences, biases, prejudices, and cultures, perceptions can be very different from person to person. Research suggests that implicit racial prejudice and stereotypes affect perception. For instance, several studies have demonstrated that non-Black participants identify weapons faster and are more likely to identify non-weapons as weapons when the image of the weapon is paired with the image of a Black person (Payne, 2001; Payne, Shimizu, & Jacoby, 2005). Furthermore, White individuals' decisions to shoot an armed target in a video game is made more quickly when the target is Black (Correll, Park, Judd, & Wittenbrink, 2002; Correll, Urland, & Ito, 2006). This research is important, considering the number of very high-profile cases in the last few decades in which young Blacks were killed by people who claimed to believe that the unarmed individuals were armed and/or represented some threat to their personal safety.

Think It Over

Have you ever listened to a song on the radio and sung along only to find out later that you have been singing the wrong lyrics? Once you found the correct lyrics, did your perception of the song change?

Figure 6. The way we receive the information from the world is called sensation while our interpretation of that information is called perception. [Image: Laurens van Lieshou]

Multi-Modal Perception

Although it has been traditional to study the various senses independently, most of the time, perception operates in the context of information supplied by multiple **sensory modalities** at the same time. For example, imagine if you witnessed a car collision. You could describe the stimulus generated by this event by considering each of the senses independently; that is, as a set of **unimodal** stimuli. Your eyes would be stimulated with patterns of light energy bouncing off the cars involved. Your ears would be stimulated with patterns of acoustic energy emanating from the collision. Your nose might even be stimulated by the smell of burning rubber or gasoline.

However, all of this information would be relevant to the same thing: your perception of the car collision. Indeed, unless someone was to explicitly ask you to describe your perception in unimodal terms, you would most likely experience the event as a unified bundle of sensations from multiple senses. In other words, your perception would be **multimodal**. The question is whether the various sources of information involved in this multimodal stimulus are processed separately by the perceptual system or not.

For the last few decades, perceptual research has pointed to the importance of **multimodal perception**: the effects on the perception of events and objects in the world that are observed when there is information from more than one sensory modality. Most of this research indicates that, at some point in perceptual processing, information from the various sensory modalities is **integrated**. In other words, the information is combined and treated as a unitary representation of the world.

Behavioral Effects of Multimodal Perception

Although neuroscientists tend to study very simple interactions between neurons, the fact that they've found so many crossmodal areas of the cortex seems to hint that the way we experience the world is fundamentally multimodal. Our intuitions about perception are consistent with this; it does not seem as though our perception of events is constrained to the perception of each sensory modality independently. Rather, we perceive a unified world, regardless of the sensory modality through which we perceive it.

It will probably require many more years of research before neuroscientists uncover all the details of the neural machinery involved in this unified experience. In the meantime, experimental psychologists have contributed to our understanding of multimodal perception through investigations of the behavioral effects associated with it. These effects fall into two broad classes. The first class—**multimodal phenomena**—concerns the binding of inputs from multiple sensory modalities and the effects of this binding on perception. The second class—**crossmodal phenomena**—concerns the influence of one sensory modality on the perception of another (Spence, Senkowski, & Roder, 2009).

Multimodal Phenomena

Audiovisual Speech

Multimodal phenomena concern stimuli that generate simultaneous (or nearly simultaneous) information in more than one sensory modality. As discussed above, speech is a classic example of this kind of stimulus. When an individual speaks, she generates sound waves that carry meaningful information. If the perceiver is also looking at the speaker, then that perceiver also has access to *visual* patterns that carry meaningful information. Of course, as anyone who has ever tried to lipread knows, there are limits on how informative visual speech information is. Even so, the visual speech pattern alone is sufficient for very robust speech perception. Most people assume that deaf individuals are much better at lipreading than individuals with normal hearing. It may come as a surprise to learn, however, that some individuals with normal hearing are also remarkably good at lipreading (sometimes called "speechreading"). In fact, there is a wide range of speechreading ability in both normal hearing and deaf populations (Andersson, Lyxell, Rönnberg, & Spens, 2001). However, the reasons for this wide range of performance are not well understood (Auer & Bernstein, 2007; Bernstein, 2006; Bernstein, Auer, & Tucker, 2001; Mohammed et al., 2005).

How does visual information about speech interact with auditory information about speech? One of the earliest investigations of this question examined the accuracy of recognizing spoken words presented in a noisy context, much like in the example above about talking at a crowded party. To study this phenomenon experimentally, some irrelevant noise ("white noise"—which sounds like a radio tuned between stations) was presented to participants. Embedded in the white noise were spoken words, and the participants' task was to identify the words. There were two conditions: one in which only the auditory component of the words was presented (the "auditory-alone" condition), and one in both the auditory and visual components were presented (the "audiovisual" condition). The noise levels were also varied, so that on some trials, the noise was very loud relative to the loudness of the words, and on other trials, the noise was very soft relative to the words. Sumby and Pollack (1954) found that the accuracy of identifying the spoken words was much higher for the audiovisual condition than it was in the auditory-alone condition. In addition, the pattern of results was consistent with the Principle of Inverse Effectiveness: The advantage gained by audiovisual presentation was highest when the auditory-alone condition performance was lowest (i.e., when the noise was loudest). At these noise levels, the audiovisual advantage was considerable: It was estimated that allowing the participant to see the speaker was equivalent to turning the volume of the noise down by over half. Clearly, the audiovisual advantage can have dramatic effects on behavior.

Another phenomenon using audiovisual speech is a very famous illusion called the "McGurk effect" (named after one of its discoverers). In the classic formulation of the illusion, a movie is recorded of a speaker saying the syllables "gaga." Another movie is made of the same speaker saying the syllables "baba." Then, the auditory portion of the "baba" movie is dubbed onto the visual portion of the "gaga" movie. This combined stimulus is presented to participants, who are asked to report what the speaker in the movie said. McGurk and MacDonald (1976) reported that 98 percent of their participants reported hearing the syllable "dada"—which was in neither the visual nor the auditory components of the stimulus. These results indicate that when visual and auditory information about speech is integrated, it can have profound effects on perception.

Tactile/Visual Interactions in Body Ownership

Not all multisensory integration phenomena concern speech, however. One particularly compelling multisensory illusion involves the integration of tactile and visual information in the perception of body ownership. In the "rubber hand illusion" (Botvinick & Cohen, 1998), an observer is situated so that one of his hands is not visible. A fake rubber hand is placed near the obscured hand, but in a visible location. The experimenter then uses a light paintbrush to simultaneously stroke the obscured hand and the rubber hand in the same locations. For example, if the middle finger of the obscured hand is being brushed, then the middle finger of the rubber hand will also be brushed. This sets up a correspondence between the tactile sensations (coming from the obscured hand) and the visual sensations (of the rubber hand). After a short time (around 10 minutes), participants report feeling as though the rubber hand "belongs" to them; that is, that the rubber hand is a part of their body. This feeling can be so strong that surprising the participant by hitting the rubber hand with a hammer often leads to a reflexive withdrawing of the obscured hand—even though it is in no danger at all. It appears, then, that our awareness of our own bodies may be the result of multisensory integration.

Crossmodal Phenomena

Crossmodal phenomena are distinguished from multimodal phenomena in that they concern the influence one sensory modality has on the perception of another.

Visual Influence on Auditory Localization

A famous (and commonly experienced) crossmodal illusion is referred to as "the ventriloquism effect." When a ventriloquist appears to make a puppet speak, she fools the listener into thinking that the location of the origin of the speech sounds is at the puppet's mouth. In other words, instead of localizing the auditory signal (coming from the mouth of a ventriloquist) to the correct place, our perceptual system localizes it incorrectly (to the mouth of the puppet).

Figure 7. Ventriloquists are able to trick us into believing that what we see and what we hear are the same where, in truth, they are not. [Image: Indiapuppet]

Why might this happen? Consider the information available to the observer about the location of the two components of the stimulus: the sounds from the ventriloquist's mouth and the visual movement of the puppet's mouth. Whereas it is very obvious where the visual stimulus is coming from (because you can see it), it is much more difficult to pinpoint the location of the sounds. In other words, the very precise visual location of mouth movement apparently overrides the less well-specified location of the auditory information. More generally, it has been found that the location of a wide variety of auditory stimuli can be affected by the simultaneous presentation of a visual stimulus (Vroomen & De Gelder, 2004). In addition, the ventriloquism effect has been demonstrated for objects in motion: The motion of a visual object can influence the perceived direction of motion of a moving sound source (Soto-Faraco, Kingstone, & Spence, 2003).

Auditory Influence on Visual Perception

A related illusion demonstrates the opposite effect: where sounds have an effect on visual perception. In the double-flash illusion, a participant is asked to stare at a central point on a computer monitor. On the extreme edge of the participant's vision, a white circle is briefly flashed one time. There is also a simultaneous auditory event: either one beep or two beeps in rapid succession. Remarkably, participants report seeing *two* visual flashes when the flash is accompanied by two beeps; the same stimulus is seen as a single flash in the context of a single beep or no beep (Shams, Kamitani, & Shimojo, 2000). In other words, the number of heard beeps influences the number of seen flashes!

Another illusion involves the perception of collisions between two circles (called "balls") moving toward each other and continuing through each other. Such stimuli can be perceived as either two balls moving through each other or as a collision between the two balls that then bounce off each other in opposite directions. Sekuler, Sekuler, and Lau (1997) showed that the presentation of an auditory stimulus at the time of contact between the two balls strongly influenced the perception of a collision event. In this case, the perceived sound influences the interpretation of the ambiguous visual stimulus.

Crossmodal Speech

Several crossmodal phenomena have also been discovered for speech stimuli. These crossmodal speech effects usually show altered perceptual processing of unimodal stimuli (e.g., acoustic patterns) by virtue of prior experience with the alternate unimodal stimulus (e.g., optical patterns). For example, Rosenblum, Miller, and Sanchez (2007) conducted an experiment examining the ability to become familiar with a person's voice. Their first interesting finding was unimodal: Much like what happens when someone repeatedly hears a person speak, perceivers can become familiar with the "visual voice" of a speaker. That is, they can become familiar with the person's speaking style simply by seeing that person speak. Even more astounding was their crossmodal finding: Familiarity with this *visual* information also led to increased recognition of the speaker's *auditory* speech, to which participants had never had exposure.

Similarly, it has been shown that when perceivers see a speaking face, they can identify the (auditory-alone) voice of that speaker, and vice versa (Kamachi, Hill, Lander, & Vatikiotis-Bateson, 2003; Lachs & Pisoni, 2004a, 2004b, 2004c; Rosenblum, Smith, Nichols, Lee, & Hale, 2006). In other words, the visual form of a speaker engaged in the act of speaking appears to contain information about what that speaker should sound like. Perhaps more surprisingly, the auditory form of speech seems to contain information about what the speaker should look like.

Glossary

closure: organizing our perceptions into complete objects rather than as a series of parts

crossmodal phenomena: effects that concern the influence of the perception of one sensory modality on the perception of another

double flash illusion: the false perception of two visual flashes when a single flash is accompanied by two auditory beeps

figure-ground relationship: segmenting our visual world into figure and ground

Gestalt psychology: field of psychology based on the idea that the whole is different from the sum of its parts<

good continuation: (also, continuity) we are more likely to perceive continuous, smooth flowing lines rather than jagged, broken lines

integrated: the process by which the perceptual system combines information arising from more than one modality

McGurk effect: an effect in which conflicting visual and auditory components of a speech stimulus result in an illusory percept

multimodal: of or pertaining to multiple sensory modalities

multimodal perception: the effects that concurrent stimulation in more than one sensory modality has on the perception of events and objects in the world

multimodal phenomena: effects that concern the binding of inputs from multiple sensory modalities

pattern perception: ability to discriminate among different figures and shapes

perceptual hypothesis: educated guess used to interpret sensory information

principle of closure: organize perceptions into complete objects rather than as a series of parts

proximity: things that are close to one another tend to be grouped together

rubber hand illusion: the false perception of a fake hand as belonging to a perceiver, due to multimodal sensory information

sensory modalities: a type of sense; for example, vision or audition

similarity: things that are alike tend to be grouped together

unimodal: of or pertaining to a single sensory modality

- Multi-Modal Perception. **Authored by:** Lorin Lachs. **Provided by:** California State University, Fresno. **Located at:** http://nobaproject.com/modules/multi-modal-perception. **Project:** The Noba Project. **License:** *CC BY-NC-SA: Attribution-NonCommercial-ShareAlike*

All rights reserved content

- Perceiving is Believing – Crash Course Psychology #7. **Provided by:** CrashCourse. **Located at:** https://www.youtube.com/watch?v=n46umYA_4dM. **License:** *Other*. **License Terms:** Standard YouTube License

- The McGurk Effect. **Provided by:** BBC. **Located at:** https://youtu.be/G-lN8vWm3m0?t=32s. **License:** *Other*. **License Terms:** Standard YouTube License

- The Rubber Hand Illusion. **Provided by:** BBC. **Located at:** https://youtu.be/sxwn1w7MJvk. **License:** *Other*. **License Terms:** Standard YouTube License

Putting It Together: Sensation and Perception

Learning Objectives

In this module, you learned to

- differentiate between sensation and perception
- explain the process of vision and how people see color and depth
- explain the basics of hearing
- describe the basic anatomy and functions of taste, smell, touch, pain, and the vestibular sense
- define perception and give examples of gestalt principles and multimodal perception

In this module, you learned about the way our senses work and the impact they have on our perception of the world. Our impressive sensory abilities allow us to experience the most enjoyable and most miserable experiences, as well as everything in between. Our eyes, ears, nose, tongue and skin provide an interface for the brain to interact with the world around us. While there is simplicity in covering each sensory modality independently, we are organisms that have evolved the ability to process multiple modalities as a unified experience.

While the information covered in this module may initially seem straightforward and stagnant, you saw in the example from Jessica Witt's research on perception that a person's perception of the size of a golf hole can impact their performance. The ways that perception can alter our behavior and the impact this has on mental processes is of particular interest to psychologists.

One current area of interest is the influence of psychological principles on virtual reality design. Think about it. How can designers create a 3-dimensional world on a 2-dimensional plane? They must first consider the way that we interpret visual cues and how we see depth. Consider Google Cardboard. In 2014, two Google engineers created a cardboard viewer lens that allows users to place their smartphones inside and view the world as if they entered a virtual reality. This was a huge leap forward in reducing the cost of and increasing access to virtual reality. But how did they do it? In order to feel like you are immersed in the gaming world, you need to remove the distractions that exist outside of the immediate visual field. Hence, the box around the phone. You also need to feel like you are inside of the world, so the box includes lenses that adjust your focal point and magnify the picture on the screen (Figure 1).

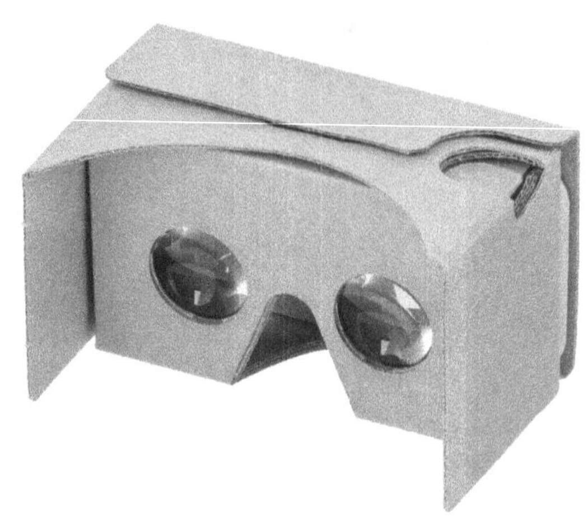

Figure 1. Google Cardboard.

You also need the world to be 3-dimensional. As you learned, your eyes rely on several monocular and binocular cues in order to see depth. Binocular disparity describes the slightly unique view of the world we see from each of our two eyes (which explains why if you hold an object near your face and close one eye, then open it and close the other, that object appears to move). To create this effect, developers put a barrier between the left and right visual fields and split the screen in two, so that the image on the screen is slightly different. The picture on your phone shows up like this: https://s3-us-west-2.amazonaws.com/courses-images/wp-content/uploads/sites/855/2016/11/26144856/16905172090_360p.mp4

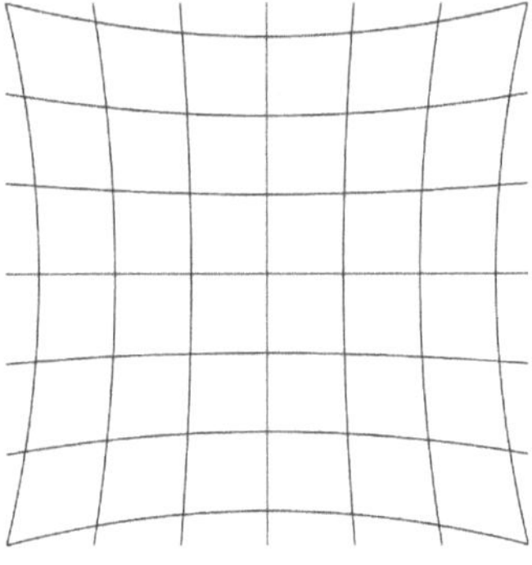

Figure 2. Pincushion distortion.

Because you are viewing the image through magnified lenses, there is a distortion called the pincushion distortion, which stretches the image in the corners of the view. To counteract that and make the work appear normal, developers apply a barrel distortion to the viewer, which explains why you see the image in the video with the pinched corners.

Advances in virtual reality are also important to psychology because virtual reality is a treatment method used to help those with psychological disorders. Consider PTSD or phobias, for example. In a virtual world, a counselor can create situations and experiences designed to recreate the triggers for specific behaviors and assist the client in using coping mechanisms to deal with threatening situations. Vir-

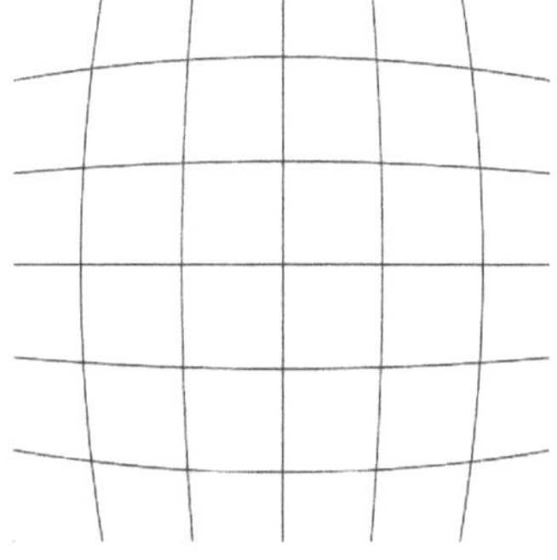

Figure 3. Barrel distortion.

tual reality therapy can be used in numerous ways as a type of exposure therapy, even assisting people with autism as they practice recognizing and interpreting social cues or helping those with depression to make choices to help them prevent negative thoughts.

Attributions

CC licensed content, Original

- Putting It Together: Sensation and Perception. **Provided by:** Lumen Learning. **License:** *CC BY-NC-SA: Attribution-NonCommercial-ShareAlike*

CC licensed content, Shared previously

- Google Cardboard VR with Camera Viewer. **Authored by:** sndrv. **Provided by:** Flickr. **Located at:** https://www.flickr.com/photos/sndrv/16905172090. **License:** *CC BY: Attribution*

- Distortion images. **Authored by:** WolfWings. **Provided by:** Wikimedia. **Located at:** https://en.wikipedia.org/wiki/Distortion_(optics). **License:** *Public Domain: No Known Copyright*

- Google Cardboard. **Provided by:** Wikipedia. **Located at:** https://en.wikipedia.org/wiki/Google_Cardboard. **License:** *CC BY-SA: Attribution-ShareAlike*

- Introductory Paragraph. **Authored by:** Adam John Privitera . **Provided by:** Chemeketa Community College. **Located at:** http://nobaproject.com/modules/sensation-and-perception. **Project:** The Noba Project. **License:** *CC BY-NC-SA: Attribution-NonCommercial-ShareAlike*

Public domain content

- Google Cardboard image. **Authored by:** Evan Amos. **Located at:** https://en.wikipedia.org/wiki/Google_Cardboard#/media/File:Google-Cardboard.jpg. **License:** *Public Domain: No Known Copyright*